Irish Catholic identities

MANCHESTER
1824

Manchester University Press

For Patrick O'Sullivan
ὑμεῖς δέ ἐστε οἱ διαμεμενηκότες μετ ἐμοῦ ἐν τοῖς πειρασμοῖς μου

Irish Catholic identities

Edited by
OLIVER P. RAFFERTY

Manchester University Press

Published by Manchester University Press
Altrincham Street, Manchester M1 7JA, UK
www.manchesteruniversitypress.co.uk

British Library Cataloguing-in-Publication Data is available

Library of Congress Cataloging-in-Publication Data is available

ISBN 978 0 7190 9731 7 *paperback*

First published by Manchester University Press in hardback 2013

This paperback edition first published 2015

Printed by Lightning Source

Contents

Notes on contributors

Thomas Bartlett is professor of Irish history at the University of Aberdeen. Previously he has been professor of modern Irish history at University College Dublin. He was elected a member of the Royal Irish Academy in 1995. His most recent book is *Ireland: A History* (Cambridge, 2010).

Fergal Casey has a Ph.D. from University College, Dublin. His research as an I.R.C.H.S.S. Government of Ireland Scholar was on the literature, economics and politics of G. K. Chesterton, Hilaire Belloc and H. E. Manning.

Caitriona Clear is a lecturer in the department of history at the National University of Ireland, Galway. She has published widely in the field of social history and women's history, including *Women of the House* (Dublin, 2000); *Social Change and Everyday Life in Ireland* (Manchester, 2007).

Revd Dr Niall Coll is senior lecturer in religious studies at St Mary's University College, Belfast. His publications include *Christ in Eternity and Time* (Dublin, 2001) and the edited collection (with Pascal Scallon) *A Church with a Future* (Dublin, 2005).

David Doyle was until his recent retirement associate professor at the school of history and archives at University College, Dublin. His books include *Irish Immigrants in the Land of Canaan: Letters and Memoirs from Colonial and Revolutionary America, 1675–1815* (New York, 2006); *Ireland, Irishmen and Revolutionary America, 1760–1820* (Dublin, 1981).

Owen Dudley Edwards was the reader in American and Commonwealth History at the University of Edinburgh, where he remains an honorary fellow and active member of the history faculty. He has published widely on the history, culture and literature of Ireland and is a recognised expert on Sir Arthur Conan Doyle, P. G. Wodehouse and Oscar Wilde. His books include: *British Children's Fiction in the Second World War* (Edinburgh, 2009); *Eamon de Valera* (Cardiff, 1988); *The Quest for Sherlock Holmes* (Edinburgh, 1983); *The Sins of Our Fathers* (Dublin, 1970).

David Finnegan has recently completed a fellowship at Trinity College Dublin, and has been working on a work entitled 'The Impact of the Counter-Reformation on the Political Thinking of Irish Catholics, *c.*1540–*c.*1640'. He is a co-editor of *The Flight of the Earls* (Derry, 2010).

Louise Fuller is an Associate Fellow of the Department of History at the National University of Ireland, Maynooth. Her published books and articles include *Irish Catholicism since 1950: The Undoing of a Culture* (Dublin, 2002); *Irish and Catholic? Towards an Understanding of Identity* (Dublin, 2006).

Raymond Gillespie is professor of history at the National University of Ireland, Maynooth. He writes on social change in early modern Ireland. His books include: *Devoted People: Belief and Religion in Early Modern Ireland* (Manchester, 1997), *Seventeenth-Century Ireland: Making Ireland Modern* (Dublin, 2006); *Ireland: Art into History* (Dublin, 1994). His latest book is (edited with R.F. Foster), *Irish Provincial Cultures in the Long Eighteenth Century* (Dublin, 2012).

Brian Jackson was awarded a Ph.D. from Trinity College, Dublin in 2007, for his work on the role of the Jesuits in the Irish Counter-Reformation. He has published in several scholarly journals, including *Analecta Hibernica*. He is director of postgraduate studies at the Institute of Technology, Carlow.

Richard Keogh recently completed a Ph.D. on Catholic loyalism in mid-Victorian Ireland, at Northumbria University.

James McConnel is principal lecturer in history at Northumbria University. He is the author of *The Irish Parliamentary Party and the Third Home Rule Crisis* (Dublin, 2013) and numerous journal articles.

Bernhard Maier is professor of religious studies and the European history of religion at the University of Tubingen. His many books and articles have appeared in English, German and Japanese. His writings include *The Celts* (Edinburgh: 2003); *Semitic Studies in Victorian Britain* (Würzburg, 2011); *Wörterbuch Schottisch–Gälisch/Deutsch und Deutsch/Schottisch–Gälisch* (Hamburg, 2011).

Patrick Maume is a researcher on the *National Dictionary of Irish Biography*. He has published numerous books and articles on nineteenth- and twentieth-century Irish history and has edited eleven titles in the UCD Press Classics of Irish History series. His is author of *The Long Gestation: Irish Nationalist Life 1891–1918* (Dublin, 1999).

James Murray is Director of Academic Affairs, Institutes of Technology Ireland. He is author of the acclaimed *Enforcing the English Reformation in Ireland: Clerical Resistance and Political Conflict in the Diocese of Dublin, 1534–1590* (Cambridge, 2009).

Éamonn Ó Ciardha is senior lecturer in history at the University of Ulster. He has written *Ireland and the Jacobite Cause, 1685–1766: A Fatal Attachment* (Dublin, 2002); he co-edited *The Irish Statute Staple Books, 1596–1687* (1999), *The Flight of the Earls* (Derry, 2010) and *The Plantation of Ulster: Ideology and Politics* (Manchester, 2012).

Donnchadh Ó Corráin is professor emeritus of medieval history at University College, Cork. He has published widely on early medieval Irish institutions, culture, law, literature, historical sources and the Viking wars. His works include: *Ireland before the Normans* (Dublin, 1972). He is founder-editor of the medieval studies journal *Peritia* (vols 1–23, 1982–2012, in progress). He has edited *Women in Irish Society: the Historical Dimension* (Dublin and Westport CN, 1979) with Margaret MacCurtain; *Irish Antiquity* (Cork, 1981); *Sages, Saints and Storytellers* (Maynooth, 1989) with L. Breatnach and K. McCone; *James Hogan: Revolutionary, Historian and Political Scientist* (Dublin, 2001); *The Viking Age: Ireland and the West* (Dublin, 2010), with J. Sheehan.

Bernard O'Donoghue is a noted contemporary Irish poet and academic. He retired as fellow and tutor in English at Wadham College, Oxford in 2011. His published work includes *The Courtly Love Tradition* (Manchester, 1982); and a number of poetry collections including *Poaching Rights* (London: 1987), *The Absent Signifier* (London, 1990); *The Weakness* (London: 1991); *Gunpowder* (London: 1995), which won the Whitbread Prize for Poetry; *Here Nor There* (London, 1999); *Outliving* (London, 2003). He is the author of a highly regarded work on Seamus Heaney, *Seamus Heaney and the Language of Poetry* (London, 1994); and also edited *The Cambridge Companion to Seamus Heaney* (Cambridge: 2008).

Ciaran O'Neill is Ussher Lecturer in history at Trinity College, Dublin. His most recent publication is *Irish Elites in the Nineteenth Century* (Dublin, 2013).

Éamon Phoenix is a political historian at Stranmillis University College, Belfast. His books include: *Northern Nationalism* (Belfast, 1994): *Two Acres of Irish History: Study Through Time of Friar's Bush and Belfast, 1570–1918* (Belfast, 2000); *Feis Na Ngleann: a century of Gaelic Culture in the Antrim Glens* (Belfast, 2005). He is co-editor of *Conflicts in the North of Ireland, 1900–2000: Flashpoints and Fracture Zones* (Dublin, 2010).

Oliver P. Rafferty, SJ has published numerous articles and five books. The most recent are *The Catholic Church and the Protestant State: Nineteenth-Century Irish Realities* (Dublin, 2008), and the edited collection *George Tyrrell and Catholic Modernism* (Dublin, 2010). He lectures on church history at Heythrop College, University of London. He has held visiting professorships at various universities in the United States, Asia and Australia.

Salvador Ryan is professor of ecclesiastical history at St Patrick's College, Maynooth. He has published numerous articles and has co-edited *Art and Devotion in Late Medieval Ireland* (Dublin, 2006) and *Devotional Cultures of European Christianity 1790–1960* (Dublin, 2012).

Frank Shovlin is senior lecturer of Irish literature in English at the Institute of Irish Studies, University of Liverpool. He is the author of *The Irish Literary Periodical 1923–1958* (Oxford, 2003), and *Journey Westward: Joyce, Dubliners and the Literary Revival* (Liverpool, 2012).

Acknowledgements

My thanks in the first place to my fellow contributors who have made the process of compiling this book a real pleasure. As with any such work, involving a large number of contributors, some individuals were more assiduous about observing deadlines than others. I should like to especially thank those whose patience has been tested by contributions that were long delayed, admittedly for a variety of legitimate reasons. 'All's well that ends well' as Shakespeare assures us.

I should also like to record my gratitude to the three anonymous readers who examined the proposal for this work and the complete typescript. Their comments were both a challenge and an encouragement.

I must also thank all those at Manchester University Press who have worked on this book at the various stages of its evolution, and whose skill has brought it to completion.

Introduction

Oliver P. Rafferty

Historians, literary critics and sociologists have in recent years given much attention to questions of identity formation as a paradigm for explaining how peoples and nations function geographically, politically and in terms of social cohesion. A number of issues are thereby raised. What are the factors that lead individuals and groups to use specific labelling devices to differentiate themselves from others? Issues of inclusion and exclusion underscore much of the preoccupation of group cohesion on which a sense of identity is constructed. Such processes are the results of long and complex factors predicated not only on common historical experiences but also within the context of literary articulation in a given culture. Often, however, attempts at drawing the contours of ethnic, cultural or political identity are the product of constructed myths as well as historical realities. Such a phenomenon gives rise to what has been described as 'historico-mythic consciousness' where nations, and groups within nations, narrate an understanding of themselves which although conforming to their sense of identity may not necessarily be an accurate reflection of the historical evolution of that particular group or nation. Equally the 'myth' may more truly represent the sense of identity than the reality of the historical experience itself.

The aim of this work is to address these issues for the Irish context and to delineate the history of identity formation in Ireland as this unfolds from the early middle ages to the present. For a large part of our history the two primary components in Irish identity, for the great majority of people who have lived on the island of Ireland, are a sense of 'Irishness' often conceived in broad terms and subject to fluctuating understanding of what constitutes such an identity, and adherence to the Catholic faith. The influence, authority and role of the Catholic Church in shaping Irish Catholic consciousness are, therefore, paramount as a template for understanding Ireland and the Irish historically. Among the issues raised is the seminal question: does it make sense to think in terms of a clear and distinct identity over time, and is this sense of identity linked with a specific political and religious unity? Is Irish identity simply a construction, an 'invented tradition', which is then read back into Irish history for purposes of nationalist and sectarian hegemony? If for the sake of argument we posit a distinct Irish identity, is this inextricably linked with the history of Catholic Christianity in the country? What then is the relationship between the specifics of Celtic/Irish culture and professing the Catholic faith? Of course it could be argued that such a question could only arise actually and historically in Ireland in circumstances where the hegemony of Catholicism was challenged as indeed it was in the sixteenth century. But, on the other hand, it could be argued that challenges to identity formation were in many ways the norm in Ireland with successive waves of invaders becoming stakeholders in the culture culminating in the twelfth-century Norman invasion.

Clearly Irish history, and therefore the sense of identity of the Irish, is complicated by the fact of the sixteenth-century Protestant Reformation so that there is no easy equation between Irishness on the one hand and Catholicism on the other. Equally, can a sense of distinct 'nationhood' be read into the history of Ireland before the sixteenth century? One of the ironic and unintended features of Henry VIII's assumption of the title king of Ireland was that it helped to foment a sense of Irish nationhood, in the sense that a king must have a kingdom, and so the kingdom of Ireland in the modern sense of a unitary state began to evolve. This kingdom was, however, for some a nation in opposition to England and some sections of the nation began to regard the English in Ireland as something foreign to Irish Catholic experience. Some aspects of this problem were of course already present in Ireland since the coming of the Normans.

What now became paradigmatic for many of the Irish was the struggle not only against England, and subsequently Britain, but the resistance to Protestantism. In that sense can we say that Irish Catholic identity was a negative construct? If the answer to that question is yes, did this negative construct remain the delimiting model for identity from the Reformation to the present? These and related questions form the context for the chapters in this volume.

I

In Part I of the work these issues are examined for the period between the coming of Christianity and the later middle ages. Bernhard Maier introduces the reader to the most important historical dates of early Christian Ireland from the fifth to the twelfth centuries. The idea here is to show the salient features of early Irish ecclesiastical organisation and some characteristic forms of liturgy, piety and devotion. These then became the constituents of how the Christian Irish were to see themselves. This is revealed by indicating the names of individuals, places and texts which would become touchstones for identity formation in the subsequent history of Ireland. Among the issues addressed is the relationship between pagan past and Christian present in early medieval Ireland. This is an essential consideration not only for the grafting of the new religion onto forms of Celtic thought and culture but also for how in later centuries the Irish would look to their 'Celtic past' for a sense of themselves. The position of Irish Christianity within a wider 'Catholic' context, including the Mediterranean and Near East indicates the ways in which Irish Christianity was or was not distinct from that practised in other areas of the Christian world. This becomes important for another theme addressed in this chapter, namely the Irish contribution to the Christianisation of north Britain and areas of mainland continental Europe. Was there a specifically Celtic form of Christianity? Furthermore, what were the formative influences of this early period on later post-Norman historical development in Irish religion and society?

Donnchdah Ó Corráin develops this trope in Chapter 2, but in his case he directly challenges some aspects of the image of early medieval Ireland as a land of saints and scholars. That particular idea, cherished by generations of Catholics in the nineteenth and twentieth centuries as a totem of a holy and learned tradition, is now open to serious question. What can be said of the early medieval period is that Ireland did indeed contribute enormously to the development of European civilisation. However, the institutional church far from being of positive benefit to early Christian Ireland was by turns domineering and rapacious. Apart from anything else it was keen to protect its place in Irish society and especially the rights to property that it had, not always honestly, acquired. Such rights it enshrined into ecclesiastical law which the church ensured would take priority over Brehon law. It is clear that ecclesiastical position was a means of enrichment and dominance in a culture whose members were all too sensitive to ideas of aristocratic lineage.

Ecclesiastics were prepared to manipulate the teachings of scripture, and the early Fathers of the church, in order to guard their position and their property. If this did not work, they did not scruple to use violence against those whom they considered their enemies, whether laity or fellow clerics and monks. Another important aspect of early medieval Ireland was slavery. The church too owned slaves and although Christianity in general had an ambiguous attitude to slavery, in Ireland scribes were not above distorting the tradition to justify contemporary practices. Thus the *Vita Tripatita* of St Patrick has the saint, who was after all a runaway slave, buying his freedom with miraculously found gold, thus preserving church practice in regard to the manumission of slaves. For some offences against church personnel Irish canon law stipulated the payment by the offender of female slaves who, as the Annals make clear, were often used for sexual purposes by their masters. Whatever about the absence of saintliness in the early medieval Irish Church, Ó Corráin is convinced that its reputation for scholarship is securely grounded.

In Chapter 3, Salvador Ryan examines the issue of cultural Catholicism in the later middle ages (*c.*1200–*c.*1550), by way of devotional cults and practices. The evidence, such as it is, does allow for an account of the distinctiveness of the Christian religion *inter hibernicos* as against its rival and equivalent *inter anglicos.* What does the devotional life of these two main groups in Ireland actually tell us about religious and cultural identity in Ireland in the high middle ages? Does the devotional landscape of Ireland in those centuries reveal that national identity gave rise to specific devotions that marked the cultural differences between the 'natives' and the English in Ireland? Were some cults and observances more popular in Anglo-Irish areas that in Gaelic territory? Were some cults confined to particular regions and wholly absent elsewhere, and can this be attributed to a devotional divide between *Gael* and *Gall* or should other factors be taken into consideration?

As Ryan explains, however, to examine late medieval cultural Catholicism in Ireland in this way should not be restricted to making facile distinctions between two communities (in itself a problematic concept); rather, this cultural Catholicism has to be judged in the wider context of later medieval European Catholicism(s) as a whole. To what extent, then, did the burgeoning European devotional cultures of the later middle ages influence and shape practical Catholicism in Ireland? Did Catholics in Ireland regard themselves as part of a larger Catholic culture and, if so, how did this identity reconcile itself with assertions of distinctiveness? Furthermore, how different was one's identity as an Anglo-Irish Catholic in the fifteenth century Pale from that of an English Catholic visitor, or indeed from the 'mere Irish' within the Pale and those outside it?

II

Without doubt the Reformation in England, evolving as it did hand in hand with Tudor state-building, had profound consequences for Irish identity. But why did the Reformation not progress as systematically in Ireland as in its sister island? Was it in fact because the Gaelic Irish manipulated the new distinction in religion as a means of emphasising linguistic and cultural differences and took the opportunity to use religious differences as an ideologically more powerful tool for distinctive identity aimed at greater political control? The resentments which had been present to a greater or lesser extent for centuries now had a coherence provided by religious difference, which had been impossible when both main groups shared the same religion. But of course the picture is much more complex than this brief synopsis would suggest. However, as David Finnegan in Chapter 4 indicates, the sixteenth century did witness a definite, if slow, transformation of the Irish political and religious landscape. However the impetus for religious reform in Ireland came not from Henry VIII but from the Observantine tendencies within some Catholic religious orders. In the face of the Henrician and Edwardian reforms, the Catholic clergy, and most laity, still asserted the pope's rights – even at political level – in Irish affairs. The essential element, however, in Tudor reform was the political transformation of the country. Even as late as Elizabeth's reign some English officials were reluctant to press religious change too rigorously.

The determination of the majority of the Irish to remain Catholic was nevertheless combined, for some, with a sense of continued loyalty to a Protestant monarchy. And although some bishops pursued such a policy, it became clear that such an attitude could not last and it imposed an enormous strain on those who tried to maintain such dual loyalty. The northern ringing of the 1590s sought to make Catholicism the unifying force among the Old English and the Gaelic Irish. However many of the clergy urged an alliance with Spain in order to frustrate Protestant political and religious ambitions in the country, which did nothing for pan-Catholic unity.

Although Raymond Gillespie (in Chapter 7) will subsequently show the difficulties in disentangling discrete lines of Catholic and Protestant influences, Finnegan demonstrates that ultimately certain sections of the Catholic clergy and laity were prepared to welcome and implement the more militant and warlike aspects of the Catholic Counter-Reformation. But Finnegan argues this was in line with a distinct political Catholicism that had already emerged in an attitude of defiance and resistance stretching back to the 1530s. By the seventeenth century, the last great European war of religion of 1618–48, had distinct cognates in the campaign waged at various levels in Ireland against Protestantism, which had its apogee in the struggles of the 1640s. The period Finnegan surveys produced what he believes was a revolution in the confessional culture of Ireland. Furthermore, the experiences of the defeat of the Confederation of Kilkenny and the rise of Cromwellian government provided the parameters for the characteristics of Catholic identity in Ireland which would endure well into the eighteenth century and beyond. The fact remains, however, that the Catholic clergy strengthened Catholic resistance to the emergent Protestant state and this in turn by the beginning of the eighteenth century emboldened the Irish government to deal with Catholic menace in the shape of the 'popery' laws.

Meanwhile for the sixteenth century James Murray is concerned to drawn attention to the main features of Anglo-Irish Catholic clerical identity in the mid-sixteenth century (Chapter 5). In particular he examines the career of Archbishop George Dowdall of Armagh, and the famous occasion on which Dowdall fled from Ireland in 1551, when the religious situation became unbearable for him. The cause of his flight was inextricably linked with his sense of religious identity. Dowdall had after all conformed under Henry and had accepted the royal supremacy. The intention here is to show that while identity was strong and long established at the outset of the Reformation, it was not impervious to change, especially in the 1540s. However, Murray argues that identity became entrenched in the mid-Tudor period in response to a complex and interrelated set of political and religious changes initiated by the Edwardian regime in Ireland. As a result, Catholicism became an essential part of Old English identity, and set in place the necessary conditions for the forging of a new, Irish Catholic identity among the Old English and Gaelic Irish communities in the following century. It would take quite some considerable time for both communities to feel at ease with this new identity and it is perhaps an irony that these two groups, so long at odds with one another, now became more enmeshed because of a common religious world-view. That world-view was not simply Gaelic and Old Irish but very much shared the religious horizons of the Old English, and in a certain sense the identification of the Irish as Catholic owes at least as much to the 'English' tradition in Ireland as it does to the 'Gaelic'.

Of course, increasingly, as the sixteenth century progressed, that world-view was being definitively forged on the anvil of the Counter-Reformation, spearheaded as this was by the Council of Trent. In the face of European Protestantism, a new sense and purpose was now envisaged by Tridentine Catholicism. The most effective instrument of the Tridentine reform was the Jesuit order, the Society of Jesus. Almost at the beginning of its existence the Jesuits had become involved in the affairs of Ireland and although the 1542 mission to the country, which lasted only one month, gave a bleak assessment of the state of

Catholicism, nevertheless Ireland would become an important centre for Jesuit activity, even though for a ten-year period (1585–95) the Jesuits were absent from the country.

Their activity and role in shaping the religious identity of Irish Catholicism in the late sixteenth and early seventeenth centuries is addressed by Brian Jackson in Chapter 6. In particular he focuses on the figure of Fr Henry Fitzsimon. Fitzsimon claimed, perhaps for purposes of controversy, that he was born and brought up a Protestant in Ireland. His family may, however, have simply been 'church-papists'. Nevertheless he attended Oxford University, was 'converted' to Catholicism on a visit to France and joined the Jesuits. He was part of the renewed Jesuit mission which landed in Ireland in 1595. A controversialist of the first order, he engaged in dispute with, among others, the Church of Ireland primate Archbishop James Ussher. Fitzsimon was a typical product of the 'church militant' and spent a good deal of his time strengthening Irish Catholic resistance to Protestantism. His work also included the reconciliation of Protestants with Catholicism and of course this also involved delicate and complex issues of political allegiance. Banished from Ireland in the early seventeenth century, he spent several years as chaplain to Irish brigades in the armies of the Holy Roman empire in the course of the Thirty Years' War. He returned to the country in 1630 imbued with the same aggressive mentality, and was clearly one of a number of Catholic priests who gave Irish Catholicism its sense of struggle against the forces of Protestantism in its political manifestations. But his was very much a Catholicism of the Old English Pale and in many ways removed from that of the 'mere Irish' Catholics.

Fitzsimons had already left Ireland by the time of the plantation of Ulster, an event which proved to be a pivotal moment in the shaping of modern Ireland. While it has been assumed that the colonisation of Ulster by settlers introduced a religious and ethnic cleavage which was fundamental for the shaping of Irish Catholic identity, and which was coterminous with the plantation, this was not in fact the case. In Chapter 7, Raymond Gillespie points to the fact that some of the settlers were Catholic, most significantly the earl of Abercorn from Scotland and the earl of Castlehaven from England. In the case of Castlehaven his religious beliefs had political implications since he supported the Confederates in the 1640s. Outside the formal plantation scheme, but within Ulster, the largest settler landowner, the earl of Antrim, was also a Catholic. Despite the apparent commonalities of religion between certain settlers and the native Irish, there were distinct differences between the types of Catholicism that existed within Ulster in the seventeenth century. Gillespie examines these divergences by using the Catholicism of the Gaelic Irish as a base from which comparisons can be made in order to understand the range of Catholic identities, both settler and native, that emerged as part of the plantation process.

III

If as Gillespie argues there was a blurring of a sense of Catholic identity in Plantation Ulster this was not the only reality. Protestant and 'British' incursions were resisted at political and cultural levels. Éamonn Ó Ciardha in Chapter 8 explores the implications of this for the development of Irish Catholic identity as preserved in Irish language texts from the early modern period until the end of Stuart pretensions. One issue which has long been disputed is the question of how much of a threat Catholicism was to the Protestant settlement in Ireland. In so far as Catholics entertained hopes of overturning what became the Hanoverian regime, those ambitions rested in loyalty to the Jacobite cause. But were such hopes realistic? Was the liberation of Catholic Ireland based on a romantic view of the Stuart monarchy? In the actual circumstances of Jacobite uprisings against the Hanoverians, Catholic Ireland proved less than reliable. The ideology of a Catholic Irish and Stuart alliance was kept alive not by displays of military prowess but by Gaelic poetry and prose. Its manifestation in the eighteenth century was drawing on a literature which emphasised distinctiveness from what was *Gall* and Protestant and which had seen something of a renaissance since the early seventeenth century.

By the mid-eighteenth century, however, it was clear that the Hanoverian settlement would not be overturned, and Pope Clement XIII, recognising the political realities, removed all vestiges of Stuart pretences and decreed that Rome would no longer recognise the Stuarts' claim with respect to episcopal appointments. This enabled some Irish Catholics, usually the better off, to protest their loyalty to the Protestant monarchy, thereby facilitating a new identity for Irish Catholics in which loyalty to both the old religion and the Protestant state could be asserted. The reality but not the romanticism of the Stuart legacy was at an end. The resurgence of 'Catholic power' in O'Connell as the 'Liberator' and of Parnell as the 'uncrowned king of Ireland', in the nineteenth century owed much to the continued hold of the Stuart romanticism of the previous century. That romanticism and the attachment to the Stuarts following 1690 had been hardened by the experience of the popery laws, following the 'betrayal' of Catholic Ireland by a failure to keep the terms of the Treaty of Limerick. But was the experience of the penal laws as universally embittering as nineteenth and twentieth-century Catholics claimed? It is to an analysis of this issue that Tom Bartlett turns his attention in Chapter 9. The laws have long been regarded as evidence of Protestant hatred of Catholicism and have been a touchstone of how Catholics regarded themselves under Protestant rule. For generations the enactments were seen as the instruments whereby a hateful and foreign minority sought to deprive the majority of its rights and liberties in respect of economic activity and religion. Catholics have long cherished the penal laws as emblematic of their centuries' long sufferings in which they are cast in the role of victims. But is the ideology of Catholic suffering at the hands of unscrupulous Protestants as enshrined in the enactments actually true? What was the purpose of the laws and how effective were they? In particular, were they actually implemented? What was the extent of persecution, and were priests and monks actually hunted down, or is this the stuff of legend? On the other hand was the symbolic value of the laws more important in the construction of eighteenth and nineteenth-century identity than any disabilities that Catholics may actually have experienced in their implementation?

The penal laws and the manner in which Catholics viewed them at the time and subsequently, became an important template and interpretative model for Irish Catholic self-understanding. Although in the subsequent history of Ireland it would be theoretically possible to differentiate between Irishness and Catholicism, the history of the penal laws would underscore the bitterness between Catholics and Protestants at times of social and political tension. The institutional Catholic Church, certainly in the Cullen and post-Cullen era, harboured profound grievances as a result of the penal enactments, and this sense of historical grievance would condition its response to subsequent enactments and would make it difficult for official Catholicism to estimate objectively London's attempts at remedial legislation.

IV

Owen Dudley Edwards in a typically bravura piece is concerned in Chapter 10 to explore nineteenth-century Irish Catholic cultural identity. He uses the penal code as a lens through which to examine Catholic attitudes to the law. Edwards demonstrates that hatred for the penal laws caused fissures to appear in Catholic attitudes to law in general and to the courts, which continued to be manifest even in independent Ireland. Despite the clear teaching of the church, and at times campaigns by reforming bishops, the Irish found it difficult, especially in forensic contexts, to see an absolute obligation to tell the truth. This gave ammunition to Protestant polemical propaganda, and became the stuff of legend for Anglo-Irish writers, and their English friends, in their observations about the Irish character.

At one level, Edwards argues, the penal code invited disrespect and perjury, since the laws were aimed at the eradication of what the majority of the Irish held dearer than life, the Catholic faith. Given the hostility to the law, the idea of perjury as a means of negating its effects entered deeply into the Irish Catholic psyche. Furthermore it is argued that so far as eighteenth-century Irish Catholic experience is concerned, perjury was regarded as theologically irrelevant. Edwards also draws attention to Gustave de Beaumont's judgement that under the penal laws the Catholic Irish lost their love for truth, since in that context truthfulness would ensure further persecution.

That acute nineteenth-century observer of rural Irish life, William Carleton took the matter further and asserted that falsehood was essential for the functioning of society. Carleton also regarded the law in Ireland as oppressive. It is with an analysis of Carleton's account of the Wildgoose Lodge murders and the role of oath swearing and perjury in that grisly episode that Edwards brings his fascinating study to an end, but not before coming to a somewhat surprising conclusion.

One aspect of Irish Catholic identity that has in the past been often overlooked is the experience of women. This is true not only in the male-dominated church but also in the equally male-dominated nationalist movement. Caitriona Clear's contribution (Chapter 11) focuses on two sets of women's experience in the 'long nineteenth century': women activists and nuns. The phenomenal increase in the number of nuns in Ireland from 100 at the beginning of the nineteenth century to 8,000 by its end, helped to transform the face of Catholic Ireland. They did so in active religious orders of Irish, French and English origin as they engaged in education, nursing and social work. In the directly religious sphere it was often they who implemented the 'devotional revolution' at the local level and encouraged a distinctive mode in faith formation of generations of Irish Catholic children.

These nuns had their counterparts in the secular sphere in ordinary working-class/farming women and also in the middle classes, in women who forged identity in the context of the home. In the later decades of the nineteenth-century the impetus for reform and social engagements was also seen in direct political involvement such as in the Women's Land League, but also in writing and publishing. Important individuals, not all Catholic, such as the Parnell sisters, Sissy O'Brien, Maude Gonne, Constance Markievicz and Alice Milligan emerge not only as substantial figures in their own right but also as significant players in the shaping of Irish consciousness. Furthermore, Clear is convinced that a particular female Catholic consciousness evolved in nineteenth-century Ireland which had mixed consequences for Ireland in the twentieth century.

If religious culture was in part shaped by women, it is also clear that Irish secular culture was undergoing deep transformations in the nineteenth century. This was caused not just by political and religious developments but also by the cataclysm of the Famine. But even here there was a tendency to read the Famine in religious as well as political and economic terms. In a certain sense the emergence of Irish Catholic identity in the modern era is perhaps uniquely a result of the historical experience of Ireland in the nineteenth century. A growing literacy in English facilitated an exchange of ideas and a reflection on ideas of identity that were expressed in newspapers, journals and books in a manner unsurpassed in any other era.

The Irish diaspora was already widespread before the Famine, but in the wake of that catastrophe millions of individuals were sent out to the USA and into the British empire. Often memories and folk memories of the inhumanity of the Famine experience conditioned and shaped the context of the diaspora and a mindset which often resulted in an identity more overtly anti-British than that of those who remained in Ireland. Those at home continued to be financially dependent on the generosity of those abroad and this facilitated important exchanges between the home and host countries. Although in many instances financial prospects improved with immigration the fact of exile often witnessed the weakening of the link with Catholicism.

Some Irish churchmen such as Cardinal Cullen saw in emigration a sort of panacea for Ireland's ills in the mid-nineteenth century, while bishops in places as far apart as London and Toronto saw the other side and warned of its dangers as the Irish appeared over-represented in the criminal classes of the host countries. In Chapter 12, David Doyle examines in particular the North American experience and especially the importance of the USA for consolidating a particular interpretation of Irish Catholic nationalist identity. But that identity was constructed also within the terms of American Catholic experience as a whole, with the Irish element competing with the Germans, Poles, Italians and other Catholic immigrant groups for a sense of what it was to be Catholic in a non-denominational, and frequently hostile, culture.

V

Catholic Ireland was not simply the passive victim of poverty and squalor in the nineteenth century. The desire for political change, for a reconfiguration of the social circumstances of the country was aligned with a growing sense of Catholic power. The question was how best to use that power for the transformation of Irish society. There was tension between the projects of a developing Catholic 'Whig' elite represented by those such as William Monsell and Lord O'Hagan, who sought to give the Catholic hierarchy some influence over the Irish administration (with which Cardinal Paul Cullen was to some extent associated), and the belief in a populist alliance between Catholicism and nationalism represented by those such as Fredrick Lucas.

Ironically, Lucas was both an Englishman and a convert to Catholicism but he was one who embraced the cause of Ireland with an ardent enthusiasm in which he represented himself as the advocate of the poor and the downtrodden. He used the Catholic newspaper which he founded, the *Tablet*, to propose an increasingly radical Catholic social agenda which engendered deep distrust on the part of English Catholic churchmen such as the Tory bishop, and future cardinal, Nicholas Wiseman, but which also proved too much for the likes of Cullen and those Irish bishops who thought like him. These bad relations with the hierarchy in two countries reflected a wider ideological dispute. Lucas, having come to Catholicism from dissenting religion, he had also been a political radical, brought with him to his new faith a refusal to accept uncritically Catholic hierarchal authority. He was convinced, as Patrick Maume argues in Chapter 13, of the need for a just and moral society supervised and influenced by the Catholic Church, but a church that was free from political alliances of any kind. Elected an MP for Co. Meath in 1852 his radical social agenda set him apart from fellow Irish MPs but especially from the Irish bishops. He was prepared to appeal to papal authority in his disputes with Cullen over the direction of Irish Catholic public life and his untimely death in 1855, much to the relief of Cullen who attributed it to divine intervention, deprived Irish Catholicism of one of its few socially radical influences.

Ireland would, however, Fergal Casey argues in Chapter 14, continue to have a deep impact in the construction of Catholic social thought in England and this is exemplified in the person who was the leader of the English Catholic Church from 1865 to 1892 Cardinal Henry Edward Manning. Manning, in trying to reconcile the English church to Cullen's Irish hierarchy and in dealing with the influx of Irish immigrants to England especially his diocese of Westminster, was radicalised at the level of political and economic theory. His *Ireland: A Letter to Earl Grey* (1868) saw him adopt all but revolutionary ideas in response to Irish conditions. This led to a more general economic radicalism as exemplified in his *The Dignity and Rights of Labour* (1874) a work which is said to have made a great impact on Pope Leo XIII in his formulation of Catholic social teaching as expounded in the encyclical *Rerum novarum* (1891). Manning's growing political activism in the 1880s, such as his mediation in the London dock strike and his 'Distress in winter' letters to *The Times,* was also linked to his growing connection to the land league and home rule movements. He was also a member of the royal commission on housing the working classes and was the principal author of its report. However, this report was too radical for other members of the commission such as the Prince of Wales and it was finally edited by another member of the commission in a manner which made it, as Manning told Sir Charles Dilke, 'pale with fear'. Manning's social justice activism was in turn to have a great influence on Chesterton and Belloc and attested to the significance of Irish Catholic affairs for English Catholic social thinking.

VI

As has been suggested, not all nineteenth-century Irish Catholic experience was universally bleak. Catholic Ireland had its share of the rich and of middle-class *arrivistes*. In looking at the educational provision of the boys from such families, Ciaran O'Neill in Chapter 15 comes to some surprising conclusions. His chapter focuses on such children in English Catholic public schools like Stonyhurst and Downside where the staunchly establishment Irish Catholics and the rising mercantile classes sought to have the characteristics of the Catholic gentleman instilled in their progeny. Like all socially ambitious groups they kept the prevailing political wind constantly before their minds, in distinct contrast to the prevailing ethos of the sons of the same class who attended equivalent schools in Ireland such as Blackrock College and Clongowes where a more general air of constitutional nationalism could be found.

Drawing on data from over one thousand schoolboys, O'Neill delineates a series of Catholic networks, informal and unstated, which served to reinforce an Irish Catholic identity based on wealth, privilege and educational advantage. Here he gives a synopsis of the political stance of these networks and charts their responsiveness to the undulations of change in the political status quo.

Some of the individuals from this group were clearly opposed to home rule and made their loyalty to the Union all too clear. This is a theme taken up by Richard Keogh and James McConnel. Their aim here is to look at the phenomenon of Catholic unionism via the Esmonde family of Co. Waterford. Chapter 16 examines Catholic unionism vis-à-vis Victorian politics, military and imperial service, the crown, and the position of the Catholic Church with relation to the structures of the state in Ireland. From a study of the Esmondes the authors extrapolate some general conclusions about the state and extent of Catholic unionism in Ireland prior to the First World War.

Continuing this idea Eamon Phoenix in Chapter 17 looks at one of the most intriguing Catholic unionists whose career spans united and divided Ireland: Denis Stanilaus Henry. Like some of those whom Ciaran O'Neill examines, Henry was from a well-to-do Catholic family in Draperstown, South Derry. One sibling became a Marist priest and another brother William, became a Jesuit. Denis himself attended the English Jesuit minor public school Mount St Mary's College in north Derbyshire. Perhaps it was his school background which confirmed him in a lifelong dedication to the interest of the Union. He stood in the conservative and unionist interest in North Tyrone in 1906 and 1907 being each time pipped at the post by a Protestant home ruler. He was eventually elected to parliament. His political adroitness, cultivated manner and unmistakeable abilities ensured that he attained to the top of his profession and he was to become successively solicitor general and attorney general for Ireland. A hardliner during the Anglo-Irish War he was a scourge of nationalist sentiment and his views served increasingly to isolate him from many of his co-religionists. He became, with the creation of Northern Ireland the first lord chief justice in the new state and rendered distinguished service on the bench. No other Catholic was to attain that rank and indeed it would be 1948 before another Catholic was even appointed as a high court judge. Henry's life and views and the office he held does indicate a greater display of openness in the early stages of Northern Ireland unionism than would ever be the case again.

VII

Historical and political developments in the nineteenth century meant that the identification of Catholic and Irish was well in place by the time of independence. Several factors would serve to reinforce this symbiosis of Irish and Catholic between the 1920s and 1960s, not least the revival of the Irish language. Independent Ireland reflected the self-identity of the majority of its citizens in its reflection of Catholic social mores. By the 1960s, however, social aspirations and economic improvements would cause cracks to appear in the too cosy coalescence between Irishness and Catholicism and indeed in the very definition of such identity. A number of factors contributed to this: changes in education, the widespread use of television and internally in Catholicism, the Second Vatican Council. One of the symbols of the change sweeping Irish Catholicism was the removal in 1970 of the ban on Catholics attending Trinity College, Dublin.

The eruption of the Troubles in Northern Ireland, as Louise Fuller maintains in Chapter 18, forced southerners to confront the unquestioned assumptions and uncomfortable realities in relation to identity and allegiance as the IRA began murdering northern Protestants and British soldiers, and indeed anyone else who opposed them, in the name of Ireland. Even in the Republic, self-propelled change would lead to the removal from the constitution in 1972 of the clause relating to the 'special position' of the Catholic Church in the Irish state. The visit of Pope John Paul II in 1979 seemed to confirm the Catholic ethos of the Republic, but even before he arrived the Family Planning Act of July that year made contraceptives legal in Ireland for the first time in defiance of Catholic moral teaching. Such trends were confirmed by the New Ireland Forum of 1983 and by the abortion referendum in September that year. Although the pro-life amendment was carried by a margin of 66 per cent, it revealed a wide divergence between rural and urban Ireland in terms of the acceptance of Catholic teaching on abortion.

This process of erosion in the Catholic mores of Irish society was at work over a sustained period of time. As Frank Shovlin points out in Chapter 19, the decline in vocations to the priesthood and religious life in Ireland over the past fifty years is mirrored in the decline in respect for Catholicism among one of the most important elements in Irish cultural articulation: Irish writers. Gone are the avuncular priests of Canon Sheehan or the committed nuns of Kate O'Brien. In their place are the forlorn suicides like Fr Walsh in Martin Donagh's Leenane trilogy or the insane paedophile Fr Tiddly of Patrick McCabe's *The Butcher Boy*. One writer who perhaps had more reason than most to feel aggrieved by his treatment at the hands of the church was John McGahern (1934–2006). Dismissed from his post as a primary schoolteacher at the behest of Archbishop John Charles McQuaid of Dublin, his second novel *The Dark* (1965) went on to become one of the last *cause célèbres* of Irish literary censorship. Yet despite his avowed atheism, McGahern, over a forty-year writing career, provided a more searching and intriguing examination of what it is to be an Irish Catholic than any writer before or since. Frank Shovlin's chapter outlines and expounds what McGahern meant when he insisted that the church was his first book and how his use of difficult concepts such as grace and benediction could exert such a powerful and moving impact on modern Irish writing.

For his part Bernard O'Donoghue in Chapter 20 illustrates the fact that the idea of the transcendent, the relationship between the world of time and eternity, between the numinous and the immanent is a central theme in the poetry of many contemporary Irish writers. Drawing on traditions as old as the medieval mystic Julian of Norwich, but reflected in the work of modern poets such as T. S. Eliot, religious images and ideas are all pervasive in the poetry of Heaney, Muldoon, Deane and others. But here the theme is the spiritual urge towards faith rather than dogmatic Christianity as such. What we have is not an easy identification between the modern Irish poet and Christianity, but rather a redefinition of the religious going beyond the categories of a particular belief system.

Often in fact in modern Irish poetry we find expressed a secular response to religious impulses. This is especially the case in the era of the Troubles, when Christianity seemed to be expressed in murderous and combative political terms. The problem, however, is that the Irish poet in representing a culture in which religious images have been so pervasive can hardly be expected to avoid the terminology of the religious. But at the same time the poet is acutely aware that such imagery has been used to bring oppression as well as liberation. It is to the working out of the implications of this dilemma, that O'Donoghue devotes his chapter in which the themes of religion and identity are central to the concerns of a group of representative Irish poets some of whom, at a rhetorical level, paradoxically no longer consider themselves practising Christians.

O'Donoghue adverts to the problems posed by the Troubles for the identification between Catholicism and Irish nationalism. In the 1960s the Catholic Church stressed the greater role that the laity should play in church affairs. The old-style clericalism whereby the priest knew best was to be confined to the dustbin of history. When the Troubles broke out, but especially with the re-emergence of the IRA and therefore the gun in Irish politics, bishops and priests sought to distinguish clearly the Catholic community from violent republicanism. The church repeatedly condemned and excoriated Republican paramilitaries as utterly unrepresentative of the church and the Irish people. The IRA responded in kind by declaring that the church was an instrument of British imperialism in Ireland and whatever its teaching on other matters, its view on the 'armed struggle' simply could not determine the right of the people to bring about change in Northern Irish society by force.

There emerged then the classic archetype of struggle between an authoritarian ecclesiastical hierarchy and a violent dissent group, most of whose members were, at least nominally, Catholic. That struggle was not simply concerned with the morality of politically motivated violence, but was preoccupied with the question of what the Irish people actually stood for. It was a struggle for the soul so to speak, of Northern

Catholicism, in which the church insisted that it and it alone could arbitrate on what was for the good of the Catholic community. In Chapter 21, Oliver Rafferty sets out the details of this conflict between the Republicans and church authority against the background of social disintegration and a growing disregard for what the church had to offer to the Catholic community. In a sense the Republicans claimed that theirs was the authentic voice of northern Catholics and not the hierarchy.

One ironic factor in the struggles between church and terrorists was precisely, as the Provincials identified, the role of the British government as it sought to manipulate ecclesiastical opinion for propaganda purposes. The problem in this, as Rafferty discovered from examining government papers in London and ecclesiastical papers in Armagh, Dublin, Derry and Belfast, was that the government did not sufficiently trust the church, nor give sufficient credence to the church's analysis of what was happening in the north in the early 1970s. Faced by hostility from the Provisional Irish Republican Army (PIRA) and from the British administration the church was unable to be a completely effective instrument for peace and reconciliation. Its relative impotence made the IRA seem the only dynamic force in the Catholic–nationalist community.

Apart from the Troubles, and the recent financial meltdown, no greater trauma has afflicted Irish society and Irish identity than the crisis in Catholicism produced by the clerical child sex abuse scandal. Can we say that institutional Catholicism as a force in Irish society is now at an end?

Will the profession of the Catholic faith no longer be regarded as an essential component in the way in which the majority of the Irish see themselves? As the theologian Nial Coll points out, in Chapter 22, the decline in the church's role in society is not simply in virtue of the abuses committed by wayward priests, and inept and misjudged episcopal cover-up. Ireland has not been immune from the growing secularisation that has swept the industrialised west since the 1960s, and perhaps for a good deal longer.

Part of the issue originated within Catholicism itself and the forces for wide-sweeping change were unleashed, perhaps in an unforeseen way, by the Second Vatican Council. The culture wars initiated by feminism in the late 1960s, the divisive referendums on abortion and divorce in the 1980s and 1990s, and the onslaughts of a 'liberal' media have all contributed to a weakening in the identification of Irishness with Catholicism. Coll argues that Irish Catholicism now exists in a state of siege, and, to say the least, the old-style Constantinian Catholicism is dead. But can organised Catholicism per se still contribute anything to the future of Irish identity? Coll thinks that if the church is to have a meaningful role it must reform itself and have a greater role for the laity. He also points to the fact that the church's continued activity as a service provider in areas such as education, social welfare and health care, will ensure that it will in some way continue to speak to Irish society and help to shape Irish identity into the future.

Despite Coll's optimism, it nevertheless remains clear that Catholicism has now less to do with Irish identity than at any other historical period surveyed in these chapters. The gradual process of secularisation, the dominance of Anglo-American culture, coupled with the virtual loss of independence owing to the financial crisis of the last few years, means that Ireland and the Irish are less secure in their own identity than arguably at any time in their history. The fact that 10 per cent of those now living in the Republic of Ireland are immigrants will, in time, have perhaps quite profound implications for Irish identity. The rapturous welcome given to Queen Elizabeth II in Dublin in 2011, however important that event was in 'maturing' the relationship between Britain and Ireland, is itself a barometer of the transformation in the way the Irish see themselves in the early twenty-first century.

For some two hundred and fifty years in the English-speaking world, the one thing that made the Irish distinct was their Catholicism. However, as will be clear from the analysis offered in this volume Irish Catholic identity has always had a great deal of fluidity about it. The relative and continued success of the resolution of the northern conflict might sow the seeds of a new form of Irish identity. An identity that will not only have room for the two main cultural traditions, in their various guises, on the island of Ireland, but one that will have a continued role for Catholicism, however modified, in the ingredients that combine to constitute Irish identity and give shape to the Irish soul.

Part I

The Celts, Catholicism and the middle ages

1

Gaelic and Catholic in the early middle ages

Bernhard Maier

When we are asked to try to visualise Ireland's material culture in what is commonly known as the early historic period, it is probably the remains of an explicitly Christian civilisation that immediately come to mind: ruins of churches and monasteries, round towers, high crosses, illuminated manuscripts, and precious metalwork serving an explicitly Christian liturgical purpose. In some instances, what we see today still looks very much as it did when it was first produced, whereas in other cases, either deliberate destruction or continuity of use and reinterpretation has all but obliterated the original appearance. When we are asked to try and visualise the people whom we know by name from Ireland's early historic period, it is probably once more some leading representatives of the Christian church that come to mind – only that in this case our image of such figures as Patrick, Columba, Columbanus and John Scotus Eriugena is conditioned not so much by any contemporary evidence, but rather by idealising nineteenth- and twentieth-century depictions, illustrating not only the central role of early Christianity in shaping our consciousness of Irish history and identity, but also the extent to which decidedly modern modes of thought and preoccupations have contributed to forming our ideas about this distant period.

In what follows, I shall first of all give a historic overview of Christian Ireland in the early middle ages. I shall then try to evoke some salient features of early Irish Christianity, both in its material and in its spiritual aspects, working my way from the visible remains of architecture, metalwork and manuscripts to the invisible realm of concepts, values and ideas, to be culled from contemporary Latin and Irish texts. Having examined both the universal Catholic mould and the distinctively Gaelic stamp of early Irish Christianity, I shall conclude by looking at some of the ways in which it has dealt with the pre-Christian past and contributed to shaping the future.

The interaction of Gaelic and Catholic in the early middle ages has to be seen in the context of a dynamic history following the Celticisation of

Ireland and the Romanisation of western Britain.[1] The Christianisation of Ireland may be taken to have begun by the third century, presumably due to contacts with Christians within the boundaries of the Roman empire both in Britain and on the continent.[2] According to the Chronicle of Prosper of Aquitaine (*c.*390–463), it was in 431 that Pope Celestine ordained Palladius, sending him to the Irish believers in Christ (*ad Scottos in Christum credentes*). This made later Irish writers assign the beginning of Patrick's mission to the year 432, but nothing is known of Palladius' activities in Ireland, and the little that we do know for certain of Patrick is based on inferences drawn from his Latin writings, hagiographical tradition about him beginning as late as the seventh century.[3]

Monasticism having developed in Egypt in the fourth century, it had come to be adapted in western Europe by the fifth century, profoundly influencing Irish Christianity from the sixth and seventh centuries. From that period onwards, monastic centres such as Bangor in Co. Down, Monasterboice in Co. Louth, Glendalough in Co. Wicklow, Clonard in Co. Meath and Clonmacnoise in Co. Offaly played an important part not only in Irish ecclesiastical organisation and the development of Christian civilisation, but also in economic terms, functioning as storehouses for local produce and valuables and as centres of crafts, art and trade.[4] Side by side with monastic structures, an episcopal system continued to function, the church as a whole existing in close symbiosis with secular structures continuing pre-Christian traditions.[5]

A by-product of monasticism in Ireland was the ideal of a voluntary lifelong exile in the name of Christ (*peregrinatio pro Christo*), which led to widespread missionary activity both in Britain and on the continent.[6] Thus Columba (*c.*520–597) founded both the monasteries of Derry and Durrow in Ireland and the monastery of Iona off the west coast of Scotland,[7] while his namesake Columba the Younger or Columbanus (*c.*543–615) established the monasteries of Luxeuil in eastern France and Bobbio in northern Italy.[8] Other Irish missionaries were Aidan (d.651), who was sent from Iona to Lindisfarne,[9] Cillian (d.*c.*689) who was active in eastern Franconia,[10] and Virgil (d.784), who became bishop of Salzburg. This early missionary activity was followed by a substantial Irish contribution to continental scholarship during the Carolingian period,[11] most notably by Dicuil, Dungal, Sedulius Scottus and John Scottus Eriugena.[12] This in turn was followed by a significant influx of Irish Benedictine monks to the continent from the late eleventh to the fifteenth century.[13]

An important factor in the development of the church in Ireland were the raids of the Vikings, which tended to affect the monasteries most severely due to their being among the most conspicuous and most easily accessible centres of affluence.[14] Between 795 and 830, the Vikings raided the Irish coast in small bands, but afterwards in ever-larger raiding expeditions, establishing bases on the coast and on rivers and taking an active part in Irish political and economic affairs. However, if ecclesiastical structures were aversely affected by the Viking raids, the eight and ninth centuries also saw the rise of a new monastic movement associated with the stern ideals of the 'companions of God' (*céli Dé*, anglicised *culdees*), which was characterised by a rigorous asceticism, but also by a considerable literary activity.[15]

Viking ambitions in Ireland having been finally crushed in 1014 in the battle of Clontarf, the eleventh and twelfth centuries witnessed a series of reforms and innovations in the Irish church, which brought ecclesiastical structures in ever-closer line with developments in Britain and on the continent.[16] As early as 1111, the Synod of Ráth Bhreasail established a national diocesan structure, divided into a northern and a southern province, comprising thirteen and twelve territorially defined dioceses respectively, with Armagh as the primatial church. At the Synod of Kells in 1152, it was decided to create the four archbishoprics of Armagh, Cashel, Dublin and Tuam, loosening the ties which until then had connected Dublin and Canterbury. By that time, the Cistercians had already founded their first Irish monastery at Mellifont in 1142, ushering in the reform of monasticism on continental models. In 1171, the arrival of the Normans was to open a new chapter in the history of the Irish church. But how are we to envisage the church in the centuries that went before, both in material and in spiritual terms?

Following traditional building techniques of the pre-Christian period, the earliest monasteries and churches would have been made of timber, roofed with wooden shingles or thatch. This is reflected by the use of the word *dairthech* 'oak-house' to designate a wooden church in the annals, stone churches making their first appearance around 800 and remaining largely confined to important sites until the tenth and eleventh centuries.[17] A conspicuous and characteristic feature of many Irish ecclesiastical sites is the round tower, designated as *cloigthech* 'bell-house' in the annals. From the tenth to the thirteenth century, perhaps as many as a hundred round towers were built, usually at some distance to the west entrance of the church to which they belonged. Of these, more than seventy may still be seen, averaging in height from 20 to 30 metres.[18] Equally well-known features of Irish monasteries are richly sculptured high crosses, dating mainly from the ninth and tenth centuries, illustrating scenes from the Bible and some non-biblical figures.[19]

Just as well known as the architectural and sculptural remains of the early medieval monasteries is the precious metalwork which was produced under their auspices, representing some of the finest specimens of what is commonly known as insular art.[20] Among the best-known examples are the so-called Tara Brooch, discovered in 1850 at Bettystown, Co. Meath, the silver communion vessel known as the Ardagh Chalice, found near Ardagh, Co. Limerick, in 1868, and the silver chalice, paten (or communion plate) and strainer, which were discovered on the ancient monastic site of Derrynaflan, Co. Tipperary, in 1980, all of these objects now being in the National Museum of Ireland.

A corollary to the central position of the scriptures and the written tradition in early medieval Christianity was the importance of manuscripts and the art of writing, which led to the development of a peculiar 'insular' script, modelled on the continental uncial and half-uncial scripts.[21] The earliest-known Irish manuscript is the so-called *Codex Usserianus Primus*, a Latin Gospel book (now in the library of Trinity College, Dublin) probably dating from the sixth or early seventh century, before the invention of the insular script. The earliest surviving insular illuminated gospel book is the Book of Durrow, dating from the late seventh century. Possibly written in Northumbria, this manuscript, consisting of 248 vellum leaves, was kept from at least the tenth century onwards in the monastery of Durrow, Co. Offaly, before it was finally presented to Trinity College, Dublin, in 1652. Closely related to the Book of Durrow, both in terms of date and provenance, are the Lindisfarne Gospels, now in the British Library, which are dated to the early eight century.[22] The art of illuminated insular gospel books reached its zenith in the late eight century with the Book of Kells, which may have been produced at Iona, but was kept at Kells from the eleventh century onwards, being kept in the Library of Trinity College, Dublin, from the 1660s.[23]

Visually less spectacular, but also of paramount historic significance, is the earliest collection of Latin prayer-formulas and hymns, illustrating the encounter between native and Latin verse composition, known since its first publication in the eighteenth century as the Antiphonary of Bangor. This is a vellum manuscript of thirty-six leaves, written *c.*690 in the monastery of Bangor, but later taken to the monastery of Bobbio and now kept in the Ambrosian Library at Milan. The earliest complete text of the New Testament from Ireland is to be found in the Book of Armagh, written in 807–08 by the scribe Ferdomnach (d.846) for the abbot of Armagh and now kept in the Library of Trinity College, Dublin. Once ascribed to St Patrick himself (and hence known as *Canóin Pátraic*), the manuscript originally consisted of 222 vellum leaves, of which 215 are still extant, containing also two Lives of St

Patrick, Patrick's *Confessio* and the Life of St Martin of Tours by Sulpicius Severus. The earliest surviving example of an Irish liturgy is the Stowe Missal, a Mass-book written in the early ninth century, which was kept in the monastery of St Ruadan at Lorrha, Co. Tipperary, and is now in the Royal Irish Academy.

In many cases, valuable manuscripts were kept in so-called book shrines (Irish *cumdach*), rectangular boxes made of wood and metal, which sometimes came to be regarded as reliquaries. Well-known surviving examples dating from the pre-Norman period include the so-called *Soiscél Molaise* (Gospel-book of St Molaise), which was made in the early ninth century, but reworked in the eleventh and fifteenth centuries, the Stowe Missal book shrine, dating from the eleventh, but reworked in the fourteenth century, and the so-called *Cathach* ('Battler', because it is said to have been taken into battle to ensure victory), the shrine for a copy of the Latin psalter long believed to have been written by St Columba, dating from the eleventh century, but repaired and altered in the fourteenth and eighteenth centuries. All of these are now in the National Museum of Ireland.

The earliest surviving Latin writings in Ireland are those of Patrick, presumably composed in the fifth century. Relating to his audience his early captivity in Ireland and his later missionary activity there in his *Confession* (*Confessio*), Patrick denounces the lawless behaviour of contemporary warlords in what is commonly known as the *Letter to Coroticus* (*Epistula ad Coroticum*). From the sixth century onwards, the widespread use of Latin in Ireland gave rise to a distinct Hiberno-Latin literature, comprising a wide variety of poems, hymns, theological treatises, grammatical works, saints' lives and penitential regulations.[24] Historically, Irish penitentials were to be of special significance, as they were of crucial importance for the development of the practice of penance in the middle ages.[25] Moreover, there may have been a considerable Irish influence on medieval ideas about kingship and on the development of the literary genre of *speculum principum* or princely mirror.[26]

At the same time, the vernacular language was cultivated in the interpretation of Scriptures, producing a considerable amount of Old Irish glosses on such Latin texts as the Pauline epistles, a commentary on the psalms and the work of the Latin grammarian Priscian. These were mainly preserved in continental manuscripts, proving to be of pivotal importance in the development of Celtic philology and comparative linguistics around the middle of the nineteenth century. Moreover, Old Irish came to be used for original compositions related to the liturgical and didactic needs of the church, such as a treatise on the Mass preserved in the Stowe Missal, the two martyrologies known as the

Martyrology of Tallaght and that of Óengus (*Félire Óenguso*), and the numerous hagiographical writings relating to Irish saints.[27] A special interest also attaches to apocryphal writings in Irish, which are numerous and sometimes present close parallels to texts current among eastern Mediterranean churches.[28]

By the end of the pre-Norman period, the gradual extension in the use of Old Irish, beside that of Latin, had led to the establishment of an extensive vernacular literature, comprising various non-theological genres, including historical and pseudo-historical writings.[29] While the medieval Irish themselves appear to have classified this material according to tale-types, modern scholars have tended to adopt a nineteenth-century classification distinguishing four 'Cycles' of tales, grouping together thematically related narratives into what is commonly known as the Finn- (or Ossianic), Ulster- and Mythological Cycles and the Cycle of the Kings. Of particular cultural importance are legal texts, which have come down to us in late medieval and early modern manuscripts only, but were often composed several centuries earlier and thus may be used to reconstruct the social and political conditions prevalent in the early middle ages.[30]

At this point it may be asked to what extent Christianity in Ireland was different – both in its material and in its social and spiritual aspects – from Christianity in western Europe as a whole. In the past, much weight used to be attached to real or alleged differences, Christianity in early medieval Ireland being taken as a representative of an alternative form of 'Celtic' Christianity. One piece of evidence which tended to be used in this context is the controversy about the proper method of calculating the date of Easter, which in the seventh and eighth centuries existed between the churches in Ireland and Britain and those on the continent.[31] Recent research, however, has tended to question the validity of any such concept as 'Celtic Christianity', as the churches in question exhibit considerable differences from as well as similarities to each other, being at he same time closely linked to non-'Celtic' churches both in structural and in theological terms. Moreover, it has come to be argued that the idea of a – geographically as well as theologically – marginal position of the early Irish, Welsh and Hebridean traditions is essentially the product of a distinctly modern and urban perspective, flimsy generalisations about the character of 'Celtic' Christianity having often been based on a highly selective use of the evidence, by lumping together features which were neither representative or characteristic nor even as old as they were made out to be.[32] However, if the idea of an alternative 'Celtic' Christianity was largely due to wishful thinking, it may also be attributed to a corresponding lack of familiarity with early Christian traditions among the general public, making certain features of the early Irish church look strange or uncommon, even though they were fairly widespread and therefore unremarkable in the early middle ages. Moreover, ideas about a distinctly Irish (or 'Celtic') spirituality have been closely related to a kind of cultural nationalism, prevalent during most of the nineteenth and twentieth centuries, which was hardly conducive to a dispassionate and critical sifting of the evidence.

Cultural nationalism, coloured by romantic ideas of continuity, has also obscured our understanding of the relationship between Christian and pre-Christian Ireland, which in many respects is still being discussed controversially.[33] While in the past it sometimes tended to be assumed that pagan myths transmitted orally survived almost intact into the early Christian period, when they came to be written down in an ecclesiastical milieu which was rather sympathetic to the pagan past, it has now come to be realised that all early Irish narratives have to be regarded as conscious and highly literary works of art, reflecting a thoroughly Christian point of view. Moreover, a closer philological attention to the texts which have actually come down to us (as opposed to their putative oral prototypes) has revealed that they can profitably be studied as reflections of the preoccupations which were prevalent at those individual points of medieval Irish history at which they originated. Thus the mythological tale of *The Second Battle of Moytura* (*Cath Maige Tuired*) once used to be derived from an unattested Indo-European prototype that might also be found in ancient Germanic, Roman and Indian traditions, the text being frequently cited as evidence for the conservative character of early medieval Irish culture and the tenacity of pagan traditions under a superficially Christian veneer. Now, however, *Cath Maige Tuired* is widely regarded as a literary reflection of social and political conditions during the Viking age, whereas the assumption of earlier oral versions linked to early Germanic, Roman and Indian tales is viewed with scepticism, if not disbelief.

The point may also be illustrated by looking at the well-known Irish tradition of a miraculous other-world island off the coast of Ireland.[34] This looms large in the eight-century tales of *Echtrae Chonnlai* and *Immram Brain*, and came to be of considerable importance in the development of the medieval Brendan legend, and was used for parodistic or satiric purposes in the (presumably) twelfth-century story of *The Vision of Mac Conglinne* (*Aislinge Meic Conglinne*). On the one hand, one purpose of the earliest texts in which this idea occurs may well have been to accommodate the pagan past within the Christian world-view, using elements of both traditions to create a novel synthesis. For this reason, it is hardly a coincidence that despite their firmly Christian setting, both *Echtrae Chonnlai* and *Immram Brain* hark back to Greek and Roman writings describing the ritual use and mythological significance of off-shore islands among the ancient Celts. Considering the treatment of the other-world island in the much later *Aislinge Meic Conglinne*, however, one has the impression not of looking backward to the pagan past, but rather of looking forward – to stories about the Land of Cockaigne, the humour of mock saints' lives, gamblers' and drinkers' masses, the French *fabliaux* and the works of Boccaccio, Chaucer and Rabelais. Looking both backward and forward, one might argue that if Ireland was one of the harbingers of the middle ages, as Ludwig Bieler once put it, she also was among the undertakers, heralding developments which were to lead right up to our own time.

Notes

1 D. Ó Cróinín, *Early Medieval Ireland, 400–1200* (London: Longman, 1995); S. Duffy, A. MacShamhráin and J. Moynes (eds), *Medieval Ireland: An Encyclopedia* (New York: Routledge, 2005); D. Ó Cróinín (ed.), *A New History of Ireland I: Prehistoric and Early Ireland* (Oxford: Oxford University Press, 2005); M. Richter, *Medieval Ireland: The Enduring Tradition* (rev. edn) (Dublin: Gill and Macmillan, 2005); P. Stafford (ed.), *A Companion to the Early Middle Ages: Britain and Ireland, c.500–c.1100* (Oxford: Wiley-Blackwell, 2009).

2 T. M. Charles-Edwards, *Early Christian Ireland* (Cambridge: Cambridge University Press, 2000), pp. 182–201.

3 *Ibid.*, pp. 202–40; T. O'Loughlin, *Discovering Saint Patrick* (London: Darton Longman & Todd, 2005); D. Howlett, *Muirchú Moccu Macthéni's 'Vita Sancti Patricii': Life of Saint Patrick* (Dublin: Four Courts Press, 2006).

4 L. M. Bitel, *Isle of the Saints: Monastic Settlement and Christian Community in Early Ireland* (Ithaca, NY: Cornell University Press, 1990); U. O'Maidín, *The Celtic Monk. Rules and Writings of Early Irish Monks* (Kalamazoo, MI: Cistercian, 1996); A. Kehnel, *Clonmacnoise: The Church and Lands of St. Ciarán* (Münster: Lit., 1997); C. Thom, *Early Irish Monasticism: An Understanding of Its Cultural Roots* (London: T & T Clark, 2006).

5 C. Etchingham, *Church Organisation in Ireland, ad 650 to 1000* (Maynooth: Laigin, 1999); Charles-Edwards, *Early Christian Ireland*, pp. 241–81; Ó Cróinín (ed.), *Pre-historic Ireland*, pp. 301–70 and 549–679; *L'Irlanda e gli Irlandesi nell'alto medioevo* (Spoleto: Fondazione Centro Italiano di Studio sull'Alto Medioevo, 2010), pp. 67–90 and 261–348.

6 P. Ní Chatháin and M. Richter (eds), *Ireland and Europe in the Early Middle Ages: Texts and Transmission* (Dublin: Four Courts Press, 2002); H. Kleinschmidt, *Migration und Identität: Studien zu den Beziehungen zwischen dem Kontinent und Britannien vom 5. bis zum 8. Jahrhundert* (Ostfildern:

Thorbecke, 2009); D. Walz (ed.), *Irische Mönche in Süddeutschland* (Heidelberg: Mattes, 2009).

7 M. Herbert, *Iona, Kells and Derry: The History and Hagiography of the Monastic Family of Columba* (Oxford: Clarendon, 1988); Charles-Edwards, *Early Christian Ireland*, pp. 282–343.

8 Charles-Edwards, *Early Christian Ireland*, pp. 344–90; M. Richter, *Bobbio in the Early Middle Ages* (Dublin: Four Courts Press, 2008).

9 J. Graham-Campbell and M. Ryan (eds), *Anglo-Saxon/Irish Relations before the Vikings* (Oxford: Oxford University Press, 2009) (Proceedings of the British Academy 157), pp. 129–50.

10 O. Meyer, *Die Christianisierung Frankens. Sankt Kilian vor dem Hintergrund des irischen Einflusses auf das frühmittelalterliche Europa* (Würzburg: Gesellschaft für Fränkische Geschichte, 2006).

11 *L'Irlanda e gli Irlandesi*, pp. 431–508.

12 F. Colnago, *Poesia e Teologia in Giovanni Scoto l'Eriugena* (Rome: Herder, 2009); H. A.-M. Mooney, *Theophany: The Appearing of God According to the Writings of Johannes Scottus Eriugena* (Tubingen: Mohr Siebeck, 2009).

13 S. Weber, *Iren auf dem Kontinent. Das Leben des Marianus Scottus von Regensburg und die Anfänge der irischen 'Schottenklöster'* (Heidelberg: Mattes, 2010).

14 Ó Cróinín (ed.), *Prehistoric and Early Ireland*, pp. 609–34, 814–41.

15 W. Follett, *Céli Dé in Ireland: Monastic Writing and Identity in the Early Middle Ages* (Woodbridge: Boydell, 2006).

16 Ó Cróinín (ed.), *Prehistoric and Early Ireland*, pp. 899–933.

17 M. Herity, *Studies in the Layout, Buildings and Art in Stone of Early Irish Monasteries* (London: Pindar, 1995); Ó Cróinín (ed.), *Prehistoric and Early Ireland*, pp. 714–43; M. Comber, *The Economy of the Ringfort and Contemporary Settlement in Early Medieval Ireland* (Oxford: Hedges, 2008); A. E. Hamlin, *The Archaeology of Early Christianity in the North of Ireland* (Oxford: Archaeopress, 2008); D. H. Jenkins, *'Holy, Holier, Holiest': The Sacred Topography of the Early Medieval Irish Church* (Turnhout, Belgium: Brepols, 2010); T. Ó Carragáin, *Churches in Early Medieval Ireland: Architecture, Ritual, and Memory* (New Haven, CT: Yale University Press, 2010).

18 B. Lalor, *The Irish Round Tower: Origins and Architecture Explored* (Cork: Collins, 1999); Tadhg O'Keeffe, *Ireland's Round Towers: Buildings, Rituals and Landscapes of the Early Irish Church* (Stroud: Tempus, 2004).

19 Hilary Richardson and John Scarry, *An Introduction to Irish High Crosses* (Cork: Mercier, 1990); Peter Harbison, *The High Crosses of Ireland*, 3 vols (Bonn: Habelt, 1992); Kees Veelenturf, *Dia brátha. Eschatological Theophanies and Irish High Crosses* (Amsterdam: Stichting Amsterdamse Historische Reeks, 1997); Rachel Moss (ed.), *Making and Meaning in Insular Art* (Dublin: Four Courts Press, 2007), pp. 153–66, 215–27; *L'Irlanda e gli Irlandesi*, pp. 707–50.

20 P. Harbison, *The Golden Age of Irish Art: The Medieval Achievement, 600–1200* (London: Thames & Hudson, 1999); M. Ryan, *Studies in Medieval Irish Metalwork* (London: Pindar, 2002); Ó Cróinín (ed.), *Prehistoric and Early Ireland*, pp. 680–713; Moss, *Marking and Meaning*, pp. 231–52; Graham-Campbell and Ryan (eds), *Anglo-Saxon/Irish Relations*, pp. 231–52.

21 Ó Cróinín (ed.), *Prehistoric and Early Ireland*, pp. 511–48; M. Slavin, *The Ancient Books of Ireland* (Montreal: McGill-Queen's University Press, 2005); *L'Irlanda e gli Irlandesi*, pp. 623–46.

22 M. Brown, *The Lindisfarne Gospels and the Early Medieval World* (London: British Library, 2010).

23 B. Meehan, *The Book of Kells* (London: Thames & Hudson, 1994); C. Farr, *The Book of Kells: Its Function and Audience* (London: British Library, 1997); H. Pulliam, *Word and Image in the Book of Kells* (Dublin: Four Courts Press, 2006); Moss, *Making and Meaning*, pp. 257–74.

24 Ó Cróinín (ed.), *Prehistoric and Early Ireland*, pp. 371–404.

25 H. Connolly, *The Irish Penitentials and Their Significance for the Sacrament of Penance Today* (Dublin: Four Courts Press, 1995).

26 F.-R. Erkens, *Herrschersakralität im Mittelalter: Von den Anfängen bis zum Investiturstreit* (Stuttgart: Kohlhammer, 2006).

27 T. O'Loughlin (ed.), *The Scriptures and Early Medieval Ireland* (Turnhout, Belgium: Brepols, 1999); J. Carey, *King of Mysteries: Early Irish Religious Writing* (rev. pbk edn, Dublin: Four Courts Press, 2000); T. O'Loughlin, *Celtic Theology: Humanity, World, and God in Early Irish Writings* (London: Continuum, 2000); J. Carey, M. Herbert and P. Ó Riain (eds), *Studies in Irish Hagiography: Saints and Scholars* (Dublin: Four Courts Press, 2001); P. Ó Riain, *Feastdays of the Saints. A History of Irish Martyrologies* (Brussels: Société des Bollandistes, 2006); J. Carey (ed.), *Apocrypha Hiberniae 2: Apocalyptica, 1: In Tenga Bithnua* (Turnhout, Belgium: Brepols, 2009); K. Ritari, *Saints and Sinners in Early Christian Ireland: Moral Theology in the Lives of Saints Brigit and Columba* (Turnhout, Belgium: Brepols, 2009); K. Overbey, *Sacral Geographies: Saints, Shrines and Territory in Medieval Ireland* (Turnhout, Belgium: Brepols, 2010).

28 M. McNamara (ed.), *Apocrypha Hiberniae 1: Evangelia Infantiae* (Turnhout, Belgium: Brepols, 2001); Carey (ed.), *Apocrypha Hiberniae*.

29 Ó Cróinín (ed.), *Prehistoric and Early Ireland*, pp. 451–510; M. Ní Bhrolcháin, *An Introduction to Early Irish Literature* (Dublin: Four Courts Press, 2009); *L'Irlanda e gli Irlandesi*, pp. 533–99.

30 Charles-Edwards, *Early Christian Ireland* pp. 68–144; Ó Cróinín (ed.), *Prehistoric and Early Ireland*, pp. 331–70; *L'Irlanda e gli Irlandesi*, pp. 67–109.

31 Charles-Edwards, *Early Christian Ireland*, pp. 391–415.

32 I. Bradley, *Celtic Christianity: Making Myths and Chasing Dreams* (Edinburgh: Edinburgh University Press, 1999); D. Meek, *The Quest for Celtic Christianity* (Edinburgh: Handsel, 2000).

33 K. McCone, *Pagan Past and Christian Present in Early Irish Literature* (Maynooth: National University of Ireland Maynooth, 1990).

34 J. Wooding (ed.), *The Otherworld Voyage in Early Irish literature: An Anthology of Criticism* (Dublin: Four Courts Press, 2000); G. S. Burgess and C. Strijbosch (eds), *The Brendan Legend: Texts and Versions* (Leiden: Brill, 2006); J. S. Mackley, *The Legend of St Brendan: A Comparative Study of the Latin and Anglo-Norman Versions* (Leiden: Brill, 2008).

2

Island of saints and scholars: myth or reality?

Donnchadh Ó Corráin

There is a view that Ireland experienced a golden age in the early middle ages, though the term is used sparingly by more recent writers. Peter Harbison's splendid study of Irish art, 600–1200,[1] is an exception in this as in other things. Historians of Northumbria's early medieval achievements have little inhibition about the expression,[2] nor had earlier generations of Irish historians.[3] The burgeoning Cullenite Irish Catholic Church of the later nineteenth century saw itself, without self-doubt, as the heir of an Irish golden age, though its attempts to expound its achievements are, to say least, immodest and uncritical.[4] The acerbic English medievalist J. H. Round dismisses the whole notion. He writes with evident satisfaction: 'Of one thing we may be sure. No fonder dream has enthralled a people's imagination than that of an Irish golden age destroyed by ruthless invaders'.[5] He may have hit the nail on the tip.

I

When the golden age began is uncertain, when it ended and what ended it evokes no agreement – not even serious discussion. But there can be no doubt about it. The achievements are in many fields: the development of two great scripts (Irish half-uncial and minuscule); the invention of a textual layout that was to change for ever how text was read and set the standard in European bookmaking;[6] the crowning accomplishment of the great calligraphic codices;[7] the creation of an astonishingly rich biblical exegetical literature (over sixty tracts survive from the seventh to the ninth centuries), a tapestry woven from the patristic threads but often to new and bold patterns[8] – a literature to be set beside a rich collection of apocrypha in Latin and the vernacular, some exceedingly rare;[9] the elaboration of a developed pedagogy in Latin grammar from which over thirty grammatical tracts and handbooks survive, evidence for the thorough teaching of Latin in Irish schools,[10] and for this the writings of Columbanus, Sedulius Scottus and many others are independent witnesses. Side by side with these undertakings, Irish schools brought the study of computistics to a high level: some twenty surviving learned tracts on computistics are primary evidence of the scholarship from which Bede acquired without admission an erudition that greatly impressed generations of his readers.[11] The Irish schools compiled a uniquely rich and innovative collection of canon law, the early eighth-century *Hibernensis*, one of the most influential law books in the West in the early middle ages.[12] The same schools created an impressive and highly sophisticated Latin literature, ranging over theology, philosophy, hymnology, even social and political theory, in prose and verse, from the seventh to the ninth centuries.[13] An early and copious corpus of hagiography and hagiology began in the seventh century and continued to the twelfth and beyond.[14] We must add the remarkable dynamic religious and cultural effect of the Irish diaspora, missionary and scholarly, in Britain and in continental Europe from the sixth to the twelfth centuries, beginning with Columba and Columbanus and not quite ending with the Irish Benedictines in the German empire in the twelfth century.[15]

Two further achievements, in the vernacular, should be added: the construction of a remarkable legal system, one with the most subtle jurisprudence of any medieval European law;[16] and the creation of the most precocious and the richest European vernacular literature in verse and in prose – a verse that includes the earliest and some of the finest vernacular lyric poetry in Europe, a prose that has, centuries before other European languages, the first vernacular grammars and metrical handbooks as well as abundant artistic narratives of a high order in many genres.[17] To this we can add achievements in the plastic arts, especially metalwork and stone sculpture, in many styles, over many centuries, much admired by art historians.[18]

And Irish scholars had a self-conscious global view of themselves and their society's past and present: they sought to give Ireland's pagan prehistory, its subsequent flourishing Christian society, and its whole elaborate network of dynastic and genealogical history, created on the model of the Old Testament, a place within the universal framework of world history, or rather the history of salvation which they had learned from their study of scripture and from Jerome, Augustine, Orosius and Isidore, of whom they were early, and perhaps the most diligent, readers.[19] The Irish achievement was described by Arnold Toynbee, with profound but fatally flawed insight, as 'the abortive Far Western christian civilization'.[20]

However, golden ages, whether the Athens of Pericles, Augustan Rome, Spain's *siglo de oro*[21] or indeed Ireland's middle ages, are the accomplishment of a small artistic and intellectual cadre, supported and patronised by a much larger and powerful extractive elite that lords it over a wretched mass of toilers, some free, many slaves, all exploited, the sweated and bloodied underbelly of a profoundly unequal society. The privileges and the freedoms these elites arrogated to themselves were denied their inferiors, a denial that may have extended not only to the goods of this life, but to the rewards of the next.

II

Here I look at some aspects of that church system and the churches that were the patrons of the Irish golden age, namely the organisation and wealth of the churches, the strategies used to acquire and defend it (including sanctions), the nature of their superiors, the way they governed, and their treatment of their many and vulnerable dependants. These are very large questions: only a brief impressionistic treatment is possible here – suggestions, rather, for future enquiries.

The churches were rich: taken together they were the largest landowning institution in early medieval Ireland. Many, perhaps most, belonged to an affiliation variously called *paruchia* (*parochia*) by medieval writers[22] and less happily 'monastic federations' by modern historians.[23] Headed, as they were, by the foundation of a great saint or church founder, they had a corporate identity like that of any large institution that has widely distributed subsidiaries, delegated responsibilities and regional centres of power. That corporate identity was carefully fostered. The hagiography of the founder had two functions: it gave the affiliation a primary cult centre by glorifying the saintly founder; and it affirmed the association of the saint with the churches of the affiliation, for example, by recounting tales of his circuits in the course of which he founded churches or foretold their foundation, visited them, made an eternal compact with their founder, worked miracles there, or left behind marks of his visit, whether physical remains such as books or relics or else *fágbála*, blessings or curses or instructions perceived to be valid for all time. Shared liturgical and devotional practices gave the affiliation even greater cohesion. Member churches maintained devotions to the saintly founder, had dedicated altars or other artefacts, for example, crosses and reliquaries associated with the saint. The feast days of the patron and of other saints linked to him were celebrated with liturgical splendour. This was reinforced by regular visitations of the affiliation by the superior and his retinue of high-ranking clerics and officials – and these were occasions of display, celebration, and feasting. The mother church collected regular dues and payments from the churches of the affiliation, and sometimes a steward of the mother church lived in the region, and in time became an officer of very considerable status, a dignitary important enough to be mentioned among the great in the annals. The mother church had rights other than income from the affiliated churches: when, for example, these could not find in their own community (founder's or donor's kin) suitable candidates for the office of superior, one could be sent from the mother church. In effect, this bound these churches to the governing elite of the head church and helped to create a corporate identity based on a shared liturgy, history and iconography that powerfully reinforced the more mundane administration that saw to it that the common interests of the affiliation were attended to, rights vindicated and dues paid. Affiliation was the key to power, wealth and patronage. How exactly the small territorial dioceses and their high-ranking bishops meshed with the affiliations, though discussed often and at length, still remains obscure.[24]

The affiliations are in place when documentation becomes available in the late seventh century and after. Some examples. Bishop Tírechán, writing on behalf of Armagh about 670, provides good evidence for an impressively extensive affiliation of churches. He lists nearly eighty individual churches said to be founded by St Patrick and thus, in the conventions of history of this kind, claimed as dependants of Armagh that owed it services and payments,[25] but his prefatory statement, 'Patrick took with him across the Shannon fifty bells, fifty patens, fifty chalices, altar-stones, books of the law, books of the gospels and left them in the new places',[26] may suggest that many other unnamed and lesser churches were claimed for Armagh. One can add more churches and estates to this list from the mid-ninth-century *Vita tripartita*,[27] and it is likely that Armagh's affiliation was indeed very much larger.

A hagiologist, of the eighth century or earlier, who heads a section of the text 'All these holy virgins whose places and names we will enumerate were subject to St Brigit', lists nearly eighty female foundations and, in addition, about twenty male ones subject to St Brigit's church at Kildare.[28] This list draws on very early records: very many churches and estates are unidentified, and some have suggestive names – Dísert Brigte i Cill Suird (in Brega), Domnach Mór Sanct Brigte (perhaps Donaghmore in Co. Kildare), Rátha Brigte (Rathbride, Co. Kildare). Kildare's affiliation was widely spread. Cogitosus's *Vita Brigitae* (written *c.*AD 670–680) grandiloquently describes Kildare as 'the head of almost all the churches of the Irish ... whose *paruchia* is spread throughout the whole land of Ireland and extends from sea to sea'; and 'it, together with all its church lands throughout the whole of Ireland, is the most secure city of refuge'.[29]

A remarkable document, the *Irish Life of St Finnbarr*, preserves an early medieval list of fifty-one churches claimed as dependants of Cork, probably extracted from the early archives of Cork to meet the property crisis of the Hildebrandine reform,[30] and clearly these are by no means all its properties.

These are evidently large and powerful affiliations, and there are many more, for example, Clonmacnoise and Glendalough.[31] Smaller affiliations were much more numerous, and sometimes formed coherent constituents of the larger. And there were free-standing churches, the *ecclesia libera* of the canon law.[32] It is clear that by the mid-seventh century, and probably long before, the churches had become property owners on a grand scale. Christianity has a long history in Ireland: Orosius provides us with impeccable evidence for large Christian foundations at the end of the fourth century, and when the indigenous record becomes more informative, in the mid-seventh century and later, the church is already handsomely endowed. It did not cease to seek and to acquire property. Besides, there is no record in Ireland of the periodic confiscations of church lands that occurred elsewhere. However, as we shall see, there were changes of ownership: churches failed; churches declined and came to be owned by others; churches lost property to rival federations or made gains, in a world of keen ecclesiastical and dynastic competition.

Wealth and power attracted ambitious superiors, royal and aristocratic ecclesiastical lineages took root in the church, and with them ambition, worldly and ecclesiastical, that led to conflict and violence in and between churches. For example, in the late seventh century, the ecclesiastical lineage, Uí Meic Brócc, a branch (at least in their own view) of the paramount Munster dynasty, the Éoganacht, established themselves as rulers of the church of Cork: Suibne (d.682) mac Maíle Umai, Ruissíne (d.687) mac Lappa, and Mend Maiche (*fl.* 697) mac Duib Dá Barc, all close relatives, were all abbots of Cork.[33] Evidence for the government of great churches and their affiliations by hereditary aristocratic lineages becomes abundant in the eighth century, but the practice is probably very much earlier and hidden from us by lack of evidence. Commonly, discarded segments of ruling dynasties, pushed out by competitors, reprised themselves in church, and often retained power and property long after their secular kinsmen had lost theirs.

Ruling families spread into the churches and tended to rule, as hereditary possessions, the important churches of the local kingdoms. We know of examples earlier than the eighth century; thus ten kindreds of Uí Garrchon, early rulers in north Leinster, held major churches in that area.[34] Furthermore we can trace the emergence of clerical lineages, early and late. For example, Cernachán mac Doilgen, *rígdamna* of the sub-kingdom of Airthir in which Armagh lay, was executed by drowning, near Armagh, in 912 by Niall Glúndub mac Aeda, king of Northern Uí Néill. He had done evil: he had violated the peace of Armagh and killed a member of the church community. His grandson, Gilla Críst (d.1028), and his lineal descendants for three further generations – Doilgen (d.1053), Mael Brigte (d.1132) and Mac Craith (d.1149) – held office as 'priest of Armagh'.[35] His fulsome obit in the annals gives no indication of Mael Brigte's family background or marriage: 'Mael Brigte mac Doilgen, noble priest of Armagh and senior of the priests of Ireland, died on 27 August in the fifth-second year of his priesthood and the eightieth year of his age'. Holders of his office, no doubt well endowed, are described as 'noble priest' (*uasalsacart*): at the least this must mean the senior priest of the primatial church of Armagh, a position of high honour and dignity. At the time of Mael Brigte's death, St Malachy of Armagh, the leading promoter of the Hildebrandine reform in Ireland, was struggling to dislodge the greatest hereditary ecclesiastical lineage in Ireland, Uí Sínaig of Armagh.[36] Its members had ruled Armagh in the late eighth century, but from 1001 to 1105 they held it without a break, passing the office to siblings, sons and grandsons.[37]

The merging of the royal, the familial, the ecclesiastical and official sanctity, is conspicuous in the unusually informative records of the church of Trim (Áth Truim):

1 Three sons of Colmán grandson of Suibne. Cormac the bishop [d.746] son of Colmán of whom Óengus ua Oíbléin said 'Everyone proclaims it as far as the great sea, the feast of Cormac, the purely good' [*Martyrology of Óengus*, 17 Feb.]; Báethchellach [d.756] son of Colmán; Rumann [d.747] son of Colmán i.e. the poet from whom descend Síl Rumainn in Trim. There are three poets of the world: Homer of the Greeks, Virgil of the Latins, and Rumann of the Gael.
2 Seven sons of Rumann i.e. Suibne the bishop [d.796] and Cenn Fáelad the bishop [d.821] and these were two deputy abbots of Clonard. Cenn Fáelad abbot of Clonard was their contemporary.[38] It is that Cenn Faelad that left the curse that time that none should hold the deputy abbacy of Clonard but a man with the licentiousness of his body, with his queens and his chariots and his studs of steeds and every other rabblement besides, and he guaranteed his brotherhood forever.[39] The names of Rumann's five [other] sons are Ruidges, Cellach, Conall, Cairpre, and Muiredach.
3 Fuinecht daughter of Máel Fithrig son of Dímma son of Colmán is the mother of Cormac and Báethchellach and Rumann. Nárblaith daughter of Feradach [king of Lóegaire, d.704] son of Máel Dúin Dergainech [d.641] is mother of the family of Báethchellach son of Colmán.

Nechtblaith daughter of Téchén of Dún Lochad is mother of Conall son of Rumann.

4 Three sons of Báethchellach son of Colmán: Airechtach, Rechtgus, Feidlimid. Indrechtach son of Rechtgus i.e. the priest.[40]

The genealogies and the annals record only the highest offices held by this lineage descended from Colmán grandson of Suibne and ultimately (at least in their own view) from Ailill (d.642), king of Lóegaire.[41] It is likely that very many others of the lineage held lesser clerical positions (and their estates and incomes) at Trim and its associated churches. Nonetheless, the record is remarkable. Colmán was married to Fuinecht, daughter of his distant kinsman, Máel Fithrig mac Dímma meic Colmáin, a hereditary church family, the owners of Cell Duma Gluinn, now Kilglyn in the parish Balfeaghan, a few miles to the south-east of Trim, and another Patrician church.[42] Fuinecht is accounted a saint of Lóegaire in her own right and again as mother of Cormac, Báethchellach and Rumann.[43] Her son, Cormac (d.746) mac Colmáin, is recorded as a saint of some distinction in the martyrologies and, in later tradition, is wrongly said, besides, to have been ruler of Armagh.[44] His brother, Bishop Báethchellach, abbot of Trim, is even more remarkable. First, he made a royal marriage to his kinswoman Nárblaith, daughter of Feradach (d.704), king of Lóegaire, and granddaughter of Máel Dúin (d.641), probably king of Lóegaire. Her brother, Óengus (d.771), was also king of Lóegaire, as was her nephew, Cú Roí (d.797). According to the Lóegaire genealogies, another brother Fergil was also a saint (*uir sanctus*).[45] Second, Báethchellach is plainly accounted a saint in the Martyrology of Donegal[46] and appears among the saints of Lóegaire in the genealogies of their saints.[47] His descendants (including a grandson, Indrechtach, described as a priest) are recorded in the Lóegaire genealogies, some for five generations or more in four lines,[48] but none appears to have held the highest offices.

Rumann (d.747) mac Colmáin, '*poeta optimus*' is the eponym of Síl Rumainn at Trim (see sections I–II above). Of his sons, two were bishops, abbots of Trim, and deputy abbots of Clonard. His grandson, Cellach (d.838), was superior (*princeps*) of Trim and left a family;[49] his great-grandson, Cairpre (d.846), was abbot of Trim, and also left a family.[50] Thereafter, no members of Síl Rumainn appear to have held high office at Trim. The rulers of the church of Trim, in the eighth and ninth centuries, combine royalty, an aristocratic lifestyle, and great wealth with extravagant claims to an uncommon sanctity, celebrated in the festologies of the saints. Seventeen saints of Lóegaire are entered as a batch in the Martyrology of Tallaght, 17 February, with the significant remark '*Hi omnes in Ath Truim requiescunt*' – an eloquent claim to the bones of the dynastic saints and to continuity with the heroic sanctity of the distant past, decisive evidence, so it appeared, of a divine favour as powerful in the next world as it was overwhelming in this.[51]

III

Inevitably, violence followed wealth and power. I look briefly at violence directed towards clergy, at succession struggles, and finally at battles between churches. Beginning in the early eighth century, the annals report violent killings of clerics. The term commonly used is *iugulatio*, which usually means to cut somebody's throat, and we can safely understand it to mean a violent death by a weapon, assassination rather than murder. We can be sure that these annals record only a small selection of violent deeds perpetrated in church on very senior clerics. In these examples the laconic annalists give neither motive nor killer's name but elsewhere, when larger issues are involved, they are more informative, as in the following disputed succession at Armagh (again one of many) that led to great bloodshed in 759 and that throws some light on the nature and seriousness of struggles among the leading clergy.

> The battle of Emain Macha between the Ulaid and the Southern Uí Néill, driven on by Airechtach, priest of Armagh, out of enmity towards abbot Fer Dá Chrích, in which Dúngal grandson of Conaing and Donn Bó were killed. Fíachnae son of Áed Rón was the victor. (ATig 759)

This was a struggle between three branches of the dynasty Ind Airthir that owned and controlled Armagh and the great offices of church and their endowments: Uí Nialláin, Uí Bressail, and Uí Echdach. Céle Petair, of Uí Bressail, abbot of Armagh, died the year before. His successor, Fer Dá Chrích (sed. 758–68) mac Suibni, was of Uí Nialláin and his father, Suibne (d.730), had been bishop of Armagh. The priest Airechtach belonged to Uí Bressail and evidently believed the office of abbot was his by right. The over-kings of Ulaid and Southern Uí Néill are likely to have their own motives, now hidden from us. In the event, Fíachnae (d.789), king of Ulaid, won the battle. Those named among the fallen are Dúngal, king of Brega (Southern Uí Néill) and Donn Bó, lord of Uí Ségáin, whose family was distantly related to the Armagh clerical dynasties[52] and belonged to a kindred that were the hereditary rulers of the church of Dunleer in the eighth and ninth centuries. Despite Airechtach's trouble-making, he eventually succeeded to the abbacy of Armagh in 793 but within a year he and the bishop of Armagh 'fell asleep peacefully on the same night', as the annalist ironically puts it.[53] Succession disputes, in which powerful kings intervened on behalf of favourites and relatives are the occasions of most conflicts that led to killings.

Writing in the late seventh century, Tírechán is much concerned about Armagh's property and its claims on its dependent churches. He laments their loss to other affiliations:

> aeclessiam sanctam Cairce quam tenuit familia Clóno Auiss (§8.1) 'the holy church of Carrac which the community of Clones held'; Fundauitque ... alternam in Campo Taidcni, quae dicitur Cell Bile, apud familiam Scire est (§16.2) 'He founded another [church], called Cell Bile, in Mag Taidcni [in Meath], now held by the community of Kilskeer'; Monachus Patricii, sed contenderunt eum familia Columbae Cille et familia Airdd Sratha (§22.4) 'He was a monk of Patrick's but the community of Columba and the community of Ardstraw fought over him' [i.e. his church and his relics at Racoon, and its estates that rightly belonged to Armagh]; non quaerebant aliquid a familia Dumiche nissi amicitiam tantummodo, sed quaerit familia Clono, qui per uim tenent locos Patricii multos post mortalitates nouissimas (§25.3) 'and they demanded nothing of the community of Dumech, only their friendship, but the community of Clonmacnoise, who hold by force many of Patrick's churches since the recent plague, demand income from it'; et est locus eorum cum familia Clono et ingemescunt uiri loci illius (§47.4) 'and their church is held by the community of Clonmacnoise, and the men of that place groan'; et reuersus est in campum Elni et fecit multas aecclesias quas Condiri habent (§48.3) 'and he [Patrick] returned to the plain of Elne and built many churches that [the clerical lineages of] Condiri own'.[54]

Tírechán declares: 'My heart inside me is filled with ardour for Patrick when I see the deserters and robbers and warlords of Ireland who bear hatred to the *paruchia* of Patrick because they have taken away from him what was rightfully his' (§18.2).[55] There is nothing innocent about this rhetoric: it cloaks a world of bitter clerical rivalry over property and power that led to killings and to battles between churches, as the clerical annals relate with unusual candour.

Here are some examples in which the conflict appears to be purely clerical. In 760 there was a battle between Clonmacnoise and Birr. In 764 there was a major conflict between Clonmacnoise and Durrow:

> The battle of *Argaman* between the community of Clonmacnoise and the community of Durrow where fell Diarmait Dub mac Domnaill and Díglach mac Duib Liss and two hundred men of the community of Durrow. Bresal mac Murchada was victor, with the community of Clonmacnoise. (AU 764.6)

Bresal mac Murchada, otherwise unknown, but likely to have been superior of Clonmacnoise, was assassinated before the year's end.

Though separated by a long distance, Cork and Clonfert came to serious blows: 'A battle between the community of Cork and the community of Clonfert of Brendan between whom there was a numberless slaughter of ecclesiastics and eminent men of the community of Cork' (AU 807.9). This account makes explicit what is implied elsewhere, namely, that the clerics themselves engaged in such battles as combatants. Elsewhere, clerics and laymen engage in pitched battle over ecclesiastical succession, and sometimes kings took offices in church, 'A battle was won by Cathal mac Dúnlainge and the community of Taghmon over the community of Ferns in which 400 were slain' (AU 817.5). Cathal mac Dúnlainge was king of Uí Chennselaig (ruler of south Leinster) since *c.*809: when he died in 819 he was king and, in addition, deputy-abbot of Ferns (*secnap Fernann*). Others combined like offices. The attempts of kings to take over churches, to dominate them, to use them as sanctuary, exacerbated the violence. The frequent burnings of churches, of which reports begin in 710, are due mainly to arson during attacks and not to unfortunate accidents.[56] Given this level of violence, it is understandable but deplorable that the Irish church should urge capital punishment with an unseemly readiness. This occurs in two forms: in the thaumaturgy of the saints and, formally, in the legal texts.

In the early Patrician hagiography, Patrick is represented as inflicting death by miracle on those who oppose his mission, and such miracles are common in the later hagiography. One occurs during his encounter with King Lóegaire and his druids, where many died:

> When holy Patrick saw that the wicked pagans were about to attack him, he rose up and said with a loud voice, 'May God arise and may His enemies be dissipated and may those who hate Him flee before His face'. And at once darkness fell and there was a horrible uproar and the impious fought among themselves, one rising against the other; and there was a great earthquake and it caused the axles of their chariots to collide and drove them violently forward so that chariots and horses rushed headlong over the plain, until in the end only a few of them escaped half dead ... and by this calamity seven times seven men perished through the curse of St Patrick, in the presence of the king ... until there remained only the king himself, and three other survivors, that is, his queen, and two of the Irish and they were in great fear.[57]

Druids who opposed Patrick are miraculously done to death. One reviled the faith: 'Holy Patrick ... with a loud voice confidently said to the Lord: "O Lord who is most powerful ... may this impious man, who blasphemes Thy name, be now raised up outside and quickly die". At these words, the druid was lifted up into the air and cast down headlong; he hit his head against a stone, and was smashed to pieces.'[58]

Tírechán relates how Patrick had the chief druid of Connacht identified: 'And behold the holy man Patrick raised his left hand to God in heaven and he cursed the druid and he fell dead in the middle of his druids and, in the sight of all, he was consumed by fire as a sign of retribution.'[59]

Such powers attach to the churches and relics of the saint long after his death:

> And Patrick left a group of his household retinue at his flagstone in Domnach Pátraic,[60] and he said this: Whoever should violate it, his life and his sovereignty should be cut short. Cináed mac Írgalaig, king of Tara, violated it, namely, he slew a man under its protection and immediately three streams of blood trickled from it and did not stop dripping until Cináed mac Írgalaig[61] granted three hereditary serfs and their land to Patrick, namely, *Úachtar Nessa* and *Ói Midgnai* and *Tír Macc Conaigg* from the church eastwards. And the third did not leave off until he himself came to be beneath his cross, that is, until Flaithbertach mac Loingsig killed Cináed mac Írgalaig at the battle of *Druim Corcán*'.[62]

Cináed mac Írgalaig was king of Tara (724–28) and belonged to a great dynasty, Síl nÁeda Sláine. None of his descendants was a king of any sort and after a generation his family disappears from the records.[63] The story is meant as a salutary warning to anybody, king or other, who violated churches or their relics, especially churches under the protection of St Patrick. Both this reification of the spiritual and the threat of immediate and terrible vengeance for any interference with the holy, church property and church personnel, are found everywhere in the hagiography of the medieval Irish church, and the power to administer such dire punishment attaches to the successors of the saint.

The death penalty was not left merely to the exhortations and threats of hagiography: it is prescribed by the laws of the church. Those who make such laws usually have good reason, and it is not far to seek: arrogant, aristocratic and grasping clergy were the object of attack by the laity and by one another. Injuries to bishops and other high-ranking clergy were punished with great severity, according to canons dated, if uncertainly, to the late seventh century. Here is no echo of the Sermon on the Mount or of Christ's command to Peter to put up his sword, or his warning on the fate of those who wield it (Mt 26:52). Hence:

> The blood of a bishop or an exalted church superior or a canon law expert which is poured out upon the ground, if it needs a bandage, the wise (*sapientes* i.e. ecclesiastical jurists) judge that he who shed the blood should be hanged or pay seven female slaves (*ancillae*). If he pays *in specie*, he shall pay a third in silver and an amount of gold equal to the width of his [the cleric's] crown and a precious jewel equal to the size of his eye;

> for the embarrassment of his bruise or wound in an assembly or in any meeting whatever up to the third year, or longer, he who has done the deed shall pay the price of a female slave, if he [the victim] does not waive his claim. If, however, the blood of the bishop does not reach the ground and he does not need a bandage, the hand of the assailant shall be cut off or he shall pay seven female slaves, if he did it deliberately; if not deliberate, he shall pay the price of one female slave. One who strikes or pushes a bishop without shedding blood shall pay half the price of seven female slaves.[64]

Only the very rich could pay fines so large; the rest will have paid with their necks. The roughly contemporary vernacular law text on status, *Miadshlechta*, is more detailed, and appears more severe.

> What is the punishment for killing a celibate bishop? Answer: that three guilty persons be hanged for each hand that slays him; half the penalty for killing him for outraging him. Anybody who stands by and does not protect him with all his strength and resources and [? or] accompanies the guilty party, each pays seven female slaves. Shedding his blood: if the blood needing a bandage reaches the ground, the guilty party is hanged for it; or the payment is seven female slaves for his sick maintenance [i.e. his nursing and medical attendance] and penalty fine. If the wound is in his face, the width of his face of silver is paid and the width of his crown of gold; and unless the victim waive his claim the guilty party pays a female slave for every time attention is drawn to his disfigurement in an assembly for a period of three years.[65]

Appropriate penalties are prescribed for offences against the lesser grades of clergy. It is worth noting that clerics set the penalties and the awards are made by clerical judges (*sapientes*).

The annals give evidence that capital punishment by hanging was carried out. For example, they report crisply: 'The violation of sanctuary at Domnach Pátraic, six condemned persons were hanged'.[66] Another, and more serious, example is recorded in 893. There was a major incident between the two dominant northern dynasties, Cenél nÉogain (Uí Néill) and Ulaid at Whitsuntide at Armagh. Many were slain. The distinguished abbot of Armagh and Iona, Mael Brigte mac Tornáin, an Uí Néill aristocrat and accounted a saint,[67] the highest-ranking figure in the Irish church, separated them, but demanded compensation for this outrage to Armagh and St Patrick:

> Mael Brigte's decision thereafter and the satisfaction of Patrick's honour by the provinces of Ireland was, together with the taking of their hostages, the payment of thirty times seven female slaves and that four of the Ulaid be hanged, besides [the handing over of] churches and *manaig* [in compensation]. The equivalent was paid by Cenél nÉogain.[68]

Unsurprisingly, neither of the royal leaders was hanged: they lived to fight and kill another day, notably the king of Ulaid who slew a rival before the year's end.

Gilla Comgáin, the thief who stole a great haul of church plate from the high altar of the stone church at Clonmacnoise in 1129, was still trying to flee the country with it in 1130 when he and his stolen treasure were found at Limerick. Conchobar Ó Briain, king of Munster, handed him over to the Clonmacnoise authorities, and he was hanged at Dún Cluana Íchtair, a fortress near Clonmacnoise. Annals from Clonmacnoise add: 'and he said in his confession before his death that he saw St Ciarán with his crosier holding back every ship in which he tried to go. So the Lord and St Ciarán slew that man.'[69] The *Annals of Clonmacnoise* make it quite clear that he was handed over by the king to the community of Clonmacnoise and they hanged him.

In 1197, Mac Gilla Étig robbed the high altar of Derry of five fine chalices. He was caught and hanged at the Cros na Riag, 'the cross of the gibbets', at Derry, 'to avenge the honour of Colum Cille whose altar had been profaned'.[70] The execution, apparently, was carried out for the church by the 'secular arm', namely, Flaithbertach Ua Mael Doraid, lord of Cenél Conaill.

The vernacular laws do not tend to use capital punishment, but it may occur, and a jurist observes: 'Three forms of execution are envisaged in secular society i.e. killing by weapons, hanging, and the pit; only one form, however, is envisaged in church, hanging.'[71] It is remarkable how early and how thoroughly the Irish canonists, in a few short sentences in the *Hibernesis*, prescribed capital punishment and justified it. The Old Testament uses capital punishment for many and varied offences, some trivial. Besides, there was a powerful tradition of capital punishment in Roman law: the Theodosian code has 120 laws that prescribe the death penalty; and centuries of sanguinary Roman legislation are codified by Justinian. Nonetheless, the Fathers are very reluctant to allow capital punishment. Not so the Irish canonists. Under the heading 'That punishment [of crimes] is not forbidden in the New [Testament] and on those fit to inflict punishment', they cite Jerome: 'Whoever strikes the evil ones in so far as they are evil and has the instruments of killing that he may strike the most wicked, is the agent of the Lord'.[72] But they, like generations of later canonists, wrench Jerome's words from their context, for he is speaking of the Lord God of Israel, and those who carry out his express wishes, and not secular or ecclesiastical powers that inflict the death penalty for offences against themselves or others. The second passage quoted by the Irish canonists, 'To punish killers and the sacrilegious (temple robbers) is not the shedding of blood but the service of the laws of God and while priests spare sinners the churches labour to bring about their own destruction',[73] is read by modern commentators as a rhetorical flourish.[74] In any event, it is not, in itself, a specific prescription of capital punishment. The additional and carefully phrased dictum, that the secular arm, not the church, should inflict the punishment, though attributed to Jerome, seems to be Irish in origin: 'Let the king restrain enemies, and bind and punish, for the church punishes nobody'.[75] This is a very early and unctuous expression of the idea of the secular arm, shocking at first, but later almost universally accepted, namely, that the church condemns to death, but the secular power executes.

We must put this beside a resounding admonition to kings, under the heading 'That the word of king, alive or dead, slays his enemy', to rule effectively and punish ruthlessly: 'The word of the king is a sword for beheading, a rope for hanging, it casts into prison, it condemns to exile'.[76] This theme is taken up again in later clerical writings. I cite one text here, an early Middle Irish poem, fathered on St Moling and thus claiming his authority, that unrelentingly urges kings to use capital punishment.[77] It opens: 'I have heard it said by one who reads books: he who spares a criminal is himself a criminal ... It has been written in the books of God [scripture]: it is not you who has slain, but He; each has been given his own judgement: each chooses life or doom'. Then he takes as example an early historic king, of whom, very suitably, little is known: 'Moínach (d.662) of Cashel is a just king; by him evil people are killed; he holds Munster in peace; may God bless the good king'. The reward is in this life as in the next: 'if a king would listen to me, his family would be prosperous after him; let him put evil people to death; let him have many good people about his table'.

This heady advice to violent kings and aristocrats reflects attitudes and practices very different from those of such Fathers as Augustine, Leo I, and Gregory the Great, and is far from the meekness of the gospels. In their theoretical justification and prescription of capital punishment the Irish churches anticipate by centuries deplorable changes in the teaching and practice of the church in general in regard to violence (including war) and the death penalty in particular. Nor could the Irish churches claim in mitigation, as did the Western Church, that their violence was directed against the threat of heresy within and the menace of Islam without: they hardly mention heresy of which they say they are free in any case (though the holy St Malachy, in the spirit of his times, did uncover some at Lismore),[78] and the Irish practically ignored the Crusades.[79]

IV

The vast estates of the churches were worked by serfs, by the semi-free, by free commoners of various grades (some of whom also owned lands of their own and mobilia),[80] and by slaves. Here I touch briefly only on slaves. Down to the late twelfth century, the Irish upper classes, clerical and lay, were slave-owners. They need have no bad conscience. Historically, the Christian church has never come clean on slavery. St Paul is ambivalent (Eph 6:5–9; 1 Cor 7:2; Col 3:22–25;1 Tm 6:1; Tit 2:9–10) and the Fathers, whatever about liberty in Christ, were too much men of the ancient world to condemn what they saw as an economic necessity and a form of property, in church as in secular society.[81] Besides, slavery was seen as a consequence of original sin.

Irish society was profoundly class conscious. One's social status was defined by one's 'honour-price' (*ainech*, *enechlann*) and that, in turn, was determined by birth and wealth: it regulated one's powers at law as well as one's social position. As one expects, detail on the lowest classes – the landless, exploited tenants, the semi-free, the serfs and slaves on church as on lay estates – is scarce. *Crith gablach* (*ante* AD 700), the best-known vernacular legal text on status and a remarkable, perhaps unique, early medieval essay on class structure – ignores all those below the *fer midboth*, the inheriting commoner who had not come (or come fully) into his inheritance.[82] Nonetheless, evidence for slavery, though scanty, is found in the laws, the hagiography and, less transparently, in the annals. The legal rights of those without, or with very little, property are severely limited: the slave, as the law texts reiterate, no more than an alien, a landless person, a cabin holder, or one who is witless or grown senile, cannot make a valid contract without the consent of his master or the superior who is held responsible for him at law.[83] Without that consent, any guarantee purporting to support such a contract is without effect. In each case, however, if the superior does not rescind the attempted contract with a specific period of time, it stands. Thus, the contract of a slave is valid if unrescinded after a month.[84] The lawyers are much concerned, like their Roman predecessors, about runaway slaves: to give a surety or a pledge for a runaway slave is a useless and profitless activity in Irish law;[85] to pay wergild for him is pointless.[86] An important legal passage classified them with other runaways:

> There are seven persons in conflict in Irish law that are most difficult to shield. Neither lord nor church nor nobles have a right, nor is there any acknowledged safe-conduct, to protect them: protection against the action of a standing surety, protection of a son who absconds from his father, protection of a daughter who absconds from her mother, protection

> of a slave who absconds from his master, protection of a *manach* who absconds from his church, protection of man who evades the law of God or man, protection of a woman who absconds from the law of marriage.[87]

Thus, nobody can harbour a runaway slave and protect him against his master's right to recover him. Nor can a male or female slave be granted as a fief by a lord.[88] As in most slave-owning societies, female slaves were used sexually by their masters[89] and the canonists are at pains to distinguish between spouses and slave concubines and their offspring.[90] The sons of slaves and other lower-class women do not succeed to lordship:

> Who are the three sons that do not succeed to the privileges of lordship in Irish law? The son of a woman slave, the son of a woman serf, the son of a scold. Why? It is impossible to have a slave woman's son in lordship because his vices equal his mother's, the son of a serf should rather be paying rent, and it is not bearable to have a sharp-tongued garrulous person in lordship.[91]

In Ireland, as in the ancient world, the main source of slaves was war, but there were others: children sold into slavery especially during famine,[92] *expositi*, those redeemed from capital punishment, debt-slaves,[93] and slaves bred in the household (*uernae*). In Roman law, the children of a female slave (*partus ancillae*), whether the father be free or servile, have the status of their mother at their birth and are the slaves of their mother's owner.[94] This appears to be the rule in Ireland. Normally, in Irish law both parents were responsible for rearing their child. However, in a list of children whose mothers do not take part in their rearing are children are female slaves.[95] Clearly, such children are slaves brought up as part of the master's household.

In running their estates and managing their households, the churches were slave-owners, like their secular peers. Estates were granted to the church with their slaves. Two excerpts from the hagiography make that clear. 'The sons of Fiachra granted to Patrick forever the northern plain between the Gleóir and the Ferne together with the slaves who served them there.'[96] 'And they gave all honours to St Carthagus, and the king Cairpre made him many grants of land and slaves.'[97] Columbanus assumes that a Christian who does penance for perjury is a slave-owner; part of his penance is done 'by offering a life for himself, that is, by freeing a man slave or a woman slave from the yoke of bondage'.[98] Even a cleric making his soul as a solitary attached to a monastic community might have a slave to look after his needs: 'that a slave who is dutiful, pious, and no talebearer should attend on you, if you can get one'.[99] The canon law envisages, among various punishments, that the thief who is caught but cannot pay the fine should be enslaved (evidently to the church), with the provision that his kin can redeem him.[100]

There is an interesting concern in Patrician hagiography, not about slavery as such, but about St Patrick's status. He was, as his *Confession* (§17) makes clear, a runaway slave, though one divinely instructed to flee his master: 'I turned to flight and I abandoned the man with whom I had been for six years'. Armagh, a slave-owning church in a slave-owning society, was very sensitive about this, and God's own instruction to run away did not suffice. It made at least two literary efforts to resolve the perceived difficulty. The first is that of Muirchú in the late seventh century. Immediately after Patrick's arrival as a missionary in Ireland, 'it seemed to him that nothing was better than that, in the first place, he should redeem himself'. He set out to find Mílucc with what Muirchú calls the 'double price of his freedom, an earthly and a heavenly one', that is, the price of his freedom in the ordinary sense and a spiritual one, rhetorically expressed, that he, a former slave, should liberate his old master from the servitude of paganism.[101] However, Mílucc evaded him by suicide. This, evidently, was not enough to lay Armagh's concerns to rest, and a second attempt was made in the mid-ninth-century *Vita Tripartita*. Here the action takes place at the end of Patrick's enslavement. The story open with the unlikely statement, based on Scripture, that 'that pagan people was accustomed to set free its manumitted slaves in the seventh year of slavery'. Patrick sought his freedom and was denied it unless he paid over to Mílucc the exact weight of his head in gold. The angel Victor, Patrick's confidant and guide, tells him how and where in the wilderness he will find the gold buried in the earth. Patrick pays his faithless and avaricious master and, emancipated, sets out joyously on his journey.[102] In the story of Mílucc's end in the *Vita Tripartita* Patrick's attempt to buy his freedom is subtly modified: he merely brought gold to win Mílucc to the faith, for he knew he was avaricious.[103]

We have seen that for attacks and injuries to its personnel the churches received compensation: that payment is described as a given number of *ancillae* or, otherwise, the price (*pretium*) of a given number of *ancillae*. It seem right to interpret the first as actual female slaves, the second as other goods, precious metals or valuables in lieu, in part or in full. According to a hagiological anecdote, an outrage was perpetrated on Semplán priest of Terryglass. In compensation, Uí Dróna paid over seven female slaves (*secht cumala*) to the abbot of Terryglass, and he paid on these seven female slaves to the superior of the dependent church of Lorum.[104]

Expositi, children rejected for many reasons – because they were the offspring of incest or adultery, because they were defective or otherwise unwanted, and this is reflected in the conventions of the hagiography[105] – were often dumped on the church, in Ireland as elsewhere. The canon lawyers ruled:

> Of the punishment of those who abandon young children in God's church. An Irish synod. Whoever abandons young children in the church of God, without the abbot's knowledge, let them do penance for three and half years, if there are bishops buried in it or present ... To whom belong children abandoned to the church. An Irish synod. A child abandoned to the church is its slave unless he is redeemed. Nor, if he be violent, shall his evil conduct stain the church if it corrected him as far as possible.[106]

These bleak canons reveal that wretched children, abandoned by their parents, become part of the church's exploited slave population, and at a tender age. They are sharply distinguished from oblates who became members of the clergy and from children fostered or educated by the church in return for payment, and who go back to their families or become members of the clerical elite.

V

The Irish churches were rich, landowners on a vast scale, and the beneficiaries of a large population of rent-payers, workers, serfs and slaves. They enjoyed, in addition, a generous income from their pastoral ministrations to the faithful at large – baptismal offerings, payments for penance, requiems, burial payments, tithes, and the like. They received the endowments, gifts and patronage of kings and nobles, and large payments for offences against their churches and persons. Church superiors, bishops, abbots and professional ecclesiastical scholars belonged, for the most part, to the lordly class, in law and status the equals of the lay nobility. Many, sprung from royal dynasties, belonged to clerical lineages that had owned and governed churches for generations, even centuries. And, if they lived the lives of hereditary aristocrats, they had the refined taste, the spirit of emulation, and the ambitions of an elite by birth, tradition and profession. A broad-church establishment was home to opulent ecclesiastical grandees, worldly scholars, learned divines, poets, austere puritans and severe ascetics. The churchmen were the patrons and exponents of the sacred sciences in the broadest sense, and of scholarship, literature and the arts. The twelfth-century Hildebrandine reformers, with ill-requited loyalty and enthusiasm, stripped the assets of the churches to fund their new episcopal organisation, and their needy though powerful bishops. It is ironic that those who would reform, in the eleventh and twelfth centuries, should, in the name of virtue, have taken from long-established centres of learning and art their essential structures and endowments, and have turned high scholarship out of the church. It is unfortunate that the papally sponsored English invasion should have exacerbated disorder and conflict, especially in the church and among the patrons of learning. The lights grew dim in these times of trouble.

Notes

1 P. Harbison, *The Golden Age of Irish Art: The Medieval Achievement, 600–1200* (London: Thames & Hudson, 1999); see also M. Ryan, *Early Irish Communion Vessels: Church Treasures of the Golden Age* (Dublin: National Museum of Ireland, 1985). Historians of literature (whether Latin or the vernacular), biblical studies, chronology and computistics, etc. are not, apparently, partial to the term. For observations on earlier ideas of a golden age, see C. O'Halloran, *Golden Ages and Barbarous Nations: Antiquarian Debate and Politics in Ireland, c.1750–1800* (Cork: Cork University Press, 2004), esp. pp. 73–96. I am grateful to Fidelma Maguire for comments and suggestions.

2 H. E. R. Davidson, *The Golden Age of Northumbria* (London: Longman, 1958); J. Hawkes, *The Golden Age of Northumbria* (Morpeth: Sandhill, 1996); P. J. Fairless, *Northumbria's Golden Age: The Kingdom of Northumbria, AD 547–735* (York: Sessions, 1994); J. Hawkes and S. Mills (eds), *Northumbria's Golden Age* (Stroud: Sutton, 1999).

3 For example, the lectures in J. Ryan (ed.), *Irish Monks in the Golden Age* (Dublin: Clonmore and Reynolds, 1963), a popular broadcast series, are essentially biographies of Irish clerics of the diaspora (SS Colmcille, Aidan, Columbanus, Gall, Virgil of Salzburg and Cathaldus), not studies of the churches at home. Nearly all the essays in another work of about the same time, H. Daniel-Rops (ed.), *Le Miracle Irlandais* (Paris: R. Laffant, 1956); translated by the earl of Wicklow as *The Miracle of Ireland* (Dublin and London: Clonmore; Burns Oates and Washbourne, 1959), belong in the Christian fairyland of the devout imagination.

4 The following are representative: Archbishop J. Healy, *The Life and Writings of St Patrick* (Dublin: M. H. Gill and Son, 1905) and *Insula Sanctorum et Doctorum or Ireland Ancient Schools and Scholars* (4th edn, Dublin and New York: Sealy, Bryers and Walker, 1902); of the golden age Healy writes: 'It was not by any means a period altogether free from violence and crime, but it was certainly a time of comparative peace and security, during which the religious communities scattered over the island presented a more beautiful spectacle before men and angels, than anything seen in Christendom before or since' (*Insula Sanctorum*, p. vi). For Healy, the golden age extends to the time of St Laurence O'Toole, archbishop of

Dublin (sed. 1162–80), and the English invasion in 1169. He has nothing to say of its ending.

5 J. H. Round, *The Commune of London and Other Studies* (London: Constable, 1899), p. 169.

6 M. B. Parkes, *Scribes, Scripts, and Readers: Studies in the Communication, Presentation and Dissemination of Medieval Texts* (London: Hambledon, 1991), pp. 1–18; P. Saenger, *Space between Words: The Origins of Silent Reading* (Stanford, CA: Stanford University Press, 1997).

7 See, for example, P. Fox (ed.), *The Book of Kells: MS 58, Trinity College Library Dublin*, 2 vols (Lucerne: Faksimile-Verlag, 1990); A. A. Luce, G. O. Simms *et al.* (eds), *Evangeliorum Quattuor Codex Durmachensis*, 2 vols (Olten: Urs Graf-Verlag, 1960); F. O'Mahony (ed.), *The Book of Kells: Proceedings of a Conference at Trinity College Dublin* (Aldershot: Scolar Press, 1994).

8 B. Bischoff, 'Wendepunkte in der Geschichte der lateinischen Exegese im Frühmittelalter', *Sacris Erudiri*, 6 (1954), pp. 189–279; C. O'Grady, 'Turning-points in the history of Latin exegesis in the early middle ages', in M. McNamara (ed.), *Biblical Studies: The Medieval Irish Contribution* (Dublin: Dominican Publications, 1976), pp. 74–160; J. F. Kelly, 'A catalogue of early medieval Hiberno-Latin biblical commentaries', *Traditio*, 44 (1988), pp. 537–71; 45 (1990), 393–434; M. W. Herren, 'Irish biblical commentaries before 800', in J. Hamesse (ed.), *Roma, Magistra Mundi: Itineraria Culturae Medievalis: Mélanges Offerts au Père L. E. Boyle à l'occasion de son 75e anniversaire*, 3 vols (Louvain-la-neuve: Collège Mercier, 1998), i, pp. 392–407.

9 M. McNamara, *The Apocrypha in the Irish Church* (Dublin: Dublin Institute for Advanced Studies, 1975); M. Herbert and M. McNamara (eds), *Irish Biblical Apocrypha: Selected Texts in Translation* (Edinburgh: T & T Clark, 1989).

10 L. Holtz, 'Grammairiens Irlandais au temps de Jean Scot: quelques aspects de leur pédagogie', in *Jean Scot Érigène et L'histoire de la Philosophie*, Actes des Colloques du CNRS, Laon 1975 (Paris: CNRS, 1977), pp. 69–78; L. Holtz, *Donat et la Tradition de L'enseignement Grammatical: Études sur l'Ars Donati et sa Diffusion (IVe–IXe siècle) et Édition Critique* (Paris: Centre National de la Recherche Scientific, 1981); L. Holtz, 'Irish grammarians and the continent in the seventh century', in H. B. Clarke and M. Brennan (eds), *Columbanus and Merovingian Monasticism* (Oxford: British Archaeological Reports, 1981), pp. 135–52; L. Holtz, 'L'Enseignement des maîtres Irlandais dans l'Europe continentale du IXe siècle', in Jean-Michel Picard (ed.), *Ireland and Northern France, AD 600–800* (Dublin: Four Courts Press, 1991), pp. 143–56.

11 D. Ó Cróinín, 'The Irish provenance of Bede's computus', *Peritia*, 2 (1983), pp. 229–47; I. Warntjes, *The Munich Computus: Text and Translation. Irish Computistics between Isidore and the Venerable Bede and Its Reception in Carolingian Times* (Stuttgart: Steiner, 2010). Computistics

was an essential, if at times inexact, science for reckoning time in the middle ages and was key for drawing up the liturgical calendar.

12 H. Wasserschleben (ed.), *Die Irische Kanonensammlung*, 2nd edn (Leipzig: B. Tauchnitz, 1885) (hereafter Hib. cited by book and section); H. Mordek, *Kirchenrecht und Reform im Frankenreich: die Collectio Vetus Gallica, Die Älteste Systematische Kanonessammlung des Fränkischen Gallien* (Berlin and New York: W. de Gruyter, 1975), pp. 143, 255–9; L. Kéry, *Canonical Collections of the Early Middle Ages (ca.400–1140): A Bibliographical Guide to the Manuscripts and Literature* (Washington, DC: Catholic University of America Press, 1999), pp. 73–80.

13 D. Howlett, 'Insular Latin writers' rhythms', *Peritia*, 11 (1997), pp. 53–116; M. Smyth, 'The date and origin of *Liber de ordine creaturarum*', *Peritia*, 17–18 (2003–04), pp. 1–39; L. Castaldi, 'La trasmissione e rielaborazione dell'esegesi patristica nella letteratura ibernica delle origini', in *L'Irlanda e gli Irlandesi nell'alto Medioevo*, Settimana di Studio ... sull'alto Medioevo, 57 (Spoleto, 2010), pp. 393–429; H. H. Anton, 'Pseudo-Cyprian: *De duodecim abusivis saeculi* und sein Einfluss auf den Kontinent, inbesondere auf die karolingischen Fürstenspiegel', in H. Löwe (ed.), *Die Iren und Europa im Früheren Mittelalter* (Stuttgart: Klett-Cotta, 1982), pp. 586–617; R. W. Dyson, *Sedulius Scottus, De Rectoribus Christianis (On Christian Rulers): An Edition and English Translation* (Woodbridge: Boydell Press: 2010).

14 R. Sharpe, *Medieval Irish Saints' Lives: An Introduction to Vitae Sanctorum Hiberniae* (Oxford: Clarendon, 1991); M. Herbert, 'The Latin and vernacular hagiography of Ireland from the origins to the sixteenth century', in G. Philippart (ed.), *Hagiographie: Histoire Internationale de la Littérature Hagiographique Latine et Vernaculaire en Occident des Origines à 1550*, 3 vols (Turnhout, Belgium: Brepols, 2001), III, pp. 327–60; J. Carey, M. Herbert and P. Ó Riain (eds), *Studies in Irish Hagiography: Saints and Scholars* (Dublin: Four Courts Press: 2001); N. Stalmans, *Saints d'Irlande: Analyse Critique des Sources Hagiographiques (viie–ixe siècles)* (Rennes: Presses Universitaires de Rennes, 2003); P. Ó Riain, *Feastdays of the Saints: A History of the Irish Martyrologies* (Brussels: Société des Bollandistes, 2006).

15 J. Kenney, *Sources for the Early History of Ireland: Ecclesiastical* (New York: Columbia University Press, 1929), pp. 486–621; A. O. Anderson and M. O. Anderson (eds and trans.), *Adomnán's Life of Columba* (Edinburgh: Nelson, 1961; 2nd edn, Oxford: Clarendon, 1991); R. Sharpe (trans.), *Adomnán of Iona: Life of St Columba* (Harmondsworth: Penguin, 1995); M. Lapidge (ed.), *Columbanus: Studies in Latin Writings*, Studies in Celtic History, 17 (Woodbridge; Boydell Press, 1997); S. Weber (ed. and trans.), *Iren auf dem Kontinent. Das Leben des Marianus Scottus von Regensburg und die Anfänge der irischen Schottenklöster* (Heidelberg: Mattes Verlag, 2010).

16 R. Thurneysen, 'Das keltische Recht', *Z Savigny-Stift Rechtsgesch*, Ger. Abt. 55 (1935), pp. 81–104; trans. as 'Celtic law', in D. Jenkins (ed.),

Celtic Law Papers (Brussels: Les Éditions de la Librairie Encyclopédique, 1973), pp. 51–70; D. Ó Corráin, L. Breatnach and A. Breen, 'The laws of the Irish', *Peritia*, 3 (1984), pp. 382–438; F. Kelly, *A Guide to Early Irish Law* (Dublin: Dublin Institute for Advanced Studies, 1988); L. Breatnach, *A Companion to the Corpus Iuris Hibernici* (Dublin: Dublin Institute for Advanced Studies, 2005) and *The Early Irish Law Text Senchas Már and the Question of Its Date*, Quiggin Memorial Lecture, 13 (Cambridge: Department of Anglo-Saxon, Norse and Celtic, 2011); N. McLeod, *Bloodshed and Compensation in Ancient Irish Law*, Inaugural Professorial Lecture (Murdoch: Murdoch University Centre for Irish Studies, 1999). Legal tracts were given final written form by professional men of letters (*filid*) and learned churchmen working in collaboration with the lawyers (N. McLeod, 'Fergus mac Léti and the law', *Ériu*, 61 (2011), pp. 1–28: 24–5).

17 R. Thurneysen, *Die Irische Helden- und Königsage bis zum siebzehnten Jahrhundert* (Halle: [Saale] M. Niemeyer, 1921); E. Knott and G. Murphy, *Early Irish Literature* (ed.) J. Carney (London: Routledge & Kegan Paul, 1966); J. Carney (ed.), *Early Irish Poetry* (Cork: Mercier Press, 1965); George Calder (ed. and trans.), *Auraicept na n-Éces: The Scholar's Primer* (Edinburgh: Grant, 1917); R. Thurneysen (ed.), *Mittelirische Verslehren*, in W. Stokes and E. Windisch (eds), *Irische Texte*, 3rd ser., 1 (Leipzig: S. Hirzel, 1891), pp. 1–182; O. J. Bergin (ed.), 'Irish grammatical tracts', supplements to *Ériu* 8 (1916), 9 (1921–23), 10 (1926–28), 14 (1946), 17 (1955).

18 F. Henry, *La Sculpture Irlandaise pendant les douze premiers siècles de L'ère chrétienne*, 2 vols (Paris: E. Leroux, 1933) and *Irish Art*, 3 vols (London: Methuen, 1965–70); F. Henry and G. Marsh-Micheli, *Studies in Early Christian and Medieval Irish Art*, 3 vols (London: Pindar, 1983–5); S. Youngs (ed.), *The Work of Angels: Masterpieces of Celtic Metalwork 6th–9th centuries AD* (London: British Museum Publications, 1989); P. Harbison, *The High Crosses of Ireland: An Iconographical and Photographic Record* (Bonn: R. Habelt, 1992); T. Ó Carragáin, *Churches in Early Medieval Ireland: Architecture, Ritual and Memory* (New Haven, CT and London: Yale University Press, 2010).

19 D. Ó Corráin, 'Creating the past: the early Irish genealogical tradition', *Peritia*, 12 (1998), pp. 177–208 and, 'The church and secular society', in *L'Irlanda e gli Irlandesi nell'alto Medioevo*, pp. 261–323.

20 A. J. Toynbee, *A Study of History* (Oxford: Oxford University Press, 1935), ii, pp. 322–40.

21 Conditions in the slave-owning societies of Athens and Rome are too well known to rehearse here; for a striking account of golden-age Spain's ruthless exploitation of the New World, its vile maltreatment of its indigenes, and its enslavement of Africans in the Americas, see C. C. Mann, *1493: How Europe's Discovery of the Americas Revolutionized Trade, Ecology and Life on Earth* (London: Granta, 2011).

22 See L. Bieler (ed. and trans.), *The Patrician Texts in the Book of Armagh* (Dublin: Dublin Institute for Advanced Studies, 1979), p. 138 (Tírechán §18.2); *Acta Sanctorum* (AASS), 1 Feb., 135, 141 (Cogitosus, *Vita Brigitae*, cited below see n. 29); cf. Annals of Ulster (AU) 787.5: *Dubh Da Bhairenn, abbas Cluana Iraird, aduisitauit paruchiam crichae Muman.* The term is common: '*Ille enim iuuencule per orationem sancti Mochutu effecte sunt uirgines, et cellas et monasteria fundauerunt. Que loca hodie sunt in parrochia sancti Mochutu. Ille enim sancte uirgines se ipsas cum suis cellis Deo et sancto Mochutu obtulerunt*' (Vita S. Carthagi, in C. Plummer (ed.), *Vitae Sanctorum Hiberniae* (VSSH), 2 vols (Oxford: Clarendon, 1910), i, p. 173 §11); '*Ecce offero me ipsum et ecclesiam meam cum mea parrochia Deo et tibi*' (*ibid.*, p. 174 §13); '*Factaque est parrochia eius magna in sua patria. Ipse enim episcopatum regionis Chiaraigi accepit*' (*ibid.*, p. 175 §15). See further VSSH, I, p. 206 §17, p. 211 §28, p. 224 §16; II, p. 40 §13, p. 44 §17, p. 51 §25, p. 52 §27, p. 72 §27, p. 74 §32, p. 192 §6, p. 229 §7.

23 C. Etchingham, 'The implications of *paruchia*', *Ériu*, 44 (1993), pp. 139–62; C. Etchingham, *Church Organisation in Ireland AD 650 to 1000* (Maynooth: Laigin, 1999), pp. 126–30, 223–37; C. Etchingham, 'Pastoral provision in the first millennium', in E. FitzPatrick and R. Gillespie (eds), *The Parish in Medieval and Early Modern Ireland: Community, Territory and Building* (Dublin: Four Courts Press, 2006), pp. 79–90; C. Etchingham, 'The organization and function of an early Irish church settlement: Glendalough', in C. Doherty, L. Doran and M. Kelly (eds), *Glendalough: City of God* (Dublin: Four Courts Press, 2011), pp. 22–53. One ought to distinguish between high-level organisation and such lower-level matters as pastoral care and the administration of the sacraments.

24 C. Etchingham, 'Bishops, church and people: how Christian was "Early Christian Ireland"?', *L'Irlanda e gli Irlandesi nell'alto Medioevo*, pp. 325–51: pp. 325–32, and the literature there cited.

25 Bieler, *Patrician Texts*, pp. 122–66; R. Sharpe, 'Churches and communities in early medieval Ireland', in J. Blair and R. Sharpe (eds), *Pastoral Care Before the Parish* (Leicester: Leicester University Press, 1992), pp. 81–109: pp. 87–9.

26 Tírechán §II.1 (Bieler, *Patrician Texts*, p. 122).

27 W. Stokes (ed. and trans.), *The Tripartite Life of Patrick*, 2 vols (London: Eyre and Spottiswoode, 1887), i, pp. 1–267; K. Mulchrone (ed.), *Bethu Phátraic: The Tripartite Life of Patrick* (Dublin: Royal Irish Academy, 1939).

28 P. Ó Riain (ed.), *Corpus Genealogiarum Sanctorum Hiberniae* (Dublin: Dublin Institute for Advanced Studies, 1985), pp. 112–18, §670.1–88.

29 *Acta Sanctorum ... a Sociis Bollandianis* (Antwerp &c., 1643–1931),1 Feb., pp. 135 (prol. §2), 141 (viii 39); S. Connolly and J.-M. Picard (trans.), 'Cogitosus's Life of St Brigit: content and value', *Journal of the Royal Society of Antiquaries of Ireland*, 117 (1987), pp. 5–27.

30 C. Plummer (ed. and trans.), *Bethada náem nÉrenn: Lives of Irish Saints*, 2

vols (Oxford: Clarendon, 1922), i, pp. 11–22; P. Ó Riain (ed. and trans.), *Beatha Bharra: St Finbarr of Cork; The Complete Life* (London: Irish Texts Society, 1993), pp. 54–91. Only nine of these can be found in the decretal letter of Innocent III (1199), setting out and confirming the possessions of the diocese, again based on the archives of Cork, and again a response to a property crisis; M. P. Sheehy, *Pontificia Hibernica*, 2 vols (Dublin: M. H. Gill, 1962–5), i, pp. 105–9 (§39); Diarmuid Ó Murchadha, 'The Cork decretal letter of 1199 AD', *Journal of the Cork Historical and Archaeological Society*, 106 (2001), pp. 79–100.

31 On Clonmacnoise, a keen rival of Armagh, see A. Kehnel, 'The lands of St Ciarán', in H. A. King (ed.), *Clonmacnoise Studies I* (Dublin: Dúchas,1998), pp. 11–17; *Clonmacnoise: The Church and Lands of St Ciarán: Change and Continuity in an Irish Monastic Foundation* (Münster: Lit, 1999); A. S. Mac Shamhráin, *Church and Polity in Pre-Norman Ireland: The Case of Glendalough* (Maynooth: Maynooth Monographs, 1996), pp. 168–215.

32 *Hib*. 29.6; for other churches bound by secular exactions, *Hib*. 42.6.

33 AU 682, AI 681; AU 687, AI 686. K. Meyer (ed. and trans.), *Cáin Adamnáin: An Old Irish Treatise on the Law of Adaman* (Oxford: Clarendon, 1905), p. 16.

34 M. A. O'Brien (ed.), *Corpus Genealogiarum Hiberniae* (Dublin: Dublin Institute for Advanced Studies, 1962), p. 24.

35 AU 912.3 = Annals of the Four Masters (AFM) 912 (907) = Annals of Clonmacnoise (AClon) 912 (904); AU 1028.2, AFM 1132, 1149; R. Atkinson (ed.), *The Book of Ballymote* (BB) (Dublin: Royal Irish Academy, 1887), p. 114 c21–31, p. 115 c22–25; K. Mulchrone (ed.), *The Book of Lecan*, Facsimiles in Collotype of Irish Manuscripts, 2 (Dublin: Stationery Office, 1937), f. 79 vc16 (genealogies of the family, Uí Chruind, compiled at Armagh).

36 This lineage is the target of St Bernard's unbridled and partisan vituperation in his *Vita S. Malachiae*, X §19; 'For a most evil custom had developed, through the diabolical ambition of certain powerful people, that the sacred see should be held by hereditary succession. For they allowed none to be bishops but members of their own tribe and family. And this accursed succession had lasted a very long time, for there have been already fifteen instances of succession in this wickedness. And so far had an evil and adulterous generation established for themselves this depraved rule, a wickedness that ought to be punished by death of any kind, that though sometimes there were no clerics of that family, there were always bishops. In a word, there had already been eight before Celsus [Cellach], married men without orders, though men of letters'. For this text, see J. Leclercq, C. H. Talbot and H. M. Rochais (eds), *Sancti Bernardi Opera*, 8 vols (Rome: Editiones Cistercienses, 1957–77) (1963), iii, pp. 307–78, X §19 (the best edition) = Jean Mabillon (ed.), *Sancti Bernardi Abbatis Claræ-Vallensis Opera Omnia*, 4th edn rev. (Paris: apud Guame Fratres. 1839), ii, cols 1465–1524, c. 1482–4, X §19 (repr. *Patrologia Latina* (PL) 182,

*c.*1073–1118; AASS Nov. ii/1, c. 135–66); H. J. Lawlor (trans.), *St Bernard of Clairvaux's Life of St Malachy of Armagh* (London and New York: Macmillan, 1920), p. 45 §19.

37 T. Ó Fiaich, 'The church of Armagh under lay control', *Seanchas Ardmhacha*, 5 (1969), pp. 75–127. Note the important corrections by Martin Holland, 'Were early Irish church establishments under lay control?', in D. Bracken and D. Ó Riain-Raedel (eds), *Ireland and Europe in the Twelfth Century: Reform and Renewal* (Dublin: Four Courts Press, 2006), pp. 128–42.

38 The translation is uncertain. If this Cenn Fáelad was abbot of Clonard, and other than Cenn Fáelad mac Rumainn, he is otherwise unknown. Mac Firbhisigh (§190.12) takes him to be Cenn Fáelad mac Rumainn and supplies an otherwise unknown Faolchú as the contemporary abbot of Clonard.

39 I cannot tell what this action may mean.

40 This is an eclectic text of an extract from (i) the genealogies of the royal dynasty of Lóegaire, BB 87d26–88a35; and (ii) the genealogies of the saints, Book of Leinster, 254c (= R. I. Best, O. J. Bergin, M. A. O'Brien and A. O'Sullivan (eds), *The Book of Leinster* (BL) 6 vols (Dublin: Dublin Institute for Advanced Studies, 1954–83), vi, p. 1588 = Ó Riain, *Corpus Genealogiarum Sanctorum*, p. 126 §690.1–5). D. Mac Firbhisigh's text of these genealogies (N. Ó Muraíle (ed. and trans.), *Leabhar Mór na nGenealach: the Great Book of Irish Genealogies*, 5 vols (Dublin: Edmund Burke, 2003–4), i, pp. 418–22, §190.1–11) is a poor copy of BB, itself faulty.

41 O'Brien, *Corpus Genealogiarum Hiberniae*, p. 166; BB 87ea45; AU 642.2.

42 Bieler, *Patrician Texts*, p. 168 §2.1 (Additamenta).

43 Ó Riain, *Corpus Genealogiarum Sanctorum*, p. 126 §690.4, p. 177 §722.74.

44 R. I. Best and H. J. Lawlor (eds), *The Martyrology of Tallaght* (London: Henry Bradshaw Society, 1931), p. 17 (17 Feb.); W. Stokes (ed. and trans.), *Félire Óengusso Céli Dé: The Martyrology of Oengus the Culdee* (London: Henry Bradshaw Society, 1905), p. 61 (17 Feb.), p. 74 (scholia); W. Stokes (ed. and trans.), *Félire hÚi Gormáin: The Martyrology of Gorman* (London: Henry Bradshaw Society, 1895), p. 38 (17 Feb.); J. O'Donovan (trans.), J. H. Todd and W. Reeves (eds), *The Martyrology of Donegal* (Dublin: Irish Archaeological and Celtic Society, 1864), p. 50 (17 Feb.).

45 O'Brien, *Corpus Genealogiarum Hiberniae*, 166, line 10; this Fergil may be identical with Virgilius of Salzburg, d.27 Nov. 784 (T. Ó Fiaich, 'Virgils Werdegang in Irland und sein Weg auf dem Kontinent', in Heinz Dopsch and Roswitha Juffinger (eds), *Virgil von Salzburg; Missionar und Gelehrter* (Salzburg: Landesregierung, 1984), pp. 17–26; A. Breen, *Dictionary of Irish Biography* (Cambridge: Cambridge University Press, 2009), ix, pp. 671–2. As Ó Fiaich points out, the genealogy is defective – a generation or two may be elided. The genealogy of Fergil preserved by the Four Masters, Paul Walsh (ed.), *Genealogiae Regum et Sanctorum Hiberniae by the Four*

Masters (Maynooth: Record Society and Dublin: H. M. Gill, 1918), p. 51 §21, is also inaccurate and their obit in AFM s.a. 789 (784) seems to be a misdated confection based on the obit of the homonymous Fergil, abbot of Achad Bó (AU 789.14).

46 *Mart. Donegal*, p. 266 (5 Oct.); he is absent in the *Mart. Óengus*; 'Baethalach', in the *Mart. Gorman*, p. 190 (5 Oct.) and 'Baethallaig', in the *Mart. Tallaght* (5 Oct.) must leave some room for doubt, but the fact that he is the only one of his name (in any of its forms) in the Irish martyrologies must tell in his favour.

47 Ó Riain, *Corpus Genealogiarum Sanctorum*, p. 126, §690.4.

48 BB p. 88a 11–35.

49 BB p. 87 ea30–6.

50 BB p. 87 ea17–23.

51 Ó Riain, *Corpus Genealogiarum Sanctorum*, pp. 126–8 §690, pp. 1–18; cf. Walsh, *Genealogiae*, pp. 49–53 §§1–40.

52 F. J. Byrne, 'Appendix 1.1: Genealogical tables', in F. J. Byrne *et al.*, *Historical Knowth and Its Hinterland* (Dublin: Royal Irish Academy, 2008), pp. 55–87: 64 (Dúngal of Brega); Donn Bó was brother of Blathmac, author of a remarkably fine poem on the Passion; see J. Carney (ed. and trans.), *The Poems of Blathmac Son of Cú Brettan* (Dublin: Irish Texts Society, 1964), pp. 1–88.

53 There had been more trouble in 793: Fóendalach, abbot of Amagh (or one of the claimants of that office) had been outraged and Armagh attacked by outside supporters of one side (AU 793.4). Abbot Fóendelach died suddenly in 795 (AU 795.4).

54 Bieler, *Patrician Texts*, pp. 130, 136, 140, 142, 160.

55 *Ibid.*, p. 138.

56 A. T. Lucas, 'The plundering and burning of churches in Ireland, 7th to 16th century', in E. Rynne (ed.), *North Munster Studies* (Limerick: Thomond Archaeological Society, 1967), pp. 172–229.

57 Muirchú, *Vita Patricii*, §1.18 (Bieler, *Patrician Texts*, p. 90); D. Howlett (ed. and trans.), *Muirchú Moccu Macthéni's 'Vita Sancti Patricii'* (Dublin: Four Courts Press, 2006), pp. 78–9). The text appropriately echoes psalm 67:2 which reiterates the message.

58 Muirchú, §1.17 (Bieler, *Patrician Texts*, pp. 88–90; Howlett, *Muirchú*, pp. 78–9); cf. Tírechán §8 (Bieler, *Patrician Texts*, p. 130) where the death of Patrick's druid opponent is more colourfully described: 'And they all saw the druid being lifted up through the darkness of the night almost to heaven and when he came back his corpse, frozen with hailstones and snow mixed with sparks of fire, fell to the ground in the sight of all, and his stone is in the south-eastern parts of Tara to this day and I have seen it with my own eyes.'

59 Tírechán §42 (Bieler, *Patrician Texts*, p. 156).

60 Now Donaghpatrick, a hamlet and parish, between Lower Navan and Upper Kells, Co. Meath, 6.4km north-west of Navan, a dependant of

Armagh. Here was a *lecc* or flagstone associated, as a relic, with St Patrick. The parcels of land, all unidentified, appear to be near the church and are the farms of serfs, now owned (with their occupiers) by the church of Domnach Pátraic.

61 The text has *Congalaig*, apparently in error.

62 Stokes, *The Tripartite Life*, i, pp. 72–5 = Mulchrone, *Bethu Phátraic*, p. 48, lines 788–97.

63 O'Brien, *Corpus Genealogiarum Hiberniae*, pp. 125, 127; AU 724.3, 728.1; F. J. Byrne, 'Historical note on Cnogba (Knowth)', in George Eogan, 'Excavations at Knowth. Co. Meath', *Proceedings of the Royal Irish Academy (C)* 66 (1968), pp. 383–400: genealogical chart and 'Genealogical tables', in F. J. Byrne *et al.*, *Historical Knowth*, p. 64.

64 Bieler, *Irish Penitentials*, p. 170 ('Sinodus Hibernensis', probably seventh century). There are like provisions in a vernacular law text from the seventh century (D. A. Binchy (ed. and trans.), 'Bretha Déin Chécht', *Ériu*, 20 (1966), pp. 1–66: 40 §31= D. A. Binchy (ed.), *Corpus Iuris Hibernici* (CIH), 6 vols [continuous pagination] (Dublin: Dublin Institute for Advanced Studies, 1978), p. 2323.16–18; fresh translation in Ó Corráin, 'The church and secular society', in *L'Irlanda e gli Irlandesi nell'alto Medioevo*, p. 309.

65 CIH p. 588.13–21.

66 AU 746.11=Annals of Tigernach (ATig) 746.

67 J. Colgan (ed.), *Acta Sanctorum ... Hiberniae* (Louvain: *apud* Everardum de Witte, 1645), 386–7 (22 Feb.); Ó Riain, *Corpus Genealogiarum Sanctorum*, §§347, 662.29, 772.87; *Mart. Gorman*, p. 40 (22 Feb.); *Mart. Donegal*, p. 54 (22 Feb.); W. Reeves (ed.), *The Life of St. Columba ... written by Adamnan* (Dublin: Irish Archaeological and Celtic Society, 1857), p. 392. His obit in AFM s.a.927 (925) lauds him as 'cend crábhaidh Ereann uile, & urmhóir Eorpa', turned into Latin by Colgan, 'caput religionis Hiberniæ, & maioris partis Europæ'; see D. N. Dumville, 'Mael Brigte mac Tornáin, pluralist coarb (†927)', *Journal of Celtic Studies*, 4 (2004), pp. 97–116; repr. in D. N. Dumville, *Celtic Essays, 2001–2007*, 2 vols (Aberdeen: Centre for Celtic Studies, 2007), i, pp. 137–58, esp. pp. 154–8.

68 Chronicon Scottorum (CS) 893; AFM 893 (889) has an entry textually very close but with some differences in detail. There is a translation of the entry into Latin (notably changing *cumala* 'female slaves' of the annals to 'boues') by Colgan in his *Triadis Thaumaturgæ Acta* (Louvain: *apud* C. Coenestenium, E. de Witte, 1647), p. 296a: '*Maelbrigidus autem, quia ita contra reuerentiam Ecclesiae Dei & S. Patricio debitam impegnarunt; ab Vlidijs accepit obsides & 210 boues; & quatuor ex delicti authoribus suspendi curarunt Vlidijs. Keneleoguin etiam in consimilem ex parte suâ consenserunt satisfactionem*'; text also in Colgan, AASS, 386; Dumville, 'Mael Brigte mac Tornáin', pp. 153–4.

69 ATig s. a. 1129–30; slightly variant version in AClon, CS, AFM s. a. 1129–30.

70 AU, Annals of Louch Cé (ALC), AFM s. a. 1197.
71 CIH p. 1101.27, p. 1927.20; cf. *Hib.* 27.5–6.
72 Jerome, *In Ezech.* 9.1; *Hib.* 27.8a.
73 Jerome, *In Ier.*, 22.3; *Hib.* 27.8c.
74 James J. Megivern, *The Death Penalty: An Historical and Theological Survey* (New York: Paulist Press. 1997), p. 34. Both passages from Jerome are cited in defence of the death penalty by Ivo of Chartres (d.1116) in his *Decretum*, compiled between 1093 and 1095 (Megivern, *Death Penalty*, pp. 86–7).
75 *Hib.* 27.8b; see Megivern, *Death Penalty*, pp. 28, 30–1, 60–1, 70–1, 82, 87–8, 119.
76 *Hib.* 25.17c; attributed to Jerome, but not his.
77 BL iii, p. 622; K. Meyer (ed. and trans.), 'Miscellanea Hibernica', *University of Illinois Studies in Language and Literature*, 2(4) (1916), pp. 559–605, 567–8.
78 Bernard, *Vita Malachiae*, xxvi §57=Mabillon, *S. Bernardi Opera*, ii, cols 1508–9 = Leclerq, Talbot and Rochais, *S. Bernardi Opera*, iii, pp. 360–1; Lawlor, *St Bernard's Life of St Malachy*, pp. 101–3; cf. G. Murphy, 'Eleventh or twelfth century Irish doctrine concerning the real presence', in J. A. Watt, J. B. Morrall and F. X. Martin (eds), *Medieval Studies Presented to Aubrey Gwynn S. J.* (Dublin: Three Candles, 1961), pp. 19–28.
79 K. Hurlock, 'The Crusades to 1291 in the annals of medieval Ireland', *Irish Historical Studies*, 37 (2011), pp. 517–34.
80 T. M. Charles-Edwards, 'The church and settlement', in P. Ní Chatháin and M. Richter (eds), *Ireland and Europe: the Early Church* (Stuttgart: Klett-Cotta, 1984), pp. 167–75; Etchingham, *Church Organisation in Ireland*, esp. pp. 363–454.
81 J. Gaudemet, *Institutions de L'antiquité*, 2nd edn (Paris: Éditions Montchrestien, 1982), pp. 542–54; J. Gaudemet, *L'Église dans L'empire romain (IVe–Ve siècles)* (Paris: Sirey, 1958), pp. 564–8; C. Munier, *L'Église dans L'empire romain (IIe–IIIe siècles)* (Paris: Éditions Cujas, 1979), pp. 73–81; G. E. M. de Sainte-Croix, 'Early Christian attitudes to property and slavery', in D. Baker (ed.), *Church, Society and Politics*, Studies in Church History, 12 (Oxford: Blackwell, 1975), pp. 1–28.
82 D. A. Binchy (ed.), *Críth gablach* (Dublin: Stationery Office, 1941); N. McLeod, 'The two *fer midboth* and their evidence in court', *Ériu*, 33 (1982), pp. 59–63; T. M. Charles-Edwards, '*Críth gablach* and the law of status', *Peritia*, 5 (1986), pp. 53–73.
83 N. McLeod (ed. and trans.), *Early Irish Contract Law* (Sydney: University of Sydney, 1992), p. 124 §1, p. 190 §53, p. 192 §54; CIH p. 593.35–8 = R. Thurneysen (trans.), *Die Bürgschaft im Irischen Recht* (Berlin: W. De Gruyter, 1928), p. 11 §37 = R. C. Stacey (trans.), '*Berrad airechta:* an Old Irish tract on suretyship', in T. M. Charles-Edwards and D. B. Walters (eds), *Lawyers and Laymen* (Cardiff: University of Wales Press, 1986), pp. 210–33: p. 213 §37; CIH pp. 522.1–4, 536.23–4 (Córus bésgnai); CIH

p. 351.24 = R. Thurneysen (ed. and trans.), 'Aus dem irischen Recht, IV', *Z Celt Philol* 16 (1926), pp. 167–230, p. 177 §12 = L. Breatnach, *The Early Irish Law Text Senchas már*, p. 6 §9 (Introduction to Senchas már).

84 McLeod, *Irish Contract Law*, p. 124 §1.

85 CIH pp. 28.11–12, 29.11.

86 CIH p. 17.18.

87 CIH pp. 46.37–47.3, 1523.17, 1847.40–1848.10; cf. Thurneysen, 'Bürgschaft', p. 55; normalised text and translation in F. Kelly and T. M. Charles-Edwards, *Bechbretha: An Old-Irish Law-Tract on Bee-keeping* (Dublin: Dublin Institute for Advanced Studies, 1983), p. 144.

88 CIH p. 27.9–24.

89 Penitential of Vinnian, §§39–40, 42, L. Bieler (ed. and trans.), *Irish Penitentials* (Dublin: Dublin Institute for Advanced Studies, 1963), pp. 88, 90; Penitential of Cummian, §§26–7 (Bieler, *Irish Penitentials*, p. 116); *Hib* p. 46.32 ; T. Ó Donnchadha (ed. and trans.), 'Advice to a prince', *Ériu*, 9 (1921–3), pp. 43–54: 46 §12.

90 *Hib.* 46.19 (citing Leo the Great's letter to Rusticus of Narbonne, PL 54, cols 1204–5).

91 CIH p. 233.4–12, 1871.40; *muccsaid*, lit. 'a pig woman', i.e. a woman who herds and feeds pigs, and she is, according to the gloss, the daughter of a very lowly serf.

92 See J. Boswell, *The Kindness of Strangers: The Abandonment of Children in Western Europe from the Roman Empire to the Renaissance* (New York: Pantheon, 1988), pp. 163, 165–7, 169–72, 201–3.

93 For a 'leading case' on debt slavery, see N. McLeod, 'Fergus mac Léti and the law', *Ériu*, 61 (2011), pp. 1–28. Dornach, who bore a son to an outsider (and thus he is kinless apart from her), is enslaved because she is unable to pay the seven *cumala* of compensation for his crime.

94 A. Watson, *Legal Origins and Legal Change* (London: Hambledon, 1991), pp. 265–8; A. Watson, *Roman Slave Law* (Baltimore, MD and London: Johns Hopkins University, 1987), pp. 8–15.

95 CIH p. 1585.12–14; cf. 2193.1–4; K. Mulchrone, 'The rights and duties of women in regard to the education of their children', in D. A. Binchy *et al.* (eds), *Studies in Early Irish Law* (Dublin: Royal Irish Academy, 1936), pp. 187–205: 191; R. Thurneysen, 'Aus dem irischen Recht IV', pp. 215–16.

96 Bieler, *Patrician Texts*, p. 170 §5 (Additamenta).

97 VSSH i, p. 184 §37 (Vita Carthagi).

98 Penitential of Columbanus, §20 (Bieler, *Irish Penitentials*, p. 104).

99 K. Meyer (ed.), 'Regula Choluimb Chille', *Z Celt Philol* 3 (1901), pp. 28–30: p. 29 §7 = E. O'Curry (ed. and trans.) in W. Reeves (ed.), *Acts of Archbishop Colton in his Metropolitan Visitation of the Diocese of Derry* (Dublin: Irish Archaeological Society, 1850), pp. 109–12: p. 110

100 *Hib.* 29.5.

101 Muirchú, §1.11 (Bieler, *Patrician Texts*, pp. 76–8; Howlett, *Muirchú moccu Macthéni's Life of St Patrick*, pp. 60–2).

102 Stokes, *Tripartite Life of Patrick*, i, p. 21 (= Colgan (ed.), *Triadis Thaumaturgæ Acta*, p. 120 §§21–22; the main Irish MS is here defective and we depend for the full narrative on Colgan's Latin translation); see Mulchrone, *Bethu Phátraic*, pp. 12, 14 (excerpts of the Irish text from *Lebor Breac* and the *Book of Lismore*). Note that the gold is uncovered in the wilderness: thus, it is legally Patrick's and none has an adverse claim to it.

103 Stokes, *Tripartite Life of Patrick*, p. 38; Mulchrone, *Bethu Phátraic*, 24.

104 BL vi, pp. 1579–80 = Ó Riain (ed.), *Corpus Genealogiarum Sanctorum*, p. 111 §668.

105 VSSH, i, pp. 46–7 §1, p. 64 §1, p. 183 §36; ii, p. 268 §26; W. W. Heist (ed.), *Vitae Sanctorum Hiberniae* (Brussels: Société Bollandistes, 1965), pp. 192–3 §40; BL v, p. 1248.

106 *Hib*. 42.22, 24. A second opinion imposes a penance of seven years on those who abandon children, and that they should suffer as much loss as they imposed on God's church (i.e. that they should bear the expense of the church in raising the children).

3

The devotional landscape of medieval Irish cultural Catholicism *inter hibernicos et inter anglicos*, *c.*1200–*c.*1550

Salvador Ryan

In his 1985 survey entitled *The Irish Catholic Experience*, Patrick J. Corish points to 'the complexity of the patterns of culture in which Christianity existed in Ireland in the fourteenth and fifteenth centuries, while noting that the source material allows little more than an impressionistic survey of what was distinctive about the Christian religion *inter hibernicos* as against its equivalent *inter anglicos*.[1] Difficulties arising from a dearth of source material will always hamper the efforts of historians who attempt to peel back the layers of time in order to catch a glimpse of medieval culture; this is particularly true in the case of medieval Ireland for which so much has been lost or destroyed. Nevertheless, the source material which does survive, when examined closely, can reveal much about a vibrant and developing Catholic devotional culture which existed in Ireland but which also had its face firmly turned in the direction of Britain and the continent.

This chapter will focus, in particular, on collections of devotional material in late medieval Ireland, which, for the most part, can be found in manuscripts which also contain a great deal of miscellaneous material of a non-religious nature. These were frequently commissioned by lay members of the aristocratic elite, and written by professional scribes. The material featured in such collections was dictated largely by the devotional tastes of those for whom they were compiled, and thus they are enormously valuable indicators of the variegated nature of late medieval Irish Catholic piety. However, while the patrons of such collections came from both Gaelic Irish and Anglo-Norman backgrounds, delineating the boundaries of religious identity and devotional taste 'across the divide' is not a simple task for, in most cases, these boundaries (if they were boundaries at all) were quite porous. This chapter will confine itself to considering what devotional interests both communities actually shared in common as part of a wider late medieval Catholic culture.

In her recent study of the transformation of the twelfth-century Irish Church, Marie Therese Flanagan contends that by the time Anglo-Norman infiltration into Ireland began in 1167 the Irish Church had already established ecclesiastical structures that were broadly in line with those of the continent. Moreover, she argues that the impetus for such a transformation should not be located solely in the external agency of the see of Canterbury, Rome or, indeed, the reformist agendas of the Cistercian order: after all, it was the initiative of Malachy to visit Arrouaise and Clairvaux in 1139 and to introduce continental monasticism to Ireland, not that of the Cistercians. Flanagan is also anxious to emphasise how much of the groundwork of ecclesiastical reform was accomplished by lay rulers such as Muirchertach Ua Briain, king of Munster, who may have been instrumental in securing the position of papal legate for Bishop Gillebertus of Limerick, who held this position until 1139. The synod of Kells in 1152 would give formal papal endorsement to the new diocesan structures which had been put in place some forty years earlier at Ráith Bressail – however, this came after Malachy had already travelled twice to the continent in a bid to secure papal approval.[2] In many important respects, therefore, the late medieval Irish Church which emerged out of a long period of ecclesiastical reform was an outward-looking church, its eyes fixed on continental developments in piety and practice; it was happy, therefore, to adopt and, as we shall see, adapt many of the features of continental Catholicism for its own purposes.

The arrival and rapid expansion in Ireland of monastic orders such as the Cistercians and, later, mendicant orders of Augustinians, Franciscans and Dominicans, played a huge part in the transformation of the religious landscape of Ireland. By the fifteenth century, the mendicant orders were, themselves, reinvigorated by the continental Observant reform movement; this advocated a return to their foundational ideals and charisms, and resulted in a flowering of devotional and didactic religious texts and the establishment of large numbers of new foundations, particularly in Gaelic Ireland, which were enthusiastically patronised by local lay rulers.[3] Between 1400 and 1508 some ninety new mendicant houses were founded in Ireland and many more established communities also allied themselves to the cause of Observant reform.[4] Henry Jefferies surmises that this burgeoning increase in mendicant clergy, who were certainly better educated and trained than their secular counterparts and were highly esteemed for their preaching skills, 'did not simply reflect an increase in lay piety in late medieval Ireland, but contributed to that increase'.[5] Yet, allowance must be made for both; for, as we shall see from the evidence of surviving manuscripts, the concerns of the lay members of wealthy Irish families of Gaelic and

Anglo-Norman stock alike often neatly dovetailed with those of the religious orders which they supported.

Fifteenth-century Gaelic Ireland has rarely been noted for the healthy state of its ecclesiastical life. In a succession of historical studies it has been invariably described as being in a state of decline and stagnation, rife with a variety of abuses ranging from familial control of dioceses and monastic institutions to the non-observance of the rule of celibacy and the poor upkeep of church buildings. Religious observance and sacramental practice are portrayed as having been haphazard, compounded by a widespread lack of parochial structures.[6] Indeed, one could argue that it represented just the sort of condition to which Jean Delumeau famously refers: one that was in need both of Christianisation and reformation.[7] This standard view has been challenged by more recent scholars who point out that, despite continuing serious organisational and moral problems in the late medieval Irish Church, evidence of lay investment in church-building programmes and other forms of patronage suggests a more vibrant scene.[8] Certainly, the fifteenth century saw the emergence of a new confidence and vibrancy among the native Irish population. Aided by a continuous weakening of English presence in Ireland, partly attributable to a preoccupation with the wars in France in the early part of the fifteenth century and, internally, with the War of the Roses in its latter decades, a Gaelic Irish pragmatic resurgence led to sporadic attacks and raids by clans eager to recapture their lands and extend their power base.[9]

It is interesting to note that fifteenth-century Gaelic expansionism was accompanied by an increase in native literary output. This was the century when the great *bibliothèques* and other literary compilations containing much religious material were completed – famous works such as the *Leabhar Breac* (*c.*1411), the Book of Ballymote (*c.*1391), the Great Book of Lecan (*c.*1397–*c.*1418), *Liber Flavus Fergusiorum* (*c.*1435–40) and the *Book of Lismore* (late fifteenth century).[10] Works such as these did not have their origin in a monastic setting as in earlier periods but were, instead, compiled by secular scholars who were commissioned by prominent Gaelic families. The *Leabhar Breac*, for instance, was connected with the MacEgans, a brehon family from Duniry in Galway who possessed the collection in the sixteenth century; the Book of Ballymote was compiled for a member of the McDonagh family of Ballymote castle, Co. Sligo, and its scribes were former pupils of the MacEgans; the Great Book of Lecan written by Giolla Íosa Mac Firbisigh who was assisted by Murchadh Riabhach Ó Cuindlis (also a scribe of the *Leabhar Breac*) under the patronage of the O'Dowds of Sligo; in the case of the *Book of Lismore*, one of whose scribes was under the patronage of Finghin Mac

Carthaigh Riabhach (d.1505) and his wife Caitilín (d.1506), daughter of Thomas, eighth earl of Desmond.[11]

Secular and religious material frequently coexisted in these works, indicative of their perceived complementary nature. The first page of the Book of Ballymote, for example, contains a drawing of Noah's ark followed by a discussion of the ages of the world, a popular medieval theme which divided world history into six distinct periods, culminating in the Christian era. Interspersed in the compilation one can find heroic sagas, treatises on the metre and profession of poets, a physical and geological survey of Ireland and a translation of the destruction of Troy and the wanderings of Ulysses. The *Book of Lismore*, meanwhile, in addition to containing twelve saints' lives, also boasts treatment of the wars between the Norse and the Irish, the conflict between Cormac Mac Airt and the king of Munster and includes a copy of the travels of Marco Polo.

The fifteenth century was also a period when many devotional works of continental origin were translated into Irish, undoubtedly to feed what was becoming a growing market. The hugely influential *Meditationes Vitae Christi*, written by the Tuscan Franciscan Johnannes de Caulibus sometime around 1300, was translated by Tomás Ó Bruacháin, a choral canon of Killala and committed to writing by one Domnal Ó Conaill about 1443; this was some thirty-three years after its first appearance in English in the form of *Mirrour of the Blessed Lyf of Jesu Christi*, the work of Carthusian prior, Nicholas Love, who translated and adapted the *Meditationes* text, expanding upon it in places to include some anti-Wycliffite material.[12] The same Ó Conaill who produced the Irish version of *Meditationes* is also thought to have collaborated with translator William MacGivney of Breifne, in producing the earliest Irish text of the *De Contemptu Mundi* of Pope Innocent III (1160/1–1216) around the same time. A famous thirteenth-century life of the Virgin Mary known as the *Vita Rhythmica* was also translated from Latin into Irish in the fifteenth century, in addition to a tract entitled *Liber de Passione Christi*, attributed to St Bernard. A devotional work comprising a literary dialogue between St Anselm and the Virgin Mary on the subject of Christ's Passion, *Dialogus Beatae Mariae et S. Anselmi de Passione*, was first translated to Irish at the end of the fourteenth century and was repeatedly copied through the fifteenth century.[13] Religious texts from England were similarly absorbed into fifteenth-century Gaelic Irish devotional culture. One good example is the *Carta Humani Generis* or 'Charter of Christ'; this is a Middle English allegory which presented the crucified Christ as concluding a peace treaty with humanity. The terms of this treaty are drawn up on a formal document: the skin of Christ's crucified body. His skin functioned as the parchment, the lance piercing his side as the pen, his five wounds the letters and his open heart-wound the inkwell from which would be drawn copious amounts of ink (blood). The 'Charter of Christ' was translated into Irish by Uilliam Mac an Leagha around 1461–63 and came to be used increasingly in the religious compositions of native Irish bardic poets in the fifteenth and sixteenth centuries.[14]

It appears incongruous that such a flowering of literary activity, particularly in the devotional sphere, should occur in a century characterised by the lamentable state of its church organization. However, two factors can, in part, explain this phenomenon. First, because Gaelic Ireland was not immune from the broader devotional trends found on the continent, fifteenth-century Irish piety became heavily influenced by European affective devotion. Such devotion highlighted the importance of mentally entering a suggested religious scene and empathising with the characters therein; for example, the duress of the flight of the Virgin and child into Egypt, the horror of the torture endured by Christ on Calvary and the heartbreak of Mary at the foot of the cross. Devotional texts, which stretched the canonical outlines of gospel narrative in order to more fully express the poignancy and emotion of events for the pious to contemplate, became increasingly sought after, especially by wealthy and educated laity. A movement towards greater interiorisation of devotion was under way, most effectively highlighted by the increasing demand in England and on the continent for books of hours with which one could retire to a private place for an intimate exchange with God. Independence in the exercise of devotion was much sought after in educated lay circles and, perhaps, in Ireland, the laxity of secular clergy actually contributed to the urgency of this need.[15]

Although having its roots in the writings of Anselm (d.1109) and Peter Damian (d.1072), affective devotion, especially to the passion of Christ, was nurtured by Bernard of Clairvaux (d.1153) and the Cistercians. Later it found its most ardent advocate in the form of the Franciscan order, which made preaching the crucified Christ their central charism, adopting as a motto '*Mihi absit gloriari nisi in cruce Domini*' ('God forbid that I should glory save in the cross of Our Lord').[16] This emphasis on associating oneself with the pain of Christ crucified and calling to mind the various scenes of his passion was, of course, as much a feature of the devotional world of those living within areas of English influence as of the native Irish. Here, too, the friars fed the religious imagination of their flocks. The well-known Franciscan collection of verse and prose, composed in a mixture of Hiberno-English, Latin and French and preserved in British Library MS Harley 913, which was assembled around the 1330s, most probably in Waterford, attests to this. One poem entitled 'Christ on the Cross', invites its hearer to 'Look at your Lord, man, where he hangs on the cross, and weep, if you can, tears entirely of blood'.[17] Such an invitation is also a common feature of the native Irish bardic religious poetry of the fifteenth and sixteenth centuries, which also places great emphasis on the sincerity of compassion for Christ, exemplified in the tears of blood shed by his grieving mother, Mary, at the foot of the cross.[18] Moreover, Alan J. Fletcher has recently drawn attention to the 'close association, even symbiosis of the material forms of two ethnic religious cultures on the island of Ireland', pointing, in particular, to Trinity College Dublin MS 667, an Irish Franciscan manuscript, perhaps compiled in Co. Clare, in which English, Irish and Latin texts appear in close proximity to each other: evidence of cultural exchange across ethnic boundaries.[19]

The spread of the Franciscan order, in both its unreformed Conventual and Observant forms, into Gaelic areas in the fifteenth century, had a notable impact on both literary and devotional trends. Quite an interesting literary network can be discerned when manuscript compilations, in addition to the identities of their patrons and scribes, are examined closely. *Leabhar Uí Mhaine*, or the 'Book of the O'Kellys' was completed sometime around 1394, the work of ten scribes. The book was commissioned by Muirchertach Ua Ceallaigh (O'Kelly) who was bishop of Clonfert 1378–94 and archbishop of Tuam 1394–1407.[20] The O'Kellys were subsequently to have close associations with the Franciscan order. In 1414 Pope John XXII instructed the bishop of Clonfert, Thomas O'Kelly, to license the foundation of the Franciscan friaries of Meelick and Kilconnell. It appears that the monastery of Kilconnell was actually founded by the incumbent O'Kelly chieftain, William, for his obit of 1420 is recorded in the book of the community.[21] It was at the request of Malachy O'Kelly, lord of Uí Maine, in 1464 that the Kilconnell friars adopted Observant reform, illustrating the concern which O'Kelly had for the progress of the order.

The spirituality of the Franciscans was likewise adopted by members of Uí Maine's ruling family, exemplified by the fact that Tadhg Caoch O'Kelly is recorded as dying in the habit of the Franciscan Third Order in 1486. Members of other native literary families often gained prominent positions in ecclesiastical life as Franciscans. In 1453 Pope Nicholas V instructed the bishop of Clonfert to license the foundation of three or four new friaries in the province of Tuam. The incumbent prelate was one Cornelius Ó Cuindlis, a Franciscan, who may have belonged to the same family of historians as Murchadh Riabhach Ó Cuindlis, scribe of the *Leabhar Breac*.[22] It is perhaps no coincidence that for many years the *Leabhar Breac* was housed at the Franciscan abbey of Kilnalahan (established 1371), where the Franciscan lay brother and scholar, Mícheál Ó Cléirigh, would consult it in October 1629.[23] Close ties between the Franciscan order and local ruling families would have an important impact on the spread of devotional trends. It has been suggested, for instance, that Tomás Ó Bruacháin of Killala, who completed the Irish translation of *Meditationes vitae Christi*, may have acquired the Latin copy from the nearby Franciscan friary of regular tertiaries at Rosserk which was established around that time.[24]

The second factor, which encouraged a flowering of devotional works in the fifteenth century, was the Observant reform movement which revitalised orders such as the Franciscans, Dominicans and Augustinians. The epicentre of the revival could be found in Gaelic areas and, more particularly in the western dioceses of Killala, Achonry and Elphin from the 1450s, Clonfert having led the way in the first half of the fifteenth century. The prominence of reform in Gaelic areas led to the appointment of a succession of Gaelic Irish Franciscan provincials from the 1440s onwards.[25] One of the consequences of reform was a greater emphasis on enlisting the laity in the Franciscan way of life. The first Irish establishment of the Third Order regulars can be found in the diocese of Clonfert in the 1420s while evidence of their secular counterparts appears in the 1460s. Franciscan tertiaries observed the seven canonical hours and were expected to attend Mass daily in addition to confessing and receiving the eucharist three times a year. For seculars, proximity to a Franciscan house was a practical requisite, in order to facilitate attendance at the liturgy. Illiterate lay members were also catered for, being required to recite twelve *Pater Nosters* and *Glorias* at Matins (seven for the other hours) in addition to a credo and psalm 50.[26] The prominence of Third Order seculars in Gaelic Ireland (which did not experience the same growth in English areas) has been identified as an 'alternative confraternal impulse' to the lay fraternities which operated in at least forty-five towns and villages in nine counties and which were associated most prominently with the *ecclesia inter anglicos* whose parochial organisation was largely modelled on that of England.[27] Urban lay fraternities in cities such as Dublin had much in common with the craft and trade guilds in their devotional interests. In the later fifteenth century, the bonds of kinship which confraternities offered to citizens of the Pale undoubtedly contributed to the fashioning not only of civic identity but also to the sense of belonging to a colonial community at a time when their English inheritance was increasingly under threat from an ever-expanding Gaelic cultural revival.[28]

Although all but six of the sixty-two lay fraternities were found within the *ecclesia inter anglicos*, the religious communities of native Irish and Anglo-Irish areas did not inhabit wholly separate devotional worlds.[29] Perhaps the most instructive instance of the diffusion of a religious cult which one might initially associate with only these areas is that of St George. The municipal ruling body in Dublin sponsored the religious fraternity of St George whose master and wardens were usually appointed from the outgoing mayor and bailiffs of the city. Members of the fraternity were also routinely employed in the defence of the Pale against rebel activities in its borderlands in the late fifteenth century.[30] Given its associations with the colonial community of the Pale, one would not expect the cult of this saint to have travelled far beyond its borders. However, the evidence of Irish manuscripts suggests otherwise. The passion of St George is found in both the *Leabhar Breac* and *Liber Flavus Fergusiorum* and a homily on the life of St George. The latter is essentially a reworking of the *Leabhar Breac* text, with the addition of the story of the saint's encounter with the dragon (first found in the thirteenth-century *Legenda Aurea*) and is found in a fifteenth-century Irish manuscript, British Library MS Egerton 91, written by one of Gaelic Ireland's most prolific scribes, Uilliam Mac an Leagha. Less surprising, perhaps, is the fact that an Irish life of St George, dating, it is thought, from the mid-fifteenth century, appears in the Book of Fermoy, written for David Mór, son of Maurice, son of John Roche, member of the Anglo-Norman Roche family whose seat was at Castletownroche near Fermoy in Co. Cork.[31]

If the evidence of native Irish manuscripts suggests that the cult of St George was not confined to the piety of Palesmen, a compilation such as Oxford Bodleian Library MS Laud. Misc. 610, which comprises a manuscript written between 1410 and 1452 for James Butler, fourth earl of Ormond ('the White Earl') and a second written in 1453–54 for his nephew, Edmund Butler,[32] demonstrates that the devotional interests of Anglo-Irish magnates often closely mirrored those of the native Irish lords with whom they were often at war. Indeed, stories found here are often present in other Gaelic Irish collections; one such is the passion of Christ's image, which is found in the *Leabhar Breac*. This relates how a Jewish community scourges, mocks and pierces a full-size icon of Christ in a re-enactment of the passion drama of the gospels, whereupon real blood and water begins to flow from the image as a sign of their condemnation. Likewise, two separate 'dialogues on the passion' – one between the Virgin Mary and St Anselm and the other between the Virgin and St Bernard, are also found in the *Liber Flavus Fergusiorum*. Bede's *De locis sanctis*, on the holy places, is here too, having also appeared in the *Leabhar Breac*. The tale of the finding of the true cross by St Helena, the *Inventio Sanctae Crucis*, was also a popular inclusion in manuscripts of this period; it is often followed by a reworking of the chivalric romance known in Middle English as the legend of Sir Firumbras and in Irish as *Stair Fortibrais*. This was set in the context of the conflict between Charlemagne and the Saracens and featured the characters of Roland and Oliver who battle against a Saracen king and his giant son. In at least three other Irish manuscripts from the period – *Liber Flavus Fergusiorum*, British Library MS Egerton 1781 and Royal Irish Academy MS 475 (*Leabhar Chlainne Suibhne*) – this tale follows that of the finding of the cross. In the White Earl's collection, the same pattern is observed.[33]

The miscellany of religious material found in British Library MS 30512 which had nothing if not a chequered history, passing from the hands of the Butlers of Ormond into those of the Fitzgeralds of Desmond (perhaps as a ransom for Edmund Butler in 1462), and then back again over the course of the fifteenth and sixteenth centuries, is also of some interest. Here, too, there is much material that is shared with devotional collections produced in the far stronger Gaelic areas of the north and north-west of the country: popular legends of martyrs such as St James Intercisus (or 'James-cut-to-pieces'), the child-and-mother martyrs Quiricus and Julitta, and the martyr to nuptial consummation, St Alexius.[34] Here, too, is contained a note on the twelve 'Golden Fridays' on which it is proper to fast, a devotion that was also dear to the Donegal Gaelic noblewoman, Máire Ní Mháille, who included it in her own personal 'Book of Piety' in 1513 and who was assiduous in observing the devotion in her own life, according to her obit.[35]

The transmission of religious ideas from learned authors to the devout laity through the medium of mendicant orders is perfectly exemplified in the case of a text listing the sixteen conditions required for a good confession. Originally enumerated in Dominican Observant Antoninus of Florence's (1389–1459) *Confessionale-Defecerunt*, where it is attributed to Thomas Aquinas, it subsequently turns up in some fifteenth-century Irish manuscripts (including the *Liber Flavus Fergusiorum*) some of which are Franciscan. One, which dates from 1475, was written at the friary of Kilcrea, Co. Cork; another mid-fifteenth-century manuscript is likely to have been produced in a Franciscan community in Co. Clare.[36] The library catalogue of the Franciscan friary in Youghal (1490–1523) shows that it possessed a copy of the *Confessionale* as does the library list of the earl of Kildare, indicating its usefulness to both clerical and lay readers.[37] The recommendations for a good confession included simplicity, humility and honesty, deep contrition and a confidence that the confessed sins would be forgiven. Most importantly, perhaps, the penitent was advised to confess at least three times a year. This last recommendation suggests that this text embraced lay tertiary members of the order, for whom this was a requirement. Apart from the text's obvious relevance as a tool in preaching, it was also to prove popular in non-clerical circles. Devout noblewoman, Máire Ní Mháille's 'Book of Piety' contains the list, illustrating that it was most probably cherished and used by her. It is likely that Máire first heard of the sixteen conditions from the Donegal Franciscans and thereafter chose to have the list included in the book that was compiled for her use.[38] Moreover, many of these recommendations are also to be commonly found in bardic religious verse dealing with penance. While the 'sixteen conditions' formula is not specifically referred to in these poems, its prescriptions, certainly are. Thus a transmission of ideas can be discerned from a learned continental author to Irish members of the Franciscan order and, in turn, to members of the educated laity, of both Gaelic Irish and Anglo-Norman stock, as evidenced above.

In religious terms, late medieval Ireland can be characterised as something of a melting pot of devotional influences from both England and the continent. The pastoral care and preaching of its new mendicant orders would greatly contribute to the transformation of the devotional landscape across the jurisdictions of both *ecclesia inter anglicos* and *ecclesia inter hibernicos*. The very latest hagiographical work, or most up-to-date cult of Christ's passion, would become highly prized commodities, which both Anglo-Norman and Gaelic Irish families of means would scramble to include in devotional collections or 'launch' in religious verse. In this, at least, the communities of both Anglo-Ireland and Gaelic Ireland were as one. In the long term, it would be the shared religious culture of both Anglo-Norman (now 'Old English') and Gaelic Irish Catholics which would come under scrutiny in the Reformation period, leading to the construction of a common Catholic identity in the seventeenth century.[39]

Notes

1 P. J. Corish, *The Irish Catholic Experience* (Dublin: Gill and Macmillan, 1985), p. 49.

2 M. T. Flanagan, *The Transformation of the Irish Church in the Twelfth Century* (Woodbridge: Boydell Press, 2010), pp. 243–8.

3 See especially R. Stalley, *The Cistercian Monasteries of Ireland: An Account of the History, Art and Architecture of the White Monks in Ireland from 1142–1540* (New Haven, CT and London: Yale University Press, 1987); F. X. Martin, 'The Augustinian friaries in pre-Reformation

Ireland', *Augustiniana*, 6 (1956), pp. 346–84; B. O'Sullivan, *Medieval Irish Dominican Studies* (ed.), H. Fenning (Dublin: Four Courts Press, 2009); C. N. Ó Clabaigh, *The Franciscans in Ireland, 1400–1534: From Reform to Reformation* (Dublin: Four Courts Press, 2002); C. N. Ó Clabaigh, *The Friars in Ireland*, 1224–1540 (Dublin: Four Courts Press, 2012).

4 J. Watt, *The Church in Late Medieval Ireland* (Dublin: Gill and Macmillan 1972), pp. 193–4.

5 H. A. Jefferies, *The Irish Church and the Tudor Reformations* (Dublin: Four Courts Press, 2010), p. 38.

6 See C. Mooney, *The Church in Gaelic Ireland: Thirteenth to Fifteenth Centuries* (Dublin: Gill and Macmillan, 1969); Watt, *The Church in Late Medieval Ireland*; A. Lynch, 'Religion in late medieval Ireland', *Archivium Hibernicum*, 36 (1981), pp. 3–15; Corish, *The Irish Catholic Experience*; P. O'Dwyer, *Towards a History of Irish Spirituality* (Dublin: Columba Press, 1995).

7 J. Delumeau, *Catholicism from Luther to Voltaire: A New View of the Counter-Reformation* (London: Burns and Oates, 1977).

8 See, in particular, H. A. Jefferies, *Priests and Prelates of Armagh in the Age of Reformations, 1518–1558* (Dublin: Four Courts Press, 1997); H. A. Jefferies, *The Irish Church and the Tudor Reformations* (Dublin: Four Courts Press, 2010). Here Jefferies' argument mirrors that of E. Duffy's *The Stripping of the Altars: Traditional Religion in England, 1400–1580* (New Haven, CT and London: Yale University Press, 2002) with respect to England.

9 Lynch, 'Religion in late medieval Ireland', p. 3; O'Dwyer, *Towards a History of Irish Spirituality*, p. 135; S. Ellis takes a more cautious approach in *Tudor Ireland: Crown, Community and the Conflict of Cultures, 1470–1603* (London and New York: Longman, 1985).

10 R. Atkinson (ed.), *The Passions and Homilies from Leabhar Breac* (Dublin: Royal Irish Academy, 1887); *The Book of Ballymote: Photographic Facsimile with an Introduction by R. Atkinson* (Dublin: Royal Irish Academy, 1887); K. Mulchrone (ed.), *The Book of Lecan: Leabhar Mór Mhic Fhir Bisigh Leacain: Facsimile Edition* (Dublin: Royal Irish Academy, 1937); for contents of *Liber Flavus Fergusiorum*, see K. Mulchrone *et al.*, *Catalogue of Irish Manuscripts in the Royal Irish Academy* (1926–70) No. 476, 1254–73; R. A. S. Macalister, *The Book of Lismore: Facsimile with Introduction* (Dublin: Irish Manuscripts Commission, 1950).

11 B. Ó Cuív, 'Observations on the Book of Lismore', *Proceedings of the Royal Irish Academy. Section C: Archaeology, Celtic Studies, History, Linguistics, Literature*, 83C (Dublin: Royal Irish Academy, 1983), pp. 269–92.

12 C. Ó Maonaigh (ed.), *Smaointe Beatha Chríost* (Dublin: Dublin Institute for Advanced Studies, 1944); for its English equivalent and for discussion of the vernacular transmission of *Meditationes Vitae Christi*, see M. G. Sargent (ed.), *The Mirror of the Blessed Life of Jesus Christ: A Full Critical Edition* (Exeter: University of Exeter Press, 2005).

13 M. Mac Conmara, 'An léann eaglasta ag baile, 1200–1500', in Máirtín Mac Conmara (ed.), *An Léann Eaglasta in Éirinn, 1200–1900* (Dublin: An Chlóchomhar Tta, 1988), pp. 113–14; Mooney, *The Church in Gaelic Ireland*, p. 33; P. O'Dwyer, *Mary: A History of Devotion in Ireland* (Dublin: Four Courts Press, 1988), pp. 38, 156; R. A. Q. Skerrett, 'Two Irish translations of the *Liber de Passione Christi*', *Celtica*, 6 (1963), pp. 82–117.

14 A. Breeze, 'The charter of Christ in medieval English, Welsh and Irish', *Celtica*, 19 (1987), pp. 111–20.

15 On the privatisation of devotion, see A. Taylor, 'Into his secret chamber: reading and privacy in late medieval England', in J. Raven, H. Small and N. Tadmor (eds), *The Practice and Representation of Reading* (Cambridge: Cambridge University Press, 1996), pp. 41–61.

16 See T. H. Bestul, 'Antecedents: the Anselmian and Cistercian contributions', in W. F. Pollard and R. Boenig (eds), *Mysticism and Spirituality in Medieval England* (Cambridge: D. S. Brewer, 1997), pp. 1–20.

17 A. M. Lucas (ed.), *Anglo-Irish Poems of the Middle Ages* (Dublin: Columba Press, 1995), p. 123.

18 M. Gray and S. Ryan, '"Mother of Mercy": the Virgin Mary and the Last Judgement in Welsh and Irish tradition', in K. Jankulak and J. Wooding (eds), *Ireland and Wales in the Middle Ages* (Dublin: Four Courts Press, 2007), pp. 246–61; S. Ryan, '"No milkless cow": the Cross of Christ in medieval Irish literature', in P. Clarke and C. Methuen (eds), *The Church and Literature: Studies in Church History 48* (Abingdon: Boydell & Brewer, 2012).

19 Alan J. Fletcher, *Late Medieval Popular Preaching in Britain and Ireland: Texts, Studies and Interpretations* (Turnhout, Belgium: Brepols, 2009), pp. 267 and 245 (see ch. 8 for the argument in full).

20 *The Book of Uí Maine, Otherwise Called the Book of the O'Kellys: Facsimile Edition* (Dublin: Irish Manuscripts Commission, 1942). For a valuable recent overview of the contribution of the friars to vernacular literary culture in late medieval Ireland, see E. Bhreatnach, 'The mendicant orders and vernacular Irish learning in the late medieval period', *Irish Historical Studies*, 37(147) (2011), pp. 357–75.

21 Ó Clabaigh, *The Friars in Ireland*, pp. 43–4.

22 Ó Clabaigh, *Franciscans*, pp. 45, 84–5.

23 F. Mac Donncha, *A Pictorial Guide to the Irish Franciscan First Order Foundations* (Dublin: Dún Mhuire, Killiney, 1982), p. 58.

24 Ó Maonaigh, *Smaointe Beatha Chríost*, p. 363; Ó Clabaigh, *Franciscans*, pp. 97, 102.

25 Ó Clabaigh, *Franciscans*, pp. 53–7; for the Gaelic Irish contribution to the reform of the Augustinians, see F. X. Martin, 'The Irish Augustinian reform movement in the fifteenth century', in J. A. Watt *et al.* (eds), *Medieval Studies Presented to Aubrey Gwynn SJ* (Dublin: C. Ó Lochlainn, 1961), pp. 230–64.

26 Ó Clabaigh, *The Friars*, 305–12.

27 C. Lennon, 'The confraternities and cultural duality in Ireland, 1450–1550', in C. Black and P. Gravestock (eds), *Early Modern Confraternities in Europe and the Americas: International and Interdisciplinary Perspectives* (Aldershot: Ashgate, 2006), pp. 36–8.
28 *Ibid.*, pp. 38–9.
29 *Ibid.*, p. 36.
30 *Ibid.*, p. 40.
31 G. Murphy, E. Fitzpatrick *et al.* (comps), *Catalogue of Irish Manuscripts in the Royal Irish Academy* (Dublin: Royal Irish Academy, 1940–58), fasc. 25, pp. 3091–3125.
32 B. Ó Cuív (comp.), *Catalogue of Irish language Manuscripts in the Bodleian Library at Oxford and Oxford College Libraries* (Dublin: Dublin Institute for Advanced Studies, 2001), part 1, pp. 62–88.
33 For manuscript parallels, see S. Ryan '"Wily women of God" in Cavan's late medieval and early modern devotional collections', in B. Scott (ed.), *Culture and Society in Early Modern Breifne/Cavan* (Dublin: Four Courts Press, 2009), pp. 31–47.
34 *Ibid.*
35 S. Ryan, 'Windows on late medieval devotional practice: Máire Ní Mháille's "Book of Piety" (1513) and the world behind the texts', in R. Moss, C. Ó Clabaigh and S. Ryan (eds), *Art and Devotion in Late Medieval Ireland* (Dublin: Four Courts Press, 2006), pp. 1–15.
36 G. Dottin, 'Le Manuscript irlandais de la bibliothèque de Rennes', *Revue Celtique*, 15 (1894), pp. 79–91; for discussion of these, see Ó Clabaigh, *Franciscans*, pp. 122–3.
37 Ó Clabaigh, *Franciscans*, pp. 160–80; G. Mac Niocaill (ed.), *Crown Surveys of Lands, 1540–41, with the Kildare Rental Begun in 1518* (Dublin: Irish Manuscripts Commission, 1994), pp. 312–14, 355–6.
38 Ryan, 'Windows on late medieval devotional practice', pp. 4–5.
39 S. Ryan, 'Reconstructing Irish Catholic origins after the Reformation', in S. Ditchfield, K. van Liere and H. Louthan (eds), *Sacred History: Uses of the Christian Past in the Renaissance World* (Oxford: Oxford University Press, 2012).

Part II

Early modern struggles

4

Irish political Catholicism from the 1530s to 1660

David Finnegan

The reconstruction of the institutions of the Irish polity attendant upon Henry VIII's pursuit of *imperium* in the 1530s presented his Irish subjects, both old and new, with fundamentally new political realities. The introduction of Reformation via the parliament of 1536–37, and the elevation of the Irish lordship into a kingdom in 1541, began the slow transformation of the island's religio-political landscape. Of more immediate consequence though was the destruction of the Fitzgeralds of Kildare – the dynasty that had effectively ruled Ireland for English monarchs since the mid-fifteenth century – following 'Silken' Thomas, the tenth earl's, ill-starred rebellion. Few in Ireland, other than the rival Butlers and their clients and a small reform-minded lobby within the Pale, were happy to see the Kildares destroyed in the name of political reform; and it was from among these groups that Protestantism drew its initial limited support. For neither Irish laymen nor clerics wished to promote thoroughgoing church reform, as the new force energising and reforming religious life in early sixteenth-century Ireland was an Observantine-inspired Catholic Reformation. The evidence suggests that in 1530 there was little possibility for a 'popular' Reformation in Ireland, especially given the depth of Ireland's Roman connection, which had emerged over the medieval era as a core element of Irish life.[1]

The Catholic clergy played an integral role in shaping Irish responses to the Henrician political and religious reforms, persuading 'Silken' Thomas to proclaim Henry VIII a heretic and to plead for papal and imperial support in opposing him. In doing so they created a new source of disaffection, which thereafter bedevilled English efforts to control Ireland. The despairing admission of George Browne, Henry's pro-schism archbishop of Dublin (1537–55) of his failure 'to procure the nobility and gentry of this nation' to recognise Henry as 'their supreme head, as well spiritual as temporal' suggests that few within the Pale accepted Royal Supremacy.[2] That the pope's right to intervene in political matters was an integral part of Irish political culture was underlined by the recrudescence of the Kildare rebels' rhetoric during the Geraldine League (1538–41).

The unprecedented unity of this native coalition brought about a constitutional revolution that envisaged the incorporation of the Gaelic lordships into a new integrative kingdom of Ireland encompassing the whole island. In return for full recognition of crown sovereignty, the 'wild Irish' were to be 'accepted as subjects, where before they were taken as Irish enemies' and re-granted their lands under the crown, in return for supporting political and religious reforms. Between 1542–48 this 'constitutional revolution' stabilised Ireland and had it reached maturity, may well have accomplished a gradual reduction of Gaelic Ireland to English ways at minimal cost. However, a more aggressive government-sponsored military policy – advocated by influential servitors in the face of perceived native backsliding on reform – saw the Gaelic lords swiftly abandon their commitment to reform and seek foreign support. This tendency resurfaced whenever local powerbrokers felt their interests threatened by the state and this disjunction eventually strangled the reform process although it persisted as an option into the 1590s.

Edwardian confessional policy also alienated the elite in the governed territories because, sharpened by greater Protestant commitment and use of the vernacular, it proved considerably less tolerant than its Henrician forbear of the difficulties of implementing reform. The unpopularity of Edwardian reform ensured that both Tudor kingdoms – which remained essentially Catholic – welcomed the Marian succession. Although there seems to have been little outward opposition to Elizabeth's re-establishment of Protestantism in Ireland contemporaries suggested that most of the English of Ireland were crypto-Catholics who treated their attendance at 'divine service as ... a may game'.[3] Political reform – for which the colonial community's support was critical – took precedence over its religious analogue, as it did down to the 1640s. Whenever Elizabeth's Protestant servants in Ireland raised the issue of compelling conformity, London always proffered some variation of Cecil's advice to 'stir no sleeping dogs in Ireland ... many things in commonweals are suffered that are not liked'.[4]

Reform in the autonomous lordships proved impossible as it was widely felt from early in Elizabeth's reign that any attempt to establish Protestantism would provoke rebellion. The lords and bishops increasingly acted in concert to oppose the introduction of reform of either stripe. The upshot was that by 1570 many English Protestant observers held that 'the minds of the Irishry be so estranged from us ... partly by reason of our religion, which those savage and wicked people do so deadly hate that they daily gape for some foreign regiment, and are willing to submit their necks to any government so they were delivered from us'.[5] This owed much to the efforts of Irish Catholic clergymen – returning to Ireland in the 1560s – educated in the seminaries of the *monarquía*. Many seminarians had hoped to promote an accommodation between their spiritual authority and that of the state. Yet the government's refusal to accept the principle of dual allegiance and Pius V's moulding of a more militant Counter-Reformation, culminating in Elizabeth's excommunication in 1570, saw this conciliatory approach quickly dissipate. Thereafter the Catholic clergy's instructions to encourage the Irish to persevere in their defence of the faith assumed a much more ambiguous colour. By 1579 many priests were advocating force as the means of restoring Catholicism; this filtered through to the lay elite providing the key context for the series of rebellions that erupted between 1579 and 1583.

The evolution of a post-Tridentine collective consciousness of Catholicism as a confessional church with its own forms of practice and discipline also proved critical to the development of a less militant – though no less committed – religio-political consciousness among the traditionally loyal community. It has been suggested that their commitment to Counter-Reformation Catholicism was more a consequence of, than a formative influence upon, their political attitudes, and that it was only after their alienation from the crown over the cess controversy that religious considerations started to influence their political position. This suggestion seems a tenuous one, resting upon anachronistic modern presumptions. The sweeping reforms proposed by Lord Deputy Sir Henry Sidney in the 1569–71 parliament had both political and religious overtones; and they were successfully opposed on precisely these grounds by 'busy headed lawyers and malcontented [sic] gentlemen ... all thwarters and hinderers of matters that should tend to the reformation of Religion'.[6]

As native-born officials displayed little enthusiasm for the radicalisation of the secular and religious policies formulated for Ireland in England, English-born Protestant officials grew in number and influence in the Dublin administration at their expense. That this increasingly alien government made ever more onerous demands upon the excluded did little to persuade them to support reform. This was categorically restated in 1585–86 when Sir John Perrot's effort to revive Sidney's legislative programme was once again thwarted in parliament. The outraged deputy complained bitterly that 'it is the rubbing of that sore (of religion) that makes them thus kick'.[7] But it was also clear that the effort to introduce penal legislation and establish a permanent commutation of the cess into a tax fused the community's growing fears regarding the crown's encroachment upon their old religion and ancient constitutional liberties.

Sir Nicholas Walsh, chief justice and the government's nominee for the speakership, delivered that parliament's closing oration. A representative of that small element of the community who retained government confidence, his view of how best to reconnect crown and community provides an insight into moderate opinion among the English of Ireland. While acknowledging Elizabeth's unquestioned right to political obedience he argued that the time had come to readmit the consultative right of 'the multitude' through their representatives – a 'brotherly Society of Commons' – and to start governing Ireland again by the customary principles that informed the community's political heritage rather than those of an unrepresentative clique. The community's political representatives employed with ever-greater conviction the discourse of Ireland as a distinct *patria* with its own rights and customs against the state's innovatory policies – and Catholicism provided the most obvious marker of that polity's autonomous tradition.[8] Edward Nugent made this abundantly clear in his statement in parliament 'that things prospered in Henry V's and other kings' times when mass was up'.[9] The government's brutal reaction to the Desmond and Baltinglass rebellions demonstrated that the rebels' analysis of their community's problems, if not their methods of remedy, had been largely correct.

Between the militancy of the rebels and the moderacy of Speaker Walsh lay a range of other opinions on matters of faith and fatherland. Some men chose to ignore the conflicting claims to their allegiance emanating from London and Rome, some were willing to settle for tacit toleration, some hoped that the vagaries of dynastic politics might bring a Catholic ruler to the throne, while others still waited for the main chance to reverse the religious settlement by force. Nevertheless almost all born in Ireland were resolved to persevere in their confessional allegiance; if not seeking separation from the English crown, they were questioning the system of government then prevailing. These heterogeneous attitudes were critical in the variegated responses of Ireland's Catholics to the 1590s crisis.

This crisis began in Ulster, the most autonomous region in Ireland, as a localised seigneurial protest, but from its outset it had a pronounced religious dimension. In 1594 most Ulster dioceses had resident and active bishops and Catholic reformation could certainly have been percolating if these took their ministry as seriously as Redmund O'Gallagher, Bishop of Derry 'legate to the Pope and Custos Armaghnen' who 'useth all manner of spiritual jurisdiction throughout all Ulster, consecrating Churches, ordaining Priests, confirming children, and giving all manner of dispensations, riding with pomp and company from place to place as it was accustomed in Queen Mary's days'.[10] Moreover, the clergy had clearly taught the natives about the wider European confessional situation because Captain Cuellar, the Armada castaway, claimed they were 'well affected to us Spaniards, because they realise that we are attacking the heretics and are their great enemies'.[11]

These bishops first persuaded Hugh Roe O'Donnell to seek Spanish support in 1593, using their contacts with Irish *émigrés* within the *monarquía*. These clerics functioned as a proto-diplomatic corps supporting those in Ireland seeking to arrest the advance of the state and its established church. Sir Francis Bacon later asserted that the 'defence of the Catholic religion ... hath made the foreigner reciprocally more plausible with the rebel'.[12] The Ulster confederates had absorbed the lessons of earlier rebellions and clearly saw in Catholicism a potent unifying force, offering the means to transcend Ireland's local particularism. Clerical support transformed the rebellion from a localised seigneurial protest into an island-wide league – allied with Spain – demanding the restoration of Catholicism. As rebel religious propaganda saturated the countryside, by 1600 many government servitors discerned a pan-insular coalition:

> not satisfied without the open exercise of the same under the Romish authority, which they strive to have supreme. This is not only plotted amongst the rebels, but amongst those whom – we term best subjects, as well abroad in the countries, as at home in corporate towns and elsewhere; and for this cause only are the rebels by all sorts of people relieved, making it a conscience not to assist them, and thinking themselves damned if they should incur excommunication.

Yet this clearly overstated the case. Although the Ulster rebels drew many to their cause, not all Ireland's Catholics saw the struggle in strictly religious terms, and many men, such as Niall Garbh O'Donnell, preferred 'the cause of kith and kin to the Catholic religion, which they embrace and revere'.[13] Equally significant, was their failure to recruit any more than a few inhabitants of the towns or Pale despite their alienation from government. Familiar with their worldview, Tyrone, with the assistance of the Catholic clergy, drew up a proclamation in late 1599 seeking Ireland's re-establishment as a Catholic kingdom, ostensibly under Elizabeth. Although they still did not join the rebels, they 'temporised with her [Elizabeth] so as not to lose their estates and they hoped that, when she would die, there would come a change of religion' and used the threat of joining the rebellion to openly practise Catholicism and to refuse to billet troops or contribute to their maintenance.[14]

The rebellion's failure meant that those Irish Catholics who survived the turmoil of Elizabeth's reign with lives and lands intact now sought a relationship with the firmly ensconced Stuart monarchy, especially after the Recusancy Revolt, a bungled attempt by a number of Irish towns to present Ireland as a Catholic kingdom to the new King. The general disengagement from military conflict in north-west Europe and the papacy's increasing retreat from militancy suited the imperatives of the Irish Catholic position under the Stuarts. Facing a retrenched Protestant state and determined to remain Catholic, they sought toleration for their faith. While James VI and I, and later Charles I, seemed open to this at times, the Irish government, now completely comprising Protestants, displayed no such sentiments. They demanded that the Stuart kings by 'some moderate co-actions' compel the laity to come in and hear the reformed clergy for 'once they were grounded in the principles of true religion ... there would be sincere obedience, loyalty, peace ... wherewith the Kingdom of England is blessed'.[15] Clearly the Irish Protestant hierarchy had still not given up on converting the natives, but contemporaneous reports from the Catholic clergy disputed this possibility.[16]

That the Catholic clergy assessment was correct was demonstrated by failure of the government's 'Mandates' policy (1605–07). Based on the principle *compelle intrare*, this involved unprecedented compulsion to break Catholicism's grip on the colonial community. This two-year trial of wills, described by a Catholic contemporary as 'the Neronian times', only ended when the privy council, disquieted by reports of a rebellious conspiracy developing among Ireland's Catholics, demanded that Lord Deputy Chichester desist.[17] Ireland's confessional demography forced those in authority in England to accept that where religion was concerned 'the same rule serveth not fitly for Ireland and for England'.

Recognition of demographic realities persuaded Ireland's Catholic leadership that if they remained united it would prove impossible for the state to compel them to embrace the reformed faith. The Catholic hierarchy also recognised the principle conceded in 1607 and sought to use it to their advantage by advertising their unwillingness to challenge the crown's political authority, a difficult task given that they sought to balance a defence of papal monarchy with the pursuit of toleration from a Protestant ruler who claimed headship of the Irish Church. Tyrone's former Roman agent, Peter Lombard, now Irish primate, framed this new strategy, which was not predicated upon any ecumenical concerns, but rather upon two pragmatic points. First, to achieve its pastoral ends the church should avoid provoking the state; and second, if granted, toleration would most likely occur only after Catholics had demonstrated that they represented no danger to the state. Therefore, the church aimed to proceed quietly with its spiritual mission in the hope that by remaining detached from secular concerns, insofar as possible, the state would permit tacit (or even official) toleration. The existence of a wing in the Catholic Church that found this compromise distasteful and continued to seek to reverse the defeats of the sixteenth century, problematised this approach. It was further undermined by the continuing hostility of Ireland's Protestants who constantly agitated for more forceful measures against recusants, invariably presented as an ever more assertive subculture hindering the officers of state and church.

That James felt conflicted was clear from the periodic bouts of persecution he permitted and from his infamous denunciation of Ireland's Catholics as 'half-subjects'. His frustration was because papal supremacy completely inverted the logic of its royal counterpart. It also undermined the state's ability to reform (socially discipline) its subjects.[18] The government's suspicion of clerical influence on Catholic MPs during the 1613–15 parliament was not unfounded; David Rothe, the bishop of Ossory and acting primate in Ireland, had schooled Catholic representatives in parliament to oppose any legislation that threatened Catholic interests.[19] The principle *Redde Caesari* underpinned the decrees of the 1614 Drogheda Synod, over which Rothe had presided, and significantly, Sir John Everard, who had resigned from King's Bench in 1605 rather than take the oath of supremacy, appealed to the principle in parliament in 1615.[20] Intolerably, then, Irish allegiance to Rome implied that Ireland's laws should actually be subject to papal approval. Finally it raised the inevitable question of what would happen if the pope ordered Irish Catholics to actively resist the state: for Rome did claim – albeit indirectly – authority to depose rulers for offences against religion. Furthermore, most Irish Catholics accepted the pope as ultimate political arbiter.[21] That 'dual allegiance' proved difficult for Protestants to accept was because it simply did not exist for orthodox Catholics in the early seventeenth century.

As the seventeenth century wore on, the political and social status of Catholics continued to decline. This, coupled with periodic bouts of persecution altered their views of monarchy and their obligations towards that institution. In his *Analecta Sacra Hibernica* David Rothe concluded that a monarch not guided by his subjects' interests was an unworthy ruler. While influenced by prevailing Catholic political theory imbibed during his formation on the continent, Rothe's vision of sovereignty also depended upon *Laudabiliter*. This papal grant stipulated that English sovereignty over Ireland was conditional upon 'the submission and acceptance of the inhabitants of Ireland themselves' (as there had been no conquest) and the preservation of the Roman interest in Ireland. Despite the Reformation's corruption of this medieval constitution, Irish Catholics continued to yield political obedience in the face of considerable provocation. Yet there were limits to how much persecution the commonwealth could reasonably be expected to tolerate and Rothe pointed out that the authority of political government:

> which guides this earthly commonwealth to temporal felicity in this mutable and mortal life granted to men may be taken from men, and may in differently be swayed amongst them according to the different manner of the original cause and the different form of government.[22]

This focus on the rights of the Irish polity informs the writings of Ireland's Catholic clergymen in the period, especially those who belonged to the 'Old English' community. They constructed a contemporary Irish Catholic political identity by borrowing heavily from the past and particularly from the pre-Norman achievements of the early Christian (and Gaelic) church in Ireland, especially its missionary endeavours in Britain and Europe. This contributed to an increasing identification of the two historic communities as one nation – a confessionally inclusive identity pointedly excluding the New English (*Nua-Ghaill*) on grounds of their Protestantism. Perhaps the most famous exponent of this new 'national' history was Seathrun Ceítinn [Geoffrey Keating]. Through combining continental concepts of sovereignty with Irish history, Ceítinn transformed the tribal and localised political institutions of the pre-Christian Irish into those of a contemporary centralised monarchy. Pre-Christian kings ruled over the entire island guided by the Brehon laws which were regulated by the triennially convened *Féis* [parliament] of Tara, the *Fianna* enforced the monarch's decisions and the *Ollamh* kept the kingdom's records.[23] Ceítinn maintained that Ireland had always been ruled by contract theory – a point reaffirmed by *Laudabiliter* – and that under the pre-Norman political dispensation the principle of the 'common good' had always been accepted. In mid-seventeenth-century Ireland, the government's recent anti-Catholic policies revealed that the 'common good' was patently not the monarchy's priority. Respect for religion underpinned Ceítinn's vision of monarchy because upholding the faith of its commonwealth was critical to monarchy's rationale. In *Foras*, politics and religion were inseparable: royalism and Catholicism were the twin pillars of Ceítinn's imagined Irish people. Given Charles I's continuing failure to honour 'the Graces' and his intransigence in the face of Catholic pleas for assurance of their status within Ireland, Ceítinn's history implicitly advocated a 'conditional royalism'.

Most of the clerical corps (and their flock) shared this 'conditional' allegiance to the crown. They accepted the pope's role as their spiritual leader and their pursuit of toleration then was entirely secondary to their loyalty to Roman orthodoxy. The centrality of this tenet to Irish Catholic identity is clear from the community's refusal to swear an oath of allegiance until Charles I offered a reformulated version that omitted the notorious clause denying the pope's deposing power. Moreover, the controversy stirred up by William Malone, SJ, when he proposed permitting Charles rights of consultation in the affairs of the Irish Church, reveals the uniformity of Irish Catholic ultramontanism and their hostility to those who challenged it.[24] Seventeenth-century Irish Catholic clergymen were clearly engaged in the construction of a Catholic 'corporate structure' into which the religious injunctions of the state could not penetrate. John Copinger's *Memoriall to the Afflicted Catholickes in Irelande* (1606) typified the opinion of his fellow clerics in describing religion as 'nothing else than a binding, and consecrating of ourselves unto God'.[25] This was to take precedence over any other form of relationship as 'we be more obliged unto [Christ] and his Church, than either the captain unto his king, or the wife unto her husband' and martyrdom was preferable to defaulting. Those who did seek to ease their way in the world by conforming to Protestantism, especially at the lower social levels, were ostracised by their communities.

The administration of Sir Thomas Wentworth (1632–40), which amplified the pressure on the Catholic elite while simultaneously refusing to accept that Catholic constitutionalism had become central to their political identity, brought these issues sharply into focus. Their parliamentary representation declined from 112 MPs in 1634 to seventy-four in 1640. Furthermore they became increasingly dependant on the whim of their untrustworthy monarch and his Irish viceroy who aimed, by the extension of plantation to the Catholic strongholds throughout the rest of the country, to reduce their socio-economic and political influence. Their changed circumstances in the later 1630s left the Irish Catholic party fumbling for a way forward and resulted in the remarkable – and desperate – parliamentary alliance with the planters of 1640–41. However they had little faith in their 'allies' and secretly negotiated with Charles. Moreover many Irish Catholics considered rebellion in summer 1641 if 'the Graces' were again denied them.[26] As well as turning them into political outsiders, the period 1615 (when they lost their parliamentary majority) to 1640 had transformed them into opportunists, with no real commitment to any political position that did not provide for their religious sensibilities and their landed interests. In joining Irish Protestants in destroying Wentworth's 'absolutist' government, Ireland's

Catholics – who misunderstood the nature of the power struggle both in Ireland and across the three kingdoms – ironically played a key role in empowering English and Scottish puritanical ideologues. The increasingly aggressive anti-Catholicism of the puritan party convinced many leading Irish Catholics that the time had now come to take arms, after the example of the Scots, to prevent their destruction.[27] Most Irish historians agree that a small clique of Ulster natives, men of 'desperate and broken fortunes' in Richard Bellings's memorable phrase, planned and executed the 1641 Rising.[28] This is not a convincing explanation, however, as considerable evidence exists to support the argument that the rebellion involved Catholics across Ireland. Although the original plot cannot definitively be recovered, it is indisputable that all Irish Catholics faced the same threat in late 1641. It seems unlikely that a handful of Ulster lords felt confident of defying the state without wider support within Ireland. Furthermore, the chief insurgents in Ulster were 'parliament men' and married into the 'Old English' community. According to Hugh Bourke, Guardian of St Anthony's College Louvain, 'the parliament [Catholic delegates] of Ireland and the insurgents ... are in collusion to compass their end betwixt peace and war'.[29] The Palesmen's failure to use the parliament as a platform to alleviate Catholic grievances, saw them drift into rebellion, unconvincingly citing the actions of 'evil counsellors' as the key reason for their defection.

Religious unity brought an increasing sense of 'national' unity from the outset of the seventeenth century. This reached its apogee in the Confederation of Kilkenny which ordered that all differences between 'Old Irish, and Old and New English, or betwixt septs or families, or betwixt citizens and townsmen and countrymen' be superseded by the fact that all members 'be professors of the Holy Church and maintainer's of the country's liberties'. That such rapprochements were still being negotiated in the 1640s can be discerned from the poems that Pádraigín Haicéad and Seathrun Ceítinn addressed to the Confederation of Kilkenny, which while highlighting the fraternal bond between the two historic communities predicated upon their shared historical experience, kinship and Catholicism, also denounced dissension between Irish Catholics as sinful.

It was this weakness that historians have traditionally argued caused the Confederation's disintegration in the late 1640s. Yet perhaps more remarkable, given the range of political opinions it encompassed, is that the organisation functioned well enough until the crippling military defeats of 1647 – the confederacy's *annus horribilis*. Although the then unrealistic aims of the Catholic clergy have been blamed for the Confederation's collapse over the Inchiquin Truce, this somewhat obscures their crucial role in establishing the Confederation. As the fortunes of the disunited Irish Catholic insurgents waned in early 1642, the intervention of the bishops brought unity and purpose to their ranks. On 22 March 1642, the Armagh suffragans met at Kells, declared the rising just, a war of self-defence against 'those who have always, but especially in recent years, plotted the destruction of the Catholics, the slavery of the Irish, and the abolition of the king's prerogatives'. The synod also called for 'the immediate establishment of a council of suitable ecclesiastics and laymen to direct the Catholic arms'.[30] Its articles and those of the Irish Congregation, convened in May 1642, envisaged substantial modification to the laws and institutions of the Irish 'state' which would privilege the interests of 'mother church'. This clearly exerted considerable influence on the subsequent emergence of the Confederation of Kilkenny as that body's founding statute made plain:

> That the Roman Catholic Church in Ireland shall and may have and enjoy the privileges and immunities according to the Great Charter, made and declared within the realm of England, in the ninth year of King Henry III, sometime king of England, and afterwards enacted and confirmed in this realm of Ireland. And that the common law of England, and all the statutes of force in this kingdom, which are not against the Roman Catholic religion, or the liberties of the natives, and other liberties of this kingdom, shall be observed throughout the whole kingdom, and that all proceedings in civil and criminal cases shall be according to the same laws.[31]

The clergy then plainly had enormous influence on political matters and their attitudes were critical in shaping opinions and events. Nevertheless, disinterested in establishing a theocracy and keen to return to their pastoral role, the Catholic hierarchy relinquished authority to a largely secular government while reserving the right to monitor that government's adherence to the confederation's Oath of Association.[32]

Collectively the articles propounded at Kilkenny revealed the confederates' vision of Ireland's ideal political future. Although willing to come to terms with Charles, whom they accepted as their monarch, this was conditional upon the kingdom's essential Catholicity being upheld.[33] Following David Rothe's Bodinian analogy of the state as a corporeal form consisting of 'many parts, dissimilar, but of substantial and quickening form', they recognised the monarch's central role as the regulator of a religiously pluralistic commonwealth:

> we may behold in a politique body or great monarchical frame in so great a diversity of nations, difference of customs, variety of delights, affections and inclinations, in which we observe men to differ, and so disagree one from another, yet that they might be all governed by one sceptre, and

> contained under the name and label of one diadem, and under the knot of one union, and dominion, in the league of concord and peace.[34]

They did not explicitly demand re-Catholicisation of the kingdom, but if their proposals were implemented – given the natural Catholic majority – this would have been the outcome of the 'free parliament' the confederates subsequently requested. The Catholic clergy would be re-established as a propertied and endowed national organisation.[35]

While this Confederate 'constitution' represented a substantial majority of Irish Catholics, especially at elite level, a wider range of political opinions existed within the ranks. Many recognised the improbable equation at the centre of the Confederate constitution and at its radical fringe, some in this grouping even rejected Charles as their king. The breakdown of order in 1641 revealed that, for some, royalism was a conveniently expendable concept, especially among the meaner sort. Some insurgents assured the settlers that 'unless the King of England be favourable unto them they would depose [him] and make a new King of their own'.[36] And it was precisely because such opinions existed that the *Disputatio Apologetica* (1645) of Cornelius O'Mahony, SJ, caused such a furore; its very orthodoxy demonstrated why Protestants categorically rejected the Irish Catholic claim to accept the Stuarts as their legitimate rulers. At the other end of the spectrum Irish Catholics whose royalism trumped their faith – usually because they had secular interests to protect – were more willing to accept a less public position for Catholicism within the state. These hoped, by concluding a swift peace, to earn the government's gratitude and commensurate rewards. As the confederacy's position collapsed in the late 1640s more of its members sought to conclude a peace with the royalists and stave off destruction at the hands of the parliament.

As the royalist coalition established by the earl of Ormond in early 1649 failed to halt the inexorable advance of parliament's forces, Ireland's Catholics once more proved willing to embrace alternatives. The Catholic hierarchy first pressurised Ormond into resigning his royal commission as lord lieutenant and, after Charles II's deal with the Scots, they requested aid from the duke of Lorraine given that his 'His Majesty throweth away the nation … [and] will have no friends but the friends of the Covenant, and no enemies, but the enemies of the Covenant'. Thereafter they proved willing to indefinitely suspend Stuart sovereignty and appoint Lorraine as 'Catholic Protector Royal'.[37] Significantly the clergy who 'would withdraw the subjects from obedience … had gained upon the people but specially in corporate towns and cities'.[38] Although it came to naught, the Lorraine project suggests that quite a number of

Irish Catholics held that sovereignty in Ireland was not unconditionally invested in the Stuarts.[39] This proved the last major political initiative of the Irish Catholic community until after the Restoration.

What occurred in Ireland between the years 1534 and 1660 truly merits the term revolutionary as the island's confessional, cultural, socio-economic and political landscapes were irrevocably altered. Two distinct and opposed conceptions of the relationship between religion and politics developed during the slow and increasingly violent maturation of the Irish state; both were shaped by the experiences and desires of two religiously defined communities. For the Protestant community, a small minority of the island's inhabitants dominated by a recently introduced colonial presence from England and Scotland, the state, and more particularly its religious injunctions, provided the vehicle through which their cultural, socio-economic and political superiority was established and then maintained. For the 'barbarous' Catholic majority, the state was an unpopular, repressive institution which undermined their position, purely on the basis of their refusal to conform to the church by law established. They refused to give it their full cooperation. So throughout the period the Irish state functioned with a congenital defect at its heart – 'institutionally' Protestant, but 'functionally' Catholic. The vested interests of the new landholding elites whose position was underpinned by the Protestant nature of the state, prevented the privatisation of religion, such as occurred in the United Provinces. It also owed to the efforts of the Irish Catholic clergy who used their enormous moral, cultural and political influence to preserve and intensify – in opposition to the state's designs – 'the common sentiments and ideals circulating in the community, adapting a wider religious doctrine and ethic to the special needs and interests of a culturally distinct and historically self-conscious population'.[40]

Notes

1 B. Bradshaw, *The Irish Constitutional Revolution of the Sixteenth Century* (Cambridge: Cambridge University Press, 1979), ch. 1.

2 R. D. Edwards, *Church and State in Tudor Ireland* (London: Longman, 1935), pp. 54–5.

3 The National Archives (London) State Papers Ireland (TNA SPI) 63/6/57.

4 TNA SPI 63/12/50.

5 TNA SPI 63/30/88.

6 W. M. Brady (ed.), *State Papers Concerning the Irish Church* ... (London: Longman, 1868), pp. 8–9. The cess controversy concerned the right of the crown to levy taxes for the upkeep of the military garrison in Ireland.

7 V. Treadwell, 'Sir John Perrot and the Irish parliament of 1585–6', *Proceedings of the Royal Irish Academy*, section C, 85 (Dublin: Royal Irish Academy, 1985), pp. 259–308.
8 TNA SPI 63/125/12.
9 D. B. Quinn (ed.), 'Calendar of the Irish Council Book, 1581–1586', *Analecta Hibernica*, 24 (1967), pp. 20–1.
10 Bodleian Library Oxford, Rawlinson MSS, C. 98, ff.26v–27r.
11 R. Crawford (trans.), 'Captain Cuellar's Letter', in B. Clifford (ed.), *A Story of the Spanish Armada* (Belfast: Athol Books, 1988), p. 37.
12 I. Hazlett, *The Reformation in Britain and Ireland: An Introduction* (Edinburgh: T & T Clark, 2003), p. 111.
13 Philip O'Sullevan Beare, *Ireland under Elizabeth*, ed. M. J. Byrne (Dublin: Sealy, Bryers and Co., 1903), p. 51.
14 M. Kerney-Walsh, *'Destruction by Peace': Hugh O'Neill after Kinsale* (Armagh: Cumman Seanchais Ard Mhacha, 1986), docs 43a, 72a, 102a.
15 TNA SPI 63/215/68.
16 H. Fitzsimons, *Words of comfort to Persecuted Catholics ...* (ed.) E. Hogan (Dublin: Gill and Son, 1881).
17 TNA SP 63/221/57 and 57i; 63/222/112. J. McCavitt, *Sir Arthur Chichester: Lord Deputy of Ireland, 1605–16* (Belfast: Institute of Irish Studies, 1998), pp. 111–28.
18 'The Philosophy of Imperial Kingship and the Interpretation of James VI and I', in R. A. Houlbrooke, *James VI and I: Ideas, Authority, and Government* (Aldershot: Ashgate, 2006), pp. 43–60. These points were explicit in the complaint of Bishop John Rider, after his 1615 visitation of his diocese of Killaloe against: 'the multitude of Popish priests within my Diocese who draw the people from their obedience to his Majesty: and then especially when any proclamation or direction comes from his Highness: hindering also the minister in the work of his calling, and drawing back those whom the minister had formerly gained' ('Visitation of Killaloe, 1615', in P. Dwyer, *The Diocese of Killaloe* (Dublin: Hodge, Foster and Co., 1878), p. 143).
19 P. F. Moran (ed.), *Spicilegium Ossoriense*, 3 vols (Dublin: W. B. Kelly, 1874–84), i, p. 272; E. Hogan (ed.), *Ibernia Ignatiana* (Dublin: Excrudebat Societas, 1880), pp. 130–1.
20 *Archivium Hibernicum*, 3, p. 284; D. McCarthy (ed.), *Collections of Irish Church History from the MSS of the Late Laurence F. Renehan*, 2 vols (Dublin: Duffy and Son, 1861–74,) i, pp. 118–19.
21 A. Clarke, *The Old English in Ireland, 1625–42* (London: MacGibbon and Kee, 1965), pp. 32–3, 37.
22 D. Rothe, 'The Analecta of David Rothe' (National Library of Ireland, MS 642, f.43r).
23 G. Keating, *Foras Feasa ar Éirinn* (ed. and trans.) D. Comyn *et al.*, 4 vols (London: Irish Texts Society, 1902–14), i, pp. 78–81, 118; ii, pp. 325–35.

24 W. Malone, SJ, *A Reply to Mr James Ussher his answere* ... (Douai: s.i. s.n. 1627), Epistle Dedicatory.
25 J. Copinger, *A Mnemosynum or Memoriall to the Afflicted Catholickes in Irelande* (Bordeaux: Arnald du Brell, 1606), pp. 150, 244.
26 M. Perceval-Maxwell, *The Outbreak of the Irish Rebellion of 1641* (London: McGill-Queen's University Press, 1994), pp. 190–212.
27 J. T. Gilbert (ed.), *The History of the Irish Confederation and the War in Ireland, 1641–1649*, 7 vols (Dublin: Dollard, 1882–91), i, pp. 237–40; iii, pp. 336–9.
28 Cited in R. Gillespie, 'The end of an era: Ulster and the outbreak of the 1641 Rising', in C. Brady and R. Gillespie (eds), *Natives and Newcomers: The Making of Irish Colonial Society, 1534–1641* (Dublin: Irish Academic Press, 1986), p. 193.
29 *Report on the Franciscan Manuscripts Preserved at the Convent, Merchants' Quay, Dublin* (Dublin: Historic Manuscripts Commission, 1906), p. 111.
30 Gilbert, *Irish Confederation*, i, pp. 290–8.
31 *Ibid.*, ii, p. 74.
32 T. Ó hAnnracháin, 'Rebels and confederates: the stance of the Irish clergy in the 1640s', in J. R. Young (ed.), *Celtic Dimensions of the British Civil Wars* (Edinburgh: John Donald, 1997), pp. 101–5.
33 Gilbert, *Irish Confederation*, ii, p. 74; *Franciscan MSS*, pp. 138–40.
34 Rothe, 'Analecta', f. 73r.
35 Gilbert, *Irish Confederation*, ii, pp. 73–84.
36 Depositions of Joseph Wheeler and Henry Robinson, Co. Kilkenny (Trinity College Dublin, MS 812, ff. 202r–208v and 223r–223v).
37 U. Burke (ed.), *The Memoirs and Letters of Ulick, Marquis of Clanricarde ... Lord Lieutenant of Ireland* (London: J. Hughs, 1757).
38 BL, Add. MSS, 4819, f. 345r.
39 *Memoirs of Clanricarde*, pp. 173–91.
40 A. D. Smith, *The Ethnic Origins of Nations* (Oxford: Basil Blackwell, 1986), pp. 35–7; F. Barth, *Ethnic Groups and Boundaries: The Social Organization of Cultural Difference* (London: Allen and Unwin, 1970).

5

The 'absenting of the bishop of Armagh': eucharistic controversy and the English origins of Irish Catholic identity, 1550–51

James Murray

In the summer of 1551, before 28 July, Archbishop George Dowdall of Armagh made a fateful decision. After eight years of service as the crown's appointee to Ireland's primatial see, the archbishop elected to relinquish his office and to flee the kingdom. The 'absenting of the bishop of Armagh' – as Lord Deputy Croft euphemistically described Dowdall's flight – was preceded, and immediately precipitated, by a meeting between the two men. The surviving notice of their interview – an instruction from Croft to his servant, Thomas Wood, to brief the English privy council on their deliberations – does not specify the particulars of their conversation, nor why it provoked such a dramatic response from Dowdall: Croft merely asked Wood to 'show' what the archbishop 'hath required of me, and mine answer to him'.[1]

Despite this, the substantive issue that they discussed is recoverable from another contemporary source: a letter from Archbishop George Browne of Dublin to John Dudley, the earl of Warwick and lord great master of Edward VI's household. Browne disclosed that on the eve of his departure Dowdall had written to Sir Thomas Cusack, the lord chancellor of Ireland, declaring 'that he would never be bishop, where the holy mass (as he called it) was abolished'. The reported declaration points to the fact that what Dowdall 'hath required' of Croft during their meeting was an assurance that the 'holy mass' would be accommodated within the state church. It also implies that Croft's 'answer to him' failed to provide that assurance.[2]

The 'absenting of the bishop of Armagh' has generally been regarded by scholars as a significant, even pivotal, event in Ireland's early modern religious history. Shared both by historians of the old, Catholic–nationalist school, and those of more recent revisionist vintage, this dominant interpretation has portrayed the event as a watershed moment through which native disenchantment with Edward VI's Protestant religious settlement crystallised into active resistance, and Ireland's Counter-Reformation was effectively inaugurated. Only the subtlest hermeneutical differences have disturbed this remarkably consistent characterisation. Thus where writers in the older tradition saw in the archbishop's action the inevitable awakening, from its late medieval slumber, of a robust, native Irish Catholicism, their revisionist successors observed that it marked the effective endpoint of what had hitherto been a thriving indigenous flirtation with the Tudor Reformation, especially in its Henrician form. Both schools were united in drawing a link between the doctrinally conservative Dowdall's rejection of the crown's radical religious policies in 1551, and his subsequent return to Ireland in 1553, as the papally appointed and crown-approved archbishop of Armagh, 'to spearhead the Counter-Reformation'.[3] It is this perceived link that has given leave to more than one generation of historians to portray Dowdall's flight as the starting point of the Irish Counter-Reformation.

And, yet, in several crucial respects, this judgement is problematical. Although it would be perverse to argue that his eucharistic beliefs were in anyway insincere, the broader argument that the stance Dowdall took in the summer of 1551 marked or even embodied the commencement of the Irish Counter-Reformation is more debateable. Certainly, Dowdall displayed none of the pro-papal attitudes that one might expect of a committed counter-reformer in the period leading up to his decision to vacate his bishopric On the contrary, he consistently defended the crown's supremacy over the Irish church against the pretensions of the papacy, including in relation to the legitimacy of his own archiepiscopal title, which had been challenged directly by the papal appointee to Armagh, Robert Wauchop, when the latter visited Ulster in the spring of 1550.[4]

It is also the case, moreover, that Dowdall conducted his defence of the eucharist without any identifiable reference to the papacy or, indeed, to any doctrinal statements emanating from Rome. Not only did he mount it before the Council of Trent's decree on the sacrament of the eucharist was promulgated in October 1551, but his subsequent reconciliation with the papacy did not take place quite as quickly, or as seamlessly as the conventional view seems to suggest. Although his erstwhile rival Wauchop died in November 1551 only a few months after he had departed Ireland, the ultimate decision by Pope Julius III to appoint Dowdall as his successor, was taken much later, on 1 March 1553, at least nineteen months after Dowdall originally left Ireland, and then only after some discordant debate in the Roman curia. Indeed, Dowdall did not actually return to Ireland until the Catholic Queen Mary succeeded her Protestant stepbrother, Edward, and had given her imprimatur both to the restoration of Catholicism and to his papal appointment to Armagh. When he again set foot in Ireland, on 3 November 1553, more than two years had elapsed since Dowdall had first fled the realm, during which time, bereft of the power and influence he had exercised as a senior royal official, he was a largely anonymous figure in Irish affairs, who was not noticeably active in promoting the teachings of the Council of Trent in his homeland from his place of exile.[5]

A desire to advance the Counter-Reformation, then, does not provide an entirely convincing explanation of Dowdall's decision to vacate his see in 1551. Indeed, the tendency to retrofit the later Dowdall on the earlier figure, obscures one of the most critical, and most problematical issues surrounding his flight from Ireland: why, and on what basis, did he make demands of Lord Deputy Croft – including his demand for the preservation of the 'holy mass' – when they met in the summer of 1551? It is this fundamental question, in particular, that this chapter considers, on the grounds that its exploration has much to reveal about the complexities of religious identity and its formation in sixteenth-century Ireland. The starting point for the study is the summer of 1550 when, with the reappointment of Sir Anthony St Leger as the crown's viceroy, the Edwardian regime inaugurated a new campaign in Ireland to enforce the reformed communion service from the first Book of Common Prayer.

This initiative was driven by the evangelical faction on the English privy council which, led by the earl of Warwick and Archbishop Thomas Cranmer of Canterbury, was now in a secure and dominant position, having successfully weathered a series of political convulsions during the previous year.[6] Thus, when St Leger negotiated his latest programme for the government of Ireland in July 1550, he encountered a situation in which the appetite and drive for further religious reform showed no signs of abating. A new Ordinal had been introduced at the beginning of the year, which confirmed that the task of reorienting the traditional liturgies of the church in a firmly Protestant direction would continue. In addition, the privy council was also engaged in an extensive campaign to purge the English church of unsupportive bishops.[7] And, at the very time St Leger's instructions were being drafted, Archbishop Cranmer published *A Defence of the True and Catholic Doctrine of the Sacrament of the Body and Blood of Our Saviour Christ*, which clarified beyond all doubt – in a way that the text of the communion rite in the first Book of Common Prayer had not definitively done – that the new communion service was not a propitiatory sacrifice; that Christ's presence in the sacrament was not substantial, but spiritually signified, and that this spiritual presence could only be received by the godly.[8]

With these and other reforming initiatives being energetically pursued in England, it was inevitable – given the fact that the new communion service had only been implemented in a patchy manner in the eastern and southern shires of Ireland – that St Leger's instructions would require him to 'set forth God's service ... according to our ordinances and proceedings ... giving straight order for the observation thereof'.[9]

St Leger had significant misgivings about the task at hand, however. Although neither of the extant, preparatory documents that were drafted prior to his departure for Ireland contain overt evidence of these misgivings, once St Leger set foot in Ireland he was not shy in revealing his doubts about a directive which compelled him to implement the king's religious proceedings in an environment that was markedly different to the English shires, and through processes which, to him, were not obviously fit for purpose.[10] These misgivings were given their most direct expression in the context of a private conversation he had with Sir John Alen less than a year after his appointment. Discussing the contemporary fear of a French invasion, St Leger reluctantly admitted that if the 'French men' landed on Irish soil:

> they shall have more friendship amongst this nation for religion's cause then for their own sakes ... and so God help me ... knowing the manner and ignorance of this people, when my lords of the council willed me to set forth the matters of religion here ... I had rather they had sent me into Spain, or any other place where the king should have had cause to make war there, than burdened me to set forth that here, and I told my lords no less before my coming away.[11]

One of the underlying reasons for St Leger's frustration was the privy council's refusal to endorse a proposal he had put forward to sanction the use of a Latin version of the English communion service in Ireland. Latin, of course, was not just the lingua franca of scholars, statesmen and ecclesiastics, but it was also the main language through which the Dublin administration communicated with the Gaelic Irish.[12] Its employment would have enabled St Leger to introduce the new service 'where the inhabitants understand not the English tongue' in a comfortingly familiar form, and thus reduce the effect of its unsettling novelty. However, his final instructions, which only permitted the use of an Irish translation of the English communion service – and not the Latin translation he had commissioned from one 'Mr Smyth' – indicates that the proposal was rejected, most likely because of fears among the more zealous members of the council that a Latin service would not have been clearly distinguishable from the Mass or, worse, would have allowed for the counterfeiting of the proscribed liturgy.[13]

Faced, then, with the privy council's demand that he should execute the king's proceedings, and the prevailing reality that the indigenous communities in Ireland were unenthusiastic about Protestant doctrine and practice, St Leger turned reflexively to the principles and actions that had informed his approach to religion since the early 1540s. Grounded on the basic axiom that religious matters should at all times be subordinate to, and support his own political imperatives, St Leger sought, through a carefully modulated approach, to balance the interests of religious conservatives and reformers alike, and to ensure that the actions of neither would interfere with his grand plan to make the kingdom of Ireland a meaningful political reality.[14] By the early 1550s, however, this strategy was becoming increasingly difficult to sustain, for one simple reason. It had been conceived at a time when Henry VIII's religious settlement intrinsically favoured the balancing of religious interests, given that that settlement was built, on the one hand, upon the radicalism of the royal supremacy and the purging of what were perceived to be the worst excesses of Catholic idolatry and superstition and, on the other, upon the preservation of essential Catholic doctrine. In effect, Henry's settlement represented a middle way between 'the old religion' and 'the new learning' of Protestantism, and his church was a place that conservatives and reformers could both lay claim and adhere to.[15] When St Leger returned to Ireland in September 1550, however, these propitious circumstances no longer prevailed. With the introduction of a more overtly Protestant religious settlement under Edward VI, religious opinion was quickly polarising in Ireland and less inclined to accept the temporising attitudes that were required to follow the deputy's way. This was certainly the case with Archbishop Browne who, up to the end of Henry VIII's reign had had no difficulty accepting St Leger's modulated approach to religion, but who now, in an era of more sharply defined religious views, regarded the deputy's reaching out to the 'papists' as a matter of real 'discouragement' to the 'professors of God's word'.[16] And it was equally true of those who favoured the 'old religion', including one of the deputy's staunchest political allies in Ireland, Archbishop George Dowdall of Armagh.

Dowdall had risen to national prominence in 1543 when, on St Leger's recommendation, he was appointed by King Henry VIII to the primatial see. The close, political relationship that existed between the pair was rooted in a shared vision of what English political reform in Ireland should entail and might achieve: the establishment of the crown's authority in every corner of the island through the peaceful assimilation and gradual acculturation of the independent Gaelic lordships. In practical terms, Dowdall had served loyally as St Leger's agent in Ulster, where he used his local knowledge, multilingualism, primatial authority and the canonical sanctions of the church, to support the incorporation of the O'Neill lordship into the kingdom of Ireland, following the ennoblement of Con Bacach O'Neill as earl of Tyrone in 1542.[17] On his return to Ireland in 1550, St Leger envisaged that Dowdall would continue to perform this role. Indeed, it was essential that he should do so, as a number of factors had combined to threaten the unravelling of the O'Neill settlement that the two men had put in place in the 1540s. Some of these were intrinsic to the settlement itself: in particular, the great difficulty of converting, into legally enforceable claims, the dues and obligations that the O'Neills had traditionally exacted by force from the lesser lords. Other factors were extrinsic to it, such as the permanent migration of the McDonnell clan from the Western Isles of Scotland to Clandeboye in the north-east of the province; and the establishment of strategic English garrisons in the same region which, initially, were intended to repulse the Scots, but which in practice also became involved in military activity aimed at reducing the Irish to obedience. These developments had the effect of weakening Con Bacach's authority, and of pushing him and his sons towards violence and disorder as they bid to maintain their traditional dominance in the province.[18] In this context, St Leger looked to Dowdall, who had developed close ties with the earl, to keep the lines of communication open with the O'Neills as his regime endeavoured to stabilise the general political situation in Ulster and re-energise the reform process.

But his plans were complicated by Dowdall's religious disposition. The deputy knew, from close to a decade's experience of working with him, that the archbishop's religious leanings were of a decidedly conservative nature. Dubbed a 'papistical fellow' by the English administration as early the late 1530s, he had only fully embraced the royal supremacy, when it became clear – following the passage of the English act of six articles in 1539 – that traditional Catholic doctrine and practices would be maintained by the established church in Ireland; and that his own politico-cultural aspirations to sustain the historic role of the Englishry in civilising the Gaelic Irish could be accommodated and fostered under Henry's kingship and his supremacy over the church.[19] This remained Dowdall's position after Edward VI succeeded his father, and he had thus persisted 'in his naughty sort', according to Archbishop Browne, 'to maintain the bishop of Rome's service' up to and beyond the point of St Leger's reappointment as the crown's viceroy.[20] It was a stance that presented the deputy with a particularly acute problem. Dowdall's loyalty to the crown, his commitment to establishing the kingdom of Ireland as a working polity and his influence with Tyrone made him an indispensable figure in the deputy's continuing efforts to reform Ulster. However, his unwillingness to embrace the reformed communion service made his position as a crown-appointed archbishop less than tenable, and appeared to place a firm onus on the deputy to secure his conformity to 'God's service' or, failing that, his removal from office.

Yet as stark and as intractable as St Leger's 'Dowdall problem' appeared, the deputy was determined that this essentially religious matter would not be allowed to restrict his freedom to act in the political sphere. Thus he decided early to stand by Dowdall. This was evident, paradoxically, in a decision taken prior to his departure for Ireland to omit the archbishop from the list of officials to be appointed to the Irish council.[21] The decision was not intended as a snub to the archbishop. Rather, it was a pragmatic tactic to ensure that Dowdall's difficulties with the official communion service would not be exposed at the council board, and thus become a lightning rod for controversy. In effect, St Leger wanted to make Dowdall an anonymous figure on religious matters, unless his actions could be presented in a positive light. And it was not long before an opportunity arose to do just that. At the end of October 1550, and despite the fact he was not a member of the Irish council, the archbishop was given leave, while on a visit to Dublin, to append his signature to a council letter, which *inter alia* recommended to the English privy council the appointment of John Brady to the bishopric of Kilmore. The reason this was done is evident from the text of the letter. Brady, it transpired, had had the bishopric conferred on him by provision from Rome, but had subsequently elected to surrender his bulls for cancellation, and to allow the then royal incumbent to enjoy the living without interruption.[22] By signing the letter, Dowdall was clearly demonstrating that he supported the appointment of a candidate who upheld the royal supremacy and that his own loyalty to the supreme head could not be questioned.

The employment of such diversionary tactics, however, could not hide Dowdall's recalcitrance on the communion service indefinitely. This issue, as St Leger well knew, would have to be confronted and managed in some fashion if it was not to erode his standing with his political masters, and derail his deputyship. Thus soon after he was sworn in, the deputy summoned Dowdall to a meeting in Dublin to discuss the matter of its implementation. The meeting, which probably took place in late October – when Dowdall was in the city and signed the council letter in support of John Brady's promotion – was a private encounter, and no contemporary minutes of the proceedings, if there ever were any, are now extant. Despite this, we do know some things about their discussion. On the critical issue of Dowdall's refusal to 'set forth the king's majesty's most godly proceedings', it was subsequently reported by Archbishop Browne that the deputy had 'advised' the primate 'as it were to the contrary'.[23] This, no doubt, was the 'official' outcome of the meeting as promulgated by St Leger, and it served, in effect, to affirm in a public manner his own commitment to his appointed task of implementing the state's communion service. Yet, while the deputy clearly wanted it to be known that he had 'advised' Dowdall to conform, their encounter actually confirmed that there was no real possibility that this would ever happen. On the contrary, he concluded that if he wanted to retain the primate in his service in Ulster he would have to create the necessary conditions to allow him to maintain his attachment to the Mass, while at the same time ensuring that this would have no detrimental effect on his own political standing.

St Leger arrived at this realisation because Dowdall had presented him, most likely during the October meeting, with a Latin tract entitled '*Fides priscorum de veritate carnis et sanguinis Christi in sacramento altaris* ...', which set out the archbishop's own deeply held and entirely immoveable convictions on the doctrines of the real presence and transubstantiation. The tract, which is known to have been in St Leger's possession before February 1551, survives now in the form of a deliberately anonymised copy of his original, which is located – after undergoing a somewhat circuitous journey – in the records of the English secretaries of state.[24] Yet, although the author's identity is protected in the extant version of the document, it can be attributed to Dowdall with confidence for the following reasons. First, '*Fides priscorum*' was written by someone who not only maintained a strong attachment to orthodox eucharistic doctrine, but who also had urgent cause to communicate his convictions to Lord Deputy St Leger during his second Edwardian viceroyalty. This was certainly the case with Dowdall who 'repaired' to St Leger for this very reason in October 1550. Second, it is also evident that the person who wrote and submitted the document to St Leger was both a trusted and trusting confidante of the deputy, for he was willing to provide him with incriminating material that confirmed he upheld proscribed theological views, in the firm belief that he would not be betrayed by the receiver. Here too Dowdall presents himself as the most likely author, given his longstanding and close relationship with the deputy. Finally, the text of '*Fides priscorum*' reveals that it was drafted primarily as a personal testimony, which was addressed directly to the deputy and was intended neither for publication or widespread dissemination. Again this points to Dowdall as the author, and is of a type with the archbishop's entire mode of communication on the issue of the communion service during 1550–51, which was not only unflinchingly discreet but was in all recorded instances – such as in his subsequent contacts with Croft and Cusack – conducted exclusively with officials in the Dublin administration away from public view. All of these features – the urgency of his address, Dowdall's status as the viceroy's confidante and the private nature of the communication – are neatly encapsulated in the final words of '*Fides priscorum*'. Here, in a subtle paraphrasing of a passage from St Jerome's letter to Pammachius and Oceanus, Dowdall boldly asserted his faith in traditional eucharistic doctrine and confirmed his loyalty to the viceroy:

> Behold! You have here truly most illustrious man the Christian faith which by the gift of God I received in baptism, which I, a young man, learned afterwards, and in which I shall die an old man. May the best and greatest God preserve your power unimpaired a long while for the world.[25]

Not surprisingly, given the author's background as a canon lawyer, the theology presented in '*Fides priscorum*' is conventional and clearly not the product of an original theological thinker. The essential argument, which is encapsulated in the final section of the tract, is that God's miraculous word converts bread and wine into the body and blood of Christ, and that to deny this is to deny the other miracles of Christ. Man, therefore, should let his intellect be captive to God and, acknowledging God's power over nature, accept the words of consecration not as a literary trope, but as the literal truth.[26] The conventional nature of '*Fides priscoum*' may also have been due to the circumstances in which it was drafted. In responding to the deputy's summons, it is likely that Dowdall had to prepare his testimony in a hurried manner, and thus he had little choice but to draw heavily on the works of other theologians, amongst which were two polemical treatises – *The Assertion and Defence of the Sacrament of the Altar*[27] and *A Defence of the Blessed Mass and the Sacrifice Thereof*[28] – written at the end of Henry VIII's reign by Dr Richard Smyth, the first regius professor of theology at Oxford.[29] Smyth's treatises were not only a source for the patristic *sententiae* that Dowdall cited in 'Fides priscorum' – Cyprian's *De Coena Domini*, Ambrose's *De Sacramentis*, Chrysostom's Mass and his homily on Matthew 26, Theophilus's commentary on the words '*Benedicens fregit*' (Mark 14:22), Augustine's *Confessions* and Clement's epiclesis[30] – but were also influential in the construction of the argument, and the illustrative examples, that he employed in the concluding discussion.[31]

Smyth's influence on Dowdall was not confined to supplying patristic references and exemplary theological arguments however. His treatises were written only a few short years before '*Fides priscorum*' at a time when traditional eucharistic doctrine – 'the true and catholic faith of Christ's church touching the blessed sacrament of the altar' – was upheld by Henry VIII and the English nobility who had 'fully and perfectly agreed' to its establishment 'by act of parliament'.[32] It was this late Henrician, conservative position, as articulated and defended by Smyth, that gave Dowdall a coherent basis for holding his own orthodox views on the eucharist, while still continuing his support for the royal supremacy. Like Smyth in 1546, he looked not in 1550 to the papacy for authoritative sanction of his eucharistic beliefs, but appealed rather to the king or, more particularly, to his viceroy, to uphold them.

While Dowdall's attachment to the 'holy mass' was clearly a manifestation of his own personal faith, it also had strong roots in the ecclesiastical culture of the English Pale. This is evident from the one distinctive feature of '*Fides priscorum*' that separates it from Smyth's treatises or, indeed, from the works of conservative, English-born writers, such as Stephen Gardiner, who set themselves the task of defending the Mass in Edward VI's reign. Where the latter writers felt compelled to follow royal diktat and the humanist fashion of only using scriptural and patristic sources to make their case, Dowdall had no compunction about going beyond these *ad fontes* sources and using scholastic authorities for his defence of the doctrines of the real presence and transubstantiation. One of the main reasons for this was his desire to protect the historical status and identity of his own community, the English-Irish of the Pale. The English community's existence in Ireland, and the religious sanction that its Anglo-Norman ancestors had received from the papacy for the conquest of the island, were entirely bound up with the Western Church of the scholastic era. For Dowdall, who was extremely sensitive about the historical identity of his community, and who had already had to abandon his support for the papacy, the rejection of much of the remainder of the ecclesiastical culture in which it had originated would have been tantamount to wiping out that historical identity.[33] And he refused to countenance it. Thus, unlike the English conservatives who, as one historian put it, were compelled to argue the case for the real presence and transubstantiation 'with one hand tied behind their backs'; or those English reformers, like Archbishop Cranmer, who saw these doctrines as abuses that originated 'specially within these four or five hundred years'; Dowdall, the English-Irishman, embraced this past passionately and was able to call upon writers like Albert the Great and Bernard of Clairvaux, as witnesses, respectively, to the truth of these doctrines, and of the value of affective devotion to the eucharist for those who accepted them.[34]

Dowdall's convictions, then, were serious matters that could not easily be overlooked by Lord Deputy St Leger if he wished to retain him in his service. Thus, in the wake of their autumn encounter, he elected to put in place two measures that would provide some basis for an accommodation with Dowdall, while simultaneously addressing the demands of his political masters in England. The first was an already sanctioned initiative to set up a printing press in Dublin, to produce English service books for use in the English-speaking areas of Ireland.[35] The second was a decision to proceed after all with the promulgation of the Latin translation of the communion service that he had commissioned before his return to Ireland. Conceived primarily with the provinces in mind, St Leger hoped that the latter initiative would not only minimise the effects of the innovatory aspects of the new liturgy upon the local communities, but also provide Archbishop Dowdall with sufficient theological latitude to enable him to embrace it; or, failing that, that its general use in the provinces would disguise his continued maintenance of the Mass in Armagh.

The Latin service was introduced in the provincial cities of Limerick and Galway in the winter of 1550–51 by Lord Chancellor Cusack and the master of the rolls, Patrick Barnewall, while journeying throughout Connacht and Munster to reform 'sundry great abuses' and settle disputes among the leading families. The initiative was, in reality, an unsanctioned experiment and St Leger was wary of the reaction that it might provoke among the more radical Protestant figures on the English privy council. Thus, in his correspondence with the crown's officials, he was exceedingly coy and opaque in what he said about it, and all statements were carefully worded so that, if the initiative ultimately received an unfavourable reaction from his political masters, it would be possible to deny that it ever took place.[36] This was even true of his most direct statement on the Latin service, where a deliberately ambiguous usage of the pronoun 'which' left it unclear – when he wrote about printing the service, or about how it had been received by the bishop and citizens of Limerick – as to whether he was referring to the Latin or English version. 'And now as touching religion', he informed Secretary Cecil:

> although it be hard to plant in men's minds herein, yet I trust I am not slack to do what I can to advance the same. I have caused the whole service of the communion to be drawn into Latin, *which* shall be shortly set forth in print. I have caused books to be sent to the city of Limerick who most gladly have condescended to embrace the same with all effect, although the bishop there who is both old and blind be most against it.[37]

The deputy's sensitivity on the matter of the Latin communion service was due to the fact that his political enemies had already identified his approach to religion, including his support for Dowdall, as a potential weakness, and had begun to accuse him of being a 'papist'. These complaints emerged, as St Leger himself identified, from among 'my late companions here now displaced', and included Sir John Alen, whom he had removed from the chancellorship on his return to Ireland in the previous summer; and the English garrison commanders, who were resentful of St Leger's support for the earl of Tyrone, particularly after he sacked Andrew Brereton, the constable of Lecale, for leading an ambush on O'Neill's troops in MacCartan's country in 1550.[38] And allied to both Alen and the soldiers in their opposition to the deputy, there also stood Archbishop Browne of Dublin, who had never forgiven St Leger for accusing him of conspiring against the deputy with Alen and the earl of Ormond in 1546. Browne, in particular, had challenged the deputy over his indulgence of Archbishop Dowdall since his return to Ireland, and it was he who encouraged Alen and other aggrieved figures like Sir Ralph Bagenal, the lieutenant of the army, to pursue their political battles with him by focusing on this potential weakness.[39]

These tensions reached their highest point early in 1551, and Browne and Bagenal were determined to bring matters to a head by exposing the deputy's tolerance of Dowdall at the council board. Thus, complaining that it 'was so much against duty to suffer the primate so to contemn the king's proceedings', they demanded that Dowdall 'mought be called before him [St Leger] and the rest'. St Leger, for his part, knew that their demand was intended to undermine his own position as much as, if not more than Dowdall's, and thus, in the period leading up to the primate's appearance at the council board, he decided to take his own pre-emptive action in a bid to distance himself from the conservative eucharistic doctrines that he knew Dowdall would inevitably propound. Around Candlemas 1551 (2 February), therefore, he arranged a private meeting with Archbishop Browne and gave him five books which he asked him to 'consider' before returning them. Among the collection was Dowdall's '*Fides priscorum*', and at least one other document compiled by the same author which, again, was indebted to Richard Smyth for the provision of references to works that raised and answered a range of theological questions on the eucharist, but which in this instance also included English translations of the same texts.[40] This second document was, in effect, a series of speaking notes for a disputation, and was prepared by Dowdall for either the October meeting with St Leger or his upcoming appearance at the council. St Leger's decision to seek Browne's professional opinion on the contents of these books, was done not with the intent of betraying his old ally – they were handed over with the author's identity excised – but with a view to positioning himself as a neutral chairman for the impending meeting, establishing his *bona fides* with the reformers and demonstrating why it was necessary to implement the king's proceedings in the provinces 'in such sort as there is great assurance the same shall be duly observed'.[41]

And, ostensibly, the strategy appeared to work. Dowdall, as expected, came to the council meeting 'and disputed plainly the massing and other things, contrary the king's proceedings'. And, equally predictably, Sir Ralph Bagenal reacted angrily to the primate's stance, calling him an 'errant traitor'. But that is as far as the matter went according to Archbishop Browne's eyewitness account of the encounter. St Leger, in the role of the neutral chairman, all the while remained silent, leaving it to Lord Chancellor Cusack, who was a kinsman of the primate, to defend his honour and reject Bagenal's charge that he was a traitor. It appears too that Archbishop Browne also kept his counsel, a development which, given his previous criticisms of St Leger, may have signalled to the deputy that the archbishop would indeed back his initiative on the Latin communion service as the best means of bringing Dowdall and other religious conservatives into the Protestant fold. If the deputy did take this view, however, he was greatly mistaken. Underestimating the extent to which Browne had established connections with the Edwardian establishment in England, and the depth of his commitment to the Edwardian religious settlement, St Leger's attempt to court the archbishop backfired spectacularly. After he gave Browne the anonymised books on the eucharist ahead of the council's meeting, the archbishop had them copied and despatched speedily to the earl of Warwick with a view to undermining his position before the English privy council.[42]

The timing of this development could not have been worse for the deputy. Already under fire for his secular policies – in particular, for defending O'Neill against the aggressive garrison commanders – St Leger's books on traditional eucharistic doctrine appeared on Warwick's desk at the very time the Edwardian regime was completing its moves to deprive the figurehead of religious and doctrinal conservatism in England, Stephen Gardiner, of the bishopric of Winchester. During his trial, on 26 January 1551, Gardiner had produced a text attacking Archbishop Cranmer's *Defence of the True and Catholic Doctrine of the Sacrament*, which he had written in prison and against which Cranmer immediately set about writing a rejoinder.[43] While engaged on this project in spring 1551, Cranmer would have been aware, through Warwick, that the lord deputy of Ireland held books in his possession which, like Gardiner's text, defended the doctrines of the real presence and transubstantiation. It was no surprise, therefore, that when the privy council met to review St

Leger's position as viceroy on 11 April 1551, a composite document was prepared and, most likely, tabled, comprising two of the books, including Dowdall's anonymised tract '*Fides priscorum*'. Archbishop Cranmer, in particular, appears to have taken an active interest in this matter. Although he had only attended twenty-five of the previous 151 council meetings that had been held since St Leger's appointment as deputy, he made it his business to attend at Greenwich when Warwick and the rest of the council decided 'upon good considerations' – including, no doubt, his much maligned approach to the advancement of the king's religious proceedings and his possession of books 'poisoned to maintain the mass with transubstantiation and other naughtiness' – that 'Sir Anthony St Leger, now deputy there, should be revoked, and that ... Sir James Croft shall supply his place'.[44]

The revocation of St Leger was, of course, a huge blow to Archbishop Dowdall. Not only did it cast a dark shadow over the future of the reform project in Ulster, but it also removed from the scene the man who had allowed the archbishop to freely maintain what was, in effect, a proscribed religious settlement in his jurisdiction, in defiance of those who had demanded that the deputy secure Dowdall's conformity to Edwardian Protestantism. Indeed, on this matter, St Leger remained unrepentant. A fortnight before he left Ireland in June 1551 – in a conversation at his lodging with one of O'Neill's servants, carried out via an interpreter, Oliver Sutton – the outgoing deputy endorsed the contribution of Dowdall as a loyal servant of the crown 'before the presence of twelve or sixteen persons'. According to Sutton's later testimony:

> the said Sir Anthony bid him ask where the primate was, who did so. And the messenger answered that he was at Armagh. Then said Sir Anthony he is a good man. And I would wish that all the Irish men in Ireland spake so good English as he, and if they do no worse than he, the king had been the better served.[45]

In these few words, St Leger revealed why he had supported Dowdall over the previous year. It was because he believed that Dowdall could always be counted upon to serve the king faithfully, and because he considered his eucharistic beliefs to be much less harmful to the crown's interests in Ireland than the general behaviour of the Irishry.

Dowdall's immediate response to the loss of his patron was naively optimistic. He engaged immediately in a flurry of activity with a view to constructing a case to put to the new lord deputy, Croft, that would allow both for the continuation of the reform project in Ulster and his attachment to the Mass. At the heart of his case was St Leger's public endorsement of him. Dowdall went to great lengths to get an accurate, legally documented version of the same, which involved seeking out Sutton and other witnesses, and securing their contribution to the preparation of two bills detailing the particulars of St Leger's conversation with O'Neill's servant.[46] In addition, Dowdall also completed a translation 'out of a Latin book into English ... found with O'Neill in Armagh', which detailed the heroic military exploits of Sir John De Courcy, the first earl of Ulster. While it is not known exactly why Dowdall undertook the translation, it is doubtful that it was simply a literary pursuit, given that it was commenced and completed during what was a period of deep crisis for him between March and July 1551. It is more likely that the translation was associated with the development of new political ideas for the reform of Ulster to put before Croft. Any such ideas would have involved the earl of Tyrone, and may have included the revival of a proposal – first mooted by the St Leger regime in the early 1540s – that O'Neill should acquire the title earl of Ulster as a means of strengthening his authority in the province, and tying him in more closely to the crown.[47] It was Dowdall's capacity to offer such ideas on political reform, together with his connections in, and knowledge of the Ulster region, that St Leger so valued. And it was this very same package, sealed with the endorsement of his predecessor, that Dowdall offered to Croft, when he met him in the summer of 1551. However, Dowdall made that offer on the same terms that he had previously agreed with St Leger. In return, he demanded that he would be allowed to maintain the 'holy mass'.

Sir James Croft, whether he was personally inclined to or not, was in no position to strike a deal with Dowdall on the Mass. The determination of the Edwardian regime to press ahead with the religious reform agenda in both of Edward's realms, and the knowledge that St Leger's revocation was, in part, due to the latter's failure to meet the regime's expectations on the implementation of 'God's service', precluded it. Thus, despite the effort and energy that he put into his case, Dowdall's overtures were rejected by Croft. This rejection was a significant turning point for Dowdall. Before it, he believed that the allegiances he held for his king and the traditional eucharistic doctrines of the Western Church were compatible. After it, their incompatibility became fully apparent, and it was this revelation that compelled him to leave the realm; the first, necessary step in his re-engagement with Rome. But whether this can be described as an Irish or English cultural process remains ambiguous. Dowdall's attachment to the Mass, and the political manoeuvres that St Leger had undertaken to accommodate him, were carried out in an Irish setting, within the confines of English government, by men who considered themselves to be English. If we maintain, then, that George

Dowdall was in any sense a progenitor of Irish Catholicism, we must also acknowledge that that phenomenon had English, as well as Irish, roots.

Notes

1 'Instructions from the lord deputy to the council', 28 Jul. 1551, The National Archives: Public Record Office (London) (TNA: PRO) SP 61/3, ff.103–6; *The Antiquities and History of Ireland by the Right Honourable Sir James Ware, Knight* (Dublin: A. Crook *et al.*, 1705), pt ii (Annals of Ireland), p. 146.

2 'Instructions from the lord deputy to the council', 28 Jul. 1551; Browne to Warwick, 6 Aug. 1551 (TNA: PRO SP 61/3, ff.103–6, 130–1).

3 P. F. Moran, *History of the Catholic Archbishops of Dublin since the Reformation*, 2 vols (Dublin: J. Duffy, 1864), i, pp. 32–3; M. V. Ronan, *The Reformation in Dublin 1536–58* (London: Longman, 1926), pp. 355, 370; R. Dudley Edwards, *Ireland in the Age of the Tudors* (London: Croom Helm, 1977), p. 68; B. Bradshaw, *The Irish Constitutional Revolution of the Sixteenth Century* (Cambridge: Cambridge University Press, 1979), p. 251; C. Lennon, *Sixteenth-Century Ireland: The Incomplete Conquest* (Dublin: Gill and Macmillan, 1994), p. 170; J. Murray, *Enforcing the English Reformation in Ireland: Clerical Resistance and Political Conflict in the Diocese of Dublin, 1534–1590* (Cambridge: Cambridge University Press, 2009), pp. 216–17.

4 Dowdall to Chancellor Alen, 22 Mar. 1550 (TNA: PRO SP 61/2, f. 116).

5 Murray, *Enforcing the English Reformation*, pp. 207–8, 218–19; D. MacCulloch, *Reformation. Europe's House Divided 1490–1700* (London: Penguin, 2003), pp. 275–6.

6 J. Guy, *Tudor England* (Oxford: Oxford University Press, 1988), pp. 212–14; D. MacCulloch, *Thomas Cranmer* (New Haven, CT and London: Yale University Press, 1996), pp. 410–53.

7 D. MacCulloch, *The Later Reformation in England* (Basingstoke and London: Macmillan, 1990), pp. 16–17; F. Heal, *Reformation in Britain and Ireland* (Oxford: Oxford University Press, 2003), pp. 329–30; MacCulloch, *Cranmer*, pp. 456–9.

8 H. Jenkyns (ed.), *The Remains of Thomas Cranmner*, 4 vols (Oxford: Oxford University Press, 1833), ii, pp. 287–463; MacCulloch, *Cranmer*, pp. 462–9.

9 B. Bradshaw, 'The Edwardian Reformation in Ireland', *Archivium Hibernicum*, 34 (1976), pp. 83–99; St Leger's instructions, Jul. 1550 (TNA: PRO SP61/2, f.135r).

10 'The humble requests of Sir Anthony St Leger, knight, touching his service in Ireland', Jul. 1550; 'Remembrances for Ireland', Jul. 1550 (TNA: PRO SP61/2, ff. 129–30, 131–2).

11 Deposition of Sir John Alen, 19 Mar. 1552, TNA: PRO SP 61/4, f. 102v.

12 Tyrone to the archbishop of Armagh, 7 Mar. 1550; Council of Ireland to Tyrone, 17 Mar. 1550 (TNA: PRO SP 61/2, ff. 122rv); Sutton's deposition, 22 Mar. 1552 (TNA: PRO SP 61/4, f. 104r).

13 'Remembrances for Ireland', Jul. 1550; St Leger's instructions, Jul. 1550 (TNA: PRO SP 61/2, f. 132r, 135r).

14 On St Leger's approach generally, see Murray, *Enforcing the English Reformation*, chs 4 and 5; for a report on and critique of his efforts in 1550–51, see Browne to Warwick, 6 Aug. 1551 (TNA: PRO SP 61/3, ff. 130–1).

15 G. W. Bernard, *The King's Reformation: Henry VIII and the Remaking of the English Church* (New Haven, CT and London: Yale University Press, 2005), ch. 6.

16 Browne to Warwick, 6 Aug. 1551 (TNA: PRO SP 61/3, f.130r).

17 Murray, *Enforcing the English Reformation*, pp. 181–7.

18 On Ulster generally, see C. Brady, *Shane O'Neill* (Dundalk: Dundalgan Press, 1996), pp. 22–34.

19 Murray, *Enforcing the English Reformation*, pp. 208–13, 216.

20 Browne to Warwick, 6 Aug. 1551 (TNA: PRO SP 61/3, f. 130r).

21 St Leger's instructions, Jul. 1550 (TNA: PRO SP 61/2, f. 135r).

22 St Leger and the council to the privy council, 28 Oct. 1550 (TNA: PRO SP 61/2, f. 159).

23 Browne to Warwick, 6 Aug. 1551, TNA: PRO SP 61/3, f.130r.

24 The full title is *Fides priscorum de veritate carnis et sanguinis Christi in sacramento altaris quam ab ipsa assensione dominica semper tenuit universalis Christi ecclesia, a vetustissimis auctoribus in suis scriptis nobis relicta*. The tract survives as the major component of a composite document in the State Papers Ireland Mary, described as the 'Book out of Ireland in Latin' (TNA: PRO SP 62/2, ff. 189r–203v, at 189r–198v). On its origins and provenance generally, see M. V. Ronan '"Booke oute of Ireland in Latten", Fresh Light on the "Reformation" in Dublin', *Irish Ecclesiastical Record*, 25 (33 and 39) (1925), pp. 501–13, 606–22.

25 'Ecce hic habes vir illustrissime fidem vere christianam quam dei munere in baptismo accepi, quam iuvenis postea didici in qua et senex moriar. Deus optimus maximus dominationem tuam diu orbi servet incolumem' (TNA: PRO SP 62/2, f.198v); P. Schaff and H. Wace (eds), *A Select Library of Nicene and post-Nicene Fathers of the Christian Church, Second Series, Volume VI, St Jerome* (New York: Christian Literature Company, 1893), pp. 175–81.

26 TNA: PRO SP 62/2, ff. 196v–198v.

27 2nd edn, London, 1546 (*STC* 22815).

28 2nd edn, London, 1546 (*STC* 22820).

29 On Smyth and his treatises, see J. A. Löwe, *Richard Smyth and the Language of Orthodoxy: Re-imagining Tudor Catholic Polemicism* (Leiden: Brill, 2003).

30 *Fides priscorum*, ff. 189r, 190r, 191rv, 195v–196r; Smyth, *Defence*, ff. 83rv,

124r, 128r; *Assertion*, ff. 22v, 28v–29r, 212v, 255r. The epiclesis refers to that part of the Mass when the Holy Spirit is invoked to change the bread and wine into the body and blood of Christ.

31 See, for example, the discussion on Christ's use of figurative language in John 15:5 (*Fides priscorum*, f. 198v; Smyth, *Assertion*, ff. 163v–164r).

32 Smyth, *Assertion*, f. 14v.

33 On this point generally, see Murray, *Enforcing the English Reformation*, pp. 210–13.

34 MacCulloch, *Cranmer*, p. 489; Jenkyns (ed.), *Remains of Cranmner*, ii, p. 292; *Fides priscorum*, ff. 193r–194v.

35 'Remembrances for Ireland', Jul. 1550 (TNA: PRO SP 61/2, f. 132r); J. R. Dasent (ed.), *Acts of the Privy Council of England 1542–1604*, 32 vols (London: Stationery Office, 1890–1907), iii, p. 84.

36 St Leger to Cecil, 19 Jan. 1551; St Leger and council to privy council, 15 Feb. 1551; St Leger to Somerset, 18 Feb. 1551 (TNA: PRO SP 61/3, ff. 9–10, 16–17, 20–1).

37 St Leger to Cecil, 19 Jan. 1551 (TNA: PRO SP 61/3, f. 9v).

38 *Ibid.*, f. 9r; Alen to privy council, Sept. 1550 (TNA: PRO SP61/2, ff. 148–9); Brady, *Shane O'Neill*, p. 28; Edwards, *Ireland in the Age of the Tudors*, pp. 67–8.

39 Murray, *Enforcing the English Reformation*, pp. 188–97, 199–20; Browne to Warwick, 6 Aug. 1551 (TNA: PRO SP 61/3, ff. 130–1); Alen's deposition, 19 Mar. 1552 (TNA: PRO SP 61/4, ff. 102–3).

40 Browne to Warwick, 6 Aug. 1551 (TNA: PRO SP 61/3, ff. 130–1); 'Book out of Ireland in Latin', untitled segment (TNA: PRO SP 62/2, ff. 199r–203r). Smyth is a reference for works by Augustine (twice), Eusebius and Chrysostom: TNA: PRO SP 62/2, ff. 199r, 200rv, 202rv; Smyth, *Defence*, ff. 110v–111r, 122v; Smyth, *Assertion*, ff. 22v–23r, 193r.

41 The phrase is the deputy's: St Leger to Somerset, 18 Feb. 1551 (TNA: PRO SP 61/3, f. 20v).

42 Browne to Warwick, 6 Aug. 1551 (TNA: PRO SP 61/3, ff. 130rv).

43 MacCulloch, *Cranmer*, pp. 484–9.

44 Dasent (ed.), *Acts of the Privy Council*, iii, pp. 96–256; TNA: PRO SP 62/2, ff. 189r–203v; Browne to Warwick, 6 Aug. 1551 (TNA: PRO SP 61/3, ff. 130–1).

45 TNA: PRO SP 61/4, f.104rv.

46 *Ibid.*, ff. 104v–105r.

47 J. S. Brewer and W. Bullen (eds), *Calendar of Carew Manuscripts: The Book of Howth* (London: Longman, 1871), pp. 36–117; Brady, *Shane O'Neill*, pp. 19–20.

6

Henry Fitzsimon, the Irish Jesuits and Catholic identity in the early modern period

Brian Jackson

In a short biographical sketch of the distinguished Irish Jesuit Henry Fitzsimon published in *Studies* in 1943, James Corboy concluded his essay with a bleak assessment of life on the Jesuit mission to Ireland in 1630. Corboy asserted that after a long literary career on the continent, Fitzsimon returned from exile to Dublin where he was so harassed by persecution that he had no opportunity to write.[1] Corboy was following in distinguished footsteps down a well-worn path. Tropes of exile, persecution and hardships endured by witnesses for the true faith were recurring themes in Irish historical writing. This should not be surprising as much of the Irish historical canon, particularly that part of it which concerns the history of the church, had been written by men who played an active role in promoting the causes for beatification of Irish martyrs. Patrick Moran, Edmund Hogan and many others had devoted much of their active research careers to this task and in the process they had helped to shape the prevailing perception of Catholic life in post-reformation Ireland, a perception that informed subsequent historians of the period, both clerical and lay, including Myles Ronan, Timothy Corcoran and Robin Dudley Edwards.

The historical writings of Hogan, Ronan, Corcoran, Corboy and Dudley Edwards, although grounded in meticulous archival research, all have a common rhetorical thread: they are faith narratives. And in each of these histories the story of the fortunes of the Catholic Church in Ireland has been explicitly, and with single-minded determination, bound to the formation of a single national consciousness and identity. But this 'faith and fatherland' narrative is something of a blunt instrument. It cannot offer an adequately nuanced explanation as to how a complex figure such as Henry Fitzsimon identified himself. And in its reliance on themes of risk, peril and danger it also loses sight of the documented reality of everyday life for at least some of the Irish Catholic clergy.

Fitzsimon's later years were not as bleak as the image Corboy seeks to project. In fact his effective retirement gave Fitzsimon the opportunity to complete two large book projects that he had begun some fifteen years beforehand.[2] The mere existence of this body of work completely undermines Corboy's assertion. The content of the books also suggests that a number of other assumptions that have been too readily accepted by historians about the realities of everyday life for Irish Catholics in the first half of the seventeenth century may need to be reconsidered.

Fitzsimon's manuscript throws a very specific and focused light on the realities of life for at least one Irish Jesuit. The text itself was written on some 750 folios of very high-quality paper manufactured in Colmar in Alsace. The raw materials themselves constitute an expensive luxury item. The papers have been stitched into quaternions of varying size and each one of these has been wrapped in endpapers. In some cases the endpapers have been recycled from lavishly illustrated printed folio volumes and internal evidence from the sheets would suggest that the pages had been removed from books in an Irish library.[3] The volumes may have belonged to, or been paid for by, Richard Nugent the earl of Westmeath, a significant patron of the Jesuits in Ireland and a close associate of Fitzsimon. The texts are heavily annotated and supported by a substantial and impressive range of marginal notation, citation and indices. At each stage of its composition, the author of the text must have had access to a well-stocked library. This was not a text that was written in hiding.

Edmund Hogan asserted that by going to Ireland as part of the Jesuit mission in 1597, Fitzsimon 'periled his liberty and his life'.[4] But his behaviour would suggest otherwise. He did not travel to Ireland in disguise. He boarded the *Brye* at Chester and sailed for Dublin in the company of a number of the city's prominent merchants.[5] The boat was becalmed and to pass the time the group debated points of religious controversy. At least one of the passengers, John Lanye, was a convinced Protestant who would later serve as sheriff of Dublin during the mandates controversy. The point at issue centred around what was to become the first of the 104 articles of religion of the Church of Ireland, that 'the ground of our Religion and the rule of faith and all saving truth is the word of God contained in the holy Scripture'. Essentially it was a chicken-and-egg debate and Fitzsimon asserted that Lanye volunteered 'pleasant evasion in support of the doctrine which if it wanted all probabilitie at least it shewed a great goodwill and industrie to maintaine infidelitie'. According to Fitzsimon's account of things, the Jesuit deployed his formidable classical rhetorical skills, the product of decades of expensive and exclusive education at Oxford, Paris, Pont-à-Mousson and Louvain to expose the flaw in this tradesman's logic and rendered him speechless 'never sheathed blade in his shoppe or sheeted carcass was more silent in disputing religion than he all the tyme of our expecting the wished wind for Ireland'.[6]

This vignette tells us a number of things. First, Fitzsimon made no attempt to conceal his identity, nor did he believe himself to be in any danger. He was travelling in the company of wealthy Dublin merchants who were his friends and family. It was John Lanye, not the Jesuit, who was the outsider. Lanye was set apart from his fellow passengers not only by his religion. He was also marked out by a perception of his lower social status as a shopkeeper and a tradesman. At another point in the text, where he seeks to draw a link between religious dissent and civil disobedience among the lower orders, Fitzsimon refers to Lanye as 'the cutler's apprentice'.[7] This characterisation of Layne reflects the prevailing social attitudes of the merchant elite and the landed gentry of the Pale.

Layne was in fact reasonably well connected. His uncle, Francis was a wealthy landowner in Laois, an associate of Francis Cosby and Peter Carew, former victualler for the army and for Walter Devereux during the Ulster campaign in the 1570s. Francis provided a marriage settlement when John married the daughter of Robert Bysse of Swords.[8] Lanye's own daughter married William Parsons, a nephew of Geoffrey Fenton.[9] But in the context of the closed, hierarchical, confident and socially exclusive culture of the Pale, irrespective of the wealth he might accrue or the political favour or offices he might enjoy, he would remain an outsider.

Fitzsimon was no outsider. The son of a wealthy alderman, he was connected by marriage to many of the leading merchant and landowning families of the city and the Pale Maghery and throughout a long and distinguished (if controversial) career, he demonstrated, in both his actions and in his writings a patrician self-confidence and an insouciance to the sensibilities of others.

Arriving in Ireland in 1597, he quickly established his mission in Dublin and commandeered a suitably appointed hall in the house of one of his patrons that he had decorated with carpets, tapestries and wall hangings. Here, on an altar adorned with rich and elaborate plate and supported by an orchestra of musical instruments including harps and lutes (although not, we are told, an organ) he celebrated masses and ran a branch of the Jesuit sodality of the Blessed Virgin.[10]

It would appear that lavish décor was not confined to the chapels in the houses where the Irish Jesuit lived. In a letter to Robert Nugent, superior of the Irish mission, the Father General, Mutio Vitelleschi, noted that it had been brought to his attention that there was an apparent culture of laxity and luxury among the personnel on the Irish mission and that this was particularly prevalent in Dublin. He asserted that the houses were lavishly stocked with overly elegant furnishings and with books and pictures donated by generous supporters and patrons. Within the houses there was an absence of appropriate decorum. Prominent laypeople were frequent guests at table and this eroded the appropriate ambience of gravity and temperance.[11] This impression of life within Jesuit residences is compounded by a request from Robert Bath to Vitelleschi asking that a Jesuit brother with expertise in decorative painting be sent to Ireland.[12] Vitelleschi appears to have eventually acceded to the request and passed it for action to Francesco de la Croix, the provincial in Brussels.[13]

Some twenty years later, Mercurian Verdier, was given the task of undertaking a visitation of the Irish mission in the wake of the censures and interdict issued by Archbishop Giovanni Battista Rinuccini. In his report to Vincenzo Carafa, Vitelleschi's successor as general, Verdier observed that the Irish Jesuits still insisted on dressing as laymen, not for reasons of security but out of preference. He asserted that the mission had a lax disciplinary culture, that subjects had their own money and that they wasted it on extravagant trinkets such as pocket watches.[14]

Life on the Irish mission in the 1630s was described, with some satisfaction, as settled and quiet.[15] The Jesuits cultivated their patrons, and the order went about its business in its residences and schools, quietly accumulating property and capital. The administrators who ran the mission, the Old English coterie around the superior, deployed an armoury of blind trusts and other legal devices to protect property, maximise returns on investments and enforce its claims and rights.[16]

By the time that Robert Nugent was appointed superior of the Irish mission, Fitzsimon was no longer a part of this inner circle. Clever and privileged though he undoubtedly was, his career within the Society of Jesus had been marked by a series of controversial spats with authority, culminating in a ferocious row with the German theologian, Jacob Keller in 1620 that threatened to derail the campaign to canonise Ignatius of Loyola, the founder of the Jesuits.[17] From this point forward, Fitzsimon's valency within the Society of Jesus was diminished. He spent the 1620s working as a military chaplain in Flanders and Hainaut, the territory of his dead patron the Comte de Bucquoy.[18] At the end of 1629, now in his early sixties, he decided that he wished to return to Ireland. Vitelleschi confided to a colleague that he did not think he could refuse the request unless the Irish superior raised strong objections.[19]

No formal objection was raised, but it is apparent that Nugent regarded Fitzsimon as an irritant and subsequently indicated to Rome that Fitzsimon's presence in Dublin represented a threat to the mission and he used this as a pretext to send him back to Douai at the end of 1632.[20] Fitzsimon was ostensibly accompanying the earl of Westmeath on a pilgrimage to Loreto, but Vitelleschi assured Nugent he would endeavour to persuade the Jesuits in Douai to keep him there.[21] Vitelleschi also attempted to prise Fitzsimon away from his wealthy patron, solicitously suggesting that at his advancing age (he was 66) the journey to Loreto might be too much of a burden.[22] But Fitzsimon ignored the general's blandishments and he continued on his journey with the earl, stopping at St Omer to arrange places for Nugent's sons at the college there before continuing south to Italy.[23] They returned to Ireland in the summer of 1635 and at that stage Vitelleschi was forced to write, somewhat apologetically, to Nugent assuring him that he would have redeployed Fitzsimon elsewhere if he could have found someone willing to take him on.[24] Nugent was forced to accept Fitzsimon back and deployed him in teaching philosophy to students in Dublin. He is listed in a 1637 catalogue of mission personnel as part of the Dublin residence and at 71 years old was described as being in vigorous good health.[25] This was the reality of life on the Irish mission for Fitzsimon, and for his colleagues. Irish Jesuits led privileged and comfortable lives. They lodged in well-appointed residences and were courted by wealthy patrons and supporters drawn from their extended families and social networks. They moved freely among their peers in the upper reaches of Irish society and they travelled back and forth with ease from Ireland to Europe.

These physical and social circumstances and the experiences of everyday life served to shape and to frame the formulation of Fitzsimon's statement and expression of his sense of identity as a Catholic, as an Irishman and as a member of the community of the Pale. The manuscript texts that today constitute Oscott MS 8 provided Fitzsimon with a vehicle for a sustained and considered disquisition over a number of key themes and issues. They afford us a rare, comprehensive and unambiguous articulation of an Irish Catholic world-view. To be more precise, it is the world-view of a highly educated, articulate and privileged individual within that very broad group. This view is expressed in an elegant, sophisticated and distinctly metropolitan manner and it is emphatically at odds with the picture of Irish Jesuit life sketched by Corboy or Hogan.

Fitzsimon's view of the world fits into the classic Old English mould. The church and the monarch are twin pillars of a well-ordered society. Each supports the other and together they form a solid and enduring bulwark against dissent and social unrest. Much of what he has to say would be familiar and give comfort to George Dowdall and the canon lawyers who presided over the Irish Church during the late medieval and high reformation periods. Fitzsimon holds fast to his Anglo-Norman or Old English heritage in his articulation of the historical relationship between church and state or papacy and monarchy. But that world-view, or sense of identity, had an inward focus and a very local point of reference. In contrast, Fitzsimon eschews arguments for the unique or special nature of the Irish Church. Rather, he offers a much broader frame of reference to help make sense of the Reformation and he chooses to present the history of events not as a seismic transformation or a body blow to the church but rather as a series of relatively minor local and isolated incidents. He considers the Reformation and the careers of its principal actors (whom he portrays as self-serving renegade regular clergy) against a specific backdrop, the history of medieval heterodoxy, the story of Cathars, Lollards and Hussites. His underlying message is clear: puritanism and contemporary schism are momentary difficulties and like the medieval examples that have preceded them – they too will pass.

For Fitzsimon, heterodoxy is symptomatic of a downward spiral into civic unrest, political dissent and social chaos. He is at pains to represent Puritanism as a particular threat to society and goes so far as to present it as ideologically alien, having more in common with Islam than with any formally organised Christian church.[26] Fitzsimon is relentless in portraying the principal personalities of the reform movement in the worst possible light, as henpecked drunkards (Luther), sexually incontinent apostates (Bucer), violent sodomites (Calvin) and forgers (Fox). Civil society with its established hierarchies, and its legal and social frameworks all risked being swept away by the lawless, faithless rabble that they led and whom he asserts were more accustomed to tippling in a tavern than expounding scripture.[27]

Fitzsimon's inherent social conservatism is apparent from his rather snobbish attitude to figures like Lanye, and it is explicit in his statement of the duties of a subject to the sovereign. This section in the manuscript appears to have been a late addition, inserted almost as an afterthought. It is appended to an examination of Ussher's assertion that William the Conqueror was 'the slave of Antichrist' and that the Norman polity was inherently hostile to the true Christian church. Ussher's perspective on the Anglo-Normans and on the medieval church was anathema to an orthodox Catholic Palesman. Fitzsimon approaches his critique of Ussher's work with a broad historical examination of the allegiance that princes, and the Anglo-Norman kings in particular, owed to the papacy. He added a passage setting out his views on the contemporary oaths of allegiance required from the subject to the sovereign. Although the piece has a particular local aspect, it is argued in a polished, fluid, rhetorical and lawyerly manner that has its origins in a much wider European context, the unabashedly literary humanist approach that the Jesuits took to the dissemination of orthodox theology.[28] Fitzsimon builds his case on a classic Thomist position. His essential point is that there is an inherent legal and logical contradiction in Irish Puritan dogma. The first Article of Religion asserts 'that the ground of our Religion and the rule of faith and all saving truth is the word of God contained in the Holy Scripture'. Yet the oath of allegiance contains within it statements concerning the powers of the papacy, excommunication, deposition and absolution, none of which can be expressly substantiated by scriptural authority alone. Fitzsimon cites the Dionysian principle used by Aquinas in his examination of lying[29] '*bonum ex integra causa, malum ex quocum que defectu*' – or as he renders it in English, 'Good must be intiere: evil chanceth by every defect'. Therefore, he asserts that if the oath is not rooted in scripture it is defective, then to take it is perjury. But he goes further:

> As for Catholikes refusing the sayd oath, what at least their Christian dutie is toward our soveraign king Charles Steward now raigning, I will sincerely and briefly manifest.
>
> We do professe to Charles our King and gratious Liege,
> Our hands, our lives, our goodes, in neede we should obliege
> And praye to God, to prosper and preserve his lyfe,
> And foes confownd, and bless his Roiall race and Wyfe,
> Gainst whom who treason knows, and doth it not disclose,
> Be he accurst and speedie foode to kytes and croes
> To this each Catholike will willingly subscribe
> Or bastard is allyed to Purists rebel tribe.
> Allegiall oath we loath to swear of other kynde
> For this sufficient is true loialtie to bynde
> Gods word our warrant is, this lawfull oath to sweare,
> Gods word doth not afford that ayene should foresweare.[30]

Fitzsimon is adamant that Catholic subjects owe allegiance to the crown and he is specific in his condemnation of misprision of treason and asserts that those guilty of it should meet a traitor's end on a gibbet. Catholics who would refuse to subscribe to such an oath are, he asserts, little better than rebel puritans who have no regard for social hierarchy which is essential to the maintenance of civil society and a well-ordered polity.

Social status and hierarchy are key motifs in Fitzsimon's writings and this reflects his patrician upbringing and his social and political values. The polity is an ordered hierarchy governed by a sacred compact between sovereign, church and people. The compact imposes obligations and duties on each party. And to illustrate the point, he relates a story framed around the failure of a landed Scottish nobleman to observe his obligations to his tenants. Driven by greed, the laird devised novel charges and increased rents to oppress his tenants and encroach on their traditional rights of commons. Opportunistically, he aligned himself with the reformed church and commissioned ministers of the kirk to preach (for a fee) in support of his extortions.[31] The moral force of Fitzsimon's argument is clear. When the compact is broken, the structure of society crumbles. Justice is overturned and mercenary heretical preachers can be procured to defend unjust and unfair impositions and to deny the existence of the traditional post-mortem deterrents for flagrant breaches of social order: purgatory and hell.

Fitzsimon's vision of the moral and political universe is essentially one in which religious heterodoxy leads inexorably to progressive social and political chaos. And in his narrative scheme the opportunistic denial of purgatory by puritans is trumped by the outright rejection of the immortality of the soul by atheists. Fitzsimon asserts that there are numerous prominent and influential atheists among the English reformers and specifically identifies Walter Raleigh as the personification of this 'school' in England.[32] Here Fitzsimon follows Robert Persons who roundly condemned Raleigh and his 'school of the night':

> How miserable a thing it is that her majesty, descending of so noble progenitors, should be brought to make laws and proclamations in matters of religion according to these men's senses and opinions and leaving all her old nobility and the ancient wisdom, gravity and learning which England was wont to have, should rule her self by these new upstarts and publish edicts so contrary and opposite to all the laws and edicts of all the kings and queens that have been in England from the first conversion therof unto this day.[33]

Fitzsimon reiterates this explicit link between religious dissent and usurped social order in a lengthy consideration of concepts of honour and specifically, its corrupted expression in the perverse cult of the duel. Within the text of Oscott MS 8 the discussion arises in a wide-ranging consideration of articles 61 and 62 of the 1615 Articles of the Church of Ireland; that the law may punish men with death for heinous and grievous offences, and that the state may require subjects to serve in just wars. His original title for this section was 'When God's laws and counsel prescribe against single combat'. But Fitzsimon had a very specific focus and intention for this section of his text, and with a playful reference to Edmund Bonner he revised his title to 'An occasioned digression not so necessary as profitable'.[34] He subsequently crossed out the entire section.

The duel was a sixteenth-century invention. Although Italian in origin, it was particularly prevalent in France where the absence of sufficient authority at the centre meant that the institutions of the state were not up to the job of mediating or controlling disputes. Duelling was viewed in some quarters as a form of satisfaction or at any rate a stylised and choreographed means for restitution for perceived slights to aristocratic honour. The church took a firm line on duelling and the Council of Trent condemned the practice.[35]

Fitzsimon's principal objections to the private duel were: that it did not limit bloodshed, that honour could not be repaired by blood and that judgement and revenge were the preserve of God not of private individuals. These were standard orthodox positions. But Fitzsimon warms to his theme, elaborating for his reader the specific royal pedigree for duelling in France and of subsequent efforts at containment. He commends Louis XIII's initiative in legislating against the practice but he holds another king, Francis I, primarily responsible for the duelling craze.

And this provides the perfect introduction to an extensive examination of the distinctions between true and false honour. True honour is the reward of virtue that cannot be blemished by any private affront. False honour can be bestowed anywhere and on anyone and is frequently showered by deluded monarchs on charming braggarts of low birth, who usurp loyal courtiers of more noble pedigree. And he gives some examples to demonstrate what he means, Proteas, Alexander the Great's favourite drinking companion, Piers Gaveston and the Despensers, all at one stage or another, special favourites of Edward II, Elizabeth's Walter Raleigh and King James's patronage of 'the earl of Craig'.[36] These examples were chosen carefully, to convey the moral and political chaos that resulted when social taboos are broken. Fitzsimon takes Person's argument and adds a veneer of sexual innuendo to embellish his own articulation of the sense of grievance harboured by the established, yet recusant, gentry and nobility who felt that they had been ousted from the seat of power and influence by these princes' playthings. These young, hungry, ruthless schemers shamelessly manipulated vain and ageing monarchs for their own ends.

Like many of his kinsmen, Fitzsimon saw that the influence and power of the traditional ruling class in the Pale and the position of its municipal and ecclesiastical establishment had been eroded by the Tudor state. In his eyes, the proper function of the monarch was to support, not to undermine the spiritual jurisdiction of the church. Fitzsimon establishes an impeccable pedigree of faithful, attentive and continuous fealty on the part of each English king from William through to Henry VII. But the rule and conduct of Henry VIII, Edward VI, Mary and Elizabeth is the subject of more critical scrutiny. Each of their episcopal appointments, their legislative and policy decisions and their court appointments are examined, assessed and found wanting. This insidious process of state incursion had been accelerated in the volatile atmosphere of increasingly factional court politics of the closing years of Elizabeth's reign. The Stuart succession was eagerly anticipated in Ireland, particularly among the Old English of the Pale. Like many prominent English recusants, the leaders of the Pale felt that they had been excluded from their proper place in government. But James, like Elizabeth before him, was an enthusiastic promoter of favourites and the new regime proved to be a disappointment to many of the new king's more prominent Catholic subjects.

Elizabeth was an excommunicate and in the eyes of the church, the product of an illegitimate union. Fitzsimon was consistently hostile about her in both his writings and in his correspondence. He adopted a more conciliatory, if slightly disparaging tone towards King James, who for all his shortcomings was baptised a Catholic, was married to a Catholic and was the legitimate child of a legitimate Catholic monarch. Ironically, it was Charles I, the only Stuart king who was baptised, lived and died as a convinced Protestant who provided Fitzsimon and his circle with the nearest thing to an ideal monarch.

Charles worked hard to create an image of kingship that was very different from his shy, awkward personality. The monarch was moral, elegant and serene, diligent and attentive to government, and a staunch defender of orthodoxy. The strict form and ritual of the Caroline royal court reflected this ethos and served to promote and maintain this construct.[37]

Fitzsimon shared King Charles's deep suspicion of egalitarian puritanism and the basic political philosophy that is advanced in the Oscott manuscript would not have struck any jarring notes in court circles. Fitzsimon articulates the virtues of enlightened, benevolent rule by an orthodox elite who ensure peace and stability in a society where baser impulses inevitably tend to chaos and disorder. But where there may have been a meeting of minds on how society should be governed, their views would have diverged on matters of religion and that is why the last element of this manuscript, the brief introduction written in 1633 or early 1634, is most intriguing. This section consists of a brief document set out in four folios. The piece is entitled 'A Revelation or Apocalyps, of fundamentall and formall contradictions, in Reformed Articles of Religion in England, and Ierland'.[38] It asserts that the Church of Ireland, in adopting puritan articles of faith that are contrary to the Thirty Nine Articles of the Church of England, has fallen into error. And by chastising Ussher and his associates Fitzsimon attempts to build some convergence with the Caroline Church establishment and would appear to be suggesting to Bramhall and to Wentworth, that unlike the unruly puritans they are seeking to control, he and his patrons, men such as Richard Nugent, the earl of Westmeath, are true and natural supporters of the regime that they represent.

Fitzsimon's writings project a sense of identity that is self-confidently and assertively Catholic. But these texts in particular are also self-consciously metropolitan or international in the way in which the author approaches his subject material. Although the two texts are concerned with very specifically Irish topics, Fitzsimon deliberately eschews Irish material or examples as he constructs his argument. Despite an Irish childhood and the strong underlying markers of the Hiberno-English dialect spoken in the Pale which unconsciously colour Fitzsimon's prose style, the text is deliberately 'located' elsewhere, in Scotland, in Italy, in Bohemia and in the Low Countries. It reflects the complex web of professional and personal networks that Fitzsimon built up over a lifetime spent working and travelling around Europe. This is in so many ways an *ad hominem* testament. In tone and in style it reflects Fitzsimon's patrician background and attitudes. In its compositional structure it owes something to the culture of formal disputation that dominated the lecture halls of Oxford, Paris and Louvain. This is folded into a historical narrative frame that serves to contextualise and to legitimate asserted positions. Stylistically it is self-consciously learned and the text is littered with classical aphorisms and quotations, each one accompanied by an elegant and well-honed translation, crafted by the author himself and designed to display his own linguistic skill, rhetorical dexterity and sophistication. And yet it also achieves a populist, even picaresque quality in its underlying narrative; an unfolding of Fitzsimon's own life experiences and his multifaceted career as scholar, missionary, controversialist, military chaplain and, latterly, as companion to the well connected and the wealthy. He self-consciously uses autobiography as a clever literary device. These anecdotes form an engaging and apparently effortless narrative thread that draws readers in and engages them in more complex theological expositions that he has artfully constructed around his own life story.

Fitzsimon had a rich and varied life. He was conscious and proud of his Irish heritage and of his family's place in the social order of Dublin.

He was assertive in his creed and had a sophisticated understanding of the intellectual origins and historical development of different strands within Christianity. His writings demonstrate layers of complexity and intellectual sophistication. His actions exhibit the contradictions and the opportunism in his character. Each of these modulated and informed his attitudes to the church and his allegiances to his homeland. 'Faith and fatherland' simply cannot explain how he identified himself in terms of either.

Notes

1 J. J. Corboy 'Henry Fitzsimon SJ, 1566–1634', *Studies: An Irish Quarterly Review*, 32(126) (1943), p. 266.

2 Oscott College, Birmingham MS 8. Physically this is a substantial item of *c*.750 folios. The papers have been gathered and stitched into 22 quaternions. Originally deposited in Douai, possibly by Fitzsimon himself when he was there with Richard Nugent in 1633, the papers were brought to Birmingham in 1792. At some stage the bundles of paper were rearranged as the manuscript, which comprises several texts, is no longer in sequence. Roughly 50 per cent of the text is a detailed examination of the Articles of Religion of the 1615 convocation of the Church of Ireland. This element of the text was begun in 1616 and was completed on 23 Aug. 1626. The second item, of similar size, is a rebuttal of James Ussher's *Gravissimae Quaestionis*, published in 1613. This text was begun when Ussher was still Professor of Divinity in Trinity, a post he resigned in 1621. It was completed on 14 Jan. 1633. The final element of the manuscript is a comparison between the 1615 Articles of Religion of the Church of Ireland and the thirty-nine Articles of the Church of England. This was written in 1633 in the run-up to the second general convocation of the Church of Ireland. The original preface to the commentary on the 1615 Articles was sliced out with a razor and this new addition to the text was inserted in its place.

3 Oscott MS 8, Q. 8, Q. 11, Q. 12, Q. 13.

4 E. Hogan 'Father Henry Fitzsimon SJ', *Irish Ecclesiastical Record*, 8 (1872), p. 284.

5 Oscott MS 8, Q. 2, f. 2r.

6 *Ibid.*

7 Oscott MS 8, Q. 4, f. 22r.

8 *The Irish Fiants of the Tudor Sovereigns during the Reigns of Henry VIII, Edward VI, Philip & Mary, and Elizabeth I*, 4 vols; introd. Kenneth Nicholls; pref. T. Ó Canann (Dublin: Edmund Burke, 1994), iii, 1586–1603, No. 4990, p. 10.

9 C. Lennon, *The Lords of Dublin in the Age of Reformation* (Dublin: Irish Academic Press, 1989), p. 259.

10 E. Hogan, *Ibernia Ignatiana* (Dublin: Excudebat Societas, 1880), p. 41. For a description of a silver chalice presented by Elizabeth, dowager countess of

Kildare (and sister of Richard Nugent earl of Westmeath) to the Irish Jesuit mission in 1634, see *Journal of the Co. Kildare Archaeological Society*, 5 (1906–8), pp. 61–2. In the same year she leased Kilkea castle to the Jesuit community and they occupied the property until 1646. She also presented two strings of pearls (containing a total of 216 pearls) to the Basilica della Santa Casa in Loreto.

11 Archivium Romanum Societatis Iesu, Rome (ARSI) Anglia 4a f. 23r.
12 ARSI Anglia 4a f. 22r.
13 ARSI Gal. Belg. 2 f. 139v.
14 Mercurian Verdier to Vincenzo Carafa, 24 Jun. 1649, Irish Jesuit Archives MS A 114 f. 2.
15 ARSI Anglia 4a f. 45r.
16 B. Jackson, 'The role and influence of the Irish Missions of the Society of Jesus on the implementation of a Counter-Reformation among the Old English in Ireland, 1542–1633', Ph.D. dissertation, University of Dublin, 2007, pp. 177–229.
17 R. Bireley, *The Jesuits and the Thirty Years War: Kings, Courts and Confessors* (Cambridge: Cambridge University Press, 2003), pp. 43–4.
18 Fitzsimon had been confessor and personal chaplain to the commander of the Imperial forces Charles-Bonaventure de Longueval, Compte de Bucquoy. He wrote two tracts celebrating Bucquoy's military prowess and victory at the White Mountain in 1620. These were published pseudonymously as *Pugna Pragensis a Candido Eblanio* (Brno, 1620) and *Buquoii Quadrimestre Iter progressuque, Authore Constantio Peregrino* (Brno, 1621). Following the dispute with Keller, Fitzsimon was instructed by his superiors not to publish these accounts again. However, he seems to have been prepared to risk flouting this directive, and material from the tracts was utilised within the Oscott MS. He also took the opportunity to reiterate his trenchant views on the mendicant orders originally published in *The Iustification and Exposition of the Divine Sacrifice of the Masse* (Douai, 1611). These views had been censured by the Inquisition following a complaint from the Capuchins.
19 Vitelleschi to Francesco de la Croix, 25 Aug. 1629. Fitzsimon was granted permission to return by Vitelleschi in a letter dated 8 Sept. 1629, ARSI Gal. Belg. 2 f. 124v.
20 Vitelleschi to Robert Nugent, 13 Nov. 1632, ARSI Anglia 4a f. 30v–31v.
21 *Ibid.*
22 ARSI Anglia 4a f. 32v.
23 Vitelleschi to Fitzsimon, 25 Jun. 1633, ARSI Gal. Belg. 2 f. 283v.
24 ARSI Anglia 4a f. 37r.Vitelleschi to Robert Nugent, 25 Jun. 1635, ARSI Anglia 4a f. 38r–v.
25 ARSI Anglia 9(i) f. 9r.
26 Oscott MS 8, Q. 6, f.37r.
27 Oscott MS 8, Q. 11, f. 11r.
28 R. A. Maryks, *St Cicero and the Jesuits: The Influence of the Liberal Arts on the Adoption of Moral Probabilism* (Aldershot: Ashgate, 2008).

29 Aquinas, *Summa Theologica*, II II Q. 110 Art. 3.
30 Oscott MS 8, Q.7, f. 27r. Playing the reformers at their own game, Fitzsimon cites scriptural authorities for his oath, Hebrews 6:16, Exodus 20:7 and Deuteronomy 5:20.
31 Oscott MS 8, Q. 10c, f. 9v–10r.
32 Oscott MS 8, Q. 10c, f. 7v.
33 R. Parsons, *An aduertisement written to a secretarie of my L. Treasurers of Ingland, by an Inglishe intelligencer as he passed throughe Germanie towards Italie* ... (Antwerp, s.n., 1592), p. 18. The text is an abridged translation of Parsons' *Elizabethae, Angliae Reginae, haeresim Calvinianam propugnantis, saevissimum in Catholicos sui Regni edictum* (London: Apud Ioannem Fabrum 1591). The Latin original was written by Parsons under the name 'Andreas Philopatrum'. The translation may be by Richard Rowlands (Richard Verstegan) who was Parson's agent in the Low Countries and was instrumental in disseminating the pamphlet.
34 The title is a play on Bonner's catechetical treatise *A Profitable and Necessary Doctryne with Certain Homilies Adjoined Thereto* (London: Excasum in aedibus Iohannis Cawodi, 1555).
35 Session 25, *Decretum de reformatione generali*, ch. 19.
36 Oscott MS 8, Q. 5c, f. 15r. The 'earle Craig' may be a reference to Sir Thomas Craig, the French-educated Scottish jurist, expert in feudal law and controversialist who defended the Stuart right of succession against Robert Person's, *A conference about the next succession to the crowne of Ingland diuided into two partes* .... (Antwerp: R. Doleman, 1594).
37 K. Sharpe, *The Personal Rule of Charles I* (New Haven, CT and London: Yale University Press, 1992), pp. 209–16.
38 Oscott MS 8, Q. 1, f. 1r.

7

Gaelic Catholicism and the Ulster plantation

Raymond Gillespie

In the historiography of early seventeenth-century Ireland the Ulster plantation has assumed a paradigmatic role. Military defeat in 1603 was followed by the flight of the earls and expropriation of the lands of the Catholic Irish and colonisation by Protestant Scots and English. There is certainly contemporary evidence to support this sort of view of seventeenth-century Ulster. From the perspective of the native Irish, the *Annals of the Four Masters*, written in the 1630s, characterised the Ulster plantation as:

> it came to pass that their [the Irish lords of Ulster] principalities, their territories, their estates, their lands, their forts, their fortresses, their fruitful harbours, their fishful bays were taken from the Irish of the province of Ulster and given in their presence to foreign tribes, and they were expelled and banished into other countries where most of them died.[1]

A second piece of evidence is provided by a poem, usually ascribed to Lochlainn Ó Dálaigh. The poem is undated but from internal comments it appears to be contemporary with the Ulster plantation. The poem is built around the rhetorical question 'Where have all the Gaels gone?' and describes the dispersal of the Irish, the decay of traditional values and the occupation of church buildings by new strangers. The real reason for these changes, according to Ó Dálaigh, is not the colonisers but rather the judgement of God upon the Irish: it is 'the wrath of God scouring them before all' in the way that the children of Israel had been punished in the Old Testament. The correct response was penance rather than retaliation.[2] A similar explanation for the flight of the earls had been advocated by the Four Masters in their annal entry for 1607.

The scheme that emerged for the lands escheated from the principal Gaelic lords in Ulster envisaged the former lords would be replaced with Protestant settler landlords. The 'Orders and conditions' for the Ulster plantation, printed in late 1608 or early 1609, stipulated that 'every of the undertakers, English or Scottish, before the ensealing of his letters patent shall take the oath of supremacy either in the chancery of England or Ireland or before the commissioners to be appointed for the establishing of the plantation and shall also conform themselves in religion according to his Majesty's laws'.[3]

The revised conditions of 1610 went even further and required that not only would undertakers be required to take the oath but that they take it as heads of families so that 'their families shall also be conformable in religion aforesaid'.[4] The plans of the plantation said little about the religion of the settlers that the undertakers were to introduce but there were sufficient hints to imply that Catholics would not be welcome among this group either. The original 'Orders and conditions' of the plantation had stipulated that each of the undertakers was required 'within two years [to] plant or place a competent number of English or Scottish tenants upon his proportion' and to remove the native Irish.[5] However, the revised conditions of 1610 were much more specific, requiring the larger undertakers to plant '24 able men of the age of 18 years or upwards being English or inland Scots' within three years. Smaller undertakers were required to settle ten families on their land. While it did not explicitly say so, the equation between English or Scottish and Protestant was clearly implied in these provisions.[6] Such arrangements, it would appear at first glance, were intended to create a Protestant elite of both landowners and tenants, leaving a Catholic underclass whose grievances would emerge only in later centuries. In short the arrangements for Ulster could be seen as the plans of the Stuart monarchy for Ireland writ small. The reality, however, was more complex.

Our understanding of both the execution and implications of this scheme for the evolution of Ulster Catholicism requires a more nuanced approach to these plans. First, it is important to realise that the Ulster plantation was an unusual construct that did not apply to all of the province. The two counties east of the River Bann, Antrim and Down, were not under the control of those who had fled in 1607 and hence were not escheated and settled. Thus the society that emerged there was very different. Estates were larger and operated with fewer restrictions. In particular the largest landowner in this area, Sir Randall MacDonnell from the Scottish Isles, was a Catholic. His landholding comprised some two-thirds of Co. Antrim (some 340,000 acres) making him, with the Catholic earls of Clanricard and Ormond and the Protestant Richard Boyle in Munster, one of the four largest landowners in Ireland in 1610.[7] MacDonnell cannot be seen as a peripheral figure. Like the earl of Clanricard he moved in elite circles. He was created earl of Antrim, and his son spent a prolonged period at court, eventually marrying the widow of the duke of Buckingham.[8] Second, within the area of the plantation itself historians have focused a great deal on the lands granted to English and Scottish planters to the exclusion of other aspects of the scheme. The Ulster undertakers received some 40 per cent of the land in the scheme the remainder going to servitors or native Irish. Of the native Irish, most remained Catholic and among the servitors there were certainly suspicions about their confessional position. The royal commission of 1622 set up to enquire into the problems of Ireland reported that 'some of them who have servitors proportions are recusants and will not take the oath of supremacy'.[9] However, further investigation of the undertaker settler community itself revealed that plans were not evolving as they might. Powerful figures in Scottish politics who applied for Ulster land could not be ignored, even on the basis of religion. James Hamilton, earl of Abercorn was not only a Catholic but had been appointed a Scottish privy councillor in 1598 and was one of the commissioners for the union between England and Scotland. His political influence and the king's close relations with him led him, and most of his family, to become undertakers, Hamilton himself being the chief undertaker for the barony of Strabane. Hamilton and his family were Catholics, introduced Catholic settlers and a Jesuit community into his estates and converted a number of prominent settler women to Catholicism.[10]

Even if all had gone well in the first generation of settler landholders this was no guarantee for the future. In 1630 the Dublin government feared that the estates of some Ulster planters might be sold to Catholics, although there seems little justification for such fears.[11] Again, the existing owners of estates could change confessional position. While George Touchet, earl of Castlehaven, may have seemed a safe pair of hands when he was granted his Ulster estates, after his death in 1616 his heir flirted with Catholicism and his brother was a committed Catholic. The third earl was likewise a committed Catholic, returning from a military career in Europe to fight for the Confederated Catholics in the 1640s. In addition, as the land market developed in the years after the plantation both English Catholics and Old English Catholics from the Pale, newly rich from the trade boom, invested in Ulster. By 1641 some 15 per cent of Cavan was in Old English, Catholic hands.[12] In addition a number of Catholic Englishmen also appear to have taken the opportunity to acquire Ulster lands in the active market.[13]

Below the level of the landholding elite a substantial proportion of the native Irish remained on the land as tenants of the new undertakers despite requirements that they were to be removed. In August 1610 a proclamation was issued requiring the Irish on the undertakers' estates to remove themselves to the lands of servitors, other natives or the church but explaining that they might be permitted to stay given the low numbers of settlers that had arrived. To ensure the harvest could be saved the older inhabitants were allowed to stay on their lands for a further year. The following year the removal date was extended yet again until May 1612. By 1618, however, little had been done to remove the, by now, illegal native Irish tenants and the following year an attempt was made to fine those native Irish on undertakers' estates. This still proved ineffectual since undertakers found it more convenient to keep their native tenants and charge higher rents than they might have got from settlers without the inconvenience and difficulty of finding settler tenants. By the 1620s the Irish were well established on the undertakers' lands and this realisation gave way to a renewed debate as to their place in the plantation scheme and whether they should be allowed to hold leases on undertakers' estates.[14] In reality the prospect of removing them seemed remote. Since the undertakers were technically in breach of the conditions of the plantation they attempted to regularise their position and an agreement was reached with the government whereby in return for a fine they could retain native Irish on one quarter of their estates, removing the rest by May 1629. However, as with previous schemes, this proved almost impossible to enforce in parts of Ulster and significant numbers of Irish tenants remained on settler estates.[15] While some of these native Irish conformed to the established church, at least to the point of taking the oath of supremacy, it is clear that most remained Catholic.[16]

All this suggests that a simple model of elite equating with Protestant and popular with Catholic within the Ulster plantation context does not capture all of the complexity of the situation. Furthermore, Catholicism in the Ulster plantation was not a simple monolithic force to be equated with dispossession, exclusion and the survival of late medieval traditional belief awaiting modernisation by Tridentine reform. Rather, there were varieties of Catholicism present in early seventeenth-century Ulster ranging from that practised by the earl of Abercorn at Strabane, through that characteristic of the Old English community of the Pale who had acquired lands in Cavan, to the more traditional world of rural Ulster Catholicism. In terms of the numbers of practitioners these were not all equal but they did all constitute expressions of belief that can be understood as aspects of early modern Catholicism.

This diversity of background, both ethnic and social, meant that there was also great diversity in the way in which Catholicism was practised in Ulster during the early seventeenth century. The earl of Abercorn, for instance, had both the wealth and the status to support Jesuits at Strabane although they may not have resided in his house. Again the few houses of friars maintained by the Franciscans in plantation Ulster required local patrons, although these clearly did not come from the same social level as Abercorn, those in the region of the Donegal friary were of enough substance to present the convent with a chalice in 1633.[17] Most communities had neither the status nor the wealth of the earl of Abercorn to maintain a gentry Catholicism and religious practice fell back on a rudimentary parish system that was reconstructed only slowly, particularly after the 1620s when pressures on Catholicism from central government lessened. By the 1630s there is evidence that numbers of clergy and places of worship were growing rapidly with perhaps 70 per cent of parishes in Kilmore having a Catholic priest although in the poorer areas of Donegal that figure was much lower. Again clergy were tightening their control on the parochial network sometimes using the civil authorities to enforce the collection of dues.[18]

The limitations of this parish system in promoting the sort of devotional world that the Council of Trent had urged on Catholics in the sixteenth century are well known. Most of the Catholic clergy in Ulster had little continental experience and those who did, such as the Franciscans, being dependent on their flock for financial support and protection, trod a narrow line between the well-known and trusted world of traditional religion and that of innovation. The result is that the Catholic devotional world of plantation Ulster tended to concentrate on maintaining traditional devotion rather than promoting innovation. Change required a much greater effort over a longer time span than the forty years after the plantation could provide. Thus at the siege of Drogheda in 1642 the religious world of the Ulster Catholic besiegers showed conservative tendencies with traditional prayers or amulets being found on the bodies of soldiers indicating devotion to the traditional cult of the measure of the wounds of Christ and offering protection from fire, water or the sword. The arrival of a statue that commanded local veneration in the Ulster camp was greeted with considerable acclamation. Holy places, usually with hagiographical origin legends, also served as foci of devotion. At Arboe, for instance, the high crosses were said to have been transported there by St Patrick and prayer there was said to be more effective than in other places.[19] Perhaps the best known of these places of devotions, the holy well, is probably the least well documented but a number of '*fons miraculosus*' are known from an early seventeenth-century list of churches in the diocese of Kilmore.[20] Such wells, statues and prayer amulets all confirm the traditional nature of Ulster Catholicism in the early seventeenth century with its focus on the tangible and coherent at the expense of more recent promotion of interiority in religious practice.

One interesting case where change could be introduced given the resources and timescale to do it was the popular pilgrimage to St Patrick's Purgatory at Lough Derg in Co. Donegal. At the beginning of the seventeenth century, folklore and hagiography reinforced each other to create a penitential experience with very tangible markers of sanctity that were visible on the island: the penitential beds, the cave, the lake and the house or tree beneath which St Patrick fasted. In 1632 the Franciscan friars assumed responsibility for the penitential pilgrimage. They had shown an interest in the penitential importance of this site as early as 1611 when it had been depicted as a frontispiece in the Franciscan Bonaventura Ó hEodhasa's catechism *Teagasc Críostaí.* In the short term the Franciscans could achieve little here, since the pilgrimage was closed in the 1630s and again during the 1650s the site was sacked. The mission was taken up again in the late seventeenth century but in a rather halting fashion as political developments interrupted progress. However, the pilgrimage had been reshaped by the Franciscans, transforming it from a set of popular rituals into an interior spiritual experience. Pilgrims were provided with instructions, printed in modern form, that urged them not simply to perform the rituals but pointed out the biblical significance attached to them and urged them to meditate on their actions, turning the ritual into an example of Tridentine interiority.[21]

The same Franciscan strategy is clear in the printed books in Irish produced in Louvain in the early seventeenth century. However, in the years after 1660, copies of some of the devotional works produced by the Louvain press entered the Ulster manuscript tradition. In particular Anthony Gearnon's *Parrthas an anma* of 1645 began to circulate in manuscript. Two or possibly three copies of this tract (or extracts from it) are known to have been made in the years after 1660. One of these manuscripts also contains poems by the early seventeenth-century Franciscan Bonaventura Ó hEoghusa and at least two others contain part of his 1611 catechism.[22] Of even more interest is the copy of Aodh Mac Aingil's 1618 work on penance, *Scáthán Shacramuinte na Naithridhe*, made for Brian Maguire of Fermanagh in 1701–02.[23] This work was intended for use by clergy rather than laity and its strong emphasis on the spiritual dimension of repentance marks it out as a clearly Tridentine text. The acquisition of such a text by a layman points to the achievement of the Franciscans in introducing such ideas to a wide community. Unfortunately there is very little evidence to suggest how these manuscripts were read but those who advocated the spiritualised world of Trent were clear that reading was better than hearing or reciting. Reading provided time for meditation and meditation led to a deepening of religious experience. However, this transformation of Ulster Catholicism was a slow, tortuous process that could not be achieved in the short term.

How this rather traditional Catholic community defined itself against both the Protestant state and the wider body of Protestant settlers varied over time and space and according to social position. At the apex of the local social order were Catholics who had benefited from the plantation scheme and who wished to assume their newly found position of social leadership, thinking their Catholicism might count for little in this world. From the 1620s few impediments appear to have been put in the way of displaying their new-found status on the political stage. Status and honour were important counterbalances to confessional position. As the Church of Ireland bishop of Derry described Sir George Hamilton, brother of the earl of Abercorn, in 1630, 'Sir George Hamilton, who is otherwise a courteous and civil gentleman, has tried to draw people to popery'.[24] In the parliament of 1641, for instance, Lord Maguire from Fermanagh and Lord Strabane, sat in the House of Lords and the Ulster MPs in the Commons included Sir Phelim O'Neill from Tyrone and Philip O'Reilly from Cavan.[25] At a lower political level these men also exercised local positions of power. Both O'Neill and O'Reilly were justices of the peace and both would have had to deal with local Protestant gentry through the local institutions of law, such as the assizes. At this political level there were possibilities of slights from those whose anti-Catholicism could be thinly veiled. Brian Crossagh O'Neill, who was granted land in the plantation and was involved in the abortive plot of 1615, seems to have become attracted to the conspiracy because he was snubbed at the assizes at Dungannon in 1614 by a Dublin judge who 'was ready to revile me like a churl' rather than the landed gentleman he perceived himself to be.[26] Again Hugh MacMahon, one of the justices of the peace for Monaghan and a substantial landowner, became involved in the 1641 rising because, as he expressed it, one Fermanagh settler 'gave him [MacMahon] not the right hand of friendship at the assize, he being also in the commission of the peace with him' and described the settler as 'proud and haughty'.[27]

Further down the social hierarchy it is more difficult to describe the reaction of Ulster Catholics to the Protestant state, mainly because confessional allegiance was rarely recorded. However, if a tenuous link can be made between those with native Irish names and Catholicism, then there appears to have been a fairly active engagement with the institution of the new state with few problems. Examples of such men can be briefly glimpsed as local administrative officials. Cormac MacDonnell of Lisnaskea, for instance, was sheriff's bailiff for Fermanagh in 1641 and others fulfilled minor offices such as that of sub sheriff. Others might act as tithe proctors for the Church of Ireland clergy. Indeed one of the reasons why the local government in Ulster collapsed so quickly in the wake of the 1641 rising was the defection of so many minor, yet essential, officials who were Catholic native Irish.[28] Again the involvement of the apparently Catholic Irish is clear in the summonister rolls that record fines levied on large numbers of individuals, both native and settlers, as a result of actions at the quarter sessions. These include fines for local misdemeanours (such as ploughing by tail) while whole communities were fined for failing to maintain roads and bridges.[29] Even clearer evidence of the engagement of the Catholic Irish with the law is provided by the few surviving gaol delivery rolls of the assizes from the second decade of the seventeenth century.[30] By this date it appears that the Irish were active players in the legal system both as accused and accuser. As a result the Irish language, for instance, contains a significant number of early seventeenth-century borrowings of legal terminology.[31]

Perhaps most intriguing is the Catholic reaction to the institutions of the Church of Ireland. Clearly where these had an impact on economic life, as with tithes, there were points of contention. However in other contexts reactions might be more ambivalent. As with secular government the holding of local parish office could confer or validate local status in a highly mobile world and hence was often valued. Since local Church of Ireland records for the plantation areas have not survived (or were never kept) it is difficult to be precise about how the Catholic Irish reacted to the civil aspect of the Church of Ireland parish. However, one episode provides an intriguing picture of how confessional relationships may have been integrated into other interests. In the aftermath of an abortive rising in Ulster in 1615 one Cnougher McGilpatrick O'Mullan, a leaseholder from the Haberdasher's Company in Co. Londonderry, gave a deposition about his very marginal involvement in the conspiracy. In the course of the deposition another episode was recounted which appears to have nothing to do with the plot. A dispute between Art McTomlen O'Mullen and Brian McShane O'Mullen became violent and the said Art uttered these speeches to the said Brian saying 'Thou art a churchwarden and yet dost not attend thy office according to thy instructions. Thou had sixteen Masses said in thy house by Gillecome McTeige, abbot, to whom thou gavest a white cow for his service and then relievest the said Gillecome and harbourest him in thy house as well as abroad.'[32]

A good deal of the detail here is vague. The identity of Gillecome McTeige is unclear but he may have been the abbot of the Cistercian house at nearby Coleraine, which had recently been dissolved and he may have been living off local charity. The number of Masses suggests that McTeige may have been invited to fulfil some specific task, such as a request in a will for a specific number of post-mortem Masses. Whatever the problems with the details of this evidence, its main thrust is clear: in the very early stages of the plantation process churchwardens of the established church were not necessarily subscribers to the confession of the established church. This may not be as strange as first appears given that before the canons of 1634 there was no requirement for parochial officials to subscribe to any doctrinal statements. Given the close linkages between parish and society existing before the plantation, it would only be normal that the native population would wish to maintain links with their own parish and to maintain burial and other rights in the parish graveyard. This implies an ability among at least some native Irish to differentiate between the idea of the parish as a building block of local society and the parish as a religious community and to participate in one without the other. At least in the early stages of the plantation the idea of the parish may have provided an area of common ground, in which local identities might have been formed within confessional contexts.

A number of caveats need to be entered around this picture. First, the surviving evidence relates to those who prospered as part of the plantation scheme mainly because they reached accommodations with it. Yet, the evidence appears to suggest that it was only a minority of those Catholics who remained in Ulster, whatever about the views of those who left, that failed to adapt to the new system. The majority of those who stayed in Ulster after 1610 appear to have used the plantation process for their own ends by assimilating or accommodating themselves to the new order. Indeed for some of the leaders of that world the result of their dealings with the new order was such that they felt it worth rising in arms in 1641 to protect their gains, appealing to the king as their protector. By definition little is known about those who refused to be part of the administrative structures. Second, the administrative machine that the plantation process created captured only rather limited slices of day-to-day experience. Again that experience can be shaped by the assumptions that historians have imposed on it. To assume that Catholic–Protestant relations in Ulster were a central issue across the province is to assume that Catholics and Protestants were also spread equally across the province. This was not so and up to 1630 there were some areas of the province untouched by Protestant settlement. The failure of Protestant settlers to dominate Ulster is clear from the lack of settlement in many parts of the province.[33] In a more localised way there emerged on some plantation estates a leasing pattern in which a number of landlords set significant tracts of land to one or more substantial local

Catholic native Irish person who then sub-let it to others. This practice seems to have been common. On the Balfour estate in Fermanagh, for example, a large tract of land was leased to Catholic Irish who sub-let it in the 1630s.[34] Again on the Brownlow estate in north Armagh a rental of 1635 appears to assign a substantial tract of land around the edge of Lough Neagh, which was later to be the core of Irish settlement of this estate, to John and Garret Barry who would appear to have been Catholic Irish.[35] Areas around Arboe also saw little settlement leaving it as a Catholic enclave.

In the early stages of the settlement there was clearly a readjustment of Catholic settlement. In some places where there had been substantial early settlement this sorting-out process made little difference.[36] In other areas it pushed those Irish who had been left on the estates of settlers in the early years of the century on to more marginal land so that by 1660 some 20 per cent of townlands in the core of Ulster in north Armagh and east Londonderry had no Irish while at the edge of the province only 5–10 per cent can be so described.[37] However, few areas were exclusively Irish and on the Balfour estate, for instance, even in the areas that were dominated by Catholic Irish there were always some intermixed settlers.[38] There are hints, though little more than that, that the confessional boundaries in Plantation Ulster were remarkably porous. Intermarriage, for instance, appears to have been common, indeed so commonplace that it was often not worth mentioning.[39] Again one settler, a tenant to the Catholic Sir Phelim O'Neill, in the early months of the rising of 1641 almost nostalgically recalled that before the rising the natives and newcomers 'differed not in anything ... save only that the Irish went to Mass and the English to the Protestant Church'.[40] In short, the situation might be described as one of rough toleration, in which everyday life was enfolding in a confessional context which might at some points be activated and at other points not as the mix of political, economic and religious sensibilities altered.

In the 1640s the boundaries between Catholic and Protestant in Ulster would thicken considerably. Following the outbreak of hostilities in 1641 fear, instability and violence (both rumoured and real) led to confessional communities turning inward and using markers of belief to protect themselves from others and to invoke divine assistance against the heretic.[41] Thus in 1642 one woman in Armagh claimed that 'Protestants ... were no Christians but those that were christened at Mass were Christians and that the Protestants should be christened over again at Mass before they could be Christians' and in other parts of Ulster attendance at Mass was regarded as a precondition for protection or restoration of goods.[42] Catholicism had become a potent marker of belonging. Symbols of Protestantism, such as bibles were attacked and Protestant corpses disinterred as pollutants in churchyards.[43] The rough tolerance that had been developed in the early seventeenth century fragmented leaving a 'black legend' of massacre and distrust that would characterise future Protestant–Catholic relations in Ulster.

Notes

1 J. O'Donovan (ed.), *Annalá Ríoghachta Éireann: Annals of the Kingdom of Ireland by the Four Masters* 7 vols (Dublin: Hodges, Smith and Co. 1851), vi, pp. 2362–3.
2 W. Gillies, 'A poem on the downfall of the Gaoidhil', *Éigse*, 14 (1969–70), pp. 203–9.
3 G. Hill, *An Historical Account of the Plantation in Ulster* (Belfast: M'Caw, Stevenson and Orr, 1877), p. 83.
4 V. Treadwell (ed.), *The Irish Commission of 1622* (Dublin: Irish Manuscripts Commission, 2006), p. 504.
5 Hill, *Historical Account*, p. 83.
6 Treadwell (ed.), *The Irish Commission*, p. 504.
7 R. Gillespie, *Colonial Ulster: The Settlement of East Ulster 1600–41* (Cork: Cork University Press, 1985), pp. 86–9, 92, 145.
8 J. Ohlmeyer, *Civil War and Restoration in the Three Stuart Kingdoms* (Cambridge: Cambridge University Press, 1993), pp. 23–9.
9 Treadwell (ed.), *The Irish Commission*, p. 608.
10 M. Perceval-Maxwell, *The Scottish Migration to Ulster in the Reign of James I* (London: Routledge, 1973), pp. 325–7.
11 *Calendar of State Papers Ireland (Cal. SP Ire), 1625–32*, p. 509.
12 R. Gillespie, *Seventeenth Century Ireland* (Dublin: Gill and Macmillan, 2006), pp. 79–82; Aidan Clarke, *The Old English in Ireland, 1625–42* (London: MacGibbon and Kee, 1966), p. 236.
13 David Edwards, 'A haven of popery: English Catholic migration to Ireland in the age of plantations', in Alan Ford and J. McCafferty (eds), *The Origins of Sectarianism in Early Modern Ireland* (Cambridge: Cambridge University Press, 2005), pp. 118–19.
14 Treadwell (ed.), *The Irish Commission*, pp. 157–8, 162, 179–80, 609.
15 T. W. Moody, 'The treatment of the native population under the scheme for the plantation of Ulster', *Irish Historical Studies*, 1 (1938–39), pp. 59–63.
16 Brian Mac Cuarta, *Catholic Revival in the North of Ireland, 1603–41* (Dublin: Four Courts Press, 2007), pp. 37–70.
17 M. Krasnodębska-D'Aughton, 'Franciscan chalices, 1600–50', in E. Bhreathnach, J. MacMahon and J. McCafferty (eds), *The Irish Franciscans, 1534–1990* (Dublin: Four Courts Press, 2009), p. 286.
18 For details of this reconstruction, see Mac Cuarta, *Catholic Revival*, pp. 93–130.

19 R. Gillespie, *Devoted People: Belief and Religion in Early Modern Ireland* (Manchester: Manchester University Press, 1995), pp. 51, 72–3, 91; R. Gillespie, 'Devotional landscapes: God, saints and the natural world in early modern Ireland', in P. Clarke and T. Claydon (eds), *Gods Bounty? The Churches and the Natural World.* Studies in Church History 46 (Woodbridge: Ecclesiastical History Society, 2010), pp. 217–36.
20 C. Mooney (ed.), 'Topographical fragments from the Franciscan library', *Celtica*, 1 (1946–47), pp. 65–7.
21 Bernadette Cunningham and Raymond Gillespie, 'The Lough Derg pilgrimage in the age of Counter-Reformation', *Eire Ireland*, 39 (2004), pp. 167–9.
22 British Library, Sloane MS 3567 (1664–65), Egerton MS 196 (1688) and possibly Royal Irish Academy, MS 24 L 28 (undated); 23 L 19 (seventeenth century); C iv 1, pp. 497–518 (seventeenth century).
23 Cambridge University Library, Add MS 4205, ff 3–90v.
24 *Cal. SP Ire*, 1625–32, p. 512.
25 For other Ulster Catholic MPs, see Clarke, *Old English*, pp. 256, 259.
26 R. Gillespie, *Conspiracy: Ulster Plots and Plotters in 1615* (Belfast: Institute of Irish Studies, 1987), pp. 32–3.
27 Raymond Gillespie, 'The murder of Arthur Champion', *Clogher Record*, 14 (1991–93), pp. 58–9.
28 Gillespie, 'Murder of Arthur Champion', p. 53; Raymond Gillespie, 'Destabilising Ulster, 1641–44', Brian Mac Cuarta (ed.), *Ulster 1641* (Belfast: Institute of Irish Studies, 1993), pp. 107–10.
29 Public Record Office of Northern Ireland, T/808/ 15090, 15120, 15126, 15130–5, 15139.
30 J. F. Ferguson (ed.), 'The Ulster roll of gaol delivery', *Ulster Journal of Archaeology*, 1st ser. 1 (1853), pp. 260–70, 2 (1854), pp. 25–9; R. M. Young (ed.), *Historical Notices of Old Belfast* (Belfast: M. Ward and Co. 1896), pp. 30–39.
31 For this wider context of legal borrowings, see Liam Mac Mathúna, *Béarla sa Ghaeilge* (Dublin, An Clóchomhar Tta, 2007), pp. 89–128.
32 *Cal. SP Ire*, 1615–25, pp. 54–5.
33 P. Robinson, *The Plantation of Ulster: British Settlement in an Irish Landscape, 1600–1670* (Dublin: Gill and Macmillan, 1984), maps on pp. 93, 94, 98.
34 J. Johnston, 'Settlement of a plantation estate: the Balfour rentals of 1632 and 1636', *Clogher Record*, 12 (1985–87), pp. 97–8.
35 R. Gillespie (ed.), *Settlement and Survival on an Ulster Estate: the Brownlow Leasebook 1667–1711* (Belfast: Public Record Office of Northern Ireland, 1988), p. 152.
36 Robinson, *Plantation of Ulster*, pp. 102–3.
37 W. J. Smyth, *Map-Making, Landscapes and Memory: A Geography of Colonial and Early Modern Ireland* (Cork: Cork University Press, 2006), p. 350.
38 Johnston, 'Settlement of a plantation estate', pp. 98, 99, 102, 105, 109.

39 Mac Cuarta, *Catholic Revival*, p. 130.
40 TCD, MS 836, f. 172.
41 Gillespie, 'Destabilising Ulster, 1641–42', pp. 107–22.
42 TCD, MS 836, f. 40v.
43 Gillespie, 'Destabilising Ulster, 1641–42', pp. 115–16.

Part III

Identity formation in the seventeenth and eighteenth centuries

8

Irish-language sources for Irish Catholic identity since the early modern period: a brief survey

Éamonn Ó Ciardha

The five decades after the 'Flight of the Earls' (1607) witnessed a marked decline in the fortunes of the professional learned classes of poets, scribes, brehons, genealogists and chroniclers. Although the wholesale destruction of manuscripts and the carelessness of subsequent generations have deprived us of much of their *œuvre*, nearly six thousand manuscripts (many of which remain unedited and untranslated) have survived the ravages of time to provide a unique insight into Gaelic Ireland in a period of extraordinary political, socio-economic and cultural change.[1] Prior to the Tudor conquest (1543–1603), the organisation of Irish learning had changed little since the middle ages. In addition to the monastic schools, secular 'academies' of poetry, genealogy, history, medicine and law operated under the control of an *ollamh*, a leading scholar of the highest status. Despite successive Tudor and early Jacobean administration attempts to curb the activities of poets, harpers, rhymers, chroniclers and bards,[2] the large corpus of surviving manuscripts and *duanairí* (poem-books) would suggest that these endeavours proved largely ineffective.[3] Likewise, the position of the *ollamh taoisigh* (chief poet) continued to be maintained across large parts of the island for most of the sixteenth century.[4] Particular learned families remained associated with specific lordships and clans: Mac an Bhaird (Ó Domhnaill), Ó hEódhasa (Mac Uidhir), Ó Gnímh (Ó Néill), Ó Dálaigh (Mac Cárthaigh, Mac Gearailt, Ó Caoimh) and Mac Bruaideadha (Ó Conchobhair).[5] However, prominent poets such as Aonghus Fionn Ó Dálaigh,[6] Godfraidh Fionn Ó Dálaigh,[7] Tadhg Dall Ó hUigínn,[8] Fearghal Óg Mac an Bhaird,[9] Eoghan Rua Mac an Bhaird,[10] Eochaidh Ó hEódhasa[11] and Tadhg Mac Bruaideadha[12] also composed verse for a host of different patrons, both in Ireland and Gaelic Scotland.[13]

The traditional conservatism of the literati and their poetic art, as manifest in their adherence to strict, conservative metres, literary motifs, allusions and concepts, often masked their appreciation of, and reaction to, contemporary events. These included the rapid expansion of English power, the onset of the Protestant Reformation and the subsequent introduction of English law, language, dress and manners. Many early seventeenth-century Irish poems and prose works carried a stark message of impending doom and despair at the continual scattering of Ireland's native aristocracy, gentry and clergy, while others bore witness to an emerging cult of loyalty to the house of Stuart.[14] Although the Irish language had still not lost its dominant position in Ireland's literary culture the successive rebellions, confiscations, plantations and emigrations had left the door ajar for rapid Anglicisation.

In spite of this, the country showed a remarkable vitality in poetic and prose composition and scribal activity in Irish and Hiberno-Latin. The Franciscan order, operating from the Irish Counter-Reformation colleges of Louvain, Salamanca and Rome, utilized members of the traditionally learned families such as the Uí Ghnímh,[15] Uí Chléirigh,[16] Uí Eodhasa,[17] Uí Mhaoil Chonaire[18] and Uí Dhuibhgheannáin,[19] in a two-pronged effort to stem the Protestant tide and promote the emerging Catholic nation's literary and religious heritage.[20] Throughout the early modern period a steady stream of confessional and theological works, religious primers, catechisms, grammatical and lexicographical works emanated from these colleges, largely directed towards the clergy as opposed to the largely illiterate laity.[21] They invariably reflected both the continental and native training of many of their authors and drew heavily on contemporary European, Counter-Reformation works.[22,23,24]

Pivotal to these continuing efforts to promote Catholicism, preserve the Irish Catholic nation's literary heritage and cultivate a new, inclusive Irish Catholic nationalist identity was the Four Masters' compilation of *Annála Ríoghachta Éireann* (Annals of the Kingdom of Ireland), assembled with the support of the Franciscan order and bankrolled by Fearghal Ó Gadhra, a Sligo nobleman.[25] Paul Walsh portrayed Micheál Ó Cléirigh, the leading luminary among the quartet as the 'minstrel boy' of later Romantic literature.[26] In fact, Diarmaid Ó Doibhlin suggests that Ó Cléirigh should instead be viewed as a renaissance man going back *ad fontes* (to the sources), and listing these and the time and place where he found them. He did not seek to build a shrine to the past, Roy Foster's 'monument to a dead civilisation', but rather sat down the basic source materials for this new, emerging Ireland.[27]

Seathrún Céitinn's (Geoffrey Keating) *Foras Feasa ar Éirinn* (Foundation of Knowledge on Ireland), another key text in this genre, attacked anti-Irish scribblers such as Giraldus Cambrensis, Edmund Spenser, William Camden, Richard Stanihurst, Edmund Campion, Meredith Hamner, Fynes Moryson who he deemed to be *dall aine-*

olach i dteangaibh na tire (blind and ignorant in the language of the country).[28] This monumental work proved immensely popular, the last 'bestseller' in the European manuscript tradition, the first book of the Old Testament of Irish Catholic nationalism and a key reference work for Irish poets until the nineteenth century.[29] In the *dionbhrollach* (foreword) Céitinn justified his extensive use of poetry, *cnáimh agus smior an tseanchusa* (the bones and marrow of history) as a source for his work, a pronouncement which should not be lost on those who wish to assess the importance of Irish literary sources as a window on early modern Ireland.[30]

The first decades of the seventeenth century also witnessed a proliferation of historical texts, hagiographical works, biographies, diaries and social commentaries. Tadhg Ó Cianáin, author of *Imeacht na nIarlaí* (The Departure of the Earls), accompanied the fugitive earls from Rathmullen to Rome and provides an invaluable eye-witness account of their travels through France, the Spanish Netherlands, Lorraine, the Swiss Confederation and the Papal States to the *Città Eterna*.[31] Lughaigh Ó Cléirigh's *Beatha Aodha Rua Uí Dhomhnaill* (The Life of 'Red' Hugh O'Donnell) comprises a hagiographical, heroic biography of the warrior-prince of Tír Chonaill,[32] while *Cin Lae Uí Mhealláin* (The Diary of Friar Mallon) provides a unique account of the military campaigns of General Eoghan Rua Ó Néill's Ulster army in the 1640s.[33] *Pairlement Chloinne Tomáis* (The Parliament of Clan Thomas), a bitter invective from the learned classes at the effects of the social revolution which occurred in the aftermath of the Cromwellian wars, lambasted Oliver Cromwell as the 'king of Churls' who had established every boor and upstart in the stead of the traditional aristocracy. It proceeded to scurrilously lampoon his main benefactors, the vile progeny of Clan Thomas, who aped the manners, dress and language of the English settlers.[34] In the religious realm the Franciscan Seán Mac Colgáin reinvigorated the cult of Ireland's patron saints Patrick, Brigit and Colum Cille,[35] Seathrún Céitinn penned two key Counter-Reformation tracts on the Mass and mortality,[36] Anthony Gernon wrote on the soul,[37] Bernard Conny on the rule of Saint Francis,[38] while Teabóid Gállduff (Theobald Stapleton) produced an Irish–Latin catechism.[39]

Poetic composition also experienced a general loosening of the traditional metres in the first half of the seventeenth century. The decline of the bardic schools and collapse of the hereditary literary families heralded the arrival of a new literary caste, some of whom sprang from the ranks of the Old English descendants of the original Anglo-Norman colonisers. Seathrún Céitinn,[40] Piaras Feiritéar,[41] Pádraigín Haicéad,[42] Muiris Mac Dháibhí Dubh Mac Gearailt,[43] Dáibhí Ó Bruadair,[44] and the named and anonymous Gaelic Irish authors of five long narrative political poems (subsequently edited by Cecile O'Rahilly),[45] continued the venerable traditions of eulogy and satire. Composing their verse in more popular language and utilising more accessible metres such as the *amhrán* (song) and *caoineadh* (lament) to reach a wider audience, these poets provide authoritative commentary on the state of Ireland, the unprecedented suffering of the Irish, the wars, massacres, transportations and transplantations and noted their effects on the Irish language, aristocracy, gentry and Catholic clergy.

This literature has been edited and translated by a whole coterie of scholars such as Osborne Bergin, Pádraig Breatnach, Eleanor Knott, Sean Mac Airt, Thomas F. O'Rahilly, Paul Walsh and many others.[46] It has also engendered much lively debate in the realms of history and literary criticism, as evidenced in the writings of Brendan Bradshaw,[47] Nicholas Canny,[48] Bernadette Cunningham,[49] Micheál Mac Craith,[50] Michelle O'Riordan,[51] Patricia Palmer[52] and Katharine Simms,[53] and a number of other scholars, too many to list here. Although the Gaelic literati had lost much of their time-honoured social status and political clout, the poet remained one of the great reflectors and moulders of public opinion in Ireland until the close of the eighteenth century. Through the accumulating social, economic and political disasters of Reformation, Tudor centralisation and Anglicisation, the collapse of the Nine Years War (1594–1603), the Flight of the Earls (1607), the Plantation of Ulster (1609), the 1641 Rebellion, the Cromwellian Conquest (1649–58), Caroline Restoration (1660–85) and the Jacobite Wars (1689–91), the poet kept a finger on the pulse of Irish political life and retained his role as political chronicler and conscience of the nation.[54]

Eighteenth-century Irish political poetry has support for the exiled house of Stuart at its core. This is no great surprise, given that Jacobitism remained the ascendant political ideology in Irish Catholic society between the Battle of the Boyne (1690) and the outbreak of the American Revolution (1776) and provides one of the key languages of disaffection throughout the three kingdoms. Irish Jacobitism, like its English and Scottish counterparts, involved far more than a blind loyalty to the house of Stuart. Many Irish Jacobites looked to their exiled king to restore their confiscated lands, reverse the political dominance of Protestantism and to rehabilitate the Catholic Church and the Irish language. The poets tailored Jacobitism to suit their community's particular needs: evoking the Stuart cause to demand the right to bear arms, to inherit lands, to take out leases and vote in elections. Seventeenth-century confiscations and the subsequent political decimation of the Irish Catholic landed interest ensured that the Irish tradition was not characterised by a gentry-led or clan-inspired movement as in England and Scotland. It became closely associated with the surviving Catholic aristocracy at home and abroad, Kevin Whelan's so-called 'underground gentry', as witnessed in the Irish brigades in France and Spain, and among the inhabitants of the Irish continental colleges, and it was vigorously promoted at home by the Catholic clergy and Jacobite literati.[55]

In spite of this, Irish Jacobite poetry, particularly the *aisling* (allegorical vision poem) has often been dismissed as lacking substantive political content, the stylised output of a literary caste. However, careful re-examination and contextualisation shows that it did not flourish in a political vacuum. Compared thematically and ideologically with Scots-Gaelic and English Jacobite writings, and with contemporary Whig and anti-Jacobite rhetoric, Irish poetry showed an astute awareness of the workings of local, British and European politics and their possible ramifications for the Stuart cause. The work of Breandán Ó Buachalla, Micheál Mac Craith, Vincent Morley and Éamonn Ó Ciardha has sought to contextualise this huge corpus of literary material and bring Irish Jacobitism and its vibrant literary culture to a similar level of serious scholarly engagement.[56] Indeed, Ó Buachalla argued that Irish historians have paid too much attention to official state documents to the neglect of literary works, newspapers and ballads. Gearóid Ó Tuathaigh, in turn, takes the view that these poems 'deserve closer scrutiny as they are, in many ways, all that we have of the voice of Gaelic Ireland in the eighteenth and early nineteenth century'.[57] Ó Buachalla's close rereadings and contextualisations have rescued Irish Jacobite poetry and prose from 'Charlie over the Waterism' and the literary nostalgia which plagued it for nearly two hundred years. Unfortunately, the inability of many Irish historians to engage with the massive corpus of source material surveyed in *Aisling Ghéar*, his *magnum opus*, means that the book is more referenced than read.

The Irish literary tradition became even more representative of the greater Gaelic-speaking polity in the eighteenth century and the poet increasingly functioned as the spokesman of his peers. This 'democratisation' has numerous manifestations. Irish poetic culture adopted a toasting and drinking component; poets regularly addressed their verse to Ireland in its various female guises (Róisín, Caitlín, Meadbhín), or to its aristocracy, clergy and people. Moreover, they often based their popular political verse on European dynastic war-news, gleaned from English-language newspapers, thereby acting as the medium for the transmission of European political and military affairs to a monoglot Irish-speaking public. In addition the messianic Jacobite literary tradition regularly sought authority from a popular prophetic, folkloric and pre-'devotional revolution' religious tradition. The dramatic quality of the '*aisling*' resembled an embryonic form of street theatre or the modern '*agallamh beirte*' (dialogue of two), while the convergence of Gaelic elite and folk culture is also borne out by the employment of a more popular metre in contemporary composition and by its survival and widespread transmission in manuscript, folkloric and oral sources. Ó Buachalla utilised his memorable hierarchical analogy of *trí ghluain ó rí go ramhainn* (three generations from a king to a spade) to represent the socio-economic decline (and democratisation) of the Gaelic literati in seventeenth- and eighteenth-century Ireland – from Dáibhí Ó Bruadair through Aogán Ó Rathaille and Séamas Dall Mac Cuarta to the hedge-school masters, scribes and *spailpíní* (casual labourers) Peadar Ó Doirnín, Art Mac Cumhaigh, Seán Ó Tuama and Eoghan Rua Ó Súilleabháin.[58]

Furthermore, Irish poets regularly employed imported English and Scottish Jacobite airs such as 'The White Cockade', 'The King Shall Enjoy His Own Again', 'Bonnie Dundee', 'Charlie Come over the Water' and 'Over the Hills and Far Away'. Wading through dusty manuscripts in the National Library of Ireland, the Royal Irish Academy or any other major collection of eighteenth-century manuscripts in Ireland, Britain, mainland Europe or North America, or perusing the numerous edited volumes of Irish or Scot-Gaelic Jacobite poetry and song, it is easily forgotten that these literary works were not composed as historical source material but for public performance or recitation. In editing two hundred Ulster songs, the Monaghan-born collector, editor and scholar Énrí Ó Muirgheasa rightly remarked that they were not composed for reading but for recital and they are now without their music as a widow is without her husband.[59]

Irish poetry provided the principal medium through which Irish Jacobites could articulate and disseminate their political sentiments with relative impunity. In spite of the allegorical nature of the verse and the protection afforded by the language itself, three poets were prosecuted in the eighteenth century for composing seditious verse, and a number of others expressed fears of prosecution. Like its Scottish and English counterparts, Irish Jacobite poetry operated at two levels, and the educated ear knew exactly who the poet meant when he referred to 'The Blackbird', 'The Shepherd', 'The Little Branch' or 'The White-backed Heifer'. Ó Buachalla has made the same point, noting that while the Jacobite ideology used many media in Britain, in pamphlets, sermons, orations, books, ballads (or indeed through art, iconography, coins, glass and touch-pieces), it manifested itself in Ireland through the exclusive medium of poetry.[60]

The lack of a comprehensive study of the Catholic Church's relationship with the house of Stuart is a yawning chasm in eighteenth-century Irish history. The close ties between Jacobitism and Catholicism had been firmly established at the outset of James II's accession to the throne (1685), not least in consequence of his Declaration of Indulgence (1687) and his restoration of the Irish Catholic episcopate. Immediately after his elevation, James II successfully petitioned Pope Innocent XI for the right to nominate Catholic bishops in his three kingdoms. James retained this right after his flight and he, his wife Mary of Modena (as regent for her son) and the future 'James III' regularly and judiciously exercised their prerogative. Indeed, of the 129 bishops and coadjutors appointed to Irish sees between 1687 and 1765 all but five were chosen by the Stuart king.[61] It is no surprise, therefore, that the Rome-based, *de jure* monarch of the three kingdoms exerted a major influence on the Irish Catholic episcopate and clergy. As a result of this hold, Jacobitism remained relevant for Catholic Ireland. Although the Stuart claimant never got the opportunity to show his appreciation and affection to those Irish who had sacrificed everything in his cause he jealously guarded and regularly exercised his right of episcopal nomination. Rome rarely refused any of his nominees and the Irish Catholic clergy understood that it was to the Stuart court and not the Holy See that episcopal hopefuls had to make their representations. In return for his favour many Irish bishops and clergy such as Sylvester Lloyd, Stephen McEgan and Ambrose O'Connor acted as the eyes and ears of the Stuart king and his allies in Europe, keeping them informed of the strength of the British garrison within Ireland; suggesting ports, towns and regions which would be most accessible and suitable for a Jacobite descent. This commitment, in addition to official Vatican policy, meant that they continued to inculcate a loyalty to the exiled monarchy within their flocks.

The close relationship between Irish Jacobite poets and the Catholic clergy has obvious implications for the links between Jacobitism, Catholicism and the penal laws.[62] Priest-poets such as Liam Inglis, Seán Ó Briain, Conchubhar Ó Briain, Domhnall Ó Colmáin and Uilliam Mac Néill Bhacaigh Ó hIarlaithe promoted the Stuart cause, which remained an intrinsic feature of Irish Catholic nationalist identity until at least 1760. The Catholic Church stepped into the breach created by the effective destruction of the Catholic aristocracy to patronise the Jacobite literati. Poets, for their part, steadfastly supported their exiled king and proscribed church. The church appreciated their loyalty and, as Father Conchubhar Mac Cairteáin recorded in his preface to the unpublished *Agallamh na bhFioraon*, held it to be a 'national' and 'spiritual' duty to patronise the native culture. The Irish Catholic clergy's influence on the main themes and the diffusion of literary output throughout the greater Catholic community had consequence for the popularisation of the sentiments expressed in Irish literature.[63] However, much more work needs to be done to evaluate properly this relationship. A reconsideration of the links between the Irish literati, Catholic clergy and Jacobite ideology might be well served by a quantitative, geographical stocktake of surviving Irish-language manuscripts. This could be conjoined to a comprehensive study of Irish Catholic institutional and clerical links with the exiled court and its ambassadorial networks, and an extensive prosopographical examination of the Irish Catholic episcopate, higher clergy and the chaplaincy of the Irish brigades in the French and Spanish service.

A great deal of archival research, editorial recovery and close literary and antiquarian reading has been completed and much more remains to be done before we can fully evaluate the Irish Jacobite legacy and the relationship between Jacobitism, popular Catholicism and Irish-language literature. Vincent Morley's seminal study of Ireland and the American Revolution has both influenced and supported my own remarks on the Jacobite 'Twilight'.[64] As well as stifling the emergence of a popular Irish Catholic Hanoverian royalism, Jacobitism was crucial to the ease with which American- and French-inspired republicanism penetrated Irish society in the 1790s. Similarly, Ó Tuathaigh's, Ó Buachalla's and Ríonach Uí Ógáin's theses show that a messianic Jacobite residue survived the collapse of United Irish republicanism and manifested itself in the popular cult of Daniel O'Connell.[65]

These relationships merit further investigation, in view of the fact that the long eighteenth century has now reached the 1830s.[66] An examination of the residual Jacobite influence on, and the motivation behind, late-eighteenth and nineteenth-century literature, folklore and antiquarian investigations might also shed light on its political, literary and cultural legacy. This would necessitate a thorough investigation of the published works, writings, manuscripts, airs, libraries and cultural milieux of Charlotte Brooke, her Irish evangelist Muiris Ó Gormáin, his peers and successors Peadar Ó Gealcháin, Nicholas Ó Cearnaigh, Thomas Davis, Emily Lawless, Thomas Moore and James Clarence Mangan, among others. There is obvious scope for comparison with English and Scottish poets and writers such as Samuel Johnson, Robert Burns, James Hogg, Lady Carolina Nairne and Sir Walter Scott, as researches and lively scholarly exchanges in these realms have provided fruitful avenues of scholarly enquiry for scholars of English and Scottish Jacobitism. Even a cursory perusal of Rolf and Magda Loeber's *Guide to Irish Fiction, 1650–1900* raises the subconscious literary spectres of Wild Goose, smuggler, outlaw and ruined Jacobite houses and families – illusive Irish versions of Scott's *Redgauntlet* and *Waverley* or Stevenson's *Master of Ballintrae*.[67] Guy Beiner's groundbreaking intellectual rehabilitation and contextualisation of Irish folk history, memory and antiquarianism and Breandán Mac Suibhne's splendid reconstruction of the fractured political landscape of post-rebellion Ulster from the Gothic writings of John Gamble and Hugh Dorian's *Outer Edge of Ulster* provide obvious templates for such scholarly endeavours.[68]

David Dickson concluded his masterful reappraisal of Jacobitism in eighteenth-century Ireland with a call to investigate the contribution of Munster writers to the shaping of Irish cultural nationalism.[69] The 'Literary Revival' and the foundation of the Irish National Theatre and Conradh na Gaeilge support his call as does Stalin's truism that writers are the engineers of men's souls. No serious scholar would recruit William Butler Yeats for the Jacobite cause (much less Jonathan Swift,[70] George Berkeley,[71] Seamus Heaney[72] or, more recently, Liam Mac Cóil)[73] although Yates did attend Charles Edward's centenary requiem Mass in 1888, flirted briefly with the White Rose Society and drew inspiration from the 'Wild Geese', 'Red Hanrahan's daughter' and the doleful laments of Aogán Ó Rathaille.[74] Dubhghlas de hÍde, founder of *An Conradh* and first president of Ireland, reached back to the Jacobite literary tradition for his nom de plume, *An Craoibhín Aoibhinn*, as did Pádraig Ó Siochfhradha, *An Seabhac*, another leading 'engineer' of Irish cultural nationalism.[75] Four of the seven signatories of the 1916 proclamation (Thomas MacDonagh, Seán Mac Diarmada, Éamonn Ceannt and Pádraig Mac Piarais) edited and translated Irish Jacobite poetry, which may explain why *Óró 'sé do Bheatha Abhaile*, a repackaged, republicanised Jacobite tune, became the anthem of the Irish Volunteers in 1916.[76]

The 1980s student of eighteenth-century Ireland encountered two different nations. The first was a Protestant nation which survived the trauma of the seventeenth century, marched confidently, if sometimes fitfully, through the eighteenth century before sleepwalking into rebellion at its end. Its Catholic counterpart had been defeated, humiliated and alienated in the same period but remained attached to the Stuarts and looked optimistically to Europe for military succour, in the manner of their royalist predecessors and republican successors. Subsequently fractured between Hanoverian accommodationalists and those seduced by the new republican ideologies of the late eighteenth century, Catholic Ireland became the problem child of the British empire. Indeed the Hanoverian dynasty to which they had never been reconciled, would sacrifice Pitt the Younger and Henry Dundas and defy the 'Iron Duke'

(Wellington) before the laurels of Catholic emancipation, the wages of Union, would be won by Daniel O'Connell, the 'Uncrowned King' and penultimate inheritor of the messianic Stuart mantle. However, the liberator's broken heart would be deposited in Rome, the mausoleum of the exiled Stuarts, after his failure to renegotiate Ireland's relationship with her sister kingdom, a failure which had also dogged James II and rendered Ireland as a fifth wheel in subsequent Jacobite politics. The Young Irelanders, Fenians and Irish Volunteers, the inheritors of Tone's Republican mantle, would repudiate the Stuarts' royalist legacy but not the messianic message with which it had been associated since the early seventeenth century.

Notes

1 The best single survey is B. Ó Buachalla, *Aisling Ghéar: Na Stíobhartaigh agus an t-aos Léinn 1601–1788* (Dublin: An Clóchomhar Tta, 1996). See also B. Ó Cuív, 'The Irish language in the early modern period', in T. W. Moody, F. X. Martin and F. J. Byrne (eds), *A New History of Ireland, III: Early Modern Ireland* (Oxford: Oxford University Press, 1976), pp. 509–42; M. Caball, *Poetry and Politics: Reaction and Continuity in Irish poetry, 1558–1625* (Cork: Cork University Press, 1998).

2 Ó Cuív, 'The Irish language in the early modern period', p. 520; T. Crowley, *The Politics of Language in Ireland, 1366–1922* (London: Routledge, 2000), p. 38.

3 L. McKenna (ed.), *Leabhar Meig Shamhradhain* (Dublin: Dublin Institute for Advanced Studies, 1947); T. Ó Cléirigh, 'A poembook of the O'Donnells', *Éigse*, 1 (1939–40), pp. 51–61, 130–42; L. McKenna (ed.), *The Book of O'Hara, Leabhar Í Eadhra* (Dublin: Dublin Institute for Advanced Studies, 1951); D. Hyde, 'The book of O'Connor Don', *Ériu*, 8 (1916), pp. 78–99; J. Carney (ed.), *Poems on the O'Reillys* (Dublin: Dublin Institute for Advanced Studies, 1950); T. Ó Raghallaigh, 'Seanchus na mBúrcach', *Journal of the Galway Historical and Archaeological Society*, 13 (1924–7), pp. 50–60, 101–38; 14 (1928–29), pp. 30–51, 142–67; J. Carney (ed.), *Poems on the Butlers of Ormond Cahir and Dunboyne, ad 1400–1650* (Dublin: Dublin Institute for Advanced Studies, 1945); A. O'Sullivan and P. Ó Riain (eds), *Poems on the Marcher Lords* (London: Irish Texts Society, 1987); T. Ó Donnchadha (ed.), *Leabhar Cloinne Aodha Buidhe* (Dublin: Oifig an tSoláthair, 1931); S. Mac Airt (ed.), *Leabhar Branach* (Dublin: Dublin Institute for Advanced Studies, 1944); D. Greene (ed.), *Duanaire Mhéig Uidhir: The Poembook of Cúchonnancht Mág Uidhir, Lord of Fermanagh* (Dublin: Dublin Institute for Advanced Studies, 1972).

4 O. Bergin, 'Introduction', in D. Green and F. Kelly, *Irish Bardic Poetry* (Dublin: Dublin Institute for Advanced Studies, 1974), B. Ó Cuív, *The Linguistic Training of the Mediaeval Irish Poet* (Dublin: Dublin Institute for

Advanced Studies, 1983); P. A. Breatnach, 'The chief poet', *Proceedings of the Royal Irish Academy*, 83, c. 3 (1983), pp. 37–79.

5 M. Caball, 'Notes on an Elizabethan Kerry bardic family', *Ériú*, 43 (1992), pp. 177–92.

6 L. McKenna (ed.), *Dánta do chum Aonghus Fionn Ó Dálaigh* (Dublin: Manusel, 1919).

7 L. McKenna, 'Historical poems of Godfraidh Fionn Ó Dálaigh', *Irish Monthly*, 1–5 (1919), pp. 102–7, 160–70, 224–8, 283–6, 341–4, 397–403, 455–9, 509–14, 563–9, 622–6, 679–82.

8 E. Knott (ed.), *The Bardic Poems of Tadhg Dall Ó Huiginn, 1550–1591*, 2 vols (London: Simpkin and Co. 1922, 1926).

9 C. Ó Baoill, 'The Mac An Bhaird family (per. c.1400–1695)', at www.oxforddnb.com/view/article/70043/72771.

10 *Ibid.*

11 M. Caball, 'Eochaidh Ó hEodhusa'; J. McGuire and J. Quinn (eds), *Dictionary of Irish Biography*, 9 vols (Cambridge: Cambridge University Press, 2009), vii, pp. 553–5.

12 V. Morley, 'Tadhg Mac Bruaideadha' (*ibid.*, v, pp. 746–7).

13 Ó Cuív, 'The Irish language in the early modern period'; Ó Buachalla, *Aisling Ghéar*.

14 Caball, *Poetry and Politics*; Ó Buachalla, *Aisling Ghéar*.

15 B. Cunningham and R. Gillespie, 'The east Ulster bardic family of Ó Gnímh', *Éigse*, 20 (1984), pp. 106–14.

16 P. Walsh, 'The O'Clerys of Tir Connell', *Studies: An Irish Quarterly Review*, 24 (1935), pp. 244–62.

17 C. McGrath, 'Í Eodhusa', *Clogher Record*, 2 (1957), pp. 1–19.

18 E. Curtis, 'The O'Maolchonaire family', *Journal of the Galway Historical and Archaeological Society*, 19 (1941), pp. 118–46.

19 P. Walsh, *The Four Masters and Their Work* (Dublin: Sign of the Three Candles, 1944).

20 J. J. Silke, 'The Irish abroad, 1534–1691', in Moody *et al.* (eds), *New History of Ireland, III*, pp. 587–632; M. MacCraith, 'Printing in the vernacular: the Louvain project', B. Kelly and É. Ó Ciardha (eds), *History Ireland*, 15:4 (2007), pp. 27–32.

21 Silke, 'The Irish abroad, 1534–1691', *New History of Ireland, III*, pp. 587–632; B. Millet, 'Irish literature in Latin, 1550–1700' (*ibid.*, pp. 561–86); M. Mac Craith, 'The Louvain book initiative: manuscript into print', in É. Ó Ciardha, F. Sewell and A. Titley (eds), *The Oxford History of the Irish Book: The Printed Book in Irish since 1567* (Oxford: Oxford University Press, forthcoming).

22 B. Ó hEodhasa, *An Teagasc Criosdaidhe* (Antwerp: Iacobum Mefium, 1611).

23 A. Mac Aingil, *Scáthán Shacramuinte na Haithridhe* (Louvain, 1618); C. O Maonaigh (ed.), *Scáthán Shacramuinte na hAithridhe* (Dublin: Dublin Institute for Advanced Studies, 1952).

24 T. F. O'Rahilly (ed.), *Desiderius, Otherwise Called Sgáthán an Chrábhaidh by Flaithrí Ó Maolchonaire* (Dublin: Stationery Office, 1941); Mac Craith, 'The Louvain book initiative: manuscript into print'; B. Hazard, *Faith and Patronage: The Political Career of Flaithrí Ó Maolchonaire, c. 1560–1629* (Dublin: Irish Academic Press, 2009).

25 B. Ó Buachalla, '*Annála Ríoghachta Éireann* is *Foras Feasa ar Éirinn*: an comhthéchs comhaimseartha', *Studia Hibernica*, 22–3 (1982–83), pp 59–105; B. Cunningham, 'The making of the Annals of the Four Masters', Ph.D., UCD, 2004; see also Cunningham, *The Annals of the Four Masters* (Dublin: Four Courts Press: 2010).

26 N. Ó Muraíle (ed.), *Irish Leaders and Learning through the Ages, P. Walsh* (Dublin: Four Courts Press, 2003), pp. 350–70.

27 D. Ó Doibhlin, 'The Plantation of Ulster: aspects of Gaelic letters', in É. Ó Ciardha and M. Ó Siochrú (eds), *The Plantation of Ulster; Politics and Ideology* (Manchester: Manchester University Press, 2012).

28 S. Céitinn, *Foras Feasa ar Éirinn*, ed. D. Comyn (London: Irish Texts Society, 1902), i, p. 42.

29 B. Cunningham, *The World of Geoffrey Keating: History, Myth and Religion in Seventeenth-Century Ireland* (Dublin: Four Courts Press 2000; pbk, 2004); P. Ó Riain (ed.), *Geoffrey Keating's Foras Feasa ar Éirinn: Reassessments* (London: Irish Texts Society 2008).

30 'Do bhrígh gurab i nduantaibh atá cnáimh agus smior an tseanchusa, measaim gurab oircheas dam cinneadh mar ughdardhás air, ag tráchtadh ar an seanchus', quoted by C. O'Rahilly (ed.), *Five Seventeenth-Century Political Poems* (Dublin: Dublin Institute for Advanced Studies, 1952), p. vii.

31 N. Ó Muraíle (ed.), *Turas na dTaoiseach nUltach as Éirinn: From Ráth Maoláin to Rome: Tadhg Ó Cianáin's contemporary narrative of the so-called 'Flight of the Earls'* (Rome: Pontifical Irish College, 2007); D. Finnegan, É. Ó Ciardha and M. C. Peters (eds), *The Flight of the Earls/ Imeacht na nIarlaí* (Derry: Guildhall Press, 2010).

32 P. Walsh (ed.), *Beatha Aodha Ruaidh Uí Dhomhnaill*, 2 vols (Dublin: Irish Texts Society, 1948–57).

33 M. Nic Cathmhaoil, 'Cin Lae Uí Mhelláin', *Seanchas Ard Mhacha*, (2006), pp. 35–54.

34 N. J. A. Williams (ed.), *Pairlement Chloinne Tomáis* (Dublin: Dublin Institute for Advanced Studies, 1980).

35 J. Colgan, *Triadis Thaumaturgae, seu Divorum Patricii, Columbae, er Brigidae ... Acta* (Louvain: Cornelium Coenestenium, 1647; repr. with introd. by P. Ó Riain, Dublin: Edmund Burke, 1997); T. O'Donnell, *Father John Colgan OFM, 1592–1658* (Dublin: Assisi Press, 1959).

36 S. Céitinn, *Eochair-Sgiath an Aifrinn*, ed. W. Halliday (Dublin: P. O'Brien, 1898); S. Céitinn, *Trí Bíor-ghaoithe an Bháis*, ed. O. Bergin, 2nd edn (Dublin: Royal Irish Academy, 1931).

37 A. Gernon, *Parrthas an Anma* (Louvain: [s. n.] 1645), ed. A. Ó Fachtna (Dublin: Dublin Institute for Advanced Studies, 1953).

38 B. Conny, *Riaghuil Threas Uird S. Froinsias* (Louvain, 1641 [facs. edn Dublin: Dublin Institute for Advanced Studies, 1953]).
39 T. Gállduff, *Cathechismus* (Brussels, 1639 [facs. edn, Dublin: Stationery Office, 1945]).
40 E. Mac Giolla Eáin, *Dánta, amhráin is caointe Sheathrúin Céitinn* (Dublin: Conradh na Gaedilge, 1900).
41 P. Ua Duinnin (ed.), *Dánta Phiarais Feiritéir* (Dublin: Oifig Díolta Foilseacháin, 1934).
42 M. Ní Cheallacháin (ed.), *Filíocht Phádraigín Haicéad* (Dublin: An Clóchomhar Tta, 1962); M. Hartnett (trans.), *Haiceád* (Oldcastle: Gallery Books, 1993).
43 N. J. A. Williams (ed.), *Dánta Mhuiris Mhic Dháibhí Dhuibh Mhic Gearailt* (Dublin: An Clóchomhar Tta, 1979).
44 J. MacErlean (ed.), *Duanaire Dháibhidh Uí Bhruadair*, 3 vols (London: Irish Texts Society, 1910, 1913, 1917).
45 O'Rahilly (ed.), *Five Seventeenth-Century Poems*.
46 See Ó Buachalla, *Aisling Ghéar*, bibliography.
47 B. Bradshaw, 'Native reaction to the westward enterprise: a case study in Gaelic ideology', in K. Andrews, N. Canny and P. Hair (eds), *The Westward Enterprise: English Activities in Ireland, the Atlantic and America, 1480–1650* (Liverpool: Liverpool University Press, 1978), pp. 65–80; B. Bradshaw, 'The bardic response to conquest and colonisation', *Bullán*, 1(1) (1994), pp. 119–22.
48 N. Canny, 'The formation of the Irish mind: Religion, politics and Gaelic Irish literature, 1580–1750', *Past and Present*, 45 (1982), pp. 91–116.
49 B. Cunningham, 'Native culture and political change in Ireland, 1580–1625', in C. Brady and R. Gillespie (eds), *Natives and Newcomers* (Dublin: Irish Academic Press, 1986), pp. 148–70.
50 M. Mac Craith, *Lorg na hIasachta agus Litríocht na* Gaeilge (Dublin: An Clóchomhar Tta, 1989).
51 M. O'Riordan, *The Gaelic Mind and the Collapse of the Gaelic World* (Cork: Cork University Press, 1991); M. Caball, 'The Gaelic mind and the collapse of the Gaelic world: an appraisal', *Cambridge Medieval Celtic Studies*, 25 (1993), pp. 87–96; B. Ó Buachalla, Poetry and politics in early modern Ireland', *Eighteenth-Century Ireland*, 7 (1992), pp. 149–75.
52 Palmer, Patricia, *Language and Conquest in Early Modern Ireland* (Cambridge: Cambridge University Press, 2001).
53 K. Simms, 'Bardic poetry as a historical source', in T. Dunne (ed.), *Writer as Witness: Literature as Historical Evidence* (Cork: Cork University Press, 1987), pp. 58–75; K. Simms, *From Kings to Warlords* (Woodbridge: Boydell, 1987).
54 B. Ó Buachalla, 'Anocht is uaigneach Éire', *History Ireland*, 15(4) (Jul.–Aug. 2007), pp. 32–4; M. Caball, 'Dispossession and reaction: the Gaelic literati and the Plantation of Ulster', *History Ireland: Ulster Plantation, Special Issue* (Nov.–Dec. 2009), pp. 24–8.

55 K. Whelan, 'An underground gentry? Catholic middlemen in eighteenth-century Ireland', in J. Donnelly and K. Miller (eds), *Irish Popular Culture, 1650–1850* (Dublin: Irish Academic Press, 1998), pp. 118–73.

56 Ó Buachalla, *Aisling Ghéar*; V. Morley, 'Idé-eolaíocht an tSeacaibíteachas in Éirinn agus in Albain', *Oghma*, 9 (1997), pp. 14–24; V. Morley, 'Catholic disaffection and the oath of allegiance of 1774', in J. Kelly, J. McCafferty and C. McGrath (eds), *People, Politics and Power: Essays on Irish History 1660–1850 in Honour of James I. McGuire* (Dublin: University College Dublin Press, 2009), pp. 122–43; V. Morley, 'The idea of Britain in eighteenth-century Ireland and Scotland', *Studia Hibernica*, 33 (2004–05); M. Mac Craith, 'Filíocht Sheacaibíteachas na Gaeilge: ionar gan uaim?', *Eighteenth-Century Ireland*, 9 (1994), pp. 57–75; Mac Craith, 'Review article, Breandán Ó Buachalla, Aisling Ghéar: Na Stíobhartaigh agus an tAos Léinn, 1603–1778', *Eighteenth-Century Ireland*, 13 (1998), pp. 166–71; É. Ó Ciardha, *Ireland and the Jacobite Cause, 1685–1766: A Fatal Attachment* (Dublin: Four Courts Press, 2002).

57 G. Ó Tuathaigh, 'Gaelic Ireland, popular politics and Daniel O'Connell', *Journal of the Galway Historical and Archaeological Society*, 34 (1974–75), p. 29.

58 B. Ó Buachalla (ed.), *Peadar Ó Doirnín: Amhráin* (Dublin: An Clóchomhar, 1970), p. 25.

59 'Chan le h-aghaidh léightheoireachta act le h-aghaidh ceoltóireachta a cumadh na h-amhráin seo, agus níl ionnta mar tá siad annseo ná fochla gan na fuinn- ach mar bheadh baintreabhach ann a mbéadh a céile pósta caillte aicí', E. Ó Muirgheasa (ed.), *Dhá chéad de cheoltaibh Uladh* (Dublin: Oifigan tSoláthait, 1974), réamhra.

60 'Ní hionadh sin freisin, mar bíodh gur saothraíodh an reitric Sheacaibíteach i bhfoirmeacha difriúla (paimfléid, seanmóirí, óráideanna, leabhair, bailéid etc.) sa Bhreatain; in Éirinn bhí an reitric sin taobh, ar an mhórgóir, le haon mhéan amháin – véarsaíocht', Ó Buachalla, *Aisling Ghéar*, p. 333.

61 C. Giblin, 'The Stuart nomination of Irish bishops, 1685–1765', *Irish Ecclesiastical Record*, 55 (1966), pp. 35–47.

62 T. Ó Fiaich, 'Irish poetry and the clergy', *Leachtaí Cholmcille*, 4 (1975), pp. 30–56; A. Heussaff, *Filí agus cléir san Ochtú hAois Déag* (Dublin: An Clóchomhar Tta, 1993).

63 C. Mac Cairteáin, 'Preface to Agallamh na bhfíoraon', *Irisleabhar Muighe Nuadhad*, 5 (1913), p. 35.

64 Ó Ciarhda, *Ireland and the Jacobite Cause*, 'Postscript'. Morley's comprehensive collection of the Irish-language poems of the American Revolution [*Washington i Gceannas a Ríochta* (Dublin: Coiscéim, 2005)] are shining examples of the untold riches which await the intrepid explorer in the unchartered, unedited collections of Irish manuscripts in Ireland, Britain, Europe and North America.

65 B. Ó Buachalla, 'From Jacobite to Jacobin', in T. Bartlett, D. Dickson, D. Keogh, and K. Whelan (eds), *1798: A Bicentenary Perspective* (Dublin:

Four Courts Press, 2003), pp. 75–96; B. Ó Buachalla, *The Crown of Ireland* (Galway: Arlen House, 2006), pp. 36–48; Ó Tuathaigh, 'Gaelic Ireland, popular politics and Daniel O'Connell', pp 21–34; R. Uí Ógáin, *Immortal Dan: Daniel O'Connell in Irish Folklore* (Dublin: Geography Publications, 1995).

66 T. Barnard, 'Farewell to Old Ireland', *Historical Journal*, 34(4) (1993), pp. 309–28.

67 R. and M. Loeber and A. M. Burnham, *A Guide to Irish Fiction, 1650–1900* (Dublin: Four Courts Press, 2006). See also J. M Cahalan, *Great Hatred, Little Room: The Irish Historical Novel* (Syracuse: Syracuse University Press, 1983).

68 G. Beiner, *Irish Folk History and Social Memory* (Madison, WI: University of Wisconsin, 2007); G. Ó Tuathaigh, 'Once upon a time in the west', *Field Day Review*, 4 (2008), pp. 315–25; B. Mac Suibhne, 'Afterworld: the Gothic travels of John Gamble (1770–1831)' (*ibid.*, pp. 63–113). See also L. Ní Dhonnchadha, 'An Míleannachas agus Meisiasachas i Litríocht na Gaeilge Idir 1780–1820', MA dissertation, National University of Ireland Galway, 2005.

69 D. Dickson, 'Jacobitism in eighteenth-century Ireland: a Munster perspective', *Éire-Ireland*, 29(3–4), Fómhar/Geimhreadh /fall/winter (2004), pp. 38–99.

70 I. Campbell-Ross, 'Was Berkeley a Jacobite? Passive obedience revisited', *Eighteenth-Century Ireland*, 20 (2005), pp. 17–30.

71 Ó Ciardha, *Ireland and the Jacobite Cause*, pp. 171–2, 202, 215–16.

72 Like Yeats, Seamus Heaney has also drawn inspiration from the Jacobite canon, as evidenced by his stunning rendition of Ó Rathaille's '*Gile na Gile*', in L. De Paor (ed.), *Leabhar Sheáin Uí Thuama* (Dublin: Coiscéim, 1997), p. 105.

73 L. Mac Cóil, *Fontenoy* (Galway: Leabhar Breae, 2005).

74 It is, therefore, no great surprise that his brief dalliance with the White Rose Society is not addressed in Foster's chapter entitled 'Secret Societies' (R. F. Foster, *W. B. Yeats, A Life, I: The Apprentice Mage, 1865–1914* (Oxford: Oxford University Press, 1997), pp. 89–112).

75 Ó Siochfhradha's cultural milieu could be explored with reference to his extensive library which has recently returned to Coláiste Íde, An Daingean; D. Ní Loinsigh, 'An exploration of the bibliographical legacy of "An Seabhac"', in Ó Ciardha *et al.* (eds), *Oxford History of the Irish Book*.

76 *Abair Ambrán, An Naoú Cló* (Belfast: Comhaltus Uldah, 1984), p. 25.

9

The penal laws against Irish Catholics: were they too good for them?

Thomas Bartlett

I

The question is not entirely facetious. At one time, the penal era of Irish history – roughly 1690 to 1770 – was denounced as a period during which, as an early twentieth-century Irish schoolbook had it, 'Ireland lay in helpless misery, ground down by an inhuman tyranny – the blackest known to history'.[1] During these decades, it was claimed that the Catholic religion was in effect proscribed while Catholic priests were ordered into exile or ruthlessly pursued by 'priest-catchers'. Lay Catholics, for their part, were firmly excluded from any state position or role, denied an education, refused access to the military or legal professions, forced, at death, to divide their estate if they refused to convert to the Established Church and, if gentle-born, stripped of recognition for their status.[2] In the last fifty years, however, this altogether bleak assessment has undergone a fundamental revision.[3] We are now assured that there was no such thing as the 'penal laws', or as contemporaries described them the 'popery laws', thus emphasising their religious rather than punitive motivation. Contrary to what was commonly asserted, there was a genuine interest in converting the 'natives' and the laws should certainly not be seen as being enacted 'in vengeance and in the unbridled licence of triumph'.[4] Furthermore, it would be incorrect to characterise these laws as a constituting a 'system' or 'code', for they were in fact 'a rag-bag of measures enacted piecemeal over almost half a century'.[5] The apparent contradiction between claiming that the penal laws lacked a coherent purpose and that they were genuinely intended to bring about the conversion of Irish Catholics can be explained by emphasising that, at least in the early part of the eighteenth century, there was no consensus among Irish Protestants on what to do about Irish Catholics. Hence, the enactment of different laws at different times in an apparent ad hoc manner – to deal with such matters as education, landowning, military service abroad and Catholic religious themselves

– reflected the pressure exerted by various interests on both sides of the Irish Sea. Those laws that targeted Catholic religious were rarely enforced, were sometimes contradictory of one another and a number of them quickly became a dead letter. Again, the remarkable recovery of the Catholic Church has often been highlighted, especially the stabilisation and improvement of its diocesan and parochial structure. The church and Catholicism, so far from expiring or declining during the period of the so-called penal laws, actually flourished.

Nor was the situation of lay Catholics with money or with land all that disastrous. The emergence of a Catholic middle class much involved in trade and commerce had long been noted.[6] And in order to circumvent the terms of those penal laws aimed at Catholic landowning, the Catholic gentry devised all sorts of survival strategies. These ranged from marriages to wealthy Catholics in adjacent counties, to service in continental armies, to trading alliances with co-religionists on the continent and beyond, to 'collusive discoveries' over illegal land transactions[7] and to lease speculation, thereby ensuring that a 'Catholic interest' in land remained strong and growing. It was during the period of the penal laws that the Catholic 'strong farmer' emerged as a key player in rural Irish politics.

Lastly, we have been urged to remember that the early eighteenth century was a profoundly unequal time everywhere, that 'numbers' barely counted in the reckoning of lawmakers, and that 'penal' legislation against dissenters who refused to embrace the state church was common throughout the Europe of the *ancien régime*. Such religious deviants were viewed as enemies to the constitution, and therefore deservedly faced civil sanctions. Seen in this comparative light, the situation of Irish Catholics may not have been all that bad. The penal laws against English Catholics lasted longer (they were always 'behind' Irish Catholics where repeal of the laws was concerned) and were much tougher – they had to pay a double land tax, for example: while French laws against the Huguenots were quite draconian. Finally, it has been argued that even if there had been no penal laws against Irish Catholics the profile and composition of the governing class in the eighteenth century would not have been much altered. So calamitous had been the collapse in Catholic landholding in the seventeenth century, with the consequent decline in the social and political standing of the Catholic gentry that only a handful of Catholics could have qualified for office or a parliamentary seat in the decades after 1690.[8] All in all, it was quite unwarranted for Irish Catholics to claim that the penal laws were 'unexampled in their inhumanity'[9] or to lay claim to victimhood for having had to endure them.

Such bracing revisionism was a welcome correction to the hyperbole and triumphalism that had accompanied the ending of the penal laws and that had echoed through the nineteenth century and beyond. Statements that Irish Catholics had incurred 'a greater share of insult and oppression that it ever was the lot of any people in any other country to be exposed to' or that 'no other nation in the universe' had had to put up with worse, were bound, especially given the horrors of the twentieth century, to attract a more sober and dispassionate appraisal.[10] So far, so good. And yet, there is still a sense that the full impact of the penal laws has not yet been properly assessed; that in a concern to normalise the penal laws and minimise their impact some unique elements have been ignored or glossed over. Were Irish Catholics' claims to victimhood all that bogus in the 1820s?

II

First, a word on nomenclature. While it is true that Protestants generally, at least until the 1770s, preferred 'popery laws', the term 'penal laws' was not entirely unknown to them, nor was it newly minted in the late eighteenth century.[11] What happened was that while Catholics had generally spoken of 'penal laws' against them or sometimes referred to 'that legislation under which we suffer', by the 1770s 'penal laws' had become common even for those who opposed their relaxation. Already, in the 1760s, the *Freeman's Journal*, no friend to Irish Catholics, had used 'penal laws' and 'popery laws' interchangeably and by the time of the first significant Catholic Relief Act in 1778, 'penal laws' had carried the day against the more offensive 'popery laws'. In any case, anti-Catholic laws in England, for example, along with legislation against Dissenters, Jews and Quakers, were always described as penal laws, and it would have been surprising if this usage had not migrated into Irish public discourse.[12] We may note in passing that by the 1770s a similar retreat from calling Catholics, at least in the public prints and parliamentary debates, 'Papists', or Romanists, and citing Catholicism itself as 'popery' was also under way. Whether any or all of this indicated a change in attitude on the part of Irish Protestants towards the penal laws, or indeed towards Irish Catholics, is a moot point. The inspiration for the Catholic Relief Acts of 1778, 1782, 1792 and 1793, which cumulatively dismantled most of the penal laws, came almost entirely from successive British governments, anxious about Britain's standing in the world or fearful of the consequences of Catholic disaffection in Ireland. Left to themselves, it is hard to see Irish (Protestant) politicians making any attempt to set in train the progressive undoing of the penal laws. It was in 1746 that an exasperated lord lieutenant,

Lord Chesterfield, complained that Irish Protestants were 'in general still in the year 1689 and have not shook off any religious or political prejudice that prevailed at that time'.[13] But nearly fifty years later, more or less the same point was being made, this time by Dr James Ryan, a Catholic spokesman. Speaking at a Catholic meeting in Dublin in 1792, he remarked that 'Catholics themselves have felt the influence of time ... They seem to have borrowed the watchword of Protestants of former times; for they are the Whigs of the present day; and this among other things serves to show the mutability of human prejudices and the folly of supposing them to be fixed to an anchor that never shifts its place'.[14] Such admonitions fell, by and large, on deaf ears. In the debates on the proposed Catholic Relief Act of 1793, the redoubtable John Fitzgibbon, after drawing a distinction between the church of Rome (tolerable) and the court of Rome (anything but), went on to claim that 'I am confident that the old Romish superstition is at this hour as rank in Ireland as it was in the year 1641'.[15] And when, following the 1798 rebellion, Union was proposed as the solution to the problem of Anglo-Irish relations, John Foster, speaker of the Irish house of commons and prominent Protestant ascendancy man, declared himself opposed to it. Instructively, he rounded on British politicians for the mess that Ireland was in, and he was not alone in blaming them. He argued that it had been they who had first agitated the Catholic question and then needlessly stirred up the Catholics by promoting Catholic relief measures. He was therefore in no mood to entrust those same politicians with the future welfare of Irish Protestants.[16] Others swore that relaxing the penal laws had allowed the 1798 rebellion to take place: 'how happy was the country while the rod of iron was held over [Irish Catholics]'.[17] It is beyond the scope of this chapter to investigate why many, perhaps most, Irish Protestants continued to defend the penal laws against Irish Catholics in terms that increasingly made little sense at the end of the eighteenth century: but it is a subject worthy of consideration.

On occasion, contemporaries described the penal laws as a 'code of oppression', a 'complete system' or even as a 'machine', but this usage has been challenged on the grounds that they were nothing of the sort.[18] As Sean Connolly remarks 'any suggestion of a coherent code is misleading', and in this he is echoing George Canning who, in the course of a debate on Catholic claims in the united parliament in 1812, urged his audience to 'never let it be forgotten ... that these laws are not one uniform and consistent and permanent code'.[19] The legislative process in Ireland was so complex, lengthy and involved, with direct inputs from the Irish privy council, the English privy council, the lord lieutenant and from individual members of the Irish parliament, that it would have been extremely difficult, even if there had been a desire, to formulate a systematic code of exclusion and penalties.[20] Oddly, what made the penal laws look like a code was the manner of their repeal, for the relief acts always recited a number of laws that were to remain as well as those to be repealed. Thus the Catholic Relief Act of 1778 commended 'papists or persons professing the popish religion ... [for] ... their uniform peaceable behaviour for a long series of years' and went on to allow them to take leases for up to five lives, and to remove the threat of a conforming son 'outing' his father. But these boons were entirely conditional on taking the 1774 oath that required Catholics to renounce allegiance to the Stuarts, to repudiate the pope's temporal authority, and to deny that it was lawful to kill heretics. At the same time the opportunity was taken to confirm that converts to Protestantism were not permitted to allow their children to be educated in the 'popish religion'.[21] The next relief act in 1782 had a similar template.[22] Edmund Burke commented that the act 'as far as it goes is good undoubtedly' and he conceded that 'it amounts, I think, very nearly to a toleration with respect to religious ceremonies'. However, he added, at the same time it put 'a new bolt on Civil Rights' for lay Catholics and riveted their chains afresh. Thus the overall effect of the 1782 act was to dispose 'the penal matter in a more systematic order' and so what ought to have been cast as 'an act of amnesty and indulgence' instead was nothing less than 'a renewd [sic] act of universal, unmitigated, indispensable, exceptionless disqualification'.[23]

The next two relief acts, that of 1792 and the hugely important one of 1793 were little different.[24] The 1792 Relief Act was largely aimed at removing restrictions on Catholics entering the legal profession and setting up schools, but the penalties for Catholic clergy officiating at marriages between Protestants and Catholics were confirmed, and the whole was conditional on taking the 1774 oath. Lastly, as is well known, by the terms of the Relief Act of 1793, Catholics were allowed the parliamentary franchise in the counties on the same terms as Irish Protestants. This was a momentous breakthrough, for it brought Irish Catholics for the first time into the constitution – a position denied their co-religionists in Britain for a further generation. In addition, 'all civil and military offices or places of trust or profit under His Majesty' were to be open to Catholics. However, this seemingly extensive concession was immediately qualified by a lengthy list of offices – from lord lieutenant down to sub-sheriffs of counties – from which Catholics would continue to be excluded. As well, the penalties for any 'popish' priest celebrating marriage between two Protestants, or between a Catholic and a Protestant, were once again confirmed.[25]

Perhaps the most striking aspect of the 1793 act was that the mandatory oath bore only a passing resemblance to the earlier one of 1774. The new test had nothing to say about the Stuarts but it did require the oath-taker to swear that he would 'defend to the utmost of my power' the existing land settlement, to renounce any desire to subvert the Church of Ireland in order to have a Catholic establishment and, further, to deny any intention to 'disturb and weaken the protestant religion and protestant government in this kingdom'. It also had much to say about (alleged) Catholic theology. A Catholic who wished to vote and who had the appropriate property qualification had to swear that 'it is not an article of the Catholic faith' that the pope is infallible, and to deny that he was required to obey 'any order in its own nature immoral' even if the pope commanded it. Moreover, a Catholic had to testify that he did not believe 'that any sin ... can be forgiven at the mere will of the pope or of any priest' and that he accepted that 'sincere sorrow ... a firm and sincere resolution to avoid future guilt and to atone to God are previous and indispensable requisites to establish a well-founded expectation of forgiveness'. To believe otherwise, the oath continued, would be 'violating a sacrament'.

Burke was furious: he roared that Catholics were being required to 'abandon all that they and their ancestors have been taught to believe sacred and to forswear it publicly in terms the most degrading, scurrilous and indecent for men of integrity and virtue and to abuse the whole of their former lives and to slander the education they have received'.[26] In short, as the penal laws were progressively repealed, Catholic anger and outrage very likely mounted, and in the immediate post-Union period the failure to yield 'Catholic emancipation', i.e. the right, if elected, to sit in the united parliament, added to a burning sense of grievance. Ironically, the penal laws may have been more acutely resented *as* they were being repealed and *after* they were repealed than during the period when they were on the statute books.[27]

III

Did numbers really not count? The penal laws against Irish Catholics were enacted in the early eighteenth century, 'a pre-democratic age' when, as Sean Connolly notes, 'numerical strength ... was less important than other considerations'.[28] Hence the claim that they were unique or unparalleled in Europe because they were directed at the vast majority of the Irish population (as much as 80 per cent) has little weight. For most of the eighteenth century 'quality' mattered far more than 'quantity' and while Irish Catholics undoubtedly possessed the latter, they were singularly lacking in the former. In addition, as Ian McBride notes, the 'coercion of large communities of religious dissenters was the norm' throughout Europe of the *ancien régime*, with some two million French Huguenots being subject to harsh penal laws, as were some Protestant communities in Habsburg lands.[29]

These arguments have merit – especially so, when applied to the period before 1750 – but once again they cannot be pushed too far. Protestant defenders of the penal laws were sensitive to the charge that the vast majority of the Irish population lay under a proscription and they were keen to play down the extent of the Catholic numerical superiority. Thus Patrick Duigenan, an anti-Catholic polemicist, protested (admittedly in 1810, a different world) that Irish Catholics were a mere 'faction', comprising far less than the reputed two-thirds of the population though they were 'all the lower orders of society'. Furthermore, 'forty-eight out of forty-nine parts out of the real property and nine out of ten of the personal property was in possession of the Protestants' and therefore Irish Protestants had a prime claim to be styled 'the people and nation of Ireland'.[30] Few others went so far. In general, a ratio of Catholics to Protestants of 2:1 was conceded, though in fact the true proportion was nearer four or five to one.[31] Even at an earlier period when numbers lacked weight, there was marked lack of enthusiasm for investigating the matter further: there were no repeats of the (very imperfect) national religious census of 1732–73, and when Catholics attempted to bring some precision to the question of numbers their efforts were viewed as entirely mischievous (which they undoubtedly were). Thus when Edward Hay, in the aftermath of the recall of the pro-Catholic lord lieutenant, Earl Fitzwilliam, proposed a census of all the denominations on the island, his proposal was viewed with undisguised alarm: his objective, it was claimed, was 'to enforce the power of numbers ... representing the Catholics as the *People* of Ireland and their present political inferiority as tyranny'.[32]

Such sensitivity on the question of the exact proportion of Protestants to Catholics in Ireland was revealing. It was just about possible in the early eighteenth century to defend (or attack) the penal laws without bothering about the relative numerical strengths of Catholic and Protestant, but from the 1750s on it became much more difficult, especially as Irish Catholics, sensing that Irish Protestants were vulnerable on this score, determined to press their claims in terms of their numerical superiority. In his *Tracts Relating to the Popery Laws*, published posthumously but probably written in the mid-1760s, Edmund Burke itemised their 'whole system' and then declared that 'the first and most capital consideration' or objection to them was that they targeted 'no small sect or obscure party, but a very numerous body of men – a body which comprehends at least two-thirds of that whole nation: it amounts to 2,800,000 souls, a number sufficient for the materials constituent of a great people'.[33] Later, under the influence of the French Revolution, Burke, more cautious now, would urge supporters of Irish Catholics' claims to 'avoid the great danger of our time, that of setting up numbers against property' and to remember that while 'numbers ought never to be neglected ... they ought not to predominate'. Even so, he concluded that 'no nation in the world has ever been known to exclude so great a body of men (not born slaves) from the civil state and all the benefits of its constitution'.[34] Others were not so reticent: at the Catholic Convention of 1792, Edward Sweetman exclaimed that 'upon that score [population], it is we that can constitute the national strength and consequence. This country would not have the name of nation but for us'.[35] The Irish Catholics' nemesis, Fitzgibbon, ever watchful and fearful, noted that in 1793 Irish Catholics 'for the first time ... stood upon their numbers and demanded as of right admission into the state'.[36] And when agitation was renewed in the new century for the remaining penal laws to be repealed (especially that an Irish Catholic be allowed to take his seat, if elected, at Westminster) the argument from numbers was central. In 1812, Denys Scully offered his calculation of the respective denominational strengths – about 4.2 million Catholics out of 5 million altogether – and he concluded that these figures proved that 'in fine, the Catholics are THE PEOPLE OF IRELAND'.[37]

Surprisingly, the British government, as it attempted to manage or head off the demand for 'Catholic Emancipation', for a time accepted this argument from numbers. In 1792, Henry Dundas, the British home secretary, explained to Westmorland, the lord lieutenant, that a substantial measure of Catholic relief was necessary because, among other reasons, 'the Roman Catholics form the great body of the inhabitants of the kingdom of Ireland ... [they were] ... the majority of the Irish Nation'. Admittedly, this argument from numbers was soon deployed to explain why full Catholic emancipation simply could *not* be conceded. By 1795, Portland at the home office was pointing to the 'superiority' of Irish Catholics as a prime reason why they could not be allowed to sit in parliament, and this argument was heard well into the nineteenth century. However, the point remains: Catholic numerical superiority was deployed in support of Catholic claims because Catholics believed it gave them the high moral ground, because the British government accepted its validity and because Protestants, despite protestations to the contrary, progressively realised that this argument constituted the Achilles heel of their defence of the penal laws.

IV

'Overall the impact of the Penal laws has been exaggerated': so Louis Cullen concluded following a valuable survey of their enforcement and material effects, together with a consideration of their operation at a regional level.[38] Similarly, Sean Connolly regarded the laws rather as 'a declaration of commitment to Protestant supremacy than as a detailed plan of action'.[39] Catholic landowning, we are told, as a result of the confiscations of the seventeenth century, was already hugely diminished before the advent of the 'penal era'. The further decline of Catholic landowning in the eighteenth century can be attributed to the admission of surviving Catholic landowners into the Church of Ireland rather than to the operation of the penal laws. Interestingly, such conversions were particularly numerous – there were around 4,000 in total recorded – as the penal laws began to be dismantled from the 1770s on. This might suggest that social or political – as well as religious – motives prompted the decision 'to turn', rather than the intolerable pressure of the penal laws. And, as noted above, Catholic gentry families devised various strategies to circumvent the letter of the laws, and Catholic religious practice was little affected. In any case, the 'reach' of the eighteenth-century Irish state was quite limited: it certainly did not have the man-power needed to enforce a large body of complicated legislation enacted against the majority population. As a result, we have been assured, the large majority of the Catholic population passed largely unscathed through the so-called penal era.[40]

There can be little doubt that this was literally the case: but note Burke's telling response to this very point: 'the mildness by which absolute masters exercise their dominion, leaves them masters still'.[41] In any case, perhaps the search for material injury done on a large scale to Catholics, lay and clerical, is mistaken; could the true impact of the penal laws lie in their psychological effects? We can accept that Ireland was part of *ancien régime* Europe: as Connolly writes, 'it was a pre-industrialised society, ruled over by a mainly landed elite in which the vertical ties of patronage and client-ship were more important than horizontal bonds of shared economic and social position'.[42] However, what is missing from this brief description is the place of honour, deference and family in these social relationships, for these were their principal supports. What the penal laws did was to turn 'honour' into disgrace, reduce 'deference' to servility, and seek to undo family ties. As Burke put it, they set up 'pride and dominion' over 'subserviency and contempt' or, as Denys Scully had it: the people were divided into 'two very distinguishable casts [sic] – the Masters and the Vassals'.[43]

In reviewing Catholic writers on the penal laws and pro-Catholic advocates for their repeal it is striking how frequently the language of insult and contempt was deployed. Here the writings of the otherwise comic Sir Richard Musgrave and his circle in England and Ireland are significant for their complete colonisation of anti-Catholic discourse, so that post-1800 the venom directed against Catholics was probably worse than that at the beginning of the penal era.[44] Denys Scully spoke of the 'humiliation of the Catholics', referred to the numerous 'vexations, insults and other mischiefs' to which they were subjected and complained that 'the laws treat the Catholics as a people at once despicable and hateful'. Catholics were regarded as 'an inferior race, unfit for trust or power, marked for the scorn, derision and opprobrium of mankind'. They were denounced, as 'superstitious, idolatrous, faithless, disloyal [and] unprincipled', so much so that even 'the very peasantry feel the stigma cast by government upon their sect and their religion'.[45] John Keogh, a pioneer in the struggle for Catholic rights, put the matter succinctly in 1807: 'Our grievance is that many men beneath us in birth, education, morals and fortune are allowed to trample upon us.'[46] The Catholic petition of 1812 echoed these remarks, pointing to 'the ignominy, insult and humiliation which the Roman Catholics of these realms are now compelled to endure'. Catholic railing against the 'humiliating and ignominious system of exclusion, reproach and suspicion which those [penal] statutes generate and keep alive' was incorporated into their petitions – and note how the very act of signing a petition gave the 'worthless' Irish peasant a standing, a status and even a voice that had heretofore eluded him. We may note that by the early nineteenth century (unlike in the early eighteenth century) there were sufficient prominent wealthy Catholics to feel acutely these slights and these exclusions. Edward Byrne, a leading Catholic activist, paid a reputed £80,000 a year in taxes but yet was dismissed as a '*quondam* grocer', an insult scarcely softened by John Foster's admission that he had relied on Byrne's professional knowledge of Irish trade in his own publications.[47]

Protestant advocates for Catholic emancipation added their voices to those of Catholic protest. Sir Henry Parnell wrote that Catholics have to submit to 'a greater share of insult and of oppression than it ever was the lot of any people in any other country to be exposed to'.[48] And Parnell's brother, William, urged his readers to remember that:

> Catholics can feel and do suffer ... not only a Protestant Lord looks down upon a Catholic Lord, and a Protestant gentleman on a Catholic gentleman, but a Protestant peasant on a Catholic peasant; and in proportion as the degrading scale descends, the expression of contempt becomes more marked and gross.[49]

In order to comprehend the mindset of Irish Catholics in the early eighteenth century, to the insult of the penal laws must be added the injury of Irish history, at least as understood by Irish Catholics. Already in 1747, Dr John Curry, an early Catholic activist, had published a short account of the 1641 rebellion in which he sought to show that the rebellion was not just (or not even) a fiendish attempt to wipe out the Protestants of Ireland.[50] Curry's assault on what was both a foundation myth of Protestant Ireland and a key justification for the penal laws of the eighteenth century swiftly elicited a number of trenchant, even vituperative, replies from Protestant writers. However, Curry was undaunted and in 1775 he published *An Historical and Critical Review of the Civil Wars in Ireland* in which he traced all Ireland's misfortunes to the English invasion in the twelfth century and its subsequent rule ('barren ... barbarous ... bloody') in Ireland. This book was reprinted in 1810 and its editor praised it warmly as having 'effected a revolution in the public mind'. The book was, he advised fellow Catholics, 'your code, your political bible, your magazine of arguments, your depot of authorities [and] your repository of facts'. 'Armed with such a book', he went on, 'the most clamorous of your enemies must be reduced to silence and the most impudent to shame'.[51] With one of the primary justifications for the penal laws – the massacres of 1641 – shown as unfounded (at least to the satisfaction of Irish Catholics), the attack then turned to the Treaty of Limerick and the flagrant breach of its terms that the penal laws allegedly represented. As Sir Henry Parnell put it: 'By the Treaty of Limerick, the free exercise of their religion was guaranteed to them; by the penal laws their chapels are shut up, their priests are banished, and hanged if they return home'. The Treaty of Limerick was claimed as a Magna Carta for Irish Catholics and this made the 'perfidy' of King William and his ministers all the more reprehensible.[52] Lastly, to the broken Treaty of Limerick and the wholesale and pernicious misrepresentation of the events of 1641 should be added the betrayal of what Catholics regarded as a binding Union engagement: Catholic emancipation to follow. As Henry Grattan remarked in a debate on the Catholic claims in 1812, 'without enquiring whether the repeal of Catholic disability was actually promised, it was the expectation of [that] measure which carried the Union'.[53] The failure to 'complete' the Union by giving Irish Catholics the right to sit at Westminster constituted yet another bitter betrayal for Irish Catholics and fed their sense of victimhood.

The Catholic nation that had emerged in Ireland by the 1830s was an aggrieved one: its resentments were grievous and its grievances were numerous. Its historical memory was constructed out of broken promises over Union, betrayals over Limerick and, especially, the galling insults of the penal laws. Schooled in victimhood, learned in resentment, emboldened by survival and thus confident of a heroic future, it was altogether unlikely that this Catholic nation could long rest easy in a Protestant state.[54]

Notes

1 Cited in M. Elliott, *The Catholics of Ulster* (London: Allen Lane, 2000), p. 163.

2 For the fullest and best documented account of the trials of Irish Catholicism in the eighteenth century, see W. P. Burke, *Irish Priests in Penal Times* (1st edn, Waterford: W. P. Burke, 1914; repr. Shannon: Irish University Press, 1968). Burke's work was supplemented by a series of articles by R. Walsh entitled 'Glimpses of the penal times' and published in the *Irish Ecclesiastical Record* between 1906 and 1911.

3 See the excellent survey of the penal laws by I. McBride in his *Eighteenth Century Ireland* (Dublin: Gill and Macmillan, 2009), pp. 194–214. For their impact in one region, see O. P. Rafferty, *Catholicism in Ulster: An Interpretative History, 1603–1983* (Dublin: Gill and Macmillan, 1994), ch. 2. Their religious impact is addressed in N. Yates, *The Religious Condition of Ireland, 1770–1850* (Oxford: Oxford University Press, 2006), pp. 24–31. P. J. Corish, *The Irish Catholic Experience: A Historical Survey* (Dublin: Gill and Macmillan, 1985), ch. 5 'A secret people', is upbeat about the Catholic Church during the eighteenth century.

4 Burke, *Irish Priests*, p. 112.

5 S. J. Connolly, *Religion, Law and Power: The Making of Protestant Ireland, 1660–1760* (Oxford: Oxford University Press, 1992), p. 263.

6 M. Wall, 'The rise of a Catholic middle class in eighteenth century Ireland', *Irish Historical Studies*, 11 (1958), pp. 91–115; David Dickson, 'Catholics and trade in eighteenth century Ireland: an old debate revisited', in T. P. Power and K. Whelan (eds), *Endurance and Emergence: Catholics in Ireland in the Eighteenth Century* (Dublin: Irish Academic Press, 1990), pp. 85–100.

7 'Collusive discoveries' involved those land transactions deemed illegal under the penal laws that were then 'discovered' by friendly searchers and thus rendered immune from further 'hostile' enquiries. At least 90 per cent of the two thousand or so discoveries in the penal era were of this type.

8 Connolly, *Religion, Law and Power*, p. 263.

9 Sir Henry Parnell, *A History of the Penal Laws Against the Irish Catholics* (1st edn, Dublin: Fitzpatrick, 1808; 4th edn, London: Longman, 1825), p. 59 [4th edn].

10 [Denys Scully], *A Statement of the Penal Laws* (Dublin: Fitzpatrick, 1812), p. 190; Parnell, *History of the Penal Laws*, p. 154.

11 Thus Archbishop William King of Dublin flatly denied that there were any real 'penal laws in matters of religion' in force in Ireland since, unlike in

France where Protestantism was outlawed, there were no laws banning the practice of the Catholic religion. Cited in Connolly, *Religion, Law and Power*, p. 263.

12 J. Kelly, 'The historiography of the penal laws', *Eighteenth-Century Ireland, Special Issue 1, New Perspectives on the Penal Laws* (2011), pp. 27–54. I am indebted to Professor Kelly for allowing me to see his essay in advance of publication. It was Burke's first editor, not Burke, who assigned the title 'Tracts Relating to the Popery Laws' to Burke's attack on them. However, it was Burke himself who entitled his second chapter, 'A view of the Penal laws'. See [Edmund Burke], 'Address and Petition of the Irish Catholics', 'Tracts relating to the Popery Laws', in R. B. McDowell (ed.), *The Writings and Speeches of Edmund Burke* (Oxford: Clarendon, 1991), ix, pp. 432, 435. Dr Patrick Duigenan, a Protestant firebrand, as late as 1810 still preferred 'Irish Popery Laws' to penal code or penal laws (Patrick Duigenan, *The Nature and Extent of the Demands of Irish Roman Catholics*, Fully Explained 2nd edn, London: J. J. Stockdale, 1810), p. 213).

13 Kelly, 'Historiography of the penal laws'.

14 Dr James Ryan in *Proceedings of the Catholic Meeting of Dublin ... 31 October 1792 ... with the Letter of the Corporation of Dublin to the Protestants of Ireland* (Dublin: H. Fitzpatrick, 1792), p. 23.

15 *The Speech of ... John Lord Baron Fitzgibbon ... March 12, 1793* (Dublin: T. T. Faulkner, 1793), p. 19. In fairness, we might note that Fitzgibbon's theological distinctions between the court of Rome and the church of Rome would not have seemed bizarre to William Pitt who inquired anxiously about the pope's alleged dispensing power: *Original Papers Relative to the Present Application to the British Parliament of Relief of Roman Catholics in England* (Dublin: William Jones, 1791), pp. 19–20.

16 A. P. W. Malcomson, *John Foster: The Politics of the Anglo-Irish Ascendancy* (Oxford: Oxford University Press, 1978), pp. 65–70.

17 Quoted, T. Bartlett, *The Fall and Rise of the Irish Nation: The Catholic Question 1690–1830* (Dublin: Gill and Macmillan, 1992), p. 243.

18 David Walshe, MP for Fethard spoke of them as 'a code of laws' in 1782, and John Law, bishop of Killala, described them as a 'coercive system' in 1793 (Kelly, 'Historiography'). Edmund Burke to Sir Hercules Langrishe, Feb. 1792, in McDowell (ed.), *Burke: Writings and Speeches*, pp. 616, 637.

19 *Debates in Both Houses of Parliament in April 1812 ... on His Majesty's Roman Catholic Subjects* (London: P. Martin, 1812), p. 456.

20 See especially J. Kelly, *Poynings' Law and the Making of Law in Ireland, 1660–1800* (Dublin: Four Courts Press, 2007); Connolly, *Divided Kingdoms*, pp. 199–203.

21 An Act for the Relief of His Majesty's Subjects of this Kingdom Professing the Popish Religion: 17/18 Geo III chap. xlix.

22 21/22 Geo III chap. xxiv: this act had the same title as the previous one.

23 Burke to Kenmare, 21 Feb. 1782 in McDowell (ed.), *Burke: Writings and Speeches*, pp. 566, 579.

24 32 Geo III chap xx1 and 33 Geo III chap. xxi.

25 The penalties for this 'crime' were removed in 1833 but the marriage was declared null and void. This remained the position until as late as 1870. Corish, *Irish Catholic Experience*, p. 124.

26 Burke to Richard Burke, post 19 Feb. 1792 in McDowell (ed.), *Burke Speeches and Writing*, p. 646. A strong case, based almost exclusively on Gaelic sources, has been made in support of the contention that the penal laws were detested at all levels of Irish society throughout the eighteenth century. See, V. Morley, 'The penal laws in Irish vernacular literature', in 'New perspectives on the penal laws', *Eighteenth-Century Ireland*, Special Issue, 1 (2011), pp. 173–96.

27 See the very elaborate and detailed list of penal laws in [Denys Scully], *A Statement of the Penal Laws*. Scully claimed that even at that late stage Catholics were excluded from over 2,500 corporate offices in Ireland (pp. 95–6).

28 Connolly, *Religion, Law and Power*, p. 260.

29 McBride, *Eighteenth Century Ireland*, p. 203.

30 P. Duigenan, *The Nature and Demands of the Irish Roman Catholics*, pp. 32–3; *Debates in Both Houses of Parliament in April 1812*, pp. 207–8.

31 Connolly, *Religion, Law and Power*, p. 144.

32 Quoted in Bartlett, *Fall and Rise*, p. 206.

33 McDowell (ed.), *Burke: Speeches and Writings*, pp. 452–3.

34 Burke to Langrishe, Feb. 1792, in McDowell (ed.), *Burke: Writings and Speeches*, pp. 628, 635.

35 Sweetman in *Proceedings at the Catholic meeting of Dublin ... 31 October 1792*, p. 28.

36 *Fitzgibbon Speech*, p. 14.

37 Scully, *A Statement*, p. ii (emphasis in original).

38 L. M. Cullen, 'Catholics under the penal laws', *Eighteenth-Century Ireland*, 1 (1986), p. 26.

39 Connolly, *Divided Kingdoms*, p. 203.

40 Connolly, *Religion, Law and Power*, p. 312.

41 McDowell (ed.), *Burke Speeches and Writings*, p. 598.

42 Connolly, *Religion, Law and Power*, p. 2.

43 McDowell (ed.), *Burke: Speeches and Writings*, p. 644: Scully, *Statement*, p. 97.

44 For Musgrave and his friends' domination of anti-Catholic rhetoric in the early decades of the nineteenth century, see James Kelly, *Sir Richard Musgrave: Ultra Protestant Ideologue* (Dublin: Four Courts Press, 2009).

45 Scully, *Statement*, pp. xx, 97, 329, 354, 347.

46 *Sketch of a Speech Delivered by John Keogh Esq at a Meeting of the Catholics of Dublin Held at the Star and Garter, Essex Street, January 24, 1807* (Dublin: H. Fitzpatrick, 1807), p. 10.

47 *Proceedings of the Catholic Meeting...31 October 1792*, p. 48; *A Speech Spoken in the House of Commons of Ireland, February 4, 1793 by Patrick*

Duigenan (Dublin: W. M'Kenzie, 1793), p. 56; *An Accurate Report of the Speech of the Right Honourable John Foster, 27 February 1793* (Dublin: R. Marchbank, 1793), p. 6.

48 Parnell, *History of the Penal Laws*, p. 154.

49 William Parnell, *An Historical Apology for the Irish Catholics* (Dublin: H. Fitzpatrick, 1807), p. 143.

50 J. Curry, *A Brief Account ... of the Irish Rebellion* (London: [s.n.] 1747). Edmund Burke admired this and other works by Curry. For further discussion of the memory of 1641 in the eighteenth century see John Gibney, *The Shadow of a Year: the 1641 Rebellion in Irish History and Memory* (Madison WI: University of Wisconsin Press, 2013), especially chapter 2.

51 J. Curry, *An Historical and Critical Review of the Civil Wars in Ireland* (Dublin: R. Connolly, 1810), Dedication. For Curry, see the article by James Quinn in the *Dictionary of Irish Biography* (Cambridge: Cambridge University Press, 2009).

52 Parnell, *History of the Penal Laws*, pp. 20, 25; see also D. McCartney, 'The writing of Irish history, 1800–30' *Irish Historical Studies*, 10(40) (Sept. 1957), pp. 347–62.

53 Henry Grattan in *Debates in both Houses of Parliament in April 1812*, p. 192.

54 My thanks to James Kelly, Sean Connolly, Daire Keogh, Kevin Whelan and the editor for their comments on this chapter. The usual disclaimer applies.

Part IV

Culture, women and the American diaspora

10

Irish Catholic culture in the nineteenth century: a study in perjury

Owen Dudley Edwards

I

The historian plays at long and short centuries with varying success. The Irish Catholic nineteenth century might seem comfortably to begin on traditional target with the Act of Union of 1800, plus appropriate retroaction from the great Catholic emancipation of 1793, or the averted potentially successful French invasion of 1796, but it would be hard to deny a greater finality than the mid-century Great Famine. Did the century itself end with the self-conscious *fin de siècle* in the 1890s (Catholic poetic revival in England, Catholic political fragmentation in Ireland), or with the First World War, or with the Easter Rising, or with the Anglo-Irish War of 1919–21, or with the Civil War of 1922–23? My generation of schoolboys in the Jesuits' Belvedere College in the 1950s could find a unity with the school described in James Joyce's *A Portrait of the Artist as a Young Man* all the more because none of us would have admitted reading it, with different worlds in the Belvedere before the 1890s and in that after the 1960s. Roy Foster's entrancing *Words Alone* integrates Yeats with the nineteenth century whose inheritance – Catholic, Protestant and pagan – he did so much to enshrine, for all of the twentieth-century credentials appropriate to the editor of the *Oxford Book of Modern Verse*.[1]

Yeats's *protégé* Frank O'Connor (pseudonym of Michael O'Donovan) was defined by Declan Kiberd in the judgement that 'O'Connor's autobiography in Ireland becomes effectively the autobiography *of* Ireland', and his early short stories caress the tough roots of a Catholic Ireland aged but undying in his youth. Thus his 1956 foreword to the Knopf anthology of his *Stories* saw a break between that date and his 1935 story 'In the Train', which 'represents a phase in which I was fumbling for a new style ... very much of its period ... I have not troubled to change it, though today I should write it in a very different way'.[2]

The story's literary value is unquestionable. The historian of Irish literature (and historical novelist of Ireland) Thomas Flanagan judged it 'as fine as any in our literature'. It witnessed an Irish Catholic mind-set surviving from much more than a century before its contemporary setting. If O'Connor spared it the revisions impairing the documentary strength of some of his early stories, his and Hugh Hunt's adaptations of 'In the Train' originally for Abbey Theatre performance on 31 May 1937 provide additional but undestructive dimension.[3]

Michael Steinman, editing O'Connor letters sixty years after 'In the Train', recalled it to show his artistic measure:

> You cannot say that the man who wrote: 'The engine shrieked; the porter slammed the door with a curse; somewhere another door opened and shut, and the row of watchers, frozen into effigies of farewell, now dark now bright, began to glide gently past the window, and the stale, smoky air was charged with the breath of open fields' was indifferent to which word he used, or to the shape of his sentences.[4]

The porter's curse is because the woman acquitted of murder breaks away from the carriage to which he had thrust her, when she sees it contains the police sergeant and his wife, the reader not yet knowing that the train carries rural police because they have been witnesses in a Dublin murder trial. O'Connor in old age remembered Yeats on the play's first night:

> 'O'Connor, you have made a terrible mistake. You should have explained in the first scene that the woman was the murderess. You must never, NEVER, keep a secret from your audience'. He said it in the tone of an American television announcer telling you you may never drive a car without consulting your local agent, but though I fancy I swore under my breath, I know he was right again. Fictional irony and dramatic irony have nothing in common.[5]

The reader of the story may not determine the moment when the woman's crime and guilt are clear, although the sergeant's unpleasantly respectable wife screams a signal: '"Quick! Quick!" she cried. "Look who it is! She's coming in! Jonathan! Jonathan!"'[6] The reader's recognition that the acquittal followed perjury by the country folk is as elusive a moment to pinpoint. Its very uncertainty hardens realisation that none of them would even consider the alternative of telling the truth. Some of her defence witnesses are ready to drive the murderess from the locality when they get back to it; some are not, and despise those who are. Yet she is no friend of any of them, and such good nature as they show her at the end of the train ride is not predictable. But we realise their perjury is predictable.

God is omnipresent in the story, invoked in context after context, yet apparently non-existent on the perjury itself. The state whose law the country folk have circumvented is the Irish Free State ruled by Irish Catholics for the past dozen years, but Munster and Connacht are no readier to obey its dictates about truth-telling in court than under the United Kingdom or its predecessor the Protestant-ruled Kingdom of Ireland.

O'Connor, a Corkman in Dublin, attended a Clarewoman's trial for murdering her husband, during whose recess a friendly prosecutor, Kevin (later Mr Justice) Haugh predicted an acquittal. Haugh made it clear he was convinced of her guilt, but said the neighbours would perjure themselves rather than testify against her. He insisted none of them were her friends, and rumour of a lover made her practically an outcast. O'Connor sat as near the front as he could get (probably in the bench behind counsel, about ten feet from the witness box). When it all ended in acquittal, O'Connor hurried from the courthouse and finished the story in a week.[7] So might a medical specialist have expounded an operation he had witnessed, from his near-perfect knowledge of anatomy. 'In the Train' makes art the conductor of reality. And it implies no hypocrisy in the continual reference to God. There is a theological dissonance as to whether the acquittal is God's work, or man's (especially Moll Mhor's), but nobody sees any serious rift between these instruments. Irish rural speech in the story and in the real life of the previous two centuries implied a continued almost visible presence of God in the lives of all. The story virtually makes public confession of sin before God in Delancey's cry of despair at the sergeant's wife, in Foley's belief he would do her grievous bodily harm were he her husband, in Moll Mhor's contrition for belittling *her* husband, even in Magner's corrupt solicitation of illegally distilled whiskey. Helena's inability to pray for her acquittal for the murder she has committed is a prayer, and clearly a redemptive one in its scruple; and she has prayed afterwards giving thanks for the acquittal she dare not think she deserves. But on the perjury God is not consulted, save in Moll's self-mockery at almost believing the lies with which she above all saved Helena. It is as though God knows that perjury is not his business.

II

The poteen drunk by Moll Mhor and Magner inspires a brief reference to its maker Dan Canty, whom the sergeant declares unconvincingly he will 'get ... yet'. It is in fact an instructive homage to Edith Somerville and (Violet) Martin 'Ross' whose Irish R. M. stories include a resourceful practitioner of this surname and trade.[8] O'Connor's discarded mentor, Daniel Corkery, would have abominated such literary piety, insisting that the 'Big House' could only spawn hopelessly prejudiced evidence. That Somerville and Ross took perjury for granted among the Catholic population was inevitable, so much so that it was used only as a grace-note in one of the finest pieces of vernacular mythologising on the Irish frontier of the English language, 'Lisheen Races, Second-Hand', opening as the R. M. entertains an old and by now pompous college friend intent on writing a novel about Ireland which he is visiting for the first time: 'I took him to hear the prosecution of a publican for selling drink on a Sunday, which gave him the opportunity of studying perjury as a fine art.'

Corkery would certainly have found Edward Carson as untrustworthy a source. Carson told his biographer of an 1883 case where he defended agrarian rebels on a charge of conspiracy to murder, the defence being aided by the prosecutions' chief witness having married and lied about his marriage to get away from it into the army and now telling the court his lie had been honest as he had not kissed the book: 'Can you tell as many lies as you like if you don't kiss the book? – Yes, sir, you can.'

Defence was a 'Tipperary alibi', producing witnesses to prove prosecution witnesses were elsewhere from the scene of the crime they declared they had witnessed. But a defence witness as to the accused's whereabouts was also vulnerable, under cross-examination from The MacDermot QC, as to an earlier statement to police that he had not cut a defendant's hair whereas he now said that he did:

> Was that a lie? – Yes.
> Intentional? – No.
> Did you also tell the police that you did not drink with him at all? – I did.
> Was that a lie? – It was.
> Did you tell that lie on purpose? – Well, I knew it was against the law to drink on Sunday.
> Do you ever tell the truth to the police? – No, I do not.[9]

This seemed almost to treat perjury as a national industry, perhaps with disputed codes. And within the same decade perjury was being churned out wholesale to meet *The Times*'s market for evidence likely to incriminate Parnell and his followers. Historians no less than contemporaries were so fascinated by the rise and fall of the master-perjurer, Richard Pigott, that the lesser fry swore themselves into oblivion, but, however derisory their evidence, its sheer volume invites respect. The perjurers seem to have taken shrewd stock of the market. Evidence to incriminate Parnell and his colleagues and followers was demanded, and standards of provenance were judged not to be high. We cannot gauge the dynamics of market assessment employed by Pigott's minor counterparts, but they began with a very old weapon, rural entrapment of urban sophistication. Individual Irish perjurers doubtless sensed rather than knew that their wealthy victims were exceptionally ripe for taking: *The Times* editor, G. E. Buckle, was a smart Oxford graduate in his twenties, the manager, J. C. Macdonald, was on the verge of septuagenarian senility, the owner, John Walter III, would continue to believe in the genuineness of forgeries by Pigott after Pigott's confession, flight and suicide, the editorial staff was driven by bright young Irish unionists convinced any evidence should incriminate their parents' rebel peasantry, and the Tory government hungered for ammunition whence to deflect Gladstone's return to political power.

The perjurers may have known none of these things, but they could judge the ineptitude of their paymasters from their agents, the solicitors Joseph Soames of London and William Shannon of Dublin, and they were sufficiently skilled in judging landlords by their agents. Carson remembered once cross-examining a farmer about cattle-dealing when his enquiry for the money's receipt was answered by a contemptuous turn of witness to judge 'Yer honour, I wonder if that man was ever in a fair, and did he ever sell cattle'. Neither Soames nor Shannon showed any signs of having sold cattle. Apart from Pigott, several of their witnesses were proved perjurers under cross-examination but many more took a gleeful pleasure in contradicting their earlier depositions in *The Times*'s interest. Some were aware of the peril of social ostracism and perhaps physical injury into which testimony adverse to Parnell and the Land League might throw them, but others made it clear they had played the game for its own sake, at *The Times*'s expense. 'I do not know anything about anybody, and only know about myself', snarled Owen Morgan caught between the two fires of opposing counsel, although the remark was plainly as truthful a statement as he made. 'Who's keeping you now?', asked Frank Lockwood, QC briefed for some of Parnell's followers. 'Do you know or don't you?' 'I suppose *The Times* is keeping me now', nodded Patrick Kennedy, now he came to think of it.[10]

In acknowledging them as perjurers, we do not venture to pronounce – and it is doubtful if anyone ever can – whether they perjured themselves in deposing for *The Times* or in retracting for Parnell, where they were not discredited in the witness box. The point is that they were perjurers and several of them showed forensic, not to say thespian, quality in their court performances. A few years later, Maurice Healy, brother of Parnell's follower and subsequent bitter enemy Tim Healy, had to attend a trial in London before Mr Justice Darling (judge 1897–1923) where Darling sought to overawe an Irish witness: 'Tell me, in your country what happens to a witness who does not tell the truth?', 'Begor, my lord', replied the Irishman with a candour that disarmed all criticism, 'I think his side usually wins'.

Maurice Healy's eponymous barrister son recalled that and a feast of other forensic glories, nonetheless valuable for being hilarious, to make up his immortal *The Old Munster Circuit* (1939), noting fashionable variants in perjury. The 'Kerry alibi', which Westmeath for one sought to appropriate, meant that 'The story was true in every respect except one: the date. The events sworn as having happened on the Tuesday were all true; but they had happened on the Wednesday or on the Monday.'

It is the subversion of the written, or formal, by the oral, or natural: most people remember events from the day of the week, especially in societies where we do this on Monday but that on Tuesday, weekly, whereas the law thinks of the day of the month. A perfectly truthful and very respectable Protestant witness might thus testify in all good faith to support a Catholic perjured alibi. Healy cited one such instance in which an unscrupulous solicitor insisted counsel must ask the witness to recall 'Tuesday, October the 4th' and, after a favourable verdict, it occurred to counsel to check his own diary where he found that the 4th was a Wednesday (or so counsel told the story, avoiding self-incrimination). Healy singled out the Kerry witness as self-conscious performer, analogous to a cricket batsman:

> To attempt to overthrow the testimony of such a highly skilled partisan by the usual 'I-suggest-that-you-are wrong' kind of cross-examination, would be to court disaster ... there would have been an indignant repetition of the question, followed by an immediate turn to the Judge, who would be swamped by a deluge of irrelevant matter, as though it were a complete explanation of the problem under examination; and by the time the witness would be brought back to the point he would have thought of a plausible answer to the actual question being asked.[11]

Protestant comment on Ireland usually blamed the Catholic priests for the mendacity of their flocks, although few openly went as far as the great Orange agitator William Johnston of Ballykilbeg whose novel *Nightshade* (1857) has a confessor demanding silver from a penitent as preliminary to absolving him of a murder before he commits it. The book undoubtedly had a profound influence on one reader, to wit its author, who proclaimed that priests should be prosecuted as accomplices of murder if they heard confessions of suspected murderers and declined (as they must decline) to disclose penitential confidences. Thomas Babington Macaulay in 1827 was mocking the same Protestant bogey as suitable hysteria among clerical opponents of Catholic emancipation:

How Catholics swear as they please
In hope of the priest's absolution.[12]

In fact, what evidence we have suggests that priests varied in opposition to perjury between complacent neutrality, weary indifference, and frustrated fury. Healy's cousin, Alexander Martin Sullivan the younger, recorded the indignation of Denis Kelly, bishop of Ross in south-eastern Cork from 1897:

> Disregard of truth in the witness-box and in the jury-box was widespread and shocking, but what was worse was the fact that nobody regarded it as wrong. When Dr Kelly became bishop he was staggered at a state of affairs which was not peculiar to any dioceses but was characteristic of all. The more scrupulous witnesses avoided kissing the Bible, and kissed their thumbs before giving false testimony; and indeed persons with very tender consciences used ambiguous words or certain set phrases in place of direct lying in plain terms. A pregnant woman always told the truth, so cases dependent on her corroboration were postponed until she was fit for falsehood ... Dr Kelly commenced a crusade ... His neighbour, the Bishop of Cork [Thomas Alphonsus O'Callaghan, bishop 1886–1916], instituted an enquiry among his clergy and was assured that the sin of perjury was unknown in the confessional. As for Dr Kelly's crusade, it created prejudice against him among his own flock. They had never heard such a row over such a trifle; this craving for truth appeared to them to be unorthodox. They wondered if Dr Kelly was a Protestant.[13]

Some other bishops before Kelly and afterwards made perjury a 'reserved' sin for which only the bishop could absolve a penitent. The result was probably that almost no one confessed it, but it would seem very few were likely to do so in any case. Catholic theology has very harsh words and sentences for supposed penitents who withhold one or more sins from the recital they give the priest. But the contrasting yet related experiences of Denis Kelly and Thomas Alphonsus O'Callaghan do not suggest concealment. The historian bereft of the methodology of William Johnston must necessarily dig harder for an explanation.

III

Daniel Corkery, after all, has more uses than inspiring Frank O'Connor (and Sean O'Faolain) first positively and then negatively. Maurice Harmon quotes his *A Munster Twilight* (1916) where the results of Wyndham's Land Purchase Act (1903) are being acknowledged even by the standard hard-bitten ancient to his hopeful son: 'You won't have to face what I had to face, the struggling with landlords, and the law – the law, that would leave a rich man poor and a poor man broken.'[14]

The law is as zealous to array itself in sacred mystification as any other church, and we let it, partly in awe, partly in indolence, partly in ignorance. Above all it likes to imply that societies, peoples, states give themselves their law, and prove their fitness for existence in so doing. The United States of America gave itself law derived and diverged from English law, but such founders as John Adams revolted from British government fired by what they saw as the dictates of law and believed their future must be fulfilled in response to that law. Scotland's place in the United Kingdom was determined by its maintenance of its own law, and today that Union is under strain partly because Scotland's present devolved rulers see the integrity of law under threat from English-induced erosion. Ireland today might tell itself its law derives from English precedent, American constitution, French concordat, in various ways (with very little input pretended for ancient Brehon or other pre-invasion institutions). But the law which held Ireland under the United Kingdom was founded on its predecessor the Kingdom of Ireland. And that law was not only imposed on the majority of the Irish population: its main purpose in the eyes of that majority was to destroy the religious faith by which that majority determined its identity, and because of which it was reduced to subordinate status. Law was not merely alien to the eighteenth-century Irish majority: it was their mortal enemy, temporal and spiritual. It was there to kill what they believed.[15]

The magnificent historiographical work of recent decades, headed by my revered and beloved tutor, the late Maureen Wall, has justly called into question the assumption of ruthless enforcement of the penal laws against Catholics.[16] But what did the Catholics and their heirs think of the penal codes? Captain Caoimhín Ó Danachair (who also wrote as Kevin Danaher) in 'The penal laws and Irish folk tradition' opened up the most intransigent aspect of the matter. His essay, now a half-century old, began on a thesis now more important for his holding of it than for its accuracy. He was a great folklorist holding fruits of vast research acquired under Irish Folklore Commission auspices. Of the penal laws he wrote:

> Even yet ... their influence is clearly observable in many of our institutions. In the past they bore down upon every Catholic, be he peer, priest, peasant or pauper, and darkened every aspect of his life, be it social, economic or religious.
>
> ... The whole period from the middle of the sixteenth to the later nineteenth century appears in folk tradition as the ominous spectre of the 'Bad Times' – 'An Droch-shaol' [literally, 'the bad life'].

Danaher noted that folk tradition:

> does not remember the Laws, as the historian might, as such and such an Act of William III or Anne, or as a particular provision to suppress or discourage this, that or the other.

It did not, but Maureen Wall (a folklorist as well as historian and married to another) told her students how popular tradition named 'the awful acts of Anne' ('poor woman, I suppose she had nothing to do with them'). Danaher summed up: Folk tradition remembers the effects of the laws; it recalls public worship suppressed, education prohibited, property confiscated, social and economic position denied.[17]

Folk tradition was involuntarily more charitable than history in one respect: it shows no knowledge of the vilest acts of the Irish parliament, proposals to brand the breasts of nuns and castrate priests, which the greater humanity of the British parliament vetoed. But folk tradition was busy enough with the horrors of legal hanging, drawing and quartering, for Jacobite tories or highwaymen, although far less (if at all) with legal burning of women in which Irish justice shared. Songs, poems and chap-books helped perpetuate such fates. Folk tradition was little concerned with the motives for the penal laws on which historians have differed so rewardingly, although private vengeance was a favourite motive, as was local greed. W. E. H. Lecky concluded in his *History of Ireland in the Eighteenth Century* (whose generous sympathy for the Catholics and condemnation of his fellow Protestants puts it among the noblest works of history ever written): 'The mass of the people gradually acquired the vices of slaves. They were educated through long generations of oppression into an inveterate hostility to the law, and were taught to look for redress in illegal violence or secret combinations.'

Lecky's great heart spoke through a classic historical discourse, professional in research no less than enlightened in philosophy, but his Irish origins may have given him some awareness of folk tradition (his earliest fruit of Irish observation had been to deplore the mid-nineteenth-century power of Roman Catholic clergy, and he evidently concluded its near stranglehold owed much to its origins in Catholic popular rage at the attempted legal eradication of priesthood):

> In Ireland, except in a few remote districts in the south and west, law was recognised by the Catholic community as a real, powerful, omnipresent agent, immoral, irreligious, and maleficent. All their higher and nobler life lay beyond its pale. Illegal combination was consecrated when it was essential to the performance of religious duty. Illegal violence was the natural protection against immoral laws. Eternal salvation, in the eyes of the great majority of the Irish, could only be obtained by a course of conduct condemned by the law.

Lecky bluntly acknowledged his intellectual debt to folk tradition in a major instance: 'One case of oppression has acquired a great prominence in Irish popular traditions, and it appears indeed to have been exceedingly flagrant'.

Thus he introduced the judicial murder of the priest Nicholas Sheehy in 1766:

> found guilty, hanged and quartered. With his last breath on the scaffold he protested the absolute innocence of the charge for which he suffered ... The circumstances of the trial, and the fact that Sheehy ... was in holy orders, left a deep and lasting resentment in the popular mind. The grave of Sheehy was honoured like that of a saint.[18]

I suspect that Lecky, like his master, Thomas Babington Macaulay, reinforced his researches by fieldwork more than his sophisticated contemporaries' avowed contempt for folklore would permit him to acknowledge. Certainly he captured a local mood whose vigorous survival was attested by Clonmel publication apparently on the appropriate date of 1984 with every page sponsored:

> By means of perjured witnesses and picked juries they finally succeeded in having the innocent Fr. Sheehy convicted of a murder. He was hanged and quartered, his head placed on a spike outside the jail (which occupied the site of the present telephone exchange opposite SS. Peter and Paul's Church).[19]

Saints Peter and Paul had some decades to wait before the law and its consequent socio-economic deprivation would permit the building of their church in the significant proximity of their fellow martyr. The telephone exchange may have been less spiritually inspired in its location, but its citation firmly puts the cult alive in ominously recent times. Modern historians agree that the Sheehy case was famous partly for being exceptional,[20] but folklore feeds on the exceptional. A story of one human being holds memory and imagination where the fate of hundreds merely falls in the scrapbook of economic history. Then the story told can be taken as typical of the sufferings of the faithful, where relevant. Nicholas Sheehy does seem to have been typical in one respect – his courage, impulsiveness, burning concern for humanity, foolhardiness, and implacable readiness to defy fashionable opinion of the day are deeply representative of his (collateral) descendents Fr Eugene Sheehy, Hannah Sheehy-Skeffington, Owen Sheehy-Skeffington and Conor Cruise O'Brien.[21]

The perjury which sealed Nicholas Sheehy's fate invited obvious Catholic replication. This is not to claim it as an example of

Irish Catholic self-instruction on English forensic convention, though some of that no doubt existed, much as in the USA the Irish immigrants were not to pioneer urban machine corruption but rather to inherit, refine and increase it. The Sheehy perjury became famous as a gross abuse, to the horror of civilised commentators such as Sheehy's distant cousin Edmund Burke, whose hatred of the penal laws and abuse of justice for colonial advantage would take him from denunciation of the system in British election speeches to indictment of the judicial murder of Nandakumar in India under Warren Hastings.

The link is the stronger because Burke had sufficient education in Catholic belief to know that the killing of a Catholic priest was a blasphemy to devout Catholics against the sacrificial celebrant in Christ's place very much as Nandakumar's co-religionists must have regarded his martyrdom as a Brahmin. It made Burke vigilant and apprehensive at the first sign of French anti-clericalism in the Revolution of 1789. But to Irish Catholics in general, lacking Burke's regard for the beneficent England of his career, Sheehy's death proclaimed standards prevailing in law to be imitated when laws fell on their heads. They had no reason to respect it: law wanted to kill their faith and showed it by killing their priest three-quarters of a century after the last Stuart claimant to the British Isles had left Ireland. Burke, son of a Catholic mother and a probable convert father, could learn the value of the law which in any case existed to cherish his fellow Anglicans.[22] The Irish Catholics who had not conformed had received at best indirect value from it. The interesting debate as to the 'devotional revolution' in Irish Catholicism is (like the hero of that supposed event, Paul Cardinal Cullen) a little apt to confuse devotion with administration. Devotion cannot be measured: the material artefact and physical exertions from which devotional revolution has been assessed are vulnerable to Our Lord's parable of the Pharisee and the publican, and his admiration for the widow's mite over the proud purses. The Catholics of Nicholas Sheehy's Ireland may have been much more irregular in their Mass attendance than their descendents a century later, but they had made a far greater sacrifice than Cullen's church collections would show: they had sacrificed hope of social advancement and political success by remaining Catholics. They remained not so much outside the law, as against it, knowing it to be the enemy of God. Perjury was an obvious precaution in any entrapment in its diabolical nets. In their belief, God would not take the slightest exception to such conduct for such a reason: he had when on earth been the victim of perjury himself, as popular Gaelic poems reminded reciters and listeners.

IV

Perjury by its nature rejects honesty, whatever its motives, and we can only deduce motivation and rationalisation in most cases. With the somewhat doubtful exception of Whittaker Chambers, perjurers come before us almost invariably as mercenaries, from Titus Oates onwards.[23] The penal code in Ireland, whatever its leniency in operation or lacunae in legislation, invited perjury for moral reasons, arising out of the perjurer's religious fidelity. The mercenary motivation would not work here, since if mercenary enough to swear falsely for gain, the perjurer could save himself from all danger by turning Protestant. Admittedly the pickings from Protestantism might prove ultimately more limited than the convert wished, and hence possible resort to perjury to augment declining income. The witnesses against Nicholas Sheehy seem to have included two if not four converts to Protestantism, as well as two female prostitutes (the piety of certain historians has confused the issue further by calling the converts 'perverts'). The Sheehy case naturally won parallel status with the French Catholic judicial murder of the Protestant Jean Calas in 1762, against which Voltaire fulminated until posthumous vindication of Calas. Thomas Moore certainly gave it a Voltairean epitaph stressing exceptionalism: 'This execution of Father Sheehy was one of those *coups d'état* of the Irish authorities, which they used to perform at stated intervals, and which saved them the trouble of further atrocities for some time to come.'[24]

The French Catholic aristocrat and fellow traveller with de Tocqueville, Gustave de Beaumont took the interesting view that the penal code itself was a form of perjury in its vagaries of practice:

> There is no real difference between direct and indirect persecution; but the first, more open and frank, has fewer chances of being endured, because it is comprehended by all; the second, not being avowed, escapes the numerous multitudes in every country, who only see what is pointed out to them, and comprehend what is told.

Nevertheless the probability is that de Beaumont was told something of the kind himself when touring Ireland with de Tocqueville and interviewing many a Protestant landlord and Catholic bishop in the 1830s.

> Far from admitting that the suspension of bad laws allows some happiness to the people, I say, on the contrary, that bad laws are never so pernicious as when they are dormant. There is no tyranny worse than that which moderates itself to become supportable. A government erected for oppression and which does not oppress, is a deceiver and a liar; it is to be reproached with the additional vice of hypocrisy. If the penal laws against

> the Catholic worship had been so faithfully executed as those of which spoliation was the object, they would have driven the Irish to revolt, who, in vindicating their religion, would have re-conquered their other rights. But it is one of the most dangerous acts of tyranny, to choose among its instruments those which plunder without wounding.

On this logic the penal code taught perjury. 'There is no need of a very deep study of the character and habits of the Irish people to discover that they are often deficient in the most simple notion of good and evil, right and wrong'.

That de Beaumont was a believing Catholic removes the allowance normally requisite for prejudice in any report on the Irish.

> The principal and most cruel tyranny that Ireland has had to endure, was that brought upon it by its creed. Does any one suppose that a man will derive sound notions of rectitude and equity from a government which he sees proscribing the religion which, according to his faith, is the only true mode of adoring God, – when he sees his mode of worshipping his Creator, in his view the first of all duties, raised into a crime; or when he sees his priests, that is to say, the men he venerates as the representatives of God on earth, driven into banishment – when, to hear the last words and the adieus of these proscribed holy men, he is obliged to shroud himself in secrecy and mystery under the most terrible penalties? Thus, in order to practice what is honourable and lawful, it is sometimes necessary to hide from human eyes; these duties are crimes punished by human law. There exist just actions which the law calls crimes, but which are not crimes! – Behold notions of morality which you may be well assured will bear their fruit.

Perjury is the logical consequence. Thus on my reading, perjury was theologically irrelevant in the eyes of Irish Catholics in the long eighteenth century. De Beaumont saw it also as sociologically imperative.

> All lost the love of truth, because frankness and veracity brought down certain persecution on their heads; almost all contracted the habit of lying, because falsehood during a century was a legitimate and necessary weapon. They assumed habit of outrage and insurrection under the influence of a tyranny which drove them into open opposition to the law. Now do not complain, if you find amongst the Irish a general aversion to truth and an absolute love of falsehood. Can the Irishman, gross and ignorant as you have made him, draw with any discretion in his mind the line between the cases in which conscience may pardon a lie and those which it cannot be justified? How is he to distinguish, amongst the crimes established by law, those which are not crimes and those which he should regard as such? How is he to distinguish among the virtues which his enemies honour, those that are real virtues from those dependent on convention and form?[25]

The last was a brilliant originality, sharpened by de Beaumont's nationality, the realisation that the height of bitterness in Irish religious conflict might be mutual incomprehension of manners.

De Beaumont's friend Alexis de Tocqueville took notes on the same journey where he found priests quoted as finding attempts to preach law and order rejected by agrarian rebels:

> a local priest discovered a gang of whitefeet [i.e. Whiteboys, Rockites or Ribbonmen]. He went to meet them and reproached them severely. Their leader, who was an educated man, replied almost word for word as follows: – 'The law does nothing for us. We must save ourselves ... Emancipation has done nothing for us ... We die of starvation just the same'.

De Tocqueville considered the human face of law as Irish Catholics must find it:

> All the rich Protestants whom I saw in Dublin, speak of the Catholics with extraordinary hatred and scorn. The latter, they say, are savages, incapable of recognising a kindness, and fanatics led into all sorts of disorder by their priest. Now these same people who speak thus are those who once controlled the government of the country and who still control part of it. How can people moved by such feelings and imbued with such opinions (rightly or wrongly, I do not know) treat those of whom they speak like that, with gentleness, with trust or even with justice?

De Tocqueville attended the Kilkenny assizes and found perjury in theory and perhaps in practice:

> a farmer dismissed his servant who appeared the next day with a Bible in one hand and a pistol in the other to force him to swear to take him back into his service. If he who has thus sworn, breaks his oath, the other believes him authorised to kill him.
>
> These crimes are very common. There is nothing which better shows the imperfect state of civilisation in Ireland. What a peculiar mixture of religion and villainy; of respect for the sanctity of an oath, which forms the foundation of every society, and of distrust for all the laws of society!
>
> Three witnesses came to prove the alibi of the accused. The general belief was that they foreswore themselves; but a false oath to save a man and to trick a justice which oppresses you and which you detest, is hardly blameworthy any more in the eyes of the population.[26]

De Tocqueville's Irish experience threw a different light on perjury. The oath in the United Kingdom law courts seems to have been what de Valera described as an 'empty formula' when taking the oath to enter Dáil Éireann in 1927 with its requirement to serve the British monarch. He would later demonstrate its emptiness by abolishing it when in power. But at the time he refused to take the oath on the bible, which reminds us of an assumption sometimes mentioned that if the bible must be kissed (as some magistrates or officials required) the intentional perjurer placed the thumb of his hand clutching the bible where he could kiss it while appearing to have his lips touch the bible. Whatever the ethical merits of de Valera's conduct (notably having entered violent rebellion in 1922 for an oath so easily discarded in 1927), his mathematics gave us a useful label for the swearing with intent of perjury. He and his fellow rebels had been excommunicated for defiance of legal authority in 1922, but what in general was Roman Catholic procedure as to perjury at least in theory?

V

The Douay catechism in abstract as used in the UK (in the early nineteenth century) was detailed in many respects but curt on the relevant second commandment (third in Protestant usage):

> The second Commandment
> Q. Say the second.
> A. Thou shalt not take the name of the Lord thy God in vain.
> W. What is forbidden by this?
> A. All false, rash, and unnecessary oaths, cursing, blaspheming, breaking of lawful oaths or vows and making or keeping unlawful ones.
> Q. What is commanded by it?
> A. To speak with reverence of God and his saints.
> Q. In what case is it lawful to swear?
> A. When God's honour, our own or our neighbour's defence requires it.[27]

If terse, it was comprehensive. Its terseness was caused in part by a circumstance ignored by the United Kingdom authorities and their Irish Protestant predecessors. Christianity is in fact hostile to oath-taking, explicitly forbidden by Jesus Christ in the Sermon on the Mount (Matthew 5:34).

Roman Catholic doctrine at least showed awareness of it in contrast to the exploitative pragmatism of the Churches of England, Wales and Ireland, and the Church of Scotland. The magisterium of the Roman Catholic Church seems to have given no clear direction: at any rate some Irish bishops were hostile to oaths of any kind, some not. Bishop James O'Gallagher of Raphoe (1725–37), later of Kildare and Leighlin (1737–51), told his mid-eighteenth-century flocks in sermons studied in both Irish and English for the next century and a half that they should follow Jesus (and indeed the Letter of James 5:12), in rejecting oaths. The maintenance of his cult by his charismatic successor in the latter see, James Doyle (1819–34), kept his brave memory green.[28] As the penal laws were weakened in theory (long after their anaemia in practice), Catholic bishops were invited to swear oaths the force of whose anti-Catholicism much divided them as grounds for acceptance or rejection: but that controversy probably put a thin scab over their conscientious imperatives to follow the general condemnation of oaths by O'Gallagher, who had had the advantage of a price on his head rather than a bribe of emancipation. From O'Gallagher's fugitive apostleship's viewpoint, it was sound politics as well as doctrine to avoid all oath-taking, full of pitfalls for outlaw churchmen in legal practice as well as in theological speculation. Nor was any oath-taking likely save in adverse circumstances. But as Catholic participation in the state increased, Catholic doctrine at least retained austerity. The Douay catechism had given fairly narrow grounds for oath-usage and it might be thought that permission to swear for God's honour and one's own and one's neighbour's defence could mean permissions to swear falsely, if such an oath could save the life of a bishop, or frustrate some legalistic thug (such as Sir Murtagh Rackrent of Maria Edgeworth's *Castle Rackrent* (1800) in his predatory claims on Catholic lands). The catechism did not spell it out but it was well known that oaths exacted under duress did not count and the self-fulfilment of penal laws surely counted as duress. In cold fact, the British state had only itself to thank, but for once it was slow in self-congratulation.[29] Douay was clear enough as to the prohibition of making or keeping 'unlawful' oaths (which very definitely meant unlawful from a Catholic, not from a state, standpoint) and no doubt a Kerry Catholic could justify perjury on the ground that it meant not keeping an unlawful oath from the moment it had been sworn.

Douay, O'Gallagher and company were chiefly concerned by the readiness to call on God to attest to some avowedly trivial matter (which court evidence usually was, but not acknowledged to be). The English 'Goddamn' came to identify that nation.[30] The extent of clerical scrupulous inquiry even went as far as deeming 'bloody' (certainly a forbidden word in polite circles until the mid-twentieth century) a contraction for 'by Our Lady', which syntactically makes little sense. The censorious clerics had the excellent point that profanity was usually induced by snobbishness, the user wanting to appear sophisticated, and sophistication a capitulation to the fashions of a hedonistic state (whose depravity, after all, needed little illustration). Yet on the lowest level of Irish Catholic society (including poets) their Catholic God was a common-sense reference for them, since they were where they were because he had been there too, in his crucifixion. They measured their deprivation by his suffering and felt their superior virtue because of similarities between the Roman rule that crucified him and the British rule that degraded them. 'In the Train' caught it perfectly. The story which so delighted G. K. Chesterton (and Patrick Corish) of the woman at the time of the Eucharistic Congress in Dublin in 1932 who remarked that if it rained he'd have brought it on himself, captured the familiar quality.[31] Strangely, the sense of Jesus not as some supernatural enforcer of state law and order, but as a friend and fellow sufferer in hard times, made for remarkable affinity between Catholics and evangelicals, mutually hostile though they were: each faith wanted its adherents to think of Jesus as a comrade.

William Carleton (1794/8–1869) went from one faith to the other, and if he wisely wrote little about Jesus (neither Catholic nor evangelical clerics cared for lay theologians) he produced the most remarkable reflection on Irish oath-taking of all. As Carleton described it, Irish Catholic perjury had become a sport as well as a lucrative talent with the first third of the nineteenth century. Carleton dissected its professionalisation and acculturation in 'An essay on Irish swearing' (1833), mingling its mildly artificial tone of scientific analysis with his own rich recollections of the rural and urban Ireland through which he had travelled, and of the Tyrone and Monaghan of his youth. More Gibbonian that most of his narrative voices, it marks a self-distancing from the ex-Catholic polemics of the late 1820s with which he began Dublin literary life. His patron, the Revd Caesar Otway (1780–1842), discovered he liked Carleton stories whichever side of the sectarian divide they seemed to favour, if any, while himself abominating Catholicism and cherishing his friendship for his local parish priest.[32] Both men knew that God is truly served in laughter.[33] Like young Maurice Healy a century later, Carleton saw perjury as delicious as it was deplorable:

> Could society hold together a single day, if nothing but truth were *spoken*? Would not law and lawyers soon become obsolete, if nothing but truth were *sworn*? What would become of parliament if truth alone were uttered there? Its annual proceedings might be despatched in a month. Fiction is the basis of society, the bond of commercial prosperity, the channel of communication between nation and nation, and not unfrequently the interpreter between a man and his own conscience.

Carleton had taken up fiction officially to tell the truth about Roman Catholicism, and stayed with it to tell the truth about the Irish people, but the fictionist can only be true if he defends fiction. The English Protestant evangelicals sometimes excluded it from their *Christian Observer*, but their doctrinal sister Hannah More had used it; their Irish brethren had been uneasy about it in their *Christian Examiner*, but

Otway was not, and hence Carleton would not be. After all, Jesus had taught by inventing and telling stories. Carleton (and, it would seem, Otway) relished the ironies:

> For these, and many other reasons which we could adduce, we say with Paddy, 'Long life to fiction!' When associated with swearing it shines in its brightest colours. What, for instance, is calculated to produce the best and purest of the moral virtues so beautifully, as the swearing of an *alibi*? Here are fortitude and love of freedom resisting oppression; for it is well known that all law is oppression in Ireland.

So far, so Catholic, culturally if not theologically. But Carleton's origins in Irish-Gaelic storytelling drew on Irish satire which varied from straightforward malediction (e.g. Seán Clárach Mac Domhnaill, '*Ar Bhás Dawson*') to panegyric ascription to the victim of every virtue for whose contrasting vice he was renowned (e.g. Riocárd Bairéad, '*Eoghan Cóir*'). Swift, who derived Gulliver's travels in part from Gaelic folklore knew how to lull an audience (as a good preacher might) into comfortable assumptions that he was targeting anyone but the listener, only to be rudely woken by the satirical lash whistling at his ear. Carleton (who did not forget his lost vocation for the Catholic priesthood) continued:

> There is compassion for the peculiar state of the poor boy, who, perhaps *only* burned a family in their beds; benevolence to prompt the generous effort in his disinterestedness to run the risk of becoming an involuntary absentee [imprisonment or transportation]; fortitude in encountering a host of brazen-faced lawyers; patience under the unsparing gripe of a cross-examiner; perseverance in conducting the oath to its close against a host of difficulties; and friendship, which bottoms and crowns them all.

He was satirising the defence of the murderous arsonists burning the Lynch family (30 October 1816), whose fate he described in livid horror ('Wildgoose Lodge' *Traits and Stories of the Irish Peasantry* (1833), ii: 'An essay in Irish swearing' first appeared in volume i). The contrast in the tone of these two essays is startling, but Swift would have recognised the changes rung from savage indignation to urbane civility. 'Irish swearing' mocked magistrates and murderers:

> Paddy's merits, however, touching the *alibi*, rest not here. Fiction on these occasions only teaches him how to perform a *duty*. It may be, that he is under the obligation of a previous oath *not* to give evidence *against* certain of his friends and associates. Now, could anything in the whole circle of religion or ethics be conceived that renders the epic style of swearing so incumbent upon Paddy? There is a kind of moral fitness in all things; for where the necessity of invention exists, it is consolatory to reflect that the ability to invent is bestowed along with it.[34]

Ironies apart, this was to point out that perjury in the government courts was of no account (unless they caught you out) but that in inverse proportion oaths within the hidden Ireland were sacrosanct. The murders of Wildgoose Lodge certainly did not enjoy Roman Catholic sanction. The parish priest, Fr Thomas McCann:

> On the Sunday after the burning of the Lynches ... ascended the altar robed in his vestments, and with accents which will never leave my ear, cursed the author, abettor and assistants of the crime! He then came down from the altar, took from his feet his shoes and stockings, desired his congregation to follow him, and he and they went in procession round the chapel, calling aloud to heaven for vengeance on the murderers.

This was the most extreme possible condemnation of sin. But the above account (*The Times*, 27 March 1818) continued:

> Guess who was next the minister of religion in this awful procession? Devan, the clerk! – the planner – the instigator – the mover – the commander in this horrible transaction! And, of the whole congregation, he appeared to be the person who reiterated Amen with the most vehement devotion.[35]

Devan (who admitted his guilt on the scaffold) had made the fullest possible use of his foul cause's Catholic context. As clerk to a church whose priest (serving also in two other parishes) was not resident, he used the building to swear his followers and enjoin the fate intended for their targets upon any who would break that oath by informing the authorities. As the local hedge-schoolmaster, he had the eloquence, the learning and – it is the right word – the mastery to compel the crowd to do their worst. 'Wildgoose Lodge' purported to be the confession of a fellow Ribbonman, agrarian conspirator of an all-Catholic Masonic-style secret society. Carleton had been a Tyrone Ribbonman with little more motivation, one suspects, than to please contemporaries and join a fellowship likely to give insurance in job-finding. He may even have still held such a view when he reached Co. Louth, enquired judiciously about Ribbonmen, and found himself looking at the gibbet on which still hung the corpse of the wretched Devan, opposite his father's door. But he had, like Devan, been a teacher as itinerant 'poor scholar' or tutor rather than a fixed local worthy classically defined in Oliver Goldsmith's *The Deserted Village* (1770) and with a harsher, more brutally scientific realism, in Carleton's own 'The hedge school', as is the profession as he knew it best in the gentler 'The poor scholar'. In his horror at local learning and scholarly status in the service of exceptionally cruel mass murder and oath-bound tyrannical fraternities, he panicked and was persuaded to write to home secretary Robert Peel suspecting literate-led social war in the growing agitation for Catholic emancipation, and to the end of his days was convinced that the hedge-schoolmaster link with agrarian secret societies he learned of in Louth and perhaps Tyrone and Monaghan, was true of all Ireland. Modern historians question this last, but his version of the Wildgoose Lodge atrocity has justly dominated its historiography.[36]

Yet the very Protestant Tories where he found a haven were best able to employ his attempts to arouse Protestant public opinion to it dangers by enabling him to tell his story as stories. His departure from Catholicism cut him off from the sacrament of confession: under Protestantism he had to confess to a print audience and affirm the truth under fictional auspices. An intelligent reader of his *Traits and Stories* should have had little difficulty in recognising the condescension to 'Paddy' (in the essay on Irish swearing) as satirical self-portraiture. But to tell the truth, as he saw it, of agrarian outrage at its worst, he seriously sought to convey as truth a fictional eyewitness identity for himself and, less explicably, recording in a final note a mother suffering her son Paddy Devan's decaying gibbeted corpse outside her door although in fact Devan's mother – fortunately for her – had died before the government answered her son's atrocity with its own official obscenity. And Carleton would have known that for all the cruelty correctly imputed to Devan in the story, and the all too plausible ascription of his mob management, a final note of maternal witness of shameful filial execution would promptly trigger popular Catholic association with Mary's vision of her crucified son Jesus, whether in a conscious reaction or not. 'Wildgoose Lodge' originally appeared as 'Confessions of a reformed Ribbonman' in the *Dublin Literary Gazette, or Weekly Chronicle of Criticism, and Fine Arts*, vol. 1, 4 (23 January 1830) and 5 (30 January 1830).[37]

The oath of the Ribbonmen was shown in a ghastly sanctity driving the story forward through its Stygian location and Gothic convention. Devan ('the Captain' in this text) tells his followers:

> 'Now brothers, you are solemnly sworn to obay me, and I'm sure there's no thrathur here that 'ud perjure himself for a thrifle; but I'm sworn to obay them that's above me, manin' still among ourselves; an' to show you that I don't scruple to do it, here goes!' He then turned round and taking the Missal between his hands placed it upon the altar.

The missal would have been the volume whence the priest read the text of each Mass, with its invariable and its variable words. It would have been regarded as in some degree sacred, certainly not with the awe given to a consecrated host, but revered above all because of its place during Mass in the host's proximity and that of the chalice holding the wine to be consecrated. Certainly a layman could legitimately hold it, and at this date would indeed be expected to, in serving the priest at Mass. Devan undoubtedly did so as part of his clerkly duties. The story went on:

> Hitherto every word was uttered in a low precautionary tone; but on grasping the book, he again turned round, and looking upon his confederates with the same satanic expression which marked his countenance before, he exclaimed, in a voice of deep determination, first kissing the book! 'By this sacred an' holy book of God, I will perform the action which we have met this night to accomplish, be that what it may; an' this I swear upon God's book, an' God's althar'.

VI

But where exactly was God in Patrick Devan's cosmos? There is his probable use of the missal (Carleton's local informants, press reports, etc. may have supplied that or he may have deduced it from his knowledge of Ribbon procedures, alternatives being holy relics, Douay bibles, etc., but it was the obvious requisite instrument available to the parish clerk at the actual meeting on 29 October 1816). We have an extract from one letter and the text of another to his father from Dublin between his murders and his arrest, and these contain natural allusions to God such as Frank O'Connor uses for 'In the Train': 'in employment at present and in hopes of better with the assistance of God. All the news you have sent about me being an informer is false, thanks to God for it.'[38]

With suspicion of his involvement or even leadership of the Wildgoose Lodge horror flying around county Louth, he might find assertion of conventional pieties useful investment especially if he was to need clerical evidence for his defence, should he be arrested. But they do not look contrived, bearing even the schoolmasterly fondness for the polysyllabic word 'assistance' where convention would say 'help'. He was presumably not anticipating that his letter would be read not by his father but by the state authorities (thus enabling them to find him). He would not wish to shock his father by an obviously false use of God's name if it were foreign to their normal speech. We know him to have orchestrated and enforced one of the most evil and cruel actions in Irish history: we have no right to call him a hypocrite unless we can prove he was one. We are a world away form his contemporary Talleyrand, saying Masses with total indifference when a bishop. Devan's secondment of the priest's curse was not hypocrisy in itself: it was simply use of unavoidable requirement for self-protection. But it reduced God to an invisible official requiring job satisfaction by performance.

Yet Carleton's story, and presumably its originating sources, carried a horrifying sense of religion about the atrocity. We must remember that however savage his subsequent break with his cradle Catholicism, Carleton learned of Wildgoose Lodge when he was still a practising Catholic (and staying with a local priest). This, irrespective of its audience, is not a Protestant story reminding its readers that people were also burned by the Inquisition. It is a Catholic story diagnosing Catholic *mentalité*. The real Devan went to his death bravely enough. He was given time to pray and apparently used it as such. He audibly discussed the height of the gallows, the place on the ladder where he should halt for execution, the length of time his body would be left opposite his father's house. He was quoted by several papers: 'I die guilty. I forgive my prosecutors. Pray for me.'[39]

The remaining question is whether he thought God opposed his murder and arson. William Johnston of Ballykilbeg would obviously assume that, being a papist, he did not, or at least that he thought that with clerical assistance God could be squared. Fathers McCann and Duffy gave him no hope of that without open confession and private reprehension of his crime. But how Catholic was Devan? He would have died rather than conform to Protestantism, clearly. (So intense was the Catholicism of Ribbonmen that in his earliest version of his story, Carleton had thought the victims of Wildgoose Lodge were Protestants.) We must remember that the crimes took place on the night of 29–30 October 1816. The 31 October was Hallowe'en, 1 November All Saints' Day, 2 November All Souls' Day. The Roman Catholic Church had in fact long ago recognised that the days ending October and beginning November had religious significance, existing before Christianity. We must remember that the return of the priests of the outlaw church to Ireland gave them obvious reassurance that few of their communicants were tempted by the legality of socio-economic attractions of Protestantism, but they found all too much evidence that their fidelity to the old faith had often carried its residue of devotion to a still older one. Father Corish drew attention to Whiteboy use of pagan deities in 1762, coupling 'Queen Sive' with the newly crowned George III (in place of his Jacobite cousins): perhaps Lewis Namier should have taken such date into account when anatomising the structure of politics at George's accession. Terence Dooley worried about Hallowe'en, quoting the proverb 'Everyone has debts at Hallowe'en' and noting a witness recalling an assassin's boast that 'he would be the first of 12 men who would stand forward to burn Lynch, his house and family to ashes, and they should not eat their supper on Holy-Eve night'.[40]

The lighting of fires was the most obvious pre-Christian survival in Hallowe'en, and even the Protestant English maintained that principle, taking it forward to the fifth of November and ensuring that their fires should be shown to have the semblance of a human figure inside it. Christianity itself had sought to eradicate pagan practice by installing what remained of them in Christian festivals. But two could play that game, and Christian paraphernalia could prove useful means of prolonging the lives of pagan ceremonies. On that showing, false evidence in court was an irrelevance to the true God, the kind, gentle, suffering God of Christianity, behind whom there was a fierce brutal god who from time to time demanded a terrible vengeance on his enemies. Paddy Devan had worshipped the gentle God when on the scaffold he prayed for his enemies who had convicted him, but the crime for which he died had been exacted by 'old god': country folk in my lifetime still spoke of ancient formulae as 'that was in old god's time'. It evidently remained a great deal more real than men in black tattered gowns with horsehair wigs hanging off their heads demanding the truth, the whole truth and nothing but the truth, something that any sensible person knows nobody has ever been able to tell, and nobody ever will.

Notes

1 See my essay in J. Bowman and R. O'Donoghue (eds), *Portraits: Belvedere College, Dublin 1832–1982* (Dublin: Gill and Macmillan, 1982); also Bruce Bradley, SJ, *James Joyce's Schooldays* (Dublin: Gill and Macmillan, 1982), whose preface by Richard Ellmann is a literary imprimatur. R. F. Foster, *Words Alone – Yeats and His Inheritances* (Oxford: Oxford University Press, 2011).

2 Declan Kiberd, introduction to Frank O'Connor [i.e. Michael O'Donovan], *An Only Child and My Father's Son* (London: Penguin, 2005), p. vii (the edition republished in one volume *An Only Child* (1961) and *My Father's Son* (1968), the latter posthumous. O'Connor, 'Foreword', *Stories* (1956), p. vii: the anthology was published in New York only. T. Flanagan, 'The Irish writer', in M. Sheehy (ed.), *Michael/Frank: Studies on Frank O'Connor* (Dublin: Gill and Macmillan, 1969), p. 150.

3 O'Connor copyrighted a play text in 1960, for S. Barnet, M. Berman and W. Burto (eds), *The Genius of the Irish Theater*, published by Mentor Books for the New American Library the same year. Hunt published an adaptation under his own name copyright himself and O'Connor's widow (1973), and with O'Connor's 1960 copyright, but the versions differ, although both cut in reminiscent voices from the trial. Samuel French produced the Hunt version.

4 M. Steinman (ed.), *Happiness is Getting Down Right: Letters of Frank O'Connor and William Maxwell* (New York: Knopf, 1996), p. 266.

5 O'Connor, *My Father's Son*, in *An Only Child* and *My Father's Son*, p. 318.
6 'In the Train', *Lovat Dickson's Magazine*, ed. L. A. G. Strong (Jun. 1935), repr. in *Bones of Contention* (New York: Macmillan, 1936, London: Macmillan and Co. 1938); *Selected Stories* (Dublin: M. Fridberg, 1946); *The Stories of Frank O'Connor* (New York: Knopf 1952; London: Hamish Hamilton, 1953); *Stories* (New York: Vintage, 1956); *My Oedipus Complex and Other Stories* (London: Penguin, 1963).
7 J. Matthews, *Voices – A Life of Frank O'Connor* (Dublin: Gill and Macmillan, 1983), pp. 111–13, and 131–2 (Abbey first night, May 1937), p. 188 (Radio Éireann transmission 1942), train sounds rendering its tape unusable twenty years after (p. 399).
8 E. Somerville and M. Ross are examined for their authenticity as observers of Irish life in C. C. O'Brien, 'Somerville and Ross' (originally a Radio Éireann talk in answer to Corkery's view (then very much Irish national orthodoxy)), *Writers and Politics* (London: Chatto & Windus, 1965). Canty is in 'The Holy Island', *Burlington Magazine* (May 1899) and *Some Experiences of an Irish RM* (London: Longman, Green, 1899).
9 E. Marjoribanks, *Life of Lord Carson* (London: V. Gollancz, 1932), i, pp. 58–9. I have argued in 'Carson as Advocate: Marjoribanks and Wilde', in S. Wichert (ed.), *From the United Irishmen to Twentieth-Century Unionism – A Festschrift for A. T. Q. Stewart* (Dublin: Four Courts Press, 2004) that the book should be judged as self-serving memoirs, but this episode was certainly based on newspaper research as well as Carson's recollection. The ensuing cattle-fair story must derive from Carson's recollection alone, but as it is clearly against himself, it seems true (*ibid.*, p. 35).
10 Great Britain. The Special Commission Act 1888, *Report of the Proceedings before the Commission Appointed by the Act* (London: George Edward Wright, 1890), i, pp. 223–4
11 M. Healy, *The Old Munster Circuit* (London: Joseph, 1939), pp. 96–7, 178, 180.
12 T. Macaulay, 'The country clergyman's trip to Cambridge' (1827), in Macaulay, *Miscellaneous Writings* (London: 1860).
13 A. M. Sullivan, *The Last Serjeant* (London: Macdonald, 1952), pp. 157–8.
14 M. Harmon, 'Cobwebs before the wind – aspects of the peasantry in Irish literature 1800–1916', in D. J. Casey and R. E. Rhodes (eds), *Views of the Irish Peasantry 1800–1916* (Hamden: Archon Books: 1977), p. 150; K. Brown, 'A blessed union? Anglo-Scottish relations before the covenant', *Anglo-Scottish Relations from 1603–1900*, T. C. Smout (ed.) *Proceedings of the British Academy* 127 (Oxford: Oxford University Press, 2005), p. 48, contrasts English and Scottish courts after 1603 'utterly indifferent to each other' with Jacobean administrators from England enforcing in Ireland 'the adoption of English law, a policy designed to deliberately undermine the Old English [Catholic] community and to attack [Catholic] Gaelic society ... Irish lawyers ... excluded from practising on account of their Catholicism'. The eighteenth-century penal laws built themselves on that precedent.

15 S. J. Connolly, *Divided Kingdom* (Oxford: Oxford University Press, 2008) and I. McBride *Eighteenth Century Ireland* (Dublin: Gill and Macmillan, 2009) are admirable surveys including fine reviews of the existing literature on the penal laws and their probable cause: gratifyingly, the Catholic-descended Connolly is less critical of the penal laws than the Protestant-descended McBride. Among older treatments, O. P. Rafferty, *Catholicism in Ulster* (Dublin: Gill and Macmillan, 1994), pp. 57–73, is a lively discussion of the question in more local terms and P. J. Corish's numerous works are like Rafferty's from the advantage of being Catholic priests as well as magnificently magisterial (Corish supplied outstanding leadership both in Irish feminist history and in awareness of pagan survival). Corish, *The Catholic Community in the Seventeenth and Eighteenth Centuries* (Dublin: Helicon, 1981) is still an essential starting point, permanently exhilarating in rereading.

16 G. O'Brien (ed.), *Catholic Ireland in the Eighteenth Century – Collected Essays of Maureen Wall* (Dublin: Geography Publications, 1989) happily draws together most of her path-finding work on its titular concern, apart from her 'The Whiteboys', in T. D. Williams (ed.), *Secret Societies in Ireland* (Dublin: Gill and Macmillan, 1973) and her 'The age of the penal laws', in T. W. Moody and F. X. Martin (eds), *The Course of Irish History* (Cork: Mercier, 1967). She also produced what were probably the best essays to come from any historian on the Easter Rising of 1916 during the decade of its golden jubilee: see her two in K. B. Nowlan (ed.), *The Making of 1916* (Dublin: Stationery Office, 1969).

17 C. Ó Danachair, 'The penal laws and Irish folk tradition', *Proceedings of the Irish Catholic Historical Committee 1961* (Maynooth: 1962), p. 10. But the several volumes as by Kevin Danaher such as *In Ireland Long Ago* (Cork: Mercier Press, 1962), *The Pleasant Land of Ireland* (Cork: Mercier Press, 1970), etc. are invaluable all the more as folklore, and have much light to throw on history as yet unused.

18 W. E. H. Lecky, *History of Ireland in the Eighteenth Century* ([London: Longman, Green, 1892] 1913), i. pp. 148, 272–3; ii, pp. 41, 44. Lecky's first edition of his *Leaders of Public Opinion in Ireland* (London: Saunders, Otley, 1861) ended with an essay on 'Clerical influences', discarded from the any subsequent editions, but reprinted (London: Longman, Green, 1911), ed. F. C. O'Brien and W. E. B. Lloyd.

19 [Dan Pyke], *Parish Priests and Church of St Mary's [Clonmel, Co. Tipperary;] 1320–1984* (1984), p. 25.

20 For Sheehy, see P. O'Connell, 'The plot against Father Nicholas Sheehy: the historical background', *Proceedings of the Irish Catholic Historical Committee 1965–1967* (Maynooth, 1968), pp. 49–61.

21 C. C. O'Brien, *The Great Melody – A Thematic Biography and Commented Anthology of Edmund Burke* (London: Sinclair-Stevenson, 1992), pp. 54–5 puts the Sheehy case in its Burkean context (without self-genealogising).

22 Edmund Burke, *Irish Affairs* (ed.), Matthew Arnold ([1881], London:

Cresset Library, 1988), introd. C. C. O'Brien. O'Brien, *Great Melody*, pp. 289–93, 379–81, 412 but the entire work – a great melody in itself – is essential to understand Burke and the Ireland from where he came and reasoned. See also O'Brien's essay on Burke and Warren Hastings in G. Carnall and C. E. Nicholson (eds), *The Impeachment of Warren Hastings* (Edinburgh: Edinburgh University Press, 1989) and his introduction to the Penguin edition of Burke, *Reflections on the Revolution in France* (London: Penguin, 1968) all of which integrate Burke's Indian and French preoccupations with his Irish antecedents. His thought and friendship have dominated my present study as well as giving me some of the greatest happiness of my life.

23 For Chambers, see C. C. O'Brien, 'The perjured saint', in O'Brien, *Writers and Politics* (London: Chatto & Windus, 1965) which raises vital questions about perjury beyond those discussed here. On Oates and his fellows, see J. Kenyon, *The Popish Plot* (London: Heinemann, 1972) though it is rewarding to pursue him through Macaulay's *History of England*.

24 [T. Moore], *Memoirs of Captain Rock* ([1824], Notre Dame: Keough-Naughton Institute for Irish Studies, 2008), E. Nolan (ed.), annotated by S. Deane, p. 85, and see Professor Deane's invaluable notes, pp. 269–70.

25 G. de Beaumont, *Ireland, Social, Political and Religious* ([1839] Cambridge, MA: Belknap Press, 2006), introd. T. Gavin and Andreas Hess, trans. W. C. Taylor, pp. 65, 71–2, 196–9, 232.

26 A. de Tocqueville, *Journeys to England and Ireland* (London: Faber and Faber, 1958), trans. G. Lawrence and K. P. Mayer, ed. J. P. Mayer, pp. 132 and 148.

27 *An Abstract of the Douay Catechism* (London: Keating and Brown, 1813), p. 29.

28 J. O'Gallagher (in some editions Gallagher), *16* (in some editions *17*) *Sermons* [or *Irish Sermons*] *in an Easy and Familiar Stile* (1736, 1795); aka *Sermons in Irish Gaelic ... with English translation* (Dublin: M. H. Gill, 1877), sermon xv, pp. 314–41, and see pp. lviii–lx for James Doyle's veneration. The 1877 edition has imprimatur from John MacHale (1791–1881) Archbishop of Tuam from 1834.

29 But the reduction of Catholic religious teaching to catechism (a blunder also followed by many Protestants) won Fr P. J. Corish's historiographical censure, *Catholic Community*, p. 109, '[older] catechisms ... were, of course, learned by rote, but they contained many texts of prayers and "facts", thereby keeping a balance between intellectual understanding of one's religion and living it which was unfortunately lost when "Butler's catechism" of the 1770s left little or nothing except question and answer'.

30 Its classic analysis is of course G. B. Shaw, *Saint Joan* (London: Constable, 1923), mostly written in Co. Kerry.

31 G. K. Chesterton, *Christendom in Dublin* (London: Sheed & Ward, 1932), p. 59.

32 Apart from Carleton's own works, G. Brand (ed.), *William Carleton: The Authentic Voice* (Gerrards Cross: Colin Smythe, 2006) is now the starting

point for Carletoniana. Otway's profile of his *protégé* (perhaps the last work he wrote) is reprinted on pp. 17–28, preceded by Samuel Ferguson on Otway. For Otway's affection for his local Catholic priest, see C. Otway, *Lecture on Miracles* (Dublin: R. M. Tims, 1823), pref.

33 Carleton's 'Essay on Irish swearing' is in fact most conveniently found in the 1844 edition of his *Traits and Stories of the Irish Peasantry* (Gerrards Cross: Colin Smythe, 1990 repr.), ii, pp. 1–12, despite its place as opening of 'Geography of an Irish oath', where previously it was printed separately. For its bibliographical adventures, see B. Hayley, *A Bibliography of the Writings of William Carleton* (Gerrards Cross: Colin Smythe, 1985), and for its historical contextualisation, Hayley, *Carleton's Traits and Stories and the 19th Century Anglo-Irish Tradition* (Gerrards Cross: Colin Smythe, 1983), pp. 204–11.

34 Carleton, *Traits and Stories*, ii, p. 3 (for all quotations). The Irish-Gaelic poems may be found in Canon P. Ó Canainn, *Filidheacht na nGaedheal* (Dublin: Press Náisiúnta, 1939).

35 A 'respectable individual from Dundalk and its vicinity' to *Weekly Freeman's Journal*, quoted in *The Times*, 27 Mar. 1818, in T. Dooley, *The Murders on Wildgoose Lodge* (Dublin: Four Courts Press, 2007), p. 150. See also R. Murray, *The Burning of Wildgoose Lodge* (Armagh: Armagh Diocesan Historical Society, 2005). However badly deceived, Fr McCann's conduct disposed of William Johnston of Ballykilbeg's thesis declaimed in *Ribbonism and Its Remedy. A Letter Addressed to the Right Hon. The Earl of Derby, First Lord of the Treasury* (Dublin: William Curry and Company, 1858): 'Does the Priest of the parish ever hand over the murderer to justice? ... Can there be told one case, even one, in which he reprobated the murder from the altar? No priest ever denounced a Ribbon murderer; for, in so doing, he would have denounced Jesuitism, Dominicanism, Inquisitionism, Rome!'

36 Carleton to William Sisson, 3 Nov. 1826 enc. memorandum to Peel, in Brand (ed.), *Carleton*, pp. 3–6. The tales cited are in *Traits and Stories*, 'The hedge school' from the first (1830) edn, the others from 1833. A. McManus, *The Irish Hedge School and Its Books 1695–1831* (Dublin: Four Courts Press, 2004), pp. 55–6 questions Carleton's generalisations but notices some agreement with him from Otway's opponent in controversy the Catholic bishop of Kildare and Leighlin James ('J. K. L.') Doyle. I am deeply grateful to Dr McManus for her courtesy and generosity in sending me her invaluable book.

37 Barbara Hayley acquits Carleton of any pretence of being the fictional narrator (Hayley, *Carleton's Traits and Stories*, pp. 124–5) but a reader of the *Dublin Literary Gazette* (then seeking to establish itself in its infancy in the demoralised Irish Protestant world just having witnessed its once revered Wellington and Peel capitulate to Daniel O'Connell over Catholic emancipation) would surely have taken the story at its face as a true confession. See also the recent works cited in n. 35.

38 Dooley, *Wildgoose Lodge*, pp. 157–8.

39 *Ibid.*, pp. 195–6, quoting *Belfast Newsletter*, 29 Jul. 1817; *Dublin Evening Post*, 29 Jul. 1817; *Freeman's Journal*, 28 Jul. 1817; *The Times*, 1 Aug. 1817. Forgiving 'my prosecutors' was of course essential as required by Our Lord in his prayer (in more frequent use among Catholics than among Protestants, in all probability, given Protestant preference for extempore prayer).

40 Corish, *Catholic Community*, p. 26; Dooley, *Wildgoose Lodge*, p. 118.

11

The voices of Catholic women in Ireland, 1800–1921

Caitriona Clear

This chapter sets out to detect the voices of those Catholic women who managed to make themselves heard by a wider audience than family and friends in Ireland in the years between the Act of Union and independence/partition. It looks at women whose words and deeds had an impact in the so-called public sphere – organisational management, work which gave them authority over others (teaching, nursing, social work/philanthropy) campaigning, politics and writing. In paying attention to these women, who were a minority, it is not the writer's intention to denigrate the importance of the majority of women, whose voices often rang loud and clear during their lifetimes, but who are silent in the historical record.

I

The most obvious Catholic women whose voices were heard between 1800 and 1921 were nuns, as religious sisters were commonly known. The increase in the number and variety of religious women over this period has been well documented over the past twenty-five years. According to Tony Fahey, numbers rose from 120 in 1800 to over 8,000 in 1901. There were more than twice as many nuns as priests, and seven times more nuns than brothers.[1] There were eleven convents in Ireland in 1800, 368 a hundred years later, and convents at the dawn of the twentieth century were much larger than they had been even fifty years earlier.[2] Applicants to the religious life had become so numerous by the 1890s that one Good Shepherd sister lamented; 'The labourers are many but the harvest is lacking' – there was not enough work, in her congregation at least, for all the candidates.[3] It became common for a number of sisters from one family to choose the religious life. In two urban convents, between 17 per cent and 22 per cent of entrants over a fifty-year period were siblings from the same family.[4] Four Fallon daughters from a Roscommon landowning family entered the Sisters of

Mercy and Loreto congregations from 1849[5] and in the Murphy family of Newmarket-on-Fergus, nine daughters of a family of twelve daughters and one son entered the religious life between 1887 and 1905.[6] Women who influenced each other in this way were not always ensuring lifelong togetherness; entering the convent, even the same convent or congregation, did not mean living together for the remainder of one's days – the Murphy sisters, for example, were scattered all over the globe in Australia, India and England. Every Irish convent founded before 1850 (and many founded after) made at least one new foundation in Ireland or abroad. The Presentation convent in Rahan, Co. Offaly, sent sisters to Madras (now Chennai) in 1842.[7] Nuns were constantly on the move; in Siobhan Nelson's memorable phrase, 'The Marthas of the nineteenth century kept quiet but they did not keep still'.[8] Quiet as far as writing and publicity was concerned, that is, although nuns did manage to present a tranquil glamour to the casual observer:

> 'Tis a beautiful life and a quiet,
> And it keeps you from going below,
> As a girl I thought I might try it,
> But ach! I dunno![9]

Percy French, himself from minor Protestant gentry, knew enough about the options available to Irish Catholic girls in the early twentieth century to pen these lines in the narrative of a girl whose father has 'made his fortune in land'. The everyday life of the convent which was involved in projects of various kinds, whatever about being 'beautiful' (or keeping one from 'going below', i.e. to hell), certainly did not lack bustle and activity. It was not for a 'quiet life' that Irish middle-class Catholic women flocked to the convent in such numbers.

In Ireland the flourishing of active congregations of women began with highly talented, energetic women of the eighteenth and early nineteenth centuries – Nano Nagle, Teresa Mullaly, Mary Aikenhead, Teresa Ball, Catherine McAuley and, in the mid-nineteenth century, Margaret Aylward. Our story begins in 1802, with the formal papal recognition, as the Presentation Sisters, of the sisterhood founded by Nano Nagle in Cork in 1776, to which Teresa Mullaly's Dublin sisterhood had already affiliated.[10] Mary Aikenhead's Irish Sisters of Charity followed in 1815, Teresa Ball's Loreto Sisters (an Irish branch of the English Institute of the Blessed Virgin Mary) in 1821, Catherine McAuley's Sisters of Mercy in 1828, and Margaret Aylward's Sisters of the Holy Faith in 1867. No individual foundress of equivalent profile is identified with the Brigidine sisters, a sisterhood with its origins in Tullow, Co. Carlow, which was recognised by Dr Daniel Delany, bishop of Kildare and Leighlin in 1807 (with papal approval in 1840), but their existence prior to the bishop's intervention suggests women of strong conviction and ability.[11] By 1850 there were ninety convents in Ireland, concentrated mostly in Leinster and Munster, and the towns of the western seaboard; over half (58 per cent) of these were either Presentation or Mercy convents. Older congregations like the Dominicans, and some convents of the Poor Clares took up new work of teaching and running orphanages in the early nineteenth century, while congregations from abroad like the Ursulines (which arrived in 1771 to take over some of Nagle's projects in Cork), the Sacred Heart nuns and the Faithful Companions of Jesus had arrived by mid-century. The following seventy years saw further expansion and growth of the native congregations, and many new arrivals from abroad such as the St Louis Sisters, the Daughters of Charity (also known as the French Sisters of Charity) and many more. Nuns ran schools for children of all social classes, hospitals, orphanages, industrial schools, and reformatories; those nuns permitted to go outside the convent nursed in workhouses, visited prisons, visited the sick poor, and held evening classes for working people. Towards the end of the century, many availed themselves of the generous government grants available under constructive unionism to build work projects, the most famous and long-lasting of which was Foxford Woollen Mills in Co. Mayo.[12]

Although convents ran projects which operated independently of state funds – and some, like the Sisters of the Holy Faith, made a point of this – most nuns, through their involvement in (and often, control of) National schools, industrial schools and workhouse hospitals, were also public servants. Nuns visited, and sometimes taught in prisons, and ran 'halfway house' hostels for women finishing up their sentences. Indeed, the only state or local authority institution in which nuns, by the end of the nineteenth century, did not have any role whatsoever, was the lunatic asylum. Nuns, seen collectively, were powerful women. Each convent had its own command structure and elected its own officers by secret ballot for three-year terms of office. Nuns in managerial roles controlled large sums of money, employed ancillary staff and negotiated with the civil authorities quite regularly. Examples of the arbitrary abuse of power by clergy and bishops over convents are legion,[13] but this should not blind us to the fact that nuns, whether they won or lost, were contenders for ecclesiastical power, a point convincingly argued by Mary Peckham Magray.[14]

For increasing numbers of Irish Catholics in the period under discussion, the face of church and state authority which they encountered most often – as schoolchildren, 'orphans', patients, paupers or poor people generally – was a female one, surrounded by a white guimp and black veil. For the smaller class of privileged Catholic girls who attended boarding schools or paying day schools, nuns were figures of authority, and often objects of deep affection during the impressionable teenage years.[15] A caveat should be entered here, however. Not all nuns exercised power; the comparatively small number of lay sisters, while they might have enjoyed the kind of informal, emotional power so difficult for the historian to measure, could not be elected to office and did not participate in the projects run by the convent, being confined to domestic and garden work, and many nuns who were not lay sisters were never elected to, and never sought, positions of authority within the convent – although they might have exercised authority in the schools, hospitals and other institutions in which they worked.

II

When it came to political and social reform movements, Protestant women's voices were the first ones raised. It is thanks to the efforts of Isabella Tod and Margaret Byers, both Protestant, that females were admitted to the school-leaving Intermediate examination in 1878 and as undergraduates with full rights to all universities in 1879 except Trinity College, Dublin and the Royal University. The Sisters of Mercy, the Dominicans, the Ursulines and the Loreto nuns were quick, in the succeeding decades, to prepare female students for examinations, even running university extension lectures, but Protestant women were in the vanguard of this particular campaign.[16] The first Irish women's suffrage movement founded by Thomas and Anna Haslam in 1876 was almost entirely Protestant.[17] Anna Parnell, from a Protestant landowning family, headed the Ladies Land League in 1881–82; her sister Fanny, before her untimely death, was its most fluent propagandist.[18] The two best-known and best-loved female political figures of the revolutionary period – that is, those whose names were best known to people at the time and who have remained in the popular memory for generations – were Maud Gonne MacBride and Constance Markievicz, both from Protestant backgrounds, though both converted to Catholicism as adults.[19] The six Gifford sisters, who were nationalists and suffragists from the early twentieth century (Katie, Nellie, Ada, Muriel, Grace and Sidney), were all reared as Protestants; their father was Catholic, and some converted to Catholicism later in life. Louie Bennett, co-founder of the Irish Women Workers Union in 1911 and lifelong political activist on behalf of women workers, was from a Dublin Protestant background.[20] And although Catholic women were involved from the very beginning (Elizabeth, Countess of Fingal, was an early patron), the original foundress of the United Irishwomen, later the Irish Countrywomen's Association, was Anita Lett, a Protestant.[21] Dr Kathleen Lynn, a member of the Irish Citizen Army, one of the first women elected to Dáil Eireann and later a well-known and much-loved founder of St Ultan's hospital for children in Dublin, was a clergyman's daughter from Connacht.[22] Nationalist and suffragist women were not the only female political activists on the island – there was also a prominent and numerous female unionist organisation in Ulster in particular.[23] However, almost all of these women in Ulster were Protestant, and though there were some Catholic unionist women on the island as a whole, they were not particularly vocal as unionists.

Catholic women's voices were also heard in almost all of these movements and in some, like the Ladies Land League, they predominated. Inginidhe na hÉireann's first massive show of nationalist strength – the Patriotic Children's Treat Committee during the king's visit in 1903 which attracted 15,000 children as opposed to the 9,000 'treated' by the Viceregal Lodge in the Phoenix Park – was brilliantly organised and conceived by Gonne (who had at this stage converted to Catholicism) and many Catholic women also participated.[24] Hanna Sheehy Skeffington one of the founders, along with her husband Frank, of the Irish Women's Franchise League in 1908, was from a Catholic background, as was Mary McSwiney, whose suffragism predated her nationalism.[25] The United Irishwomen/Irish Countrywomen's Association prided itself on having Catholic and Protestant women working alongside each other (hence its original title).[26] Though Protestants were active in it also, Catholics were founders of Cumann na mBan – Agnes O'Farrelly, its first president, was a former convent 'girl', and one of the first female graduates of the Royal, later the National, University of Ireland.[27] Many, if not most of the women who assumed leadership of the nationalist movement in the years 1916–18 when most of the male leaders were imprisoned in the anti-conscription and by-election and election campaigns of 1917–18, were Catholic. Constance Markievicz was the first woman elected to the Dáil but, of the women elected to the Second and Third Dáils, all were Catholic; one, Ada English, was one of the first female psychiatrist in the country.[28] Catholic women also took part in the various organisations which were set up to render support to the soldiers and sailors in the Great War, as leaders and as rank and file, in hospitals in Ireland and abroad as Voluntary Aid Detachment nurses. Indeed, Marie Martin, later foundress of the Medical Missionaries of Mary, got her first experience of hospital life as a Voluntary Aid Detachment nurse in Malta.[29] All women over 30 of certain property qualifications were granted the parliamentary franchise and permission to sit in both houses of parliament in the United Kingdom of Great Britain and Ireland in 1918; the Irish Free State, in common with many other new post-war democracies, granted Irish women full political equality with men (over 21) in its constitution of 1922. Women in Britain and Northern Ireland were not granted full political equality until 1928.

III

Ann Colman's groundbreaking research of the early 1990s shows definitively that Irish women, Catholic and Protestant, wrote and published vigorously – and were widely read – throughout the nineteenth and into the twentieth century.[30] The Nun of Kenmare, who wrote under the name M. F. Cusack, published thirty-five volumes, mainly of history, with some biography and fiction. Katharine Tynan published 184 volumes of fiction, biography and poetry, her sister Nora Tynan O' Mahony although less prolific was also popular. Colman tells us of the Downing sisters, who published poetry and devotional verse and one of whom, Janice, worked as a secretary to the Nun of Kenmare.[31] Rosa Mulholland (who published fifty volumes), the Sweetman sisters, the Furlong sisters and many others were encouraged (as were Protestant women writers) by Fr Matthew Russell SJ, editor of the *Irish Monthly*, which commenced publication in 1873. Catholic women also published in the *Catholic Bulletin* and the *Irish Rosary*.[32] These are only a few examples, which omit the growing number of Catholic women journalists at the end of the nineteenth century, but they indicate that Catholic women, while they might have been comparatively silent, were not silenced. It was not the Nun of Kenmare's writing which led to her eventual ostracisation; her biography of St Patrick won her a letter of congratulation from the pope, and her works were well received by bishops and clergy.[33]

IV

When Beatrice Burke, the heroine of Mary Butler's popular 1906 novel, *The Ring of Day*, wants a life more meaningful than the sociability of the Dublin season, she considers first the religious life, and then decides to dedicate herself to Ireland with equal fervour. Butler, a journalist, novelist and member of the Gaelic League, is credited by Arthur Griffith with having thought up the title Sinn Féin for his organization; this is one Catholic woman whose voice resonates to this day. Butler and her sister Belinda were educated at the Protestant Alexandra College; Belinda was a high academic achiever – she won the Archbishop Trench scholarship – and she entered the convent at the age of 40. The Butler sisters were not, however, representative of Catholic Irish women of their time. Their origins in the landed gentry of the west and the fact that neither of them had to earn a living, place them far away not only from farmers' daughters, labourers' womenfolk, domestic servants and factory workers, but from the secretaries, nurses, teachers and all the other 'white-blouse' working women whose numbers increased so rapidly, in Ireland as elsewhere, in the late nineteenth and early twentieth centuries. Their experience is important nonetheless because it illustrates that, even under optimal conditions (excellent education, freedom from financial anxiety and familial responsibility, and an atmosphere of political and cultural revival) the convent exercised a powerful pull on devout Catholics. Mary's initial reaction to the news of her sister's vocation in 1912 was one of horror: 'I argued and entreated and sobbed, praying her not to do this thing and that she would be miserable and utterly wretched in a convent – she with *her independent and intellectual tastes and cultural environment.*'[34] Belinda's withdrawal from the world at such an exciting time seemed to her sister like voluntary incarceration. Around this time also, Mary herself (who had married in 1907 at the age of 34) was praying that she might have a child who would grow up to enter the Carmelite convent and devote herself to God.[35] For this Catholic woman at least, at this time, the religious life which was so ideal for a fictional heroine or hypothetical child was unthinkable for a flesh-and-blood sister.

After the revolutionary period, as before (and even to a certain extent throughout it, as Belinda Butler's experience illustrates), the energy which might have propelled many Catholic women into politics and activism was channelled into the religious life. It must also be remembered that entering the convent, especially an active congregation which worked directly with the poor, was considered outlandish by many genteel Catholics; accounts of struggles with reluctant parents and guardians are very common in the annals and histories. Catholic women who entered convents were not always following a safe and socially acceptable path.[36] And once in the convents, women did not give up all interest in political affairs. Ní Chinnéide attributes Mary Butler's independence of mind to the fact that she was not convent educated,[37] but many of Butler's contemporaries who were much less conventional than she was, and took more risks than she did, attended convent schools in the last quarter of the nineteenth century – Mary McSwiney and Hanna Sheehy Skeffington lost their jobs, for example, many others went to prison. The young, mainly working-class Dublin women who made up the Cumann na mBan presence at Jacobs Mills in 1916 and who joined the Irish Citizen Army, must have been educated by the Presentation, Mercy, Charity or Holy Faith Sisters in the inner city. They might have been taught by somebody like Kate O'Brien's Aunt Fan, a Presentation nun in Limerick: '"Hurrah – let England quake" was very much her idea, even on Christmas Day and from her enclosed convent'.[38] The fee-paying convent school which O'Brien herself attended, although run by a congregation which was originally French, housed at least one very nationalist sister in the early twentieth century, showing that nationalist feeling was not necessarily confined to Irish congregations.[39]

Whatever about nationalism, however, the memory of early twentieth-century Irish Catholic feminism was so short-lived in independent Ireland that a young Catholic woman writer, born in 1901, could state confidently in 1933 that women in Ireland had acquired political equality in 1922 'without their having had to lift a finger to secure it'.[40] Ward, Cullen Owens, Murphy, and others have since demonstrated this to be patently untrue, while Clancy, Beaumont and this writer have documented how women – Catholic and Protestant – struggled not only to hold onto their newfound political rights in the Free State of the 1920s and 1930s, but to define feminism for a new generation.[41] However, the unchallenged ignorance of a popular writer like Alice Curtayne makes us wonder why Catholic feminists in particular (Curtayne was writing for a Catholic audience) sank so completely from the public memory in so short a space of time. There were prominent, well-known women of Catholic background in government and outside it, who drew attention to women's issues in the 1920s and 1930s – Kathleen Clarke, Jenny Wyse-Power, Brigid Redmond, for example – but the women's organisations (political, social, reforming) which survived the revolutionary period and went on to give evidence to government commissions and to lobby in the popular press up to the 1950s, contained a number of Protestants vastly out of proportion to their presence in the population.[42]

As far as Catholic lay activism (i.e., in religious activity) was concerned, the reason for the 'silence' or low level of organisation of Catholic lay women is the same as that for the silence of Catholic lay men – overwhelming clericalism and strong obedience to clerical and episcopal authority, though Catholic women in Ireland participated enthusiastically in lay and charitable organisations where these existed.[43] As nuns, Catholic women enjoyed unparalleled and increasingly, unchallenged authority; their voices rang loud and clear. But in political and reforming activity which involved public meetings, organisations, media campaigns, petitions, and liaising with politicians, Protestant women were almost invariably the instigators. Catholic women eagerly took up the tune and joined in the chorus, but Protestant women wrote the words and music, and called the tune.

Notes

1 T. Fahey, 'Nuns in the Catholic Church in Ireland in the nineteenth century', in M. Cullen (ed.), *Girls Don't Do Honours: Irish Women in Education in the Nineteenth and Twentieth Centuries* (Dublin: Argus Press, 1987), pp. 7–30.
2 C. Clear, *Nuns in Nineteenth-Century Ireland* (Dublin: Gill and Macmillan, 1987), p. 36.
3 *Ibid.*, p. 135.
4 *Ibid.*, p. 144.
5 K. Tynan, *A Nun, Her Friends and Her Order: Being a Sketch of the Life of Mother Xaveria Fallon* (London: Kessinger Publishing, 1892).
6 C. Clear, 'My mother taught me how to pray: the nine Murphys of Newmarket-on-Fergus', in *The Other Clare: Journal of the Shannon Archaeological and Historical Association*, 19 (1995), pp. 64–68.
7 T. J. Walsh, *Nano Nagle and the Presentation Sisters* (Monasterevan: Presentation Generalate, 1959), pull-out map on inside front page.
8 S. Nelson, *Say Little, Do Much: Nursing Nuns and Hospitals in the Nineteenth Century* (Philadelphia, PA: University of Pennsylvania Press, 2001), p. 31.
9 J. N. Healy, *Percy French and His Songs* (Cork: Barrie Jenkins and Mercier, 1966), p. 47. The date of the poem is around 1905.
10 All the information on the various congregational histories is taken from T. J. Walsh, *Nano Nagle*; Sr M. Pius O'Farrell, *Nano Nagle: Woman of the Gospel* (*Cork: Cork Publishing*, 1996); Sr M. Kieran Harnett, *Nano Nagle, Woman of Vision* (Dublin: Irish Messenger Office, 1975); S. Atkinson, *Mary Aikenhead: Her Life, Her Work and Her Friends* (Dublin: Brown & Nolan, 1911); A Member of the Order of Mercy/Mother M. Austin Carroll, *Leaves from the Annals of the Sisters of Mercy* (New York: Catholic Publication Society, 1881); H. Concannon, *The Poor Clares in Ireland* (Dublin: M. H. Gill, 1929); M. Gibbons, *Life of Margaret Aylward* (London: Sands, 1928); J. Prunty, *Lady of Charity, Sister of Faith: Margaret Aylward 1810–1889* (Dublin: Four Courts Press, 1999); R. B. Savage, *A Valiant Dublin Woman: The Story of George's Hill* (Dublin: M. H. Gill, 1940); A Loreto Sister, *Joyful Mother of Children: Mother Frances Mary Teresa Ball* (Dublin: M. H. Gill, 1961); Sr M. B. Degnan, *Mercy Unto Thousands* (Dublin: Newman Press, 1958); M. C. Sullivan (ed.) *The Correspondence of Catherine McAuley 1818–1841* (Dublin: Four Courts Press, 2004); M. MacCurtain and R. Raughter (eds), *Religious Women and their History: Breaking the Silence* (Dublin: Irish Academic Press, 2005).
11 Brigidine convent, Tullow, Co. Carlow, *Gleanings from the Brigidine Annals* (Carlow: 1945).

12 Clear, *Nuns*, pp. 36–68, 100–34; B. Joyce, *Agnes Morrogh-Bernard 1842–1932: Foundress of Foxford Woollen Mills* (Foxford: Foxford Integrated Resource Development, 2002).
13 Some examples are given in Clear, *Nuns*, pp. 53–68.
14 M. P. Magray, *The Transforming Power of the Nuns: Women, Religion and Cultural Change in Ireland, 1750–1900* (Oxford: Oxford University Press, 1998).
15 K. Tynan, *A Nun*, goes into great detail on this phenomenon, p. 95; for a fictional treatment, see K. O'Brien, *The Land of Spices* (London: Doubleday Doran, 1941).
16 A. V. O'Connor, 'The revolution in girls' secondary education in Ireland 1860–1910', in M. Cullen (ed.), *Girls*, pp. 31–54; M. Luddy, 'Isabella M. S. Tod', in M. Cullen and M. Luddy (eds), *Women, Power and Consciousness in 19th-Century Ireland* (Dublin: Attic Press, 1996), pp. 197–230; C. Clear, *Social Change and Everyday Life in Ireland, 1850–1922* (Manchester: Manchester University Press, 2007), pp. 42, 46–7. Women could take degrees from Trinity College Dublin and the Royal University but in extension colleges affiliated to these universities, not in the universities themselves.
17 R. C. Owens, *Smashing Times: A History of the Irish Women's Suffrage Movement 1889–1922* (Dublin: Attic Press, 1984), pp. 19–32; C. Quinlan, *Genteel Revolutionaries: Thomas and Anna Haslam, Pioneers of Irish Feminism* (Cork: Cork University Press, 2002).
18 M. Ward, *Unmanageable Revolutionaries* (Dingle: Brandon, 1982 and London: Pluto Press, 1983), pp. 4–39; D. Hearne (ed.), *Anna Parnell: The Tale of a Great Sham* (Dublin: Arlen House, 1986).
19 M. Ward, *Maud Gonne: Ireland's Joan of Arc* (London: Pandora Press, 1990); A. Marreco, *The Rebel Countess: The Life and Times of Constance Markievicz* (Philadelphia, PA: Chilton, 1967).
20 A. Hayes (ed.), *The Years Flew by: Recollections of Madame Sidney Gifford Czira or 'John Brennan' Journalist and Broadcaster* (Galway: Arlen House, 2000): R. M. Fox, *Louie Bennett, Her Life and Times* (Dublin: Talbot Press, 1958); R. C. Owens, *Louie Bennett* (Cork: Cork University Press, 2002).
21 S. McNamara, *Those Intrepid United Irishwomen* (Parteen: S. McNamara, 1995); A. Heverin, *ICA, The Irish Countrywomen's Association: A History* (Dublin: Merlin, 2000); M. Jones, *These Obstreperous Lassies: A History of the Irish Women Workers Union* (Dublin: Gill and Macmillan, 1988).
22 M. O hOgartaigh, *Kathleen Lynn: Irishwoman, Patriot, Doctor* (Dublin: Irish Academic Press, 2006).
23 D. Urquhart, *Women in Ulster Politics 1890–1940: A Story Not Yet Told* (Dublin: Irish Academic Press, 2000).
24 M. Ward, *Unmanageable Revolutionaries*, pp 47–50
25 L. Levenson and J. Natterstad, *Hanna Sheehy-Skeffington: Irish Feminist* (Syracuse: Syracuse University Press, 1986); C. Fallon, *Soul of Fire: A Biography of Mary McSwiney* (Cork: Mercier Press, 1986).
26 McNamara, *Intrepid Irishwomen*; Heverin, *ICA*; see also, G. Mitchell,

Deeds Not Words: The Life of Muriel Gahan (Dublin: Town House, 1997).

27 Ward, *Unmanageable revolutionaries*, pp. 88–118, chapter on Cumann na mBan.

28 M. McNamara and P. Mooney, *Women in Parliament: Ireland 1918–2000* (Dublin: Wolfhound Press, 2000), pp. 74–83.

29 C. Clear, 'Fewer ladies, more women', in J. Horne (ed.), *Our War: Ireland and the Great War* (Dublin: Royal Irish Academy, 2008), pp. 157–71; M. Purcell, *To Africa with Love: The Biography of Mother Mary Martin* (Dublin: Gill and MacMillan, 1987).

30 A. Colman, 'Nineteenth-century Irish women writers: an overview', in *UCG Women's Studies Centre Review*, 3 (1995), pp. 129–40; A. U. Colman, *A Dictionary of Nineteenth-Century Irish Women Poets* (Galway: Kennys Bookshop, 1996).

31 M. F. Cusack, *The Nun of Kenmare: An Autobiography* (London: Hodder & Stoughton, 1889), p. 147; *The Story of My Life* (London: Hodder & Stoughton, 1891), pp. 99–103.

32 Colman, 'Nineteenth-century', pp. 136–7, p. 138.

33 The story of Margaret Anna Cusack, the Nun of Kenmare, is too complicated and tortuous to go into here. Various versions of it can be found in Cusack's two autobiographies (see n. 31); I. ffrench Eager, *Margaret Anna Cusack: A Biography* (Cork: Cork University Press, 1970); and in Sr P. McCarthy OSC, *The Nun of Kenmare: The True Facts* (Killarney: Killarney Printing Works, 1989).

34 M. Butler, *The Ring of Day* (London: Hutchinson, 1906), p. 65 (my italics). All the information on Butler is taken from M. Ní Chinnéide, *Máire de Buitléir: Bean Athbheochana* (Dublin: Comhar Tta, 1993), pp. 1–22. See p. 23 for Mary's comment on her sister's vocation. Although the biography is written in Irish, Mary's writings, from which this extract is taken, were in English.

35 Ní Chinnéide, *Máire de Buitléir*, p. 107. Belinda entered first the Carmelite convent in Ranelagh, Dublin, and left it later to become a Benedictine, ending up in Brittany.

36 Ní Chinneide, *Máire de Buitléir*; Magray, *Transforming Power*, discusses this; for other examples, see B. Joyce, *Agnes Morrogh-Bernard*, pp. 3–4, and for more modern, twentieth-century examples, Y. McKenna, *Made Holy: Irish Women Religious at Home and Abroad* (Dublin: Irish Academic Press, 2006).

37 Ní Chinnéide, *Máire de Buitléir*, p. 23.

38 K. O'Brien, *Presentation Parlour* (Dublin: Poolbeg Press, 1994), p. 76.

39 K. O'Brien, 'Memories of a Catholic education', *Stony Thursday Book*, 7 (1981), pp. 28–32.

40 A. Curtayne, *The New Woman: The Text of a Lecture Given in the Theatre Royal, Dublin October 22 1933 Under the Title 'The Renaissance of Woman'* (Dublin: Catholic Truth Society, 1933), p. 4.

41 Ward, *Unmanageable Revolutionaries*, pp. 199–262; M. Clancy, 'Aspects of women's contribution to Oireachtas debate in the Irish Free State 1922–37', in M .Luddy and C. Murphy (eds), *Women Surviving: Studies in Irish Women's History in the Nineteenth and Twentieth Centuries* (Dublin: Poolbeg Press, 1990), pp. 226–32; C. Beaumont, 'Women and the politics of equality: the Irish women's movement 1930–1943', in M. G Valiulis and M. O'Dowd (eds), *Women and Irish History: Essays in Honour of Margaret MacCurtain* (Dublin: O'Brien Press, 1997), pp. 173–88; L. Ryan and M. Ward (eds), *Irish Women and the Vote: Becoming Citizens* (Dublin: Irish Academic Press, 2007), pp. 231–50; C. Clear, *Women of the House: Women's Household Work in Ireland, 1922–61* (Dublin: Irish Academic Press, 2000), pp. 13–91, 202–16.

42 Clear, *Women of the House*, pp. 27–67.

43 J. H. Whyte, *Church and State in Modern Ireland* (Dublin: Gill and Macmillan, 1971); L. Fuller, *Irish Catholicism since 1950: The Undoing of a Culture* (Dublin: Gill and Macmillan, 2002). Regarding Catholic women's activism in lay religious organisations, see, e.g. Margaret MacCurtain 'Fullness of life: defining female spirituality in twentieth-century Ireland', in Luddy and Murphy (ed.), *Women Surviving*, pp. 233–63.

12

Irish diaspora Catholicism in North America*

David Doyle

I

In their global faiths as in their insular polities, the experiences of the Irish at home entailed a series of unstable 'identities' to ease relations with others. This was so despite their obligation of due deference to political authority, regardless of those exercising it. The search for status and prestige imposed choreography of positioning in social life which weakened any consistent outward witness to Catholic values. Impoverished political identities exacerbated this, regardless of their provenance or their loyalties. At best, the reasoned will to virtue, the resources of sacrament and scripture, and the example of associates and of family, led to vitality and variety, often individualised. Thus the real identities of Catholics were never solely those of their changing collective characteristics, often problematic and unstable. Yet the press of such group behaviours restricted the range of Catholic variety, as of openness to others, in every era.

The post-1800 emigration brought new worlds. Largely modest people and often ill-equipped they came to countries in which the *same* domestic constraints no longer applied. Most left young, before social responses and fears had hardened. If abler Irish migrants could forge their own adaptive character and negotiate their new experiences, all chose in time whether to embody, modify or abandon their received religious beliefs, whether by design or default. These processes were repeated among their offspring born overseas. Plainly the range of their new lands, and the differences within them, bounded all responses. If potentially broader than at home, the

* This is an edited and redrafted version of 'Il cattolicesimo Irandese in Nord America', in L. Vaccardo (ed.), *L'Europa e la sua Espansione nel Continent Nord America*, 2 vols (Milan: Centro Ambrossiano, 2011), ii, pp. 449–76. The author and editor wish to thank Dr Luriano Vaccoro and the *Centro Ambrossiano* for permission to reproduce material already published.

range of accessible Catholic vitalities abroad was often limited by country.

We will focus on North America, and especially on the United States. Although parallel Irish experiences elsewhere were many and real, they are only now subject to a fully disciplined comparative scrutiny, which should be extended to similar work as between the Irish in Britain's dominions and in the United States.[1] Comparisons between these and those of the Irish in Britain are much more problematic.[2]

Isolation, cultural archaisms and then perception of long repression by Protestant England had given the Irish themselves a merited sense of singularity. Many Irish identified this defensive sensitivity with maintenance of their religious commitment, as England was officially Protestant after 1559. Yet much of positive modernity came to them in Protestant and post-Protestant forms which they then equivocated or contested. This was so at home. But it proved more so for most who went abroad. After 1707, a united Great Britain undertook a drive to economic growth and to maritime empire. It thus created the English-speaking contexts, and the economic culture and opportunities, into which around 9 million Irish later emigrated from 1815–1960. Of these, 6.5 million went to the United States and Canada, four-fifths of them directly to the US, almost all for good.[3]

Before the age of revolutions from 1789, the traditional Catholicity of non-Reformation Europe was comprehensive. Ireland has had an ambiguous relationship with mainland Europe. If many continental church–state tensions did exist, the average Mass-goer little worried either about their connections to state power or to the cohesion of social classes. The Irish had to worry about all of these together. As late as the 1850s, Catholics, and Presbyterians did not enjoy full freedom and opportunity, much less the advantages or otherwise of a state religion which was 'their own'. Even before the 1770s, this inclined many to mistrust top-down polities, established religion, and related socio-economic elites, despites their own innate conservatism, and their pragmatic adjustments to England's hegemony. The collapse of royalist France and later defeat of Spain in 1809 removed the partial exceptions to this outlook. All this complicated Irish Catholic relations with a papacy which from 1792–1884 saw royalist legitimacy as a bulwark against revolutionary de-Christianisation. In America (and partly in Presbyterian heartlands in Ireland), such conservatism in Rome added freshly to an anti-Catholicism, otherwise in decline well before 1800. It also led American Catholics after 1783 to attempts to distinguish the basics of their faith from conflicted 'old world' contexts.

For both Irish Catholics and Presbyterians, networks of shared belief and kinship remained natural mechanisms of group survival in hostile worlds. Both groups were predisposed to favour America's experiments in a republican, decentralised and finally democratic order. The precedent was first set by eighteenth-century Presbyterian emigrants. But Catholics too sought horizons free of disdain and unjust legal constraints, and arenas of advancement and subcultural community, such as Irish Presbyterians had won generally between 1765 and 1801. Mutual mistrust had largely kept Irish Catholics away from all British North America, but after 1783 this diminished in both the United States and in English-speaking areas of future Canada. From 1815, Irish Catholics decided all North America now offered such horizons (not just past enclaves in Newfoundland, Maryland, Pennsylvania and Louisiana). They began to flood there, continuing to do so into the 1920s. Used to dominant British law, power and commerce at home, they had some means to cope with what was familiar overseas. Whereas the Quebecois, the Mississippi Valley French and the Spanish on the Gulf and California coasts won time and space to develop *their* own traditions, the Irish never generally managed this, if Newfoundland is excepted. Yet while they avoided such geographic separation after the 1780s, some would seek a measure of specific community, a mild version of *survivance*, or experienced their need of these.

Such tendencies were reinforced by the effects of the Famine emigration, which, as elsewhere, built on foundations growing from the 1790s, and already more fully provided for by churchmen, from 1833–43.[4] The new outflows enhanced the possibility of more and faster growing Irish urban communities, with their own outlook, subculture and politics, all dependent upon a greatly increasing industrial expansion.[5] Yet only around one million immigrants of upwards to two million of the Famine era going to North America (1846–55) were Famine refugees proper, as many of the rest would have come at the rates already underway in the early 1840s.[6] This million was well under one-sixth of the total immigration, 1815–1960, and accounted for less again of overall descendants, given the unequal Irish mortality in urban America, 1845–70.

The now forgotten writer O. Henry (William S. Porter) depicted the United States around 1900 as a land of perpetual human collisions.[7] Irish Catholics long took this as a fact of life from first arrival. This made them well fit for religious survival, but often further narrowed their reactions to their fellow North Americans. As one of their own priests (raised in America) described them in 1848: 'Their nationality is intense, touchy, suspicious, unreasoning, morbid'.[8] Their picture of the world thus overplayed their own role in the North Atlantic Christian *oikumene* (an outlook reinforced by their early North American experiences). Their past isolation, and lack of languages, also left many laypeople unaware of their deep bonds with incoming continental Catholics. Their very increase in the US lent gradual force to their outlook. In 1900, certainly half of America's twelve million Catholics were of Irish birth or descent. In 1995, around fifteen million held they were so, among sixty-five million US Catholics, if by then, only one-third of all Irish-descended Americans reported themselves as Catholic.[9] If the Irish Catholic self-image in North America thus took only partial account of transatlantic realities, their strong sense of the interdependence of faith and ethnicity was well warranted before 1940.

II

The year 2008 saw the 200th anniversary of New York as a diocese, later an archdiocese, ruled unbrokenly since 1842 by Irish and Irish-American prelates. Through Manhattan came most Irish immigrants after 1847.[10] If four out of five then moved on, enough remained in New York to give its Catholicism an Irish-stock plurality for over a century after 1808. Already 45 per cent of the city's *total* population was Catholic in the mid-nineteenth century, if many but nominally. Churchmen were hard-pressed to provide for all this.

What manageable issues can be identified as central to this protean story? They may be grouped into two. *First*, there are those directly dependent upon church structure, and, second, those characteristic of the lay Catholic community. On the first, we examine episcopal leadership in education, and the rise of religious sisterhoods, its chief support. On the second, we will look at family life as its bedrock, and identify social politics as its distinctive expression, together inseparable from the 1830s on.

John Hughes, the first archbishop of New York, said in 1857: 'In our age, the question of education is the question of the Church.'[11] A slick historiography once sought to link authoritarianism, ghetto-formation, limited intellectuality and a new devotionalism with an Irish (or more broadly, immigrant) era in the American church. The main instrument of this supposed scenario was said to be episcopal control of schools.[12] Such a polemic tells us little. Nor do the character and aims of the episcopate over time support such notions. Sometimes quieter churchmen did most: Patrick Ryan, archbishop in Philadelphia 1884–1911, built the larger and more multi-ethnic school system; he also pioneered the Catholic high school. Some of the most commanding prelates, such as John Hughes himself, schooled rather fewer. There was also a time lag in the rise of Irish-American predominance in the hierarchy, which was clearly emergent only by the early 1880s,[13] and already in decline by the 1950s. In those years, from the Third Plenary Council of 1884, the emphasis on Catholic education, as in Ireland, was encouraged from Rome. The hierarchy held a range of opinions as to how best to attain this.

Even before this, Irish immigrant priests turned bishops had notable salience between 1842–1870s. Yet while they held major sees, in Philadelphia, New York, Cincinnati, St Louis and Chicago,[14] they were neither a majority, nor even a bloc, nor were they wholly agreed on educational objectives, nor even on whether a comprehensive parochial system was practicable. Links on such questions tended to be across, not within, ethnic groups in the still small hierarchy.

From the 1820s up to 1840, bishops had all prioritised education, whether they were of 'old' American background, or from France, England, Ireland or Italy, but problems of costs inclined them to make provision first for colleges and academies funded by the better off. Rising liberal hostility to belief might have predisposed them to seek parochial schooling, but they were reluctant to challenge the popularity of neighbourhood common schools in America. When they did so, it was not from dogma, or European outlook, much less from the influence of a putative Irish tribalism, but from actual experience of America itself. Bishops stated this clearly in their rationale for such schools at the Fourth Provincial Council of Baltimore in May 1840. It emerged as part of a heightened sense of transatlantic Catholic interests, well before Pope Pius IX's time (1846–78).

But an issue of European schooling touched more closely. The Irish Church was then divided over the new system of national primary schools provided by the British state in 1831.The majority of Irish bishops accepted a joint church–state scheme, as it allowed pastors to become patrons and managers of such schools. Bishops could not themselves fund the universal system so urgently required. The archbishop of Tuam John MacHale from a traditional, still Irish-speaking region, rejected it, but would find by 1852 that he too could not finance any alternative. Probably acting as agent of fellow Dubliner and his new bishop, Francis Kenrick, Fr Patrick Moriarty, an Augustinian lately come from Madras sought the view of the Baltimore council.[15] The council responded in support of MacHale's principle of 'Catholic schools for Catholic children under Catholic auspices'.

In 1840, the US had only 200 parochial schools, for 660,000 Catholics. The recent Irish model did not arise, given America's society, laws and politics. Instead the council urged pastors to provide directly for the young, and encouraged Catholic parents to realise that their own rights as citizens were in jeopardy when they lacked alternatives to the common schools as they were then. It was not until the 1860s that bishops *expected* pastors, where possible, to build schools, and not until 1884 *required* them to do so, although parents were left free to avail of them or not. The attendance of children of Irish parents was never uniformly related to the numbers of such children, being by 1906–08 high (over 60 per cent), in Philadelphia, Newark, Pittsburgh, Cleveland and Baltimore, but low in most other major cities (below 45 per cent), and skeletal or absent in rural areas.[16] These were children of recent Irish immigrants, coming from a Catholic Ireland almost universally catechised and practising. Earlier, however, in post-Famine years (from the 1850s to 1870s), fewer Irish children attended such American Catholic schools, indeed just 20 per cent in New York city. German speakers, not the Irish, were the trendsetters in parochial school provision. Irish American churchmen who saw their good results supported the system's mandatory spread from 1884.[17]

III

For a century, the practicality of the Catholic school system was dependent upon expanding religious sisterhoods.[18] In that time, 1850s–1950s, a majority of Irish American family heads were transport, industrial, and construction workers of modest income. By 1950, sisters provided well over four-fifths of the system's 67,000 elementary teachers, and thousands of its high school ones.[19] Such religious did not reflect the ethnic balances of immigration: the Irish relied on others before roughly 1890, and after that Irish Americans sisters made return to new immigrant Catholics. At least 4.5 million Irish Catholics came to the US from 1820–1920, with another half-million arriving as second-stage migrants from Britain and Canada. Perhaps up to 2.5 million Catholics came from Germany in the same century (including Poles from East Prussia, Posen and Silesia). Another 4.1 million came from Italy, if half of these later went home. Only half a million came from France and under 150,000 from Spain.[20] Yet between 1800–1975 one-third of women's orders and congregations active in the US originated within the country itself (if some were 'granddaughter' orders of European ones). Strikingly, over one-fifth came from France, which sent so few emigrants, and only one-sixth from Italy, which sent so many.[21] England, Switzerland, Austria, Poland and Hungary each provided 2 per cent of the congregations. Ireland and Germany, the main sources of nineteenth-century emigration, church growth and its demographic increase, provided only 7 per cent of the orders in Germany's case and 4 per cent in Ireland's.

Nineteen orders came from Canada (principally from Quebec), which *did* match the two million immigrants coming from there before 1920.[22] Notably, some orders based in France came to Ireland in the same century, so that their engagement with the Irish took place at home also.

Rich in vocations, new foundations and varied skills, French (and Quebecois) nuns and sisters proved assets to American bishops seeking aid in schools, orphanages, social care and hospitals. Indeed, of necessity Irish American bishops required them to undertake such tasks, creating some tension where contrary rules and customs were strongly held. But the process also enabled American Irish girls to get to know the congregations which taught them, e.g., the Sisters of St Joseph drew many entrants from ordinary families. By the 1890s, most 'French' orders were largely Irish American. The process was slower in German and German-American orders, whose response to diocesan needs often varied. In more numerous American-founded congregations, Irish sisters were present from the beginning. Italian sisterhoods, coming later, attracted or recruited few Irish, partly because few Irish American girls knew them. Ethnic interactions varied also within orders. Quebec-based congregations seem to have absorbed the Irish happily, both there and in English-speaking houses in the US.[23]

By contrast the two largest Irish orders of Irish origin, the [Irish] Sisters of Charity and the Sisters of Mercy had begun and then spread in response to the overwhelming practical needs of both poorer or simply plainer Irish and their children in both continents.[24] From the start their superiors usually saw eye to eye with bishops focused on those same issues, such as Daniel Murray in Dublin, John Hughes in New York, and Francis Kenrick in Philadelphia.

The ratio of nuns and sisters to population rose rapidly from the pre-Famine years until the Second World War. The decline came much more recently. In 1840, there was at most one such consecrated woman for every 735 Catholics, and by 1880, one per 287 of the faithful. These are optimal ratios, as numbers of Catholics are calculated from older minimal estimates.[25] The peak ratio was of one per 128 in 1940, or roughly one nun to every twenty or so Catholic households. This latter ratio is more certain as it uses reliable church figures; it also reflects a known increase of American Irish Catholic commitment, as increased parish schooling after 1900 interacted with now almost wholly practising migration from Ireland. The rapid decline after 1970 mirrored the growing secularisation, even loss of the faith, in parts of the Catholic community since then. Although numbers (not ratios) of sisters did increase to the mid-1960s, vocations were no longer equal to bishops' needs during these 'baby boom' years. Catholic school enrolments rose sixfold between 1900 and autumn 1960, to over five million, which prompted increasing reliance on more costly lay teachers.[26] The nuns' dedication had made possible the provision, without public financing and with few constraining state conditions, of a vast school system, and a major health care system. The whole church in the US has suffered from their decline.[27]

IV

Family life was the grounding and context of the life of the church and its community. Such realities, and their transitions from Ireland to Irish America, have been recovered as they have become contested. Much relevant 'family reconstitution' history has been driven by fashionable demographic preoccupations. These were anticipated by the US Senate's Dillingham Commission reports of 1911–13. Its express motivation was to match immigration to the real needs of the economy, by filtering supposed oversupplies of unskilled labour from Europe. Some of its members and witnesses sought to manage population and tilt towards eugenics, to thereby maintain existent ethnic hierarchies.[28] Dillingham's reports on marital fertility by ethnic group confirm this.[29]

In Ireland, the same pressures of population and unequal impoverishment that triggered mass migration from Ireland from around 1828–30, had led the country's eastern areas to delayed marriage and to the practice of inheritance of farm holdings by one male heir only (with dowry negotiated as accompaniment to an incoming bride). This system became more general after the Famine. The young delayed, even avoided, family formation. Scarce livelihoods were protected by mass emigration, by widespread rural celibacy, and by marriages negotiated by elders. Inextricably the church itself became partner in the moral anxieties and social controls of this situation. By contrast, in America more natural patterns were retained, as abundant jobs and housing allowed general marriage and early family formation. There, in 1855, as many as 85 per cent of Irish women could expect to marry, apart from in the poorest slums. Fertility rates were high, up to twice those of native-born New England women.[30] There was some delay in marriage age, and about one in ten never married, while labourers' families were smaller. Infant mortality was high, and remained so well into the 1920s. But the contrast with Ireland was deep and growing.[31] By the twentieth century, one-quarter of women remaining in Ireland who were 20 to 40 before 1936, never married; in America, still 85 per cent of their emigrated contemporaries did so. Among men the contrast was even greater.

In the next generation, the non-marrying rate of the American-born Irish was high by American standards, consistently fifteen 15 per cent in the early twentieth century. If this was normal enough by the traditional standards of old Europe, it was low by the then high rates of Irish spinsterhood. There was a tendency by more American-born Irish men than women to approach the almost universal marriage of adult Americans.[32] Overall, emigration, coupled with managed inheritances at home, seems to have been a strategy for family creation and maintenance for those who went, if it did not always ensure it, as many emigrants hoped, for those siblings remaining in Ireland. Numbers of children born to marriages in both countries confirm the attachment to family life.[33] America allowed for many more, and freely chosen matches, and large families were common there, if by 1910 marginally highest among second-generation rural Minnesota Irish.[34]

For the emigrants' basic regard for family was transmitted to the next generation, in an America generally friendly to it. Early twentieth-century social workers and novelists depicted such responses, however hardened, even in high-stress, impoverished situations.[35] The naturalness of it all hallmarked Catholic Irish-America, if there was needed a full church life to ballast it, and social justice to avert its jeopardy from casual or exploitative employments. Into the 1930s, Irish and Irish-American women had offered one of several bulwarks for marriage. They worked until they married, and then all but five in a hundred of these devoted themselves to child-raising, unless early widowhood or a husband's incapacity or desertion supervened. After major disruption during depression and wartime, 1929–45, such patterns were then re-established with church support, but in suburbanising contexts of inter-ethnic fusion, so that *Catholic* community receptivity remained strong into the 1970s.

V

Into the 1950s Catholicism itself was seen by Catholics as the vital contribution the Irish brought to the United States.[36] But it was *not* exclusive to their coming alone. Hence the distinctively vital theme was other than this. It was that of the consistent linkage of the 'family economy', orthodox Catholic commitment, and practical politics. The precedents lay in Ulster Presbyterian politics in colonial and post-revolutionary America. From the 1790s, party machines secularised their members' activities, including those of Catholic newcomers.[37] In English-speaking upper Canada, Irish Protestants likewise early set precedents for responsible and meliorist politics, in a milieu more sensitive to the Christian dimensions of public life and of legislation, and to a more activist role for the state, and for a new liberal elite. Irish Catholic influence on these freedoms proved more difficult given a vein of anti-Catholicism in both elite and popular assumptions. But Irish–Quebecois divisions also haltered adjustment.[38] Any estimates of nineteenth-century Canadian possibilities depend on whether one holds with Donald Akenson that most Famine and post-Famine Catholic Irish in upper Canada settled and assimilated successfully as had their predecessors before it, or conclude with Murray Nicholson that many now set up more marginalised, self-conscious and often poorer urban subcultures, there and elsewhere, which advanced with circumspection. Houston and Smyth, since refined by Bruce Elliott and others, long ago showed it could be a spectrum of both.[39]

By contrast, the American separation of church and state in the federal sphere had begun to influence state law and politics by the 1830s. Here a distinct social politics took real shape. For the Irish, 'keeping body and soul together' was the bedrock of family survival, prior to all real gains within a polity. In new, contested landscapes, with business cycles causing a flux of employments, the politician as councilman or state assemblyman made cities amenable to growth, and as 'fixer' found both public and contract jobs for his followers. The churchman respected these functions, even as he aimed to move souls. Both agreed their work was more easily done in familiar neighbourhoods. The Democratic party, while assertively secular, was open to the Irish as vehicle to these needs.

Most Whigs and the new (1850s) Republicans were less friendly, despite their emphasis on the merit of churches as contexts of order and disciplined enterprise. When the Civil War saw federal power used as an instrument of social reform, many Irish began to see in the Radical Republicans possible friends to pro-labour laws in industrial states. Others sought to broaden the northern Democrats' search for social protections, through actions in states and cities. These were necessary as managerialism often made short shrift of the claims of trade unions, and of the security needs of families. First the main miners' unions, next the Knights of Labor and then American Federation of Labor unions were heavily Irish American. Their members were often also sympathetic to transatlantic Irish nationalist and land reform movements.

The sequel is well known. Most Irish American Catholics, whether politicians or churchmen, editors or union leaders, shared a loyalty to the existent laws and processes of their society, were conscious of their minority status and scattered geography, and feared jeopardising their own improvements by a publicly active Catholic politics.[40] They too had to handle strong cycles of anti-Catholicism.[41] All these same constraints operated in Canada, outside Quebec, to an even greater degree. The issues were at first canvassed cautiously. While upholding church bans on fully 'secret societies', North American bishops divided as to whether such proscription ought be imposed generally or case by case on labour and nationalist organisations.[42] Led by archbishops James Gibbons in Baltimore and John Lynch in Toronto,[43] a key group recognised that Catholic people must both be protected in their public structures and activism while being strengthened in their faith and education. As cardinal designate, Gibbons memorialised Rome in February 1887:

> Since it is acknowledged by all that the great questions of the future are not those of war, of commerce or finance, but the social questions which concern the improvement of the condition of the great masses of the people ... the church should always be found on the side of humanity, of justice toward the multitudes who compose the body of the human family.[44]

The church leader of the London Irish, Cardinal Henry Edward Manning, and of Victoria's Irish in Australia, Archbishop Thomas Carr of Melbourne, had provided approaches Gibbons held to be supportive.

Unlike the American nationalists, Bishop John Ireland and Mgr Denis O'Connell, Gibbons did not press the view that church–state separation and democratic processes should become the norm elsewhere. In any case Pope Leo XIII condemned these latter propositions in 1895, and in 1899 linked them to a supposed spread in America of over-reliance on the Holy Spirit without church direction, on active rather than supernatural virtues, even on human nature without grace. Yet within a decade (1908) this warning was balanced by full recognition that the churches of the United States, Canada and England were fully component ones of the universal church, and no longer subject to the Congregation *Propaganda Fide*.

The modest public faith among Irish Americans was a realist adjustment to the scattered energies of minority status. It was brought to birth in family, and found its life in parishes, in Catholic schools, in trade unions and in political connection. It was long and influentially joined to an emphasis on human rights which were politicked well and protected in public law. Their active possession of constitutional liberties, while enjoying good church governance, gave Irish Americans the resilience, autonomy and partial cohesion to answer the fears of some about the United States itself.[45] This also partly tutored many Irish Canadians on how to conduct themselves in different, but also sometimes difficult, circumstances.

Notes

1 M. Campbell, *Ireland's New Worlds: Immigrants, Politics and Society in the United States and Australia, 1815–1922* (Madison, WI: University of Wisconsin Press, 2008); D. N. Doyle 'Cohesion and development in the Irish diaspora', *Irish Historical Studies*, 31 (1999), pp. 411–34. The pre-1776 situation was quite different: N. Canny, 'The British Atlantic world: working towards a definition', *Historical Journal*, 33(2) (1990), pp. 479–97. For earlier migrations, Nicholas Canny, *Europeans on the Move: Studies on European Migration, 1500–1800* (Oxford: Clarendon, 1994), brought a valued counter-framework.

2 D. N. Doyle, 'Small differences? The study of the Irish in the United States and Britain', *Irish Historical Studies*, 29 (1994), pp. 115–17, 119.

3 A. Bielenberg (ed.), *The Irish Diaspora* (Harlow: Longman, 2000), table 11.1, p. 224, which the editor himself adapts from D. H. Akenson, *The Irish Diaspora: A Primer* (Belfast: Institute of Irish Studies, 1993), table 11, p. 56, for 1815–1910, with additions Bielenberg explains at p. 233 n. 54. Further additions for 1911–60 are made here from standard national series, in want of comparative collation. Irish migration series would indicate up to 1.5 million leaving, 1911–60, but use varying criteria, and suffer data gaps in both post-1921 jurisdictions (J. J. Sexton, 'Emigration and immigration in the twentieth century', in J. R. Hill (ed.), *A New History of Ireland, VII: Ireland, 1921–1984* (Oxford: Oxford University Press, 2003), pp. 796–806). For official US incoming data to 1996, see P. Blessing, 'Irish in America', in M. Glazier (ed.), *Encyclopedia of the Irish in America* (Notre Dame, IN: University of Notre Dame Press, 1999), table 1, p. 454. For non-return patterns, see D. Fitzpatrick, 'Emigration, 1901–1870', in W. E. Vaughan (ed.), *A New History of Ireland V: Ireland under the Union, I, 1801–1870* (Oxford: Oxford University Press, 1989), pp. 566–67 and 'Emigration, 1871–1921', in W. E. Vaughan (ed.) *A New History of Ireland VI, Ireland Under the Union II, 1871–1921* (Oxford: Oxford University Press, 1996), pp. 633–37, modifying standard work by J. D. Gould and M. T. Hart.

4 D. N. Doyle, 'The Irish in North America, 1776–1845', in Vaughan (ed.), *Ireland Under the Union I 1801–70*, pp. 695–6, 713–14, 724–5.

5 D. N. Doyle, 'The Irish in North America, 1845–1880', in Vaughan (ed.), *Ireland Under the Union II, 1870–1921*, pp. 725–30, 740–3, 750–4; contrast H. R. Diner, '"The most Irish city in the Union": the era of the great migration, 1844–1877', in R. H. Bayor and T. J. Meagher (eds), *The New York Irish* (Baltimore, MD: Johns Hopkins University Press, 1996), pp. 87–106.

6 Doyle, 'Irish in North America, 1845–1880', pp. 732–5; James S. Donnelly, 'Excess mortality and emigration', in Vaughan (ed.), *Ireland under the Union, I, 1801–1870*, p. 353.

7 O. Henry, *100 Selected Stories* (Ware: Wordsworth Classics, 1995). The reading is my own.

8 Fr John McCaffrey to Orestes Brownson, 15 Dec. 1848, in D. A. Wilson, *Thomas D'Arcy Magee* (Montreal and Kingston: McGill-Queen's University Press, 2008), i, p. 94.

9 D. H. Akenson, 'Irish immigration to North America, 1800–1980', in A. Bielenberg (ed.), *The Irish Diaspora*, p. 113, table 6.1; Patricia Wittberg, 'Catholic population, historical growth', in M. Glazier and T. J. Shelley (eds), *Encyclopedia of American Catholic History* (Collegeville: Liturgical Press, 1997), p. 288, tables 1 and 2.

10 Before then, a majority had come to the future Canada, if many later re-migrated south.

11 F. D. Cohalan, *A Popular History of the Archdiocese of New York* (Yonkers, NY: US Catholic Historical Society, 1983), p. 56. Hughes was coadjutor bishop there, 1838–50, and first archbishop thereafter until 1864.

12 M. Dezell, *Irish America Coming into Clover* (New York: Doubleday, 2000), pp. 166–73, 239–40 captures and sources the clichés.

13 T. T. McAvoy first distinguished their inter-ethnic pattern in the 1850s, and the 'Rise of the American Irish, 1872–1884', in his *A History of the Catholic Church in the United States* (Notre Dame, IN: University of Notre Dame Press, 1969), pp. 174, 176–9, 226–62.

14 Baltimore, the primatial see, which set regional and national agendas in church law and in its directives, was in 'Irish' hands between 1851–63, and again only after 1874. Francis Kenrick and James Gibbons, the archbishops involved, were each so long-serving by their accessions as to be comprehensively American in outlook.

15 J. George, 'Very Rev. Dr Patrick E. Moriarty, OSA, Philadelphia's Fenian spokesman', *Pennsylvania History*, 48(3) (Jul. 1981), p. 222.

16 D. N. Doyle, 'Irish diaspora Catholicism', in B. Bradshaw and D. Keogh (eds), *Christianity in Ireland: Revisiting the Story* (Dublin: Columba Press, 2002), table 2, p. 239, with analysis, pp. 238–42.

17 Notably James Gibbons in Baltimore, John Purcell in Cincinnati, Peter Kenrick in St Louis, and Bernard McQuaid in Rochester, New York. An exception was John Ireland of St Paul, although he knew German towns in Minnesota well. He was an open Republican party supporter.

18 J. P. Dolan, *The American Catholic Experience* (Garden City, NY: Doubleday, 1985), p. 277; H. A. Buetow, *Of Singular Benefit* (New York and London: Macmillan, 1970), pp. 115–16, tabulates the forty-five congregations already active which made the new 1884 policy feasible.

19 [US Bureau of the Census], *The Statistical History of the United States from Colonial Times to the Present* (New York: Basic Books, 1976), series H535–44, p. 377; Buetow, *Singular Benefit*, pp. 249–50, provides somewhat higher numbers by including those teaching in a wider range of institutions, such as private academies, but the proportions (religious–lay) are constant.

20 The working assumptions are that baptised Catholics included four-fifths of Irish immigrants, between 37 per cent and 45 per cent of German ones (it varied by decade), and almost all Italian, French and Spanish ones. For

details on immigrant numbers, see *Statistical History of the United States*, series C89–119, pp. 105–6.

21 Nine-tenths of parishes in the Archdiocese of New Orleans were French speaking as late as 1880, as were two-fifths of parochial schools in New England in 1909 (C. E. Nolan, in J. P. Dolan (ed.), *The American Catholic Parish* (New York: Paulist Press, 1987), i, p. 283); Dolan, *American Catholic Experience*, p. 279.

22 Calculations are from the data provided in *The Official Catholic Directory* (New York: P. J. Kenedy, annual), and the *Catholic Almanac* (Huntington: Our Sunday Visitor, annual), summarised in 'Women, religious orders and congregations of', in Glazier and Shelley (eds), *Encyclopedia of American Catholic History*, pp. 1498–1517, as supplemented from the websites of the bodies listing incomplete foundation data.

23 This was not always reciprocal. French-speaking Acadian sisters left the New Brunswick Sisters of Charity in 1924, as that dominantly Irish Canadian order spread through Canada under new pontifical status (T. J. Fay, *A History of Canadian Catholics* (Montreal: McGill-Queen's University Press, 2002), p. 106).

24 M. C. Sullivan, RSM, *Catherine McAuley and the Tradition of Mercy* (Dublin and Notre Dame, IN: University of Notre Dame Press, 2000), pp. 294–328, provides both McAuley's original rule, 1835, and the emendations by Archbishop Murray of Dublin, 1837. The two major congregations led to new jurisdictions carved off by bishops seeking closer direction of their members, as by Thomas Connolly in Halifax and (in his later years) by John Hughes in New York. Both sisterhoods also provided models for others, such as Dubliner Mary Clarke's Sisters of Charity of the Blessed Virgin in Iowa.

25 Calculated from P. Wittberg, 'Catholic population', in Glazier and Shelley (eds), *Encyclopedia of American Catholic History*, table 1, p. 288, set against G. C. Stewart, 'Women religious in America: demographic overview' (*ibid.*, p. 1496) and R. Fink and R. Stark, *The Churching of America, 1776–1990* (New Brunswick: Rutgers University Press, 1992), p. 135, table 4.3.

26 R. J. Regan, *American Pluralism and the Catholic Conscience* (New York: Macmillan, 1963), p. 106. Public school enrolment had roughly doubled to thirty-five million (*ibid.*).

27 Bishops' many demands from 1840–1960 for changes of task, even of rule and customs, provided unfortunate precedents as congregations fractured and divided in the wake of Vatican II. Rome and local bishops now sought to avoid past dictation, to understand each congregation in its own traditions, and to guide them to a balance of evangelical deepening with appropriate updating, using a thoughtful set of 1978 directives, *Mutuae Relationes*. The hyper-politics of all American life increased the strains between the bishops, the Leadership Conference of Women Religious and the organisation *Perfectae Caritatis*.

28 A. R. Zolberg, *A Nation by Design* (Cambridge, MA: Harvard University Press, 2006), pp. 199–238, 248–9.

29 US Senate, *Reports of the Immigration Commission*, vol. 28 (Washington, DC, 1911), 'Fecundity of immigrant women', tables 39–41, pp. 816–826.

30 D. N. Doyle, 'The remaking of Irish America, 1845–1880', in J. J. Lee and M. Casey (eds), *Making the Irish American* (New York: New York University Press, 2008), pp. 237–8 and reference nn. 84–5, at p. 250.

31 See D. Mageean's balanced contrasts, alert to Catholic contexts, between Irish women in Munster and Chicago in C. Harzig (ed.), *Peasant Maids, City Women* (Ithaca, NY and London: Cornell University Press, 1997), pp. 57–97, 223–60.

32 This seems to have been reversed in New England (T. J. Meagher, *Inventing Irish America* (Notre Dame, IN: Notre Dame University Press, 2001), pp. 120–1).

33 R. E. Kennedy, *Selective Migration and the Acculturation of Immigrants: The Overseas Irish Family*, Working Paper 1; series 4, Cushwa Center for the Study of American Catholicism (University of Notre Dame, 1978), tables 3 and 5, pp. 25, 27.

34 Senate, *Reports of the Immigration Commission*, xxviii, 'Fecundity', table 40, at p. 82. Elsewhere, and even in rural Ohio, there was a small decrease between generations. Modern regression controls, connecting fertility to numbers of years married, show that the second generation was then as fertile as the immigrant one, at least in New England (Meagher, *Inventing Irish America*, pp. 120, 420, n. 123, tables).

35 T. J. Curran, *The Irish Family in Nineteenth Century Urban America: The Role of the Catholic Church*, Working Paper 2, series 6, Cushwa Center for the Study of American Catholicism (University of Notre Dame, IN, 1979); E. H. Biddle, 'The American Catholic Irish family', in C. M. Mindel and R. Habenstein (eds), *Ethnic Families in America* (New York: Elsevier, 1976), pp. 89–123; J. A. Nolan, *Ourselves Alone: Women's Emigration from Ireland, 1885–1920* (Lexington, KY: University of Kentucky Press, 1989); R. Ebest, *Private Histories: The Writing of Irish Americans, 1900–1935* (Notre Dame, IN: Notre Dame university Press, 2005), pp. 27–54, 107–25.

36 See, for the whole diaspora, D. Murphy, *A History of Irish Emigrant and Missionary Education* (Dublin: Four Courts Press, 2000), posthumously published, which is undocumented. Often incorrect on American matters, it is better on Canada (if somewhat less so on Australia, despite local research).

37 M. J. Bric, *Ireland, Philadelphia and the Re-invention of America, 1760–1800* (Dublin: Four Courts Press, 2008), pp. 149–51, 157–61, 163–9, 186–96, identifies key parts of this sequence.

38 Doyle, 'Irish in North America, 1776–1845', in Vaughan (ed.), *Ireland Under the Union I 1801–1870*, pp. 703–8; J. R. Miller, 'Anti-Catholic thought in Victorian Canada', *Canadian Historical Review*, 66 (1985), pp. 474–94; T. Fay, *Canadian Catholics*, pp. 50–1, 88–91, 121–2, 127–31, 136–42.

39 D. H. Akenson, *The Irish in Ontario: A Study in Rural History* (Montreal: McGill-Queen's University Press, 1984); M. W. Nicholson, 'The Irish experience in Ontario: rural or urban?', *Urban History Review/Revue d'histoire urbaine*, 14 (1985), pp. 35–45, and his 'Growth of Roman Catholic institutions in the archdiocese of Toronto, 1841–1890', in T. Murphy and G. Stortz (eds), *Creed and Culture: The Place of English-Speaking Catholics in Canadian Society, 1750–1930* (Montreal: McGill-Queen's University Press, 1993), pp. 152–70; B. P. Clarke, *Piety and Nationalism...Toronto, 1850–1895* (Montreal: McGill-Queen's University Press, 1993); R. J. Grace, *The Irish in Quebec: An Introduction to the Historiography* (Quebec: Pul Diffusion, 1993); T. M. Punch, *Irish Halifax: The Immigrant Generation, 1815–1859* (Halifax: St Mary's University, 1981); P. M. Toner, 'The origins of the New Brunswick Irish, 1851', *Journal of Canadian Studies*, 23 (1988), pp. 104–19; C. J. Houston and W. J. Smyth, 'The Irish abroad: better questions through a better source, the Canadian Census', *Irish Geography*, 13 (1980), pp. 1–19, refined by B. Elliott, *Irish Migrants in the Canadas: A New Approach* (Montreal and Belfast: McGill-Queen's University Press, 1988).

40 D. N. Doyle, 'Catholicism, politics and Irish America since 1890', in P. J. Drudy (ed.), *The Irish in America: Emigration, Assimilation and Impact* (Cambridge: Cambridge University Press, 1985), pp. 195–6, 197–211, with sources and studies cited pp. 220–8, nn. 24–74. Contrast J. P. Dolan, *American Catholic Experience*, pp. 321–45, learned, and stimulating, if with some premises derived from theories of liberal social Protestantism (Rauschenbusch) and civil religion (Bellah).

41 G. F. Fogarty, 'Reflections on contemporary Anti-Catholicism', *US Catholic Historian*, 21(4) (2003), pp. 37–9, 44.

42 H. J. Browne, *The Catholic Church and the Knights of Labor* (Washington, DC: Catholic University of America Press, 1949); Fergus Macdonald, *The Catholic Church and the Secret Societies in the United States* (New York: US Catholic Historical Society, 1946), each early contextualised by J. E. Roohan, *American Catholics and the Social Question, 1865–1900* (New York: Arno Press, 1976) [a Yale Ph.D. of 1952], pp. 62–71 (John Hughes), 73–95, 161–206 (Molly Maguires), 281–333 (Knights of Labor), if misreading the centrality of the McGlynn affair, pp. 332–83.

43 J. J. Lynch was an Ulsterman by birth, educated as a Vincentian in Dublin and Paris. He came to Toronto in 1859, shaped by time in Texas, Missouri and Niagara Falls, New York (G. Stortz, '"Improvident Emigrants": John J. Lynch and Irish immigration to British North America, 1860–1888', in Murphy and Stortz (eds), *Creed and Culture*, p. 172). Roohan, *Social Question*, pp. 85–6, saw him as first North American bishop sympathetic to unions (in 1873); Clarke, *Piety and Nationalism*, pp. 227–30, notes his defence of Parnell's home rule efforts; Stortz, his (unrealised) dream of a prairie refuge from the city ('Improvident Emigrants', pp. 173–4).

44 Gibbons to Cardinal Giovanni Simeoni, 20 Feb. 1887, in Browne, *Knights*

of Labor, p. 373. Both Cardinal Manning and Archbishop Lynch quickly wrote endorsing the memorial (Browne, pp. 255–7).

45 D. C. Cochran, 'Ethnic diversity and democratic stability: the case of Irish-Americans', *Political Science Quarterly*, 110 (1996), pp. 587–604; D. N. Doyle, 'Towards democracy: Irish-born elites in Canada and the United States, 1820–1920', in J. Devlin and H. B. Clarke, *European Encounters* (Dublin: University College Dublin Press, 2003), pp. 155–84.

Part V

English Catholics and Irish identity

13

Brethren in Christ: Frederick Lucas and social Catholicism in Ireland

Patrick Maume

It is often asked why Catholicism and Irish nationalism are widely equated, since many leading nationalists have not been Catholics, some Irish Catholics have not been nationalists, and there has often been tension between church authorities and nationalist movements. Nevertheless, both were seen by adherents as representing 'natural' loyalties, whereas the motives of those who upheld the British connection were regarded as artificial or corrupt, based on personal advantage; and under the Union both Catholics and nationalists liked to contrast the professed principles of British liberals with the practice of the same liberals when confronted with uncongenial groups such as Catholics and Irish nationalists.

There would be no such contrast between theory and practice, it was maintained, in an Ireland ruled by nationalists and/or Catholics; the rulers and governing classes would be bound by natural sympathy with the mass of the people and therefore ruled with greater fairness than under the Union. 'Faith and fatherland' Irish Catholic nationalism had many tensions. Two concerned the 'Catholic Whig' project, associated with higher-class Catholic schools and the upper clergy, of creating an Irish Catholic professional class to participate in the administration of Ireland and the wider British world; and relations between Irish and English Catholics.

The prestige and influence of the English Catholic revival was a source of strength to Irish Catholicism, while English Catholic apologists often cited Irish popular Catholicism as shaming British unbelief. At the same time, Irish Catholics were widely considered by their English brethren to be ignorant peasants useful for supplying numbers (and, before the rise of the home rule party, Irish seats in parliament for English Catholic spokesmen) but otherwise an embarrassment to be kept at arms' length; and English clerics influenced the Vatican against Irish nationalist aspirations.

In the nationalist version of Irish history, one English Catholic was particularly honoured. Frederick Lucas (1812–55) founding editor of the *Tablet*, was recalled as sacrificing himself for the Irish poor, opposing Castle bishops and their place-hunting lay protégés. Arthur Griffith, who had anti-clerical tendencies and thought English sympathisers with Ireland mostly humbugs, wrote:

> Frederick Lucas is a unique memory in Ireland. Other Englishmen have from time to time honestly allied themselves with the Irish cause for a space, but they did not cease to be Englishmen – well-intentioned Englishmen – in their attitude of mind. Lucas merged himself in Ireland. The phrase 'More Irish than the Irish themselves' applies more to him than to almost any other Englishman in centuries.[1]

This chapter outlines how Lucas's social Catholicism led him to identify with the Irish poor as fellow members of the body of Christ, and how he tried to embody that fellowship.

I

Frederick Lucas was born into a London Quaker merchant family in 1812; he was educated at a Quaker academy at Darlington in Yorkshire and University College London, then read for the bar. At university Lucas experienced religious scepticism and became a utilitarian exponent of enlightened self-interest. He found neither satisfactory; the poetry of Wordsworth and the Anglican apologetics of Bishop Butler restored his Christian faith, but he remained undecided between denominations.[2]

Under the influence of Thomas Carlyle, Lucas turned against the 'pig philosophy' of political economy. Carlyle preached that the nineteenth century was experiencing social and moral disintegration and must be regenerated by heroic leaders awakening all classes to their duties. Carlyle drew a contrast with the middle ages, when Abbot Sampson of Bury St Edmunds could harness a living faith to remould society. Carlyle believed Catholicism was now outworn; from 1837 Lucas wondered whether living Catholicism might answer his and society's problems. On 22 December 1838 Lucas was received into the Catholic Church and in an open letter to the Society of Friends, Lucas stated that Quaker belief in direct divine inspiration led to directly opposed principles claiming divine authority; only a divinely inspired church provided certainty.[3]

Lucas remained in contact with Carlyle for some years after his conversion, and by introducing Young Ireland intellectuals such as Charles Gavan Duffy to the sage contributed to Carlylean influence on their thought. When Carlyle denounced Catholic revival as frivolous antiquarianism, however, Lucas expressed hope that in eternity his soul would not be with Carlyle's (presumably holding that since Carlyle understood how medieval religious orders accomplished great things by faith, his view that modern religious orders must be insincere constituted wilful bad faith).[4]

In 1840 Lucas founded and became the first editor of the weekly *Tablet*, and set about criticising the English aristocratic Catholic establishment led by John Talbot, earl of Shrewsbury, patron of Pugin and generous benefactor of Catholic causes. Shrewsbury and his associates were conciliatory in their attitude towards the state church, held Catholics should be grateful to the British state for emancipation, and disliked O'Connell's post-1829 agitations. As an ex-Quaker, Lucas had no fondness for the established order in church and state. He announced (quite correctly) that the Whig government and other high-political supporters of Catholic emancipation were just as determined as its opponents to undermine the Catholic Church's mission and subordinate it to the state, differing only on tactics; Catholics should regard both parties with equal distrust. In 1847–48 Lucas tried to organise a middle-class-dominated lay body, the Association of St Thomas of Canterbury, to challenge the existing aristocrat-led Catholic Institute.[5]

Lucas, like other nineteenth-century ultramontane journalists (and ultra-Protestant journalists writing on Catholicism) reinforced readers' self-definition by demonising adversaries. The *Tablet*'s invective was extreme even by the standards of nineteenth-century *odium theologicum*. When Michael Alexander became the first Protestant bishop in Jerusalem in 1841–42, Lucas not only ridiculed Alexander's indeterminate mandate and non-celibate status, but made snide remarks about Alexander's wife for being married to him, pregnant by him, and threatened with miscarriage as the result of hostile riots. Lucas's official biography proudly reproduces this as a masterpiece of satirical invective.[6]

Lucas's aristocratic opponents rapidly grew to loathe him. When the *Tablet*'s backers failed in 1841, there was conflict over its ownership; until 1843 Lucas's paper appeared as the *True Tablet*, while a rival *Tablet* was supported overtly by Lord Shrewsbury and covertly by Bishop Nicholas Wiseman.[7]

Where the old Catholic establishment disapproved of continental-style Catholic popular devotions, Lucas practised them enthusiastically and caused controversy by adding a large picture of the Madonna and Child (holding a rosary) to the *Tablet* editorial page. Where the aristocrats looked to 'throne and altar' Catholicism, Lucas believed, with contemporary French liberal Catholics such as Charles Montalembert and Frederick Ozanam, that *ancien régime* support for the church corrupted and enslaved; the church must detach itself from state control, assert itself as independent moral arbiter, and appeal to the people by working for them and relying on them. In 1844 Lucas encouraged the introduction of the Society of St Vincent de Paul to England (he declined its national presidency).[8] It is not clear whether Lucas participated in the Society's introduction to Ireland, but the Young Irelander Charles Gavan Duffy, a close friend, was an early member. (Through Lucas Duffy underwent a renewal of Catholic faith in 1844. Lucas always defended Duffy's Catholic *bona fides* even when this caused him considerable trouble.) Like Ozanam, Lucas hailed the early popularity of the 'liberal pope' Pius IX and the absence of anti-clerical manifestations from the February 1848 French revolution (in contrast to the 1830 revolution when the church attracted the same hostility as the deposed Bourbons). Like Ozanam, Lucas supported repression of radical French republicans in July 1848 and was disappointed at the Roman uprising against papal temporal power, but continued to advocate popular government after 1848.[9] However, Lucas favoured the Papal States, thinking the pope needed them to fulfil his duties. Curiously when Pius IX fled from Rome in 1848 Lucas initially suggested he should permanently abandon the undeserving Romans for 'some small Mediterranean island or peninsula – a farm rather than a kingdom' rather than reimpose himself by force.[10]

His populism and nonconformist mindset caused Lucas to identify with the Irish Catholics. He survived the 1841–3 dispute through the support of Daniel O'Connell and many Irish clergy. Lucas particularly admired Archbishop John MacHale of Tuam and his suspicions of state aid; he echoed O'Connell and MacHale's denunciations of Peel's post-1843 concessions to Irish Catholic interests as 'divide and conquer', and denounced as dupes the faction, led by Archbishop Daniel Murray of Dublin, who accepted these concessions. Their acceptance of the 'Godless' Queens' Colleges was particularly denounced as ignoring the fact that religion was based on education.[11]

Lucas's 1840 manifesto-editorial opposed repeal of the Union, saying it might have been unjust in its origin, yet benefit both nations; without the Union Irish Catholics might have been emancipated sooner but their English counterparts not at all. English Catholics lay under a vast debt to the Irish which they were duty-bound to acknowledge.[12] He argued this case with the Belfast *Vindicator*, a journal founded by Gavan Duffy.[13] In 1843, however, Lucas visited Ireland and was horrified at its sheer poverty. After some self-questioning, he decided a Union which tolerated such misery could not be justified, and became the most prominent of the few English repealers. English friends who said a self-governing

Ireland would be torn apart by faction were told an Irish parliament would understand its own people as no British legislature could.[14]

Lucas responded to the Great Famine with fierce indignation, suggesting that it had been sent by God to show the futility of patchwork measures and force Britain to do her duty towards Ireland.[15] Lucas thought Britain – including his co-religionists – was failing the test.

In the *Tablet* of 26 December 1846 Lucas recalled for his readers the birth of Jesus into poverty; as members of the Body of Christ, the Irish poor suffered with him while English co-religionists were indifferent:

> If our Blessed Lord were here on earth again, and we knew that He lay in destitution somewhere within our reach, should we care to relieve His sufferings? We fancy that we should, and spurn from us as an evil thought the notion that we could endeavour to see Him suffer or hear of His sufferings without doing our part to alleviate them ... In Ireland, at this moment, Christ suffers many deaths by famine, and endures the agonies of the most pinching want, but we put forth no hand to help Him. The bitter blast which on the great day of the Nativity made Him shiver, blows now in Skibbereen, in Bantry, in Macroom ... and the members of Christ tremble beneath its biting rigour, while, famished and foodless, they ask for the food which we make no effort to bestow. In how many hundred or thousand Irish cabins, more squalid than the beast-stall in Jewry, is Christ now perishing for want! ...
>
> God has appointed us to keep watch over one another, and has bound us together as by chains of adamant by the obligations of charity. The feeling of charity doubtless is a great bond; the natural affection which humanity spontaneously develops links men without effort ... But to supply the defect of these sentiments, to fill up the gaps left by selfishness, to stimulate and corroborate these fitful natural impulses into a regularity of action that never intermits; to convert the service of our neighbour into an act of worship to God, there overrides us that sublime law of Heaven which makes charity a duty even when it may be nauseous and revolting to the natural sense, and which, while it invites us to do much that is not of compulsion, fastens on us with the stern gripe of a severe necessity, and, under the penalty of hell, scourges us to certain appointed tasks.

After reminding readers that they would go to hell if they did not do more to assist the starving, and expressing scruples about whether he himself had done enough, Lucas recalled the invocations of medieval charity which drew him to Catholicism:

> It is our especial boast that works of charity are the prerogative of the Faith, and that in every age the Church had made known its divine mission by the deeds of mercy it had done. We point to the memorials of former times, to the munificent foundations, the almshouses, the hospitals, the lazar-houses, the monks, the nuns, the laymen and laywomen who have

> devoted life and substance to the service of their fellows ... We become bloated with pride through the recollection of the great things accomplished by better Christians than ourselves. But when the present hour shakes before our eyes a ghastly spectacle of woe ... we fold our hands in pharisaical content and address ourselves again to sleep.

Lucas concludes that only the Quakers had 'borrowed from the Catholics of other days an example which we ought to be ashamed not to follow'.[16]

Lucas was scornful of the 'famine fatigue' experienced by British philanthropists as the Famine dragged on and the Irish appeared ungratefully rebellious. He stated that what had been given was simple duty, deserving no gratitude.[17] Lucas's own (noticeably Carlylean) view was that the government should organise large-scale productive works, paying standard wages; he apparently believed reclamation of Irish wastelands would justify the cost, and in any event the government was duty bound to save the people. He maintained that tenants should be given fixity of tenure, and that ongoing mass evictions showed the inhumanity of the view that landlord–tenant relations were just another commercial enterprise.[18] Lucas's Catholic aristocratic opponents declared him a communist. When a landlord, Major Denis Mahon, was shot in Roscommon and Lord Shrewsbury blamed incitement by the local parish priest and claimed other Irish priests were accessories to agrarian violence, Lucas returned to the attack, claiming priests restrained violence.[19] Lucas organised a public meeting in London to deny that the seal of the confessional encouraged crime. The veteran Protestant O'Connellite Thomas Steele pointed out that by travelling Ireland at O'Connell's behest to persuade Whiteboys to disband, he laid himself open to the same accusation – failing to report self-confessed criminals – brought against priests.[20]

Throughout the Famine the *Tablet* published accounts of sufferings in Ireland (from local papers or clerical correspondents) and appeals on behalf of Catholic relief projects – such as the Poor Clares of Newry, who sought contributions to their school, where 'during these last years of famine from 120 to 150 young girls daily receive breakfast and dinner, and from 70 to 100 young girls are taught embroidery and various kinds of needlework, by the sale of which they are able to maintain themselves and contribute to the support of their parents'.[21] Lucas supported O'Connell against the Young Irelanders, saying that since insurrection could not succeed, threats of physical force unintentionally assisted the government. In 1848 Lucas stated that the government's failure to safeguard lives would justify a rising with any chance of success, but military considerations made success impossible. After the failure of the 1848 rising, Lucas advised jurors to acquit Young Irelanders because resisting such a government was not treason.[22]

In 1849 Lucas moved the *Tablet* to Dublin; amidst the last stages of the Famine he campaigned for the newly formed Tenant Right League which sought fixity of tenure. The League, led by Gavan Duffy, won the support of some Ulster Protestant tenant-right activists such as the Derry newspaper editor James MacKnight. The League also allied with the Catholic Defence Association formed by some Irish MPs, including John Sadleir and William Keogh, after Lord John Russell's Whig government responded to the 1850 re-establishment of the English Catholic hierarchy by banning the use of territorial titles by Catholic bishops. (Lucas hailed this as vindicating his insistence that Whigs were as bad as Tories.) Lucas, Duffy and their allies advocated an independent Irish party, refusing office and supporting or opposing British parties as circumstances dictated.

In the 1852 general election Lucas became MP for Meath. Initially seen at Westminster as a crank, he rapidly proved a forceful spokesman for Catholic interests. One project of Lucas's brief parliamentary career was the extension to Ireland of industrial schools run by religious orders, to counteract proselytisation of the Catholic poor in state institutions and exemplify Catholic philanthropy. He visited Belgium, where such institutions already existed, and studied them enthusiastically; although Lucas died before these proposals could be implemented, his brother claimed he shared credit for their later development.[23]

The Independent Irish Party split after the fall of a Conservative minority government in December 1852, when Sadleir and Keogh took office in a Peelite–Whig coalition. The League's Presbyterian allies also maintained that refusing office irrespective of circumstances was excessive; Lucas promptly accused them of being bribed by government grants to Presbyterian interests. Many Irish Catholic priests and bishops openly sympathised with Sadleir and Keogh, including Archbishop Paul Cullen of Dublin, whom Lucas had regarded as an ally because of their shared opposition to Archbishop Murray's policy of compromise. In 1853 Cullen as papal legate restricted the political activities of priests, wishing to protect clerical prestige from public criticism and unseemly disputes between priests; Lucas and Duffy complained the ban primarily affected their clerical supporters and would cripple the Independent Irish Party by silencing the only body of support which countered landlord influence.

Lucas appealed to Rome; he was received respectfully and asked to prepare a fuller statement of his case (excerpted at length in his official biography). This argued that in Ireland priests were a quasi-gentry, natural leaders of the people, and the only force strong enough to secure parliamentary representation capable of safeguarding the interests of 'the church and the poor'. Lucas accused many of his lay and clerical opponents of exhibiting corrupt self-interest, and he argued that acceptance of office by Catholics was undesirable even if undertaken from honest motives, since officeholders would have to subordinate their views to the British administration, necessarily unfriendly to Catholic interests.

Lucas's argument indicates how his clash with Cullen was not merely about clerical discipline,[24] but touched on an abiding fault-line within Catholic and nationalist politics under the Union. Irene Whelan points out that the decision of the Catholic bishops to support O'Connell's populist campaign for Catholic emancipation in the 1820s rather than rely on continued negotiations with government reflected fear that the state administration (including the education system) would be captured by hostile evangelical Protestants unless powerful Catholic political influence could be brought to bear.[25] From this viewpoint, the rationale of Catholic emancipation was precisely to safeguard the faith by opening administration to a Catholic professional class educated by religious orders. Similar tension between opposition to British administration as such and desire to have administrators responsive to public opinion (while shutting out hard-line opponents) recurred in nationalist politics; accusations of place-hunting had been made against O'Connell and were repeated against the later home rule party. Sadleir and Keogh acquired lasting symbolic resonance not only because their later careers spectacularly contradicted their professed piety and patriotism but because, for Catholic lay and clerical elites, securing Catholic administrators by using political influence to acquire government appointments continued to have attractions as an alternative (or rather, supplement) to forcing concessions by mass agitation, and this strategy remained open to the reproach that officeholders were likely to be politically and religiously assimilated to the administration, and the populace were sacrificing themselves for self-seeking job-hunters.

Lucas alternated between hope of success at Rome and fear that Cullen's influence would prevail. It is indicative of Roman political attitudes that Lucas's memorandum finds it necessary to explain that parliamentary opposition was not seditious factionalism but a vital part of the British political system. Lucas returned to England in failing health, suffering from cardiac disease brought about by overwork. He died on 22 October 1855 before the Vatican ruled on his appeal, essentially favouring Cullen. In his later correspondence, Cardinal John Henry Newman recalled how Lucas was left to wear his heart out in Rome, despite his ultramontane loyalty, to explain why Newman himself preferred to avoid entanglement in Roman bureaucracy.[26]

II

After Lucas's death the *Tablet* changed ownership and returned to England. It abandoned his Irish nationalist sympathies, and in the late nineteenth and early twentieth centuries was conservative in politics and suspicious of Irish enthusiasms.

In significant respects, Lucas anticipated the course of English Catholicism in the later nineteenth century, when under Cardinal Henry Edward Manning old-style aristocratic leadership gave way to clerical dominance. The standard life of Lucas, published by his brother Edward (also a convert) in 1886, presents Lucas as vindicated by Gladstone's land legislation, conceded to land league and Parnellite agitations. It also implicitly presents Lucas as a forebear of Manning's social-Catholic advocacy of workers' interests (including promoting Catholic industrial schools in England to safeguard against proselytism) and the cardinal's post-1886 support for home rule (regarded by most English bishops as proof of senile dementia).[27]

Parnell often cited Lucas as prefiguring his creation of an Irish party pursuing independent opposition towards all British administrations. (Parnell had been MP for Meath and some of his local clerical backers had worked with Lucas.) Edward Lucas's use of letters from Lucas to Gavan Duffy shows that the former Young Irelander assisted in the composition of the book. In his own memoirs Gavan Duffy praised Lucas's commitment to the Irish cause and the tenant league and denounced his treatment by Cullen. These set the tone for subsequent accounts such as John J. Horgan's chapter on Lucas in *Great Catholic Laymen* (1913) and Griffith's eulogy, in articles denouncing 'Place-hunters in Irish politics'.

Lucas emerged from these accounts considerably idealised. Griffith claimed Lucas:

> devoted himself to the Irish cause and the advancement of Catholic interests – not as the scoundrels Sadleir and Keogh affected to do by increasing dissension and misunderstanding between Catholic and Protestant, but by uniting Irishmen and exhibiting Catholicity in its spirit and charity and tenderness towards all good men – substituting to the vision of the long-prejudiced for the hideous and bloody hag they had conjured up before them as Catholicity, the angelic embodiment of a creed which gave Francis of Assisi and a hundred souls as beautiful to the salvation of man; until Irishmen who did not accept the creed of the Catholic Church yet could

learn to respect and revere its spirit and live in harmony and goodwill with their Catholic fellows – for peace and goodwill are not begotten of uniformity in thought and creed, but understanding and respect … .

Unhappily since Lucas died, the thing that in Ireland calls itself a Catholic Press has been and is – with one or two honourable exceptions – remarkable only as reproducing under the name of 'Catholic' all the vices that the rabid organs of Orangeism swelter in – and for adding to them a defence of that violation of public morality involved in the circumstances of Ireland in place-hunting.[28]

This version of Lucas, which would have surprised Bishop Alexander or James McKnight, was aimed at Griffith's rival D. P. Moran, whose weekly *Leader* combined aggressive promotion of the view that Irishness was essentially Catholic and Gaelic with exposing anti-Catholic discrimination in the public and private sectors, and arguing that since Ireland could never achieve complete independence from British power, it should pursue economic power and cultural distinctiveness to strengthen the case for home rule. Moran was certainly less populist (and less fiercely devotional) than Lucas; he spoke for an upwardly mobile Catholic lower middle class formed in the burgeoning Catholic secondary school sector, itself much more extensive, confident and consolidated than in Lucas's day. In that sense Griffith had a point in calling Moran a heir to Sadleir and Keogh, though Cullen might have been a better patron; but Moran's aggressive journalism, employing vituperation to attack deference and police politico-religious boundaries, had affinities to Lucas.[29]

As the opening of archives brought greater understanding for Cullen's position, and Gavan Duffy's memoirs were criticised, Lucas diminished in stature. Sheridan Gilley's paper on Lucas, which encapsulates this approach, points out Lucas's ability to raise enemies through intolerance and vituperation. He also notes that by treating all classes of Irish peasantry as synonymous Lucas failed to realise that tenant right was not a comprehensive solution since it would only benefit better-off tenants, and he argues that Lucas's view of the political role of the church was in a sense more 'theocratic' than Cullen's. However, Gilley does not address Lucas's point that the church had already intervened when the peasantry were instructed, with Cullen's participation, that it was their religious duty to defy their landlords at the polls even if this ruined them and their families; could such sacrifices be legitimately demanded simply to secure a few more Catholic officeholders of doubtful reliability?

In fact, Lucas fell foul of two questions which were to beset European Christian Democrat politics (and indeed, which beset any political organisation linked to external social movements and defined in ideological terms) – what should be the relationship between the authority of clerics and party leaders, and how should a balance be struck between ideological purity, risking impotence, and compromise, risking corruption?

Lucas's belief that philanthropy inspired by Catholic faith could overcome class differentiation and the social ills of modernity was over-optimistic; while such beliefs could inspire beneficial and self-sacrificing social action, they could also be misused to obscure differences between the official image of Catholic institutions and their actual limitations and abuses. Catholics proved just as capable as Protestants of making charity not a sacred duty towards the suffering members of Christ's body, but a self-serving exercise in patronage. Whatever the limitations of Lucas's vision, the central point in his favour is that he lived it himself, and that behind his anger and vituperation lay a sense that Christ starved in the slums or amid Famine victims.

Notes

1 *Sinn Féin*, 18 Oct. 1913, p. 7.
2 C. J. Riethmuller, *Frederick Lucas: A Biography* (London: Bell and Daldy, 1862), pp. 19–24.
3 S. Gilley 'Frederick Lucas, *The Tablet* and Ireland: a Victorian forerunner of liberation theology', in Stuart Mews (ed.), *Modern Religious Rebels* (London: Epworth Press, 1993), pp. 56–87, see pp. 58–9.
4 E. V. Lucas, *The Life of Frederick Lucas*, 2 vols (London: Burns and Oates, 1886), i, pp. 46–57, 207–8.
5 Lucas, *Life of Frederick* Lucas, i, p. 296.
6 *Ibid.*, pp. 93–7.
7 Gilley, 'Lucas, *The Tablet* and Ireland', p. 66.
8 Lucas, *Life of Frederick Lucas*, i, pp. 161–2.
9 T. E. Auge, *Frederick Ozanam and His World* (Milwaukee, WI: Bruce Pub. Co., 1966); Lucas, *Life of Frederick Lucas*, i, pp. 327–8. Both Lucas and Ozanam were denounced by the hard-line ultramontanist editor Louis Veuillot as subversive.
10 *Tablet*, 9 Dec. 1848, p. 792.
11 Lucas, *Life of Frederick Lucas*, i, pp. 163–86.
12 *Ibid.*, p. 67
13 *Ibid.*, p. 197.
14 Riethmuller, *Frederick Lucas*, pp. 85–9.
15 Lucas, *Life of Frederick Lucas*, i, pp. 226–7.
16 *Ibid.*, pp. 236–42
17 *Ibid.*, pp. 292–3.
18 *Ibid.*, pp. 220–31
19 R. J. Schiefen, *Nicholas Wiseman and the Transformation of English*

Catholicism (Shepherdstown, VA: Patmos Press, 1984), pp. 165–8; accusation of communism in Shrewsbury to Wiseman 16 Mar. 1848, quoted *ibid.*, p. 168 .

20 *Tablet*, 25 Mar. 1848, pp. 195–8 (Steele, p. 197).

21 *Tablet*, 13 May 1848, p. 320.

22 *Tablet*, 26 Aug. 1848, p. 552; Lucas, *Life of Frederick Lucas*, i, pp. 316–24.

23 Lucas, *Life of Frederick Lucas*, ii, pp. 53–6, 61, 85–6, 94–5.

24 This was an issue on which Cullen was always likely to prevail over Lucas's argument that Rome should overrule local episcopal decisions influenced by a primate and legate with significant curial connections, and allow priests to publicly oppose their own bishop politically and go into other dioceses to publicly oppose candidates supported by local bishops.

25 I. Whelan, *The Bible War in Ireland: The 'Second Reformation' and the Polarisation of Catholic–Protestant Relations, 1800–1840* (Dublin: Lilliput Press, 2005).

26 Newman to Emily Bowles, S. Gilley, *Newman and his Age* (2nd edn, London: Darton, Longman and Todd, 2003), p. 328.

27 See. R. Grey, 'Henry Edward Manning', in J. Jolliffe, *English Catholic Heroes* (Leominster: Gracewing, 2008).

28 *Sinn Féin*, 18 Oct. 1913, p. 7

29 P. Maume, *D. P. Moran* (Dundalk: Dundalgan, Press, 1995).

14

The 'greening' of Cardinal Manning

Fergal Casey

Henry Edward Manning, son of a governor of the Bank of England, graduate of Harrow and Oxford, ended his life being denounced for home rule politics and socialistic economics. Manning expected to 'sink to the bottom and disappear'[1] when he resigned as Anglican archdeacon of Chichester in 1850 before converting to Catholicism, but in 1865 the pope personally intervened to appoint him archbishop of Westminster and leader of the Catholic Church in England, and in 1875 created him a cardinal. Manning's increasing radicalism arguably constitutes a 'greening' – the application to England of insights gleaned from his engagement with Ireland. His pamphlet *Ireland: A Letter to Earl Grey* (1868) adopted politically radical ideas in response to Irish conditions, and this essay will offer a preliminary sketch of how in the service of a new Irish Catholic identity his economics radicalised, beginning with the pamphlet *The Dignity and Rights of Labour* (1874). His activism in the 1880s such as his mediation in the dock strike and his letters to *The Times* went side by side with growing engagement with the Land League and home rule movements, leading to a nascent anti-imperialism later developed, along with his economic positions, by G. K. Chesterton and Hilaire Belloc.

Manning recorded in his 1847 diary that serious illness 'made me realise much more than I otherwise should the state of the famishing in Ireland'.[2] In the 1850s he encountered refugees from that famine in Bayswater. In 1865 he became head of an English Catholic Church of nearly 750,000 souls, swollen by Irish immigration from a tenth of that figure in 1770.[3] Manning prioritised rapprochement with the Irish hierarchy.[4] His predecessor Cardinal Nicholas Wiseman had strained relations by failing to prevent post-emancipation Old Catholic sniping at Irish political radicalism and immigration which they saw as debasing 'their' church.[5] Manning struck up a friendship with Archbishop Paul Cullen and initiated Tuesday night soirees for Irish MPs, but, as Alan McClelland argues, Manning still needed a concrete measure to publicly signal the rapprochement. 'Cullen and his bench of bishops issued Pastorals condemning Fenianism and its consequent violence. This action provided a good opportunity for Manning to identify himself with the policy of the Irish bishops'.[6] His pastoral letter for Easter 1866 united the Irish and British hierarchies in denunciations of Fenianism. His careful phrasing, however, condemned only the violence of the outrages; he regarded the Fenians as goaded sinners redeemable by constructive legislation for Ireland. McClelland reads a Cullen letter to Manning as justifying his tactic of disowning the Fenians *because* their violence prevented necessary reforms that would remove their spawning-ground of discontent.[7] Oliver Rafferty persuasively argues Cullen prioritised his church's wellbeing over 'any romanticized view of Irish nationalism'.[8] Manning was not content simply to condemn, he wished to eliminate the Fenians by tackling the land question, even amidst violence.

Manning's *Ireland: A Letter to Earl Grey* was 'rather more open to the idea of state intervention in land contracts than was usual … an area which even quite advanced critics of *laissez-faire* in England were inclined to leave alone'.[9] Published in March 1868 it became famous as a radical pamphlet. The implications for English land-laws of its remedies for Irish agrarian unrest frightened the establishment, but Manning insisted 'upon the future of Ireland hangs the future of the British Empire'.[10] John Hammond, in emphasising the radical nature of W. E. Gladstone's conversion to this proposition, quotes his 1870 letter to Lord Granville; 'the state of Ireland … [is] a danger so absolutely transcending all others, that I call it the only real danger of the noble Empire of the Queen'.[11] The first third of Manning's *Letter* attacks a polemic by the future Chancellor of the exchequer Robert Lowe.[12] Manning adopts nationalist rhetoric to tackle Lowe's assertion that: 'It has been the pleasure of Ireland to pass upon herself a sentence of perpetual poverty'.[13] Manning furiously retorted; 'Who checked its agriculture, its cattle trade, its fisheries, and its manufactures by Act of Parliament? If poverty was ever inflicted by one nation on another, it has been inflicted on Ireland by England'.[14] This anticipates Arthur Griffith's 1905 assertion; 'to effectually destroy all power of competition in Ireland, the great capitalists of England determined to undersell the Irish in their own markets'.[15] Manning argued forcefully in his pamphlet, and in a letter attached to the copy he sent Gladstone, for the disestablishment of the Protestant Church in Ireland.[16] Four days after receiving it Gladstone told the Commons, 'The time has now come when the Church of Ireland as a Church in alliance with the State must cease to exist.'[17] Gladstone's action was radical as:

> the disestablishment of the Irish Church was, like the abolition of the Slave Trade, a reform that seemed almost insuperably difficult until a Minister, who combined power and zeal, undertook it, and then it was achieved with such apparent ease as to make everybody wonder why it had been looked upon with such apprehension.[18]

Manning believed in curbing the rights of the strong to prevent abuses against the weak, but his pamphlet sounded quasi-revolutionary:

> every people has a right to live of the fruits of the soil on which they are born and in which they are buried [...] A starving man commits no theft if he saves his life by eating of his neighbour's bread so much as is necessary for the support of his existence. The civil law yields before the higher jurisdiction of the divine.[19]

That passage 'raised the ire of *The Times* ... "a veritable encouragement of Fenianism and reprisals"'.[20] The idea became a touchstone of Manning's economics, but he downplayed its political radicalism:

> If at any time the civil laws shall so define the property of private persons as to damage the public weal, the supreme civil power has both the power and the duty so as to modify those private rights as to reconcile them with the public good ... The poor law ... charged the general estate with a rent-charge for the younger children of the realm. Nothing can be conceived more just; and yet, when it was proposed in 1838 for Ireland, it was called 'confiscation'.[21]

Manning noted that Irish tenants can be evicted 'for any passing reason ... which can arise in minds conscious of absolute and irresponsible power'[22] and asks if this would be tolerated in England. His faith that the English would demand reform if educated about Irish injustices was justified by Gladstone's landslide victory after this pamphlet started a national debate on Disestablishment. Manning quotes from *Land Tenure in Ireland* by Isaac Butt; 'In a country like Ireland, to give the power of doing such things is to ensure that they will be done';[23] and distrust of giving unfettered rights to the powerful resonates through Manning's thought. His peroration reprises his speech from May 1866:

> No greater self-deception could we practise on ourselves than to imagine that Fenianism is the folly of a few apprentices and shop-boys. Fenianism could not have survived for a year if it were not sustained by the traditional and just discontent of almost a whole people.[24]

This was quoted in the house of lords by the duke of Marlborough, 26 June 1868, as 'words ... of almost revolutionary incitement'.[25] Manning defended his political activism by reference to the Irish Catholic identity of his flock:

> I am day by day in contact with an impoverished race driven from home by the land question ... the despair and wildness which spring up in the hearts of the poor when legal force, like a sharp harrow, goes over the most sensitive and vital rights of mankind.[26]

Manning was approached by some Fenians and admitted he was 'identified with them in their general objects, but differed as to the means'[27] so that in the house of commons on 15 April 1869 Charles Newdegate thundered, 'He left the question open, and said he would consider it: is not this aiding treason?'[28] Manning regarded the Fenians as a medium of discontent. Cullen saw them as rivals bent on marginalising the church politically.[29] However, he disavowed Bishop David Moriarty's 'eternity is not long enough' sermon, fearing 'high condemnation of Fenianism at that critical moment, would enhance the increasing disaffection of the Catholic people from their pastors'.[30] Cullen eventually adopted the approach of Manning and his own lower clergy and so was once more 'united with popular political aspirations'.[31]

Gladstone disestablished the Church of Ireland using Manning as an intermediary with Cullen but passed his 1870 land act while those prelates and their colleagues attended the Vatican Council. Gladstone wrote to Manning on 16 February 1870 explaining his land act (and contacting Cullen *through* Manning):

> I send you 2 copies ... of the Irish Land Bill [...] The policy of the Bill is this, to prevent the Landlord from using this terrible weapon of undue and unjust eviction by so framing the handle that it shall cut his hands with the sharp edge of pecuniary damages [...] Please give one copy to Cardinal Archbishop Cullen.[32]

Manning conveyed from Rome the Irish bishops' amendments, ideas which might have been in the bill originally had he been mediating. 'We might as well propose the repeal of the Union'[33] replied Gladstone exasperatedly though these amendments included provisions he would pass in 1881. Manning's 1868 pamphlet underpinned the Liberals' developing Irish policy more than Lord John Russell's *A Letter to the Right Hon. Chichester Fortescue on the State of Ireland* pamphlet series calling for concurrent endowment, because Manning both understood Irish grievances and knew the 'texture of Gladstone's opinions and ... how to seize on the weak points in his political theory'.[34] Gladstone's fatal weakness was that while he sponsored liberal insurrections in Europe, 'he was at the same time blinded to the fact that the Irish movement was a liberal rising of an oppressed people'.[35] Hammond corroborates this interpretation: 'This wound ... was kept open by friends and opponents alike ... Butt, pleading for the Fenian prisoners recalled his attack on the

Bourbon government in Naples [...] Manning too made use of the Irish analogy for Gladstone's embarrassment'.[36]

Manning and Gladstone corresponded closely from first meeting in Oxford to Manning's death in 1892, save for 1851–61, after Manning converted to Catholicism, and 1875–85, after a furious row over 'Vaticanism' repaired by Gladstone's 'conversion' to home rule. Hammond notes of the last period that there were only two men 'to whom Gladstone signed himself at this time habitually "Yours affectionately". They were Argyll and Manning'.[37] Despite this intermittent friendship Shane Leslie endorsed Lord Salisbury's judgement, 'As to Cardinal Manning, no one can say of what Party he is',[38] and David Newsome notes that even in the 1830s Manning 'eschewed all party connections',[39] whereas Edward Norman sees Manning as a Liberal. Norman argues that Manning spoke on the platforms of the UK Alliance in 1867, attracted by its temperance mission, and became its vice-president because it 'was also a radical political movement whose integration with similar pressure-groups helped to give a popular basis to Gladstonian Liberalism'.[40] Norman asserts that Manning's 1889 declaration 'I am a Mosaic Radical. My watchword is, For God and the People' meant 'adhesion to traditional institutions, suitably adapted to the circumstances'.[41] Manning certainly had more influence with Liberal administrations than Tory, but he repaired relations with Disraeli during his Beaconsfield government, 1874–80, and went to extremes that Gladstone's Whig-dominated second government could not, *because* he was above party politics: indeed he regarded party politics as legislating for a class rather than the entire commonwealth.

Manning became involved with unions in 1872 to Gladstone's disapproval. Colin Matthew notes that Gladstone met with union delegations as chancellor of the exchequer, but only encouraged those wishing for minor modifications to his economic ideal, 'those that challenged it he disparaged'.[42] Gladstone regarded interventionism as almost sinful because he had substituted the free-trade minimalist state for his original impracticable goal of a confessional Anglican state.[43] Manning defended himself to Gladstone with reference to his Irish flock: 'I had been so much out of England ... that I did not know how far this reached. I found last week that even my Irish hodmen are organised'.[44] His identification with the Irish and the conditions under which they laboured in London made Manning into a radical social commentator of the age. His identification with labour was deep; he subscribed to the National Agricultural Labourers' Union in 1878 and 1879, and spoke publicly in favour of its dissenting leader Joseph Arch in 1872 and 1874. By contrast the bishop of Gloucester, Charles John Ellicott, 'whom

Disraeli soon afterwards proposed to make Archbishop of Canterbury, told the farmers to put the trade union speakers in the horse pond'.[45] Manning believed the church ought to side with the people and felt such displays of Toryism prevented Anglicanism being a popular church but that 'the example of Ireland ... was of a union of sentiment between people and religion'.[46] He sought to emulate that union by applying to England the interventionism he had advocated for Ireland. His 1845 archdiaconal charge had addressed the land-laws, 'The possessors of land are the natural guardians of the poor who live and die upon their soil',[47] but it was Irish influence that made him unmercifully interrogate them. Manning consulted Archbishop William Walsh, the Irish hierarchy's economics expert, for advice on Michael Davitt and Henry George's rival land-nationalisation schemes,[48] but on industrial economics he needed no counsel. Between 1841 and 1851 over 100,000 Irish immigrated to London, most 'came as paupers, and many lived and died as paupers'.[49] Manning was thus representing a new Irish Catholic identity, a purely urban working class.

Manning's pamphlet *The Dignity and Rights of Labour* originated as a speech at the Mechanics' Institute Leeds. Manning's preamble exemplifies his Catholicised economics, promising to speak of labour 'as a political economist would' before defining labour as 'the honest exertion of the powers of our mind and of our body for our own good and for the good of our neighbour'.[50] No economist would so boldly rewrite Adam Smith's belief that the invisible hand of the free-market transformed individual greed into societal prosperity. Manning emphasised his heterodoxy, 'if he does not put forth those powers for his own good, and also for the good of his neighbours, I call it selfishness'.[51] Manning claimed that the 'first agency and factor' of Britain's 'great commercial wealth ... is labour'.[52] This goes beyond the thought of David Ricardo, Manning's avowed touchstone. Just as Karl Marx developed Ricardo's dangerous idea, unleashed against the corn laws, of an economic system where landlords parasitically thrived off subsistence workers. Marx's address to the 1865 International, published as *Value, Price and Profit* demonstrated his labour theory of value as a logical development from Ricardian economics. Manning posits labour as the origin of all wealth. Marx asserts that labour is the source of all value; diamonds are priceless and water is cheap because value is determined by the crystallised social labour invested therein. This is the basis for the theory of surplus value which explains capitalist exploitation, and Manning nears it by aligning the church with labour.

Manning thus reassuringly quotes Adam Smith; 'The property which every man has in his own labour, as it is the original foundation of all other property, so it is the most sacred and inviolable'; in order to 'claim for labour the rights of property'.[53] He then invades sacred ground, 'I claim for labour ... the rights of capital', and plays with the etymology of 'capital' to dub:

> the strength, and the skill in the honest workman 'live money'. It is capital laid up in him; and that capital is the condition of production. For capital which is in money, which I will call dead capital, or dead money, receives its life from the living power and skill of the labourer.[54]

Marx, however, acidly made the same point: 'capital is dead labour which, vampire-like, lives only by sucking living labour, and lives the more, the more labour it sucks'.[55] 'Every labourer has a right to work or not to work'[56] Manning asserted, and to judge whether he 'can subsist upon certain wages'.[57] Inseparable is the right to organise. Marx despised union advocates but regarded them as heralds of revolution.[58] Manning, however, aimed to stave off revolution with economic reform as surely as he wished to stave off Irish republicanism with political reform. He situates unions in Roman law, making them an ancient institution re-instated against rapacious capitalists. Manning advocated 'interference' in the free-market by quoting Pitt's incendiary 1800 arbitration act speech:

> The time will come when ... it will be in the power of any one man in a town to reduce the wages ... and then farewell to our commercial state [...] Parliament ... if it cannot redress your grievances; its power is at an end. Tell me not that Parliament cannot; it is omnipotent to protect.[59]

Manning thus urged intervention to curb English working-hours:

> if the hours of labour resulting from the unregulated sale of a man's strength and skill shall lead ... to turning fathers and husbands into ... creatures of burden ... who rise up before the sun, and come back when it is set, wearied and able only to take food and lie down to rest – the domestic life of men exists no longer.[60]

Marx used identical language, 'A man ... whose whole lifetime, apart from the mere physical interruptions by sleep, meals, and so forth, is absorbed by his labour for the capitalist, is less than a beast of burden'.[61] Marx noted that the working day has never been limited except by legislation, which proves that in its 'merely economical action capital is the stronger side'.[62] Manning would agree, and that means the church must side with the workers, violating *laissez-faire* precepts with government intervention.[63] This pamphlet sent a 'shock-wave through the respectable and propertied classes, in both his own church and the Establishment.'[64] Here was a trade unionism that challenged

Gladstone's economic pronouncements: 'As to the condition of the workpeople, experience has shown, especially in the case of the Factory Acts, that we should do wrong in laying down any abstract maxim as an invariable rule'.[65]

Hammond notes that Gladstone's 1881 Land Act gave the Irish peasant rights 'not yet gained by the English workman'[66] while Matthew notes that 'what is striking in the 1880s is the absence of sustained or systematic political challenge to the Gladstonian minimal central state ... Only in Ireland was there significant demand for central government money for social purposes'.[67] Manning, in service of a new Irish Catholic identity, systematically challenged economic theory which forbade government intervention for his flock. Newsome notes that extensive Irish immigration effectively split English Catholicism into a 'prosperous upper class and a massive urban labouring class'.[68] Manning's 'Relief of distress in winter' letter to *The Times* in November 1886 arose from evidence to a Mansion House committee on the labouring class, which saw him propose relief for 'those who would work if work could be found for them',[69] contravening classical economic theory. Manning, like Marx, saw depression as a consequence of overproduction. J. K. Galbraith lucidly summarises Marx:

> A progressively increasing productive power returned ... a diminishing fraction – of the value of the goods so produced to labour. From the inability of workers to buy what they produced and the tendency of the capitalists' savings to go into ever greater expansion of plant and product came cumulative over-stocking, diminishing profits and crises.[70]

But Say's law holds that overproduction is impossible. The maxim that 'supply creates its own demand' implies that 'from the proceeds of every sale of goods, there was paid out to someone somewhere in wages, salaries, interest, rent or profit ... the wherewithal to buy that item'.[71] Such theoretical certitude neglects human misery: 'Men, women, and children are starving or suffering bitterly by cold and hunger ... Is nothing to be done?'[72] Manning was *avant-garde* in urging intervention in a recession. The Liberals refused to recognise the 'existence of "unemployment" in the 1880s' because economic orthodoxy deemed it was merely a 'temporary dislocation to the balance of equilibrium, and they believed that the re-establishment of that balance needed only the corrective forces of the free market'.[73] They boycotted Lord Salisbury's 1885 Royal Commission on the Depression of Trade because it 'dignified a nonsense'.[74] Paul Krugman notes that in the 1930s:

> many prominent economists subscribed to a sort of moralistic fatalism ... recovery, declared Joseph Schumpeter, 'is sound only if it [comes] of

> itself. For any revival which is merely due to artificial stimulus leaves part of the work of depressions undone and adds, to an undigested remnant of maladjustment, new maladjustment of its own which has to be liquidated in turn.[75]

Manning presented the choices in this *laissez-faire* approach's with brutal clarity:

> To those who are willing to work, but can find no work, relief must be given either in the form of work, or without work; but relief without work, we are told, like alms and doles, is demoralising. The alternative, then, is to give relief in work or give no relief.[76]

The choice, influenced by his flock's experiences, is that of the Irish Famine: make the starving poor build follies, to survive without being demoralised, or let them die, to rebalance supply and demand. Would the rich, behind a Rawlsian 'veil of ignorance', agree with Manning that being given relief without work is less demoralising than dying? In 'The problem of the unemployed', three February 1888 letters, Manning disdains the posturing of *The Times* at the height of their campaign fraudulently linking Parnell with terrorism. He informed the newspaper that he preferred breaking from orthodoxy 'in times of severe and transient distress'[77] rather than prioritising theory over human misery, as their offending editorial did. Manning interrogated their platitude that the only solution was for the employed to maximise profit to spend on employing others, by pointing out that no trade was producing this surplus, and that if even a surplus did accumulate assurances that it would create employment in London contradicted freedom of capital.[78] Sir Robert Giffen riposted that giving relief would be socialistic. Manning quoted back J. S. Mill's 'Vindication of the French Revolution of February 1848' which defended the revolutionary government's recognition of an 'obligation on society to find work and wages for all persons willing and able to work'.[79] Mill maintained that intractable mass unemployment as opposed to this recognition led to socialism; therefore Manning's intervention to relieve transient distress represented neither socialism nor its cause but the means of its prevention. Manning proposed saving capitalism from its worst excesses against the wishes of the establishment, as he sought to save Ireland from misrule by that establishment.[80]

Manning excelled at such social activism, perhaps because of his personal stake in such undertakings. In 1868 he contended that the Irish revered their church because 'they know that no human power and no worldly interest separates their Church and their clergy from themselves'.[81] In London too if the Irish went on strike their clergy felt the hardship through unpaid dues. Manning instigated the formation of the Mansion House Committee of Conciliation in the 1889 dock strike. McClelland notes that four fifths of the dockers were Irish by birth or ancestry.[82] The bishop of London, Frederick Temple, abandoned the talks when the men rejected an inordinate postponement of a pay increase. Manning, aged 81, convinced an east end meeting of truculent dockers, which involved over four hours of debate, to concede ground on the date of implementation, then shamed the joint committee of directors into accepting this compromise with a full day of haranguing.[83]

In 1871 Manning had asked Cullen about Isaac Butt's Home Rule Association, only to be told it was a ragtag of Orangemen and communists. Cullen urged him to hold aloof from it. The Irish clergy 'had tended to ally the blessings of the Church to the aspirations of the country ... Cullen tried to reverse the flow'[84] but Manning 'felt that the Church ought always to identify itself with the legitimate aspirations of the laity'.[85] Manning approved of Butt's movement, especially after Davitt ('a frequent visitor at Archbishops' House')[86] succeeded in diverting Fenians towards politics. Manning's support for the land league caused a growing estrangement from Gladstone. When Salisbury took office one of new Viceroy Carnarvon's first visitors was Manning, delivering the 'views of the Irish Bishops'.[87] Gladstone was secretly willing to grant home rule, if it was desired *after* reform. Gladstone believed Carnarvon's Irish policy constructive and refused to 'bid' for Parnell's endorsement resulting in a scabrous manifesto repudiating the Liberals. Manning wrote to Archbishop Walsh of Dublin, '*You may rely on me* for refusing to subordinate the Irish movement to any English question',[88] sacrificing his Catholic education campaign to support Parnell's manoeuvrings. Manning publicly followed Gladstone's 'conversion' to home rule, and, just as he had put Ireland before Gladstone, in December 1890 put Ireland before Parnell. Manning urged Gladstone to sideline the scandal-ridden Parnell with the pledge: 'I will endeavour to frame a scheme of home rule which shall be *acceptable to the people of Ireland*. If *they* shall *refuse to accept it* I will relinquish the work to other hands'.[89] The Irish bishops wrote Manning daily and he held their condemnations at bay until Parnell attacked Gladstone. Such cross-channel leadership had been acknowledged by Gladstone in an 1885 private memorandum: 'I did not calculate upon Parnell and his friends, or upon Manning and his Bishops'.[90]

Manning was simultaneously active in the National Association for Promoting State Directed Colonization. Despite following the Vatican in supporting Disraeli's Turcophile policy in 1876,[91] contact with the realities of Irish expropriation erased India and Africa from his imperial horizons. He advocated planned emigration in 'Distress in Winter'[92] as the solution to London's overcrowded poverty, but only to the 'empty spaces' of Canada and the Antipodes. Active expropriation was unthinkable so he chose areas where the damage had arguably already been done. Chesterton and Belloc adopted Manning's social justice activism and developed this retreat from Beaconsfieldism into anti-imperialism, so that the immigrant Irish Catholic identity he served influenced another generation of English Catholic social thought. Archbishop Walsh had written in 1887, 'We can never make him a suitable return for what he has done, and is doing to help the Irish cause'.[93] England's poor could have expressed similar sentiments regarding the transformative influence on Manning of a diasporic urban Irish Catholic identity.

Notes

1 D. Newsome, *The Convert Cardinals: John Henry Newman and Henry Edward Manning* (London: J. Murray, 1993), p. 184.
2 S. Leslie, *Cardinal Manning: His Life and Labours* (Dublin: Clanmore and Reynolds, 1953), p. 31.
3 Newsome, *Convert Cardinals*, p. 189.
4 V. A. McClelland, *Cardinal Manning: His Public Life and Influence, 1865–1892* (Oxford: Oxford University Press, 1962), p. 162.
5 O. P. Rafferty, *The Catholic Church and the Protestant State: Nineteenth-Century Irish Realities* (Dublin: Four Courts Press, 2008), pp. 70, 79.
6 McClelland, *Cardinal Manning*, p. 163.
7 *Ibid.*, p. 163.
8 Rafferty, *Catholic Church and Protestant State*, p. 157.
9 E. R. Norman, *The English Catholic Church in the Nineteenth Century* (Oxford: Clarendon, 1984), p. 280.
10 H. E. Cardinal Manning, *Ireland: A Letter to Earl Grey* (London: Longman, Green and Co., 1868), p. 3.
11 J. L. Hammond, *Gladstone and the Irish Nation* (London: Longman, Green and Co., 1938), p. 85.
12 R. Lowe, 'What shall we do for Ireland?', *Quarterly Review*, 124 (Jan. 1868), pp. 255–86.
13 Manning, *Ireland*, p. 8.
14 *Ibid.*
15 A. Griffith, *The Resurrection of Hungary: A Parallel for Ireland* (Dublin: University College Dublin Press, 2003), p. 84.
16 Manning also politically counselled Gladstone during the bill's eventful passage. Rafferty, *Catholic Church and Protestant State*, pp. 192–3.
17 McClelland, *Cardinal Manning*, p. 171.
18 Hammond, *Gladstone and the Irish Nation*, p. 88.
19 Manning, *Ireland*, pp. 28–9.

20 McClelland, *Cardinal Manning*, p. 170.
21 Manning, *Ireland*, pp. 29–30.
22 *Ibid.*, p. 32.
23 *Ibid.*, p. 31.
24 *Ibid.*, p. 42.
25 E. R. Norman, *The Catholic Church and Ireland in the Age of Rebellion, 1859–1873* (London: Longman, 1965), p. 89.
26 Manning, *Ireland*, p. 40.
27 Norman, *Church and Ireland*, p. 126.
28 *Ibid.*, p. 127.
29 Rafferty, *Catholic Church and Protestant State*, p. 174.
30 Norman, *Church and Ireland*, p. 119.
31 *Ibid.*, p. 123.
32 H. C. G. Matthew (ed.), *The Gladstone Diaries with Cabinet Minutes and Prime-Ministerial Correspondence: Volume VII January 1869–June 1871* (Oxford: Clarendon, 1982), pp. 238–9. Matthew's selection of letters from Gladstone to Manning in 1870 clearly shows their friendship faltering over 'Vaticanism'.
33 Hammond, *Gladstone and the Irish Nation*, p. 103.
34 McClelland, *Cardinal Manning*, p. 176.
35 *Ibid.*, p. 176.
36 Hammond, *Gladstone and the Irish Nation*, p. 110.
37 *Ibid.*, p. 137.
38 Leslie, *Cardinal Manning*, p. 198.
39 D. Newsome, *The Parting of Friends: A Study of the Wilberforces and Henry Manning* (London: Murray, 1966), p. 212.
40 Norman, *English Catholic Church*, p. 274.
41 *Ibid.* Manning seems to echo the Liberal 'Mosaic view of political life, with Gladstone leading a purged party through the wilderness', but biblical comparisons abounded in the heightened political discourse of the day. H. C. G. Matthew, *Gladstone, 1809–1898* (Oxford: Clarendon, 1997), p. 550.
42 Matthew, *Gladstone*, p. 133.
43 *Ibid.*, p. 76.
44 Leslie, *Cardinal Manning*, p. 149.
45 Hammond, *Gladstone and the Irish Nation*, p. 180.
46 Norman, *English Catholic Church*, p. 275.
47 Newsome, *Convert Cardinals*, p. 148.
48 Leslie, *Henry Edward Manning*, p. 152.
49 Newsome, *Convert Cardinals*, p. 191.
50 H. E. Cardinal Manning, *The Dignity and Rights of Labour and Other Writings on Social Questions* (London: Burns, Oates and Washbourne, 1934), pp. 4–5. This edition is the 1874 text and subsequent open letters.
51 *Ibid.*, p. 5.
52 *Ibid.*, p. 4.
53 *Ibid.*, p. 16.

54 *Ibid.*, p. 17.
55 K. Marx, *Capital: A Critique of Political Economy* (Harmondsworth: Penguin, 1976), i, p. 342.
56 Manning, *Dignity of Labour*, p. 18.
57 *Ibid.*, p. 19.
58 K. Marx and F. Engels, *The Communist Manifesto* (London: Verso, 1998), p. 50.
59 Manning, *Dignity of Labour*, p. 27.
60 *Ibid.*, p. 29.
61 K. Marx, *Value, Price and Profit* (London: George Allen and Unwin, 1899), p. 81.
62 *Ibid.*, p. 89.
63 Manning, *Dignity of Labour*, p. 31.
64 Newsome, *Convert Cardinals*, p. 148.
65 Matthew, *Gladstone*, p. 118.
66 Hammond, *Gladstone and the Irish Nation*, p. 219.
67 Matthew, *Gladstone*, p. 419.
68 Newsome, *Convert Cardinals*, p. 192.
69 Manning, *Dignity of Labour*, p. 36.
70 J. K. Galbraith, *Money: Whence It Came, Where It Went* (London: Deutsch, 1975), p. 114.
71 *Ibid.*, p. 230.
72 Manning, *Dignity of Labour*, p. 37.
73 Matthew, *Gladstone*, p. 372.
74 *Ibid.*, p. 416.
75 P. Krugman, *The Return of Depression Economics* (London: Allen Lane, 1999), p. 12.
76 Manning, *Dignity of Labour*, p. 39.
77 *Ibid.*, p. 44.
78 *Ibid.*, pp. 44–5.
79 *Ibid.*, p. 49.
80 By contrast Gladstone sent the duke of Bedford 'Giffen's "masterly" refutation' of Henry George's *Progress & Poverty* (New York: Doubleday, McClure and Co., 1879); Manning had intervened to keep the work off the Vatican's index of forbidden books (Matthew, *Gladstone*, p. 357).
81 Manning, *Ireland*, p. 12.
82 McClelland, *Cardinal Manning*, p. 144.
83 Purcell's documented but hostile account records Manning saying of the directors, 'I never in my life preached to so impenitent a congregation'. E. S. Purcell, *Life of Cardinal Manning, Archbishop of Westminster* 2 vols (London: Macmillan, 1895), ii, p. 662.
84 Norman, *Church and Ireland*, p. 9.
85 McClelland, *Cardinal Manning*, p. 178.
86 *Ibid.*, p. 174.
87 Hammond, *Gladstone and the Irish Nation*, p. 378.

88 McClelland, *Cardinal Manning*, p. 188.
89 *Ibid.*, p. 191.
90 Hammond, *Gladstone and the Irish Nation*, p. 369.
91 R. T. Shannon, *Gladstone and the Bulgarian Agitation 1876* (London: Nelson, 1963), p. 192.
92 Manning, *Dignity of Labour*, pp. 41–2.
93 McClelland, *Cardinal Manning*, p. 198.

Part VI

Faith, wealth and Catholic Unionism

15

Power, wealth and Catholic identity in Ireland, 1850–1900

Ciaran O'Neill

Life is too short to follow a lisp into Burke's Peerage.[1]

Arthur E. Clery, 1921

Catholics with money can be a rare sight in Irish history – a sort of mythical, unlikely creature. The preoccupation with connecting poverty to Catholicism suggests an institutional reliance within Irish historiography on the language of 'endurance and emergence' that has been passed down from, among other sources, the widely-read Christian Brothers schoolbooks of the early twentieth century.[2] As Ian McBride has recently noted, the ubiquitous postcolonial perspectives on Irish history have also tended to overlook the diversity of social position and class hierarchy in Ireland, creating instead a 'flattened out picture of Irish society, split into monolithic blocs of dominators and resisters'.[3] This chapter will query the reasons for this binary impulse in Irish historiography, confining its analysis to the second half of the nineteenth century, a period in which class lines were being drawn more clearly, and more publicly, than ever before. It will argue for a more nuanced treatment of the whole spectrum of Irish Catholic wealth and for a considered reappraisal of the role played by the richest Catholic families in Irish society in this period. It will attempt to do so by highlighting the importance of education in relation to Catholic social mobility in the period.

I

The temptation for historians interested in the dynamics of Irish Catholic power and wealth is to focus almost exclusively on the secular clergy. This overemphasis on the loudest and most obvious source of Catholic opinion is regrettable and it has obscured discussion of the Catholic laity. Where the flock and the shepherd are mentioned, it is often assumed that the former followed the latter at all times. The historian Patrick Corish complained of such lazy assumptions in the early 1980s. The church, he quite correctly noted, 'is not the same as the clergy, there is the laity as well', and, as John Henry Newman once pointed out, the church would, after all, 'look foolish without them'.[4] In the post-Famine era Catholic social thought in Ireland and Britain revolved primarily around ideas of anti-materialism and subsidiarity that would later find expression in the outpourings of intellectuals such as G. K. Chesterton and Hilaire Belloc. These ideas formed the basis of the Social Catholic Movement which came to prominence in the early decades of the twentieth century but the ideas it espoused were, in reality, the product of a much longer gestation period. The definitive Vatican statement on social distribution in this period was Pope Leo XIII's encyclical *Rerum Novarum* (1891). Entitled 'The Rights and Duties of Capital and Labour', *Rerum Novarum* is commonly believed to have been issued at the request of Cardinal Henry Edward Manning, who had made the issue of social justice the defining one of his twenty-seven-year reign as archbishop of Westminster between 1865 and 1892 and was partly influenced by the plight of many Irish Catholics in Britain.[5] *Rerum Novarum* outlined a strand of Catholic economic and social thought that has remained influential for over a hundred years. Leo XIII was the first pope to recognize directly the suffering of the poor and the working classes, in the context of modern industrialisation, and from this point onwards the papacy has moved progressively further away from its aristocratic affinities. Its message was reaffirmed by the encyclical *Quadragesimo Anno* in 1931, which was issued by Pius XI in the wake of the Wall St crash in the summer of 1929. *Quadragesimo Anno* called for a 'redistribution of the social order', in response to the failure of capitalism with workers and employers expected to work together to close the yawning gap between rich and poor.

Although John Whyte has argued for the importance of *Quadragesimo Anno* in relation to Irish society in his seminal work *Church and State in Ireland 1923–70*, the original document, *Rerum Novarum*, is arguably just as important.[6] It copper-fastened the position of Catholic social teaching as primarily concerned with the poor. It admitted the right to accumulate capital, but its sympathy was entirely with those that had not yet managed to do so. As the central Vatican message percolated down to national and local levels the public speeches of Cardinal Manning in England consistently emphasised the poverty of Catholics in the post Famine era, as did his Irish counterparts in Dublin. The most prominent Irish clerics such as Cardinal Paul Cullen frequently bemoaned the plight of the poor, as did Cardinal Edward McCabe and Archbishop William Walsh.[7] Crucially, this created a public discourse in which wealthy Catholics were never mentioned and suited no political agenda. The rich, this seemed to indicate, could fend for themselves. Like any papal encyclical *Rerum Novarum* was interpreted in a variety of different ways across the Catholic world, but in Ireland its core argument was particularly suited to bolstering a long-held conviction that a Protestant-dominated industrialised state was fundamentally antagonistic to the spiritual wellbeing of its Catholic citizens and, not insignificantly, this was also compatible with a nationalist reading of Irish history. Tom Garvin has characterised the Irish Catholic Church in the twentieth century as espousing a 'curiously empty rhetorical democratic radicalism or national populism'.[8] This marriage of conservative and populist economic thought with the increasingly nationalist rhetoric of the virtuous downtrodden Catholic produced a rather unfortunate mixture. It has led to a situation in Irish popular culture whereby the idea of a pre-Celtic Tiger 'rich Catholic' can somehow seem an oxymoron, or at the very least incongruent.

Recent interpretations of nineteenth-century Ireland have done little to alter this view. The most recent publication to deal with the problem of the Catholic elite is Fergus Campbell's *The Irish Establishment 1879–1914*. Drawing on the sociological canon of elite theory he argues that the Irish 'establishment' or ruling class was a disproportionately non-Catholic and closed elite. He disagrees with the popular 'greening' theory of, among others, Laurence McBride, and sets out to disprove that any systematic or dramatic process of Catholic infiltration took place in the highest echelons of society prior to Independence.[9] In order to disprove this particular hypothesis Campbell systematically compiled biographical information on 1,200 or so of the top layer of powerful people across the landed, clerical, business, political, administrative and policing elites in Ireland from 1879–1914. From this position Campbell argues that under the Union aspirant Catholics were effectively repelled by a Protestant-dominated ruling caste. The only powerful positions in Ireland that could be genuinely considered open to the meritocratic advancement of any Irish Catholic, from any background, were either in the religious elite, or, to a much lesser extent, the political elite.[10] Campbell's thesis is an important contribution that poses significant challenges for those interested in Catholic mobility under the Union. His central argument rests, however, on one very debatable assumption – that the wealthiest members of the Catholic laity *wanted* to be centrally involved in any or all of the categories he has identified. This assumption is problematic, as it characterises the Catholic elite as aspirational, but ultimately failing to wield influence in Ireland under the Union. In short, Campbell has demonstrated where the Catholic elite are absent, the challenge he presents to Irish historians is to ask where they might be.

Marianne Elliott also sees the Irish Catholic laity as aspirational. Her recent work, *When God Took Sides,* acknowledges the lengthy tradition of wealthy Irish Catholics sending their sons overseas to English public schools such as Stonyhurst. Elliott remarks '[i]t was the same story as of old, rather than overthrowing the establishment, Catholics wanted to join it'.[11] Elliott's conviction implies that a relatively small group of wealthy Catholics constituted an ambitious rival elite, as opposed to an existing elite with its own internal normative behaviour. Elsewhere, Patrick Maume has compared such upwardly mobile Catholics to sunflowers, 'turned towards the source of professional opportunity'; and using education as a means to achieve it.[12] The effect of this is to contribute to an overarching legitimisation of a particular mantra in Irish history, one cultivated by a wide array of popular writers from Sean O'Faolain to C. S. Andrews and Conor Cruise O'Brien. The mantra insists that Independence from British rule in 1922 meant that a generation of Christian Brothers-educated Catholic boys replaced a Protestant-dominated closed elite by leapfrogging an expectant Catholic elite comprised of educated, moderately nationalist middle-class families. Such a reading of Irish history renders the discussion of an established and competitive Catholic elite in the decades preceding Independence rather difficult. The recent writings of Campbell, Elliott and Maume do little to address this, and in fact cement it by endorsing the bit-part offering that although some Catholics had climbed a rung or two under the Union, this was mainly a result of an aberrant, denominationally disloyal and somewhat suspect professional ambition. The vast majority of Irish Catholics, we might infer from all this, were stuck in traffic somewhere on the wrong side of a social mobility roadblock. Only independence, and with it the destruction of that closed elite, would see that traffic clear.

II

In part, this difficulty in categorising and understanding the behaviour of elite Catholics prior to Independence stems from an inability to define exactly what social grouping constituted the Catholic elite in the nineteenth century. Kevin Whelan has argued for the idea of an underground Catholic gentry in the eighteenth century, but nothing as substantial has ever been attempted for the centuries that followed.[13] This confusion is somewhat understandable, as Catholic wealth and status sometimes traduced social class and incorporated *nouveaux riche*, *nouveaux pauvres*,

Old English and Old Irish alike. Depending on their business contacts and familial network the *arriviste* could easily mix with the gentrified and thus defy straightforward categorisation. Irish historians have dealt with this by focussing attention on the rising middle class in the nineteenth century. In Senia Pašeta's *Before the Revolution* the Irish Catholic elite are characterised as an essentially middle-class cohort, predominantly based in Dublin, and educated in the major Irish Catholic schools such as Clongowes, Blackrock and Castleknock, or at the very least at the newly constituted National University of Ireland.[14] Pašeta's conclusion is that this group of university-educated Irish Catholics gravitated gradually towards moderate and advanced nationalism, conforming to the 'blocked mobility' thesis of revolutionary nationalism previously advocated by both John Hutchinson and Tom Garvin in their influential work in the 1980s.[15] This theory holds that a generation of mainly Catholic lower middle class became progressively more revolutionary in outlook when frustrated by a social structure that did not allow for upward social mobility commensurate with their increased access to education. This, combined with the placement of home rule in political purgatory in 1914, is, according to the theory, what produced a rebellion in 1916 and all that followed. This theory has much merit though it implies that Catholics were a homogenous, oppressed sect. The comparatively underdeveloped area of social history in Ireland has suffered for its commitment to this idea of the Catholic 'national struggle', one which apparently conforms to the official Catholic line.

Alan O'Day, also influenced by Hutchinson's blocked mobility thesis, provides a very good example of this interpretation of Irish history:

> Catholic Ireland within the British *imperium* is a classic instance of non-dominance – of a small peoples' quest to break the thraldom of a mighty neighbour ... Throughout the period of the union there were successive cadres of men who were determined to throw off the yoke of English rule or at the very least to modify its effect on their country ... The national struggle is a tale of how an Irish elite evolved, articulated its aspirations, persuaded and mobilised the masses and ultimately conducted a successful assault on the integrity of the United Kingdom.[16]

In his recent work on the issue of Catholic loyalty James McConnel has argued that Irish historians might move away from this rhetoric of Catholic homogeneity, endurance, and emergence. On the eve of the Great War he finds Catholic loyalty in the nineteenth century deriving from 'a confluence of gentlemanliness, economic self interest' and 'political tensions dating from the O'Connell era'.[17] The issue of Catholic loyalism has long been avoided by Irish scholars, and is dealt with elsewhere in this collection, but what of those Catholics who had no outstanding issues with social mobility, and were predominantly politically neutral?

III

Irish educational history provides a plentiful but undervalued source of information on the Irish Catholic elite. The quality and range of education on offer to Irish Catholics goes some way towards pointing to the complexity of wealth distribution. In general, historians of Irish education have tended to concentrate much more on the provision of elementary education and, to date, there exists no large-scale examination of elite education in Ireland.[18] Throughout the nineteenth century the majority of Ireland's wealthiest Catholic families educated their sons either on the continent or (more usually) in England at a network of elite Catholic colleges the most important of which were Stonyhurst, Beaumont, Downside and Oscott. Typically, Irish boys accounted for between a fifth to a third of all boys attending these English colleges in any given year between 1850–1900.[19] The most desirable domestic choices were Clongowes and Castleknock, and, at various points, the Jesuit school at Tullabeg, and the French College at Blackrock.

Those travelling abroad were following a precedent established in the sixteenth century, when the Catholic gentry were often found in continental seminaries in Spain and elsewhere as a result of penal subjugation.[20] A minority of wealthy Irish families continued to send their sons to English schools, even beyond the Second World War. For girls, the continental tradition also remained relevant well into the twentieth century, with Irish families 'finishing' their daughters in Bruges, Ypres, Switzerland and elsewhere.[21] The pursuit of a privileged or choice education strongly suggests a high degree of class consciousness in elite Catholic families, about which we know precious little. The remainder of this chapter will sketch the lives of some prominent graduates of elite schools in England in order to demonstrate the complexity of Catholic power and influence in the second half of the nineteenth century.

IV

The list of prominent Catholic families sending their sons to England contains some striking names. They are noteworthy, perhaps, for the lack of a clear pattern in their patronage. They are united by income and creed rather than any socio-political outlook. Edward Martyn (1859–1923), first president of Sinn Féin, was educated in the 1870s

Figure 1 The network of Catholic elite schools (boys)

near London, at the Jesuit Beaumont College and at an extravagant cost. His cousin, the celebrated novelist and revivalist, George Moore, was thought a 'dunce' when boarding at the prestigious diocesan seminary, Oscott College, in Birmingham. It is clear that while those travelling abroad for their education were united by their financial muscle, the origin of their wealth was variable. In the nineteenth century an education abroad was up to twice as expensive as at the domestic alternatives such as Clongowes Wood. In the 1870s a year's tuition at Beaumont College was about £120 on average per year. If a boy was to spend five years at Beaumont the total outlay on education would be in the region of £600.[23] The sums expended by these families on an English education were enormous relative to regular income levels. As late as the 1890s the average income of a small farming household in Woodford, near Galway, was just over £38.[24] The expense involved in sending these boys abroad for their education for anywhere up to five or six years effectively ruled out all but the wealthiest Catholic families from this defining social cache.

An irony of all this was that an English education could produce prominent nationalist figures in the nineteenth century who were loud in their denunciation of the Union. Thomas Francis Meagher had attended Stonyhurst in the 1830s and an apparently affected English accent remained with him through an eventful and rebellious life spent undermining various forms of authority in Ireland, America and Van Diemen's Land.[25] The future plenipotentiary of the Anglo-Irish Treaty of 1921, George Gavan Duffy (1882–1951), attended Stonyhurst in 1890s, and was followed by the poet of the 1916 Rising, Joseph Mary Plunkett (1887–1916).[26] These ideological cleavages did not emerge in adulthood, but were present throughout their schooldays as well. Writing home to his mother from the Benedictine school at Downside in 1881, an Irish boy, Lucien Bonaparte-Wyse (grandson of Sir Thomas Wyse, the politician and educationalist) noted the division caused among the Irish boys by the death of Disraeli. 'I am also sorry that Lord Beaconsfield is dead', he wrote, 'All the boys seem to go against him, such as the FitzGeralds and nearly all the other boys'.[27]

If political loyalty provides little that allows us to generalise, then neither does any form of 'ethnic' division. Downside educated a broad range of Irish Catholic families. In the 1840s the eponymous nephew of the Liberator, Daniel O'Connell, was a classmate of Valentine Augustus Browne, the future 4th earl of Kenmare of 'Old English' descent and holder of 118,000 acres in counties Kerry and Cork.[28] In 1852 Charles Owen O'Conor, a descendant of an 'Old Irish' dynasty and holder of the title of 'the O'Conor Don, Prince of Connacht' also attended Downside. At schools such this, or the Jesuit Beaumont College, Irish boys mingled with an international blend of elite Catholics. Beaumont, in particular, recruited from an astonishing array of families across Europe and the new world. In the class of 1881 sat Prince Jaime de Borbon, Carlist pretender to the throne of Spain, and legitimist claimant to the throne of France. Alongside him was Beauclerk Upington, son of Sir Thomas Upington, the Cork-born prime minister of the Cape Colony, South Africa 1884–86.[29] Together with boys of this background sat many Irish-born boys, who usually accounted for about one-fifth of the student body at Beaumont College at any one time. One such classmate was Count Patrick O'Byrne, son of Count John O'Byrne, possessed of a 3,905 acre estate split unevenly between Roscrea, Co. Tipperary and Allardstown in Co. Louth. His son would later rebel against the system that had served his family by siding with the 'irregulars' in the Irish Civil War.[30]

The many 'types' of Catholic mingled most comfortably at Stonyhurst College in Lancashire. The very existence of Henry MacDermot-Blake testifies to this phenomenon. He attended the school in 1882, the first son of the Hugh Hyacinth O-Rorke-MacDermot, who claimed the 'Old Irish' title prince of Coolavin, by his second wife Henrietta, nee Blake.[31] The Blakes were an Old English family, whose many branches included some of the largest Catholic landholdings in Connacht. Hugh's first wife, Mary, nee Howley, was a daughter of Edward Howley JP, of Belleek Castle, Ballina. This informal practise of intermarriage between major Catholic landowners had the entirely natural effect of consolidating Catholic power and influence on a local level. Several Irish boys at English schools inherited vast estates. Maurice Charles Blake, at Stonyhurst in 1852, owned 11,888 acres between the counties of Galway and Mayo in 1882. A more typical inheritance was that of George Patrick Lattin Mansfield who in the same year succeeded to 5,639 acres split between the counties of Waterford and Kildare.[32] G. P. L. Mansfield had been educated at Oscott, but sent his son George to Stonyhurst in 1864. His grandsons followed suit in the 1890s.[33]

The Mansfield family is typical of a sizable portion of the rural Catholic elite. Their land was acquired gradually in the early nineteenth century. The Mansfields were an Anglo-Norman Waterford family, thus 1,097 of the total acreage was still located in that county in 1882, though it was largely administered by agents. The rest they had gained by a mixture of luck and astute marriage. An estate at Yeomanstown in north Co. Kildare was inherited through the maternal line from the Eustace family – the nearby Morristown holding was brought into the family by Alexander in 1817 when he married the heiress Paulina Lattin.[34] His son George Patrick Lattin Mansfield was therefore able to live the life of a leisured gentleman. His pocket diary for 1837 indicates very little outside of an extensive and perhaps exhausting series of hunts, steeplechases and balls.[35] By 1882 G. P. L. Mansfield's only son George Lattin Mansfield, enjoyed a rental income of almost £4,500 yearly, more than enough to cope with the expensive education of his sons at Stonyhurst in the 1890s. The family took a full part in county life in Kildare, corresponding with families such as the Thunders, Sweetmans and the More-O'Ferralls, all of whom had sons at Stonyhurst.[36] That such prominent 'county families' should choose to send their sons to Jesuit schools in England, rather than to Clongowes Wood (little over ten miles from any of their estates) indicates the allure of an expensive education outside of Ireland. All four generations of Mansfields also participated in the local establishment and acted as authority figures in the local community and were active members of the Kildare Street Club in Dublin. George Lattin Mansfield followed in his father's footsteps by accepting a post as deputy lieutenant of the county in 1894, as did his son Eustace in 1908, who had scribbled 'Ireland forever' and surrounded it with shamrocks and harps on his copybook at school.[37] These networks of landed families exercised great power in nineteenth-century rural Ireland, and much scholarly work must be done before we can dismiss them as a non-competitive rival elite to the Protestant ascendancy.

Alongside this established and well-connected group of rural landowning families were the rising merchant classes. Some of these families also sent boys to English Catholic schools, thereby buying into the Catholic elite having clearly identified education as a means to solidify their new status in the next generation. This was far from a new phenomenon, and has been noted by Lawrence Stone and David Cannadine in their standard-bearing work on the British aristocracy.[38]

The demonstrable success of elite schools in securing their graduates prominent roles in the professions and in the competitive financial world meant that an education there became all the more attractive to those generally excluded from it by socio-economic circumstances. A pertinent example of this phenomenon is the rise and fall of the Scally family of Eustace Street and Deepwell, Blackrock Co. Dublin. Thomas E. Scally appears to have made a great deal of money trading as a wine merchant and, later, as a whiskey merchant, selling a product that was aggressively marketed as Scally's 'Swan and Crown Whiskey'.[39] In addition to this between 1884 and 1889 Scally earned approximately £100,000 through prodigious trading on the stock exchange, and then solidified his new-found social status by purchasing a landmark property in the prominent south Dublin suburb of Blackrock, named Deepwell. This house was originally built in 1810 by the Guinness family.

As cashflow was no longer an issue Scally now had free rein as to the education of his nine year old son, John Joseph Scally, and he was sent to Downside College. The dramatic change in the family fortune did not pass by without prompting allegations of impropriety. A subsequent trial proved those allegations founded in fact, and by 1892 the nascent Scally empire was up for sale at auction. When questioned by the presiding judge (Lord Chief Justice Peter O'Brien, a former Clongowes student) as to how he had managed to procure in excess of £20,000 a year on the stock exchange Mr Scally replied, to uproarious laughter in court: 'Perhaps if I told your lordship the whole Bar would go on the stock exchange'.[40] The spoils of Mr Scally's enterprise were impressive. The notice of sale counted among the amenities at Deepwell an extensive pleasure-ground and three tennis courts. Among the items for auction were costly silk curtains and no less than two pianofortes – one by Collard and Collard and the other by Schiedmayer.

The Scally family story indicates that class lines were clearly delineated in Ireland, as were the accepted routes of upward social mobility. Thomas Scally had chosen Downside for a very specific reason: it was one of the most recognisable elite schools that catered for Irish Catholics in the nineteenth century and its graduates were among the wealthiest and most influential men in Ireland. There is no record of what became of his expensively educated son, but his eldest daughter married well despite her father's financial embarrassment.[41] Such dramatic changes in family fortunes are, it should be emphasised, rather rare. They nevertheless betray a long-established formula that guaranteed either the maintenance of existing social status or the transformation from cash rich to respectable in just one generation in nineteenth-century Ireland.

V

Neil Fleming has recently argued against the common assumption in Irish historiography that ultimate power in Ireland remained in the hands of a non-Catholic elite, as it 'too easily elides the varied and relatively dispersed nature of power in late-nineteenth- and early-twentieth-century Ireland'.[42] This view has much merit, and indeed is the most suitable response to the problems posed by the excellent work of Campbell, Pašeta and Elliott, among others. Social stratification and the distribution of power in Irish society have often been overlooked by nineteenth-century scholars, or discussed narrowly in relation to political history. Power, wealth, and influence were distributed in myriad ways in the nineteenth century, and often through localised elites or social networks. Until these networks are thoroughly examined we ought not to abase the idea that many elite Catholics had found and maintained a strategic position of power under the Union, however unassuming or shrouded. If the experience of those boarding at English public schools between 1850 and 1900 can teach us anything, it is that, as a group, these elite Irish Catholics had identified education as just one method by which family fortune, power and influence might be restored, maintained or created.

Notes

1 A. E. Clery, 'Accents: Dublin and otherwise', *Studies: An Irish Quarterly Review*, 10(40) (1921), p. 545.

2 One of the most popular of these was the Irish History Reader published in 1905. It routinely used absolute terminology to describe a Catholic 'struggle'. In its treatment of St Patrick, for example, it recalls an unlikely Moses moment in Irish history when 'Almighty God promised the Saint that his faithful Irish people should never lose the Catholic faith', while he was on retreat at the summit of Mount Crualach, now renamed Croagh Patrick. Quite ahead of its time, it used terms such as 'systematic extermination of the Catholic Irish', to describe the plantation of Queen Mary in Laois and Offaly. Christian Brothers, *Irish History Reader* (Dublin: M. H. Gill and Son, 1905), pp. 45, 147.

3 I. McBride, *Eighteenth-Century Ireland: The Isle of Slaves* (Dublin: Gill and Macmillan, 2009), p. 153.

4 P. J. Corish, *The Catholic Community in the Seventeenth and Eighteenth Centuries* (Dublin: Helicon, 1981), pp. 1– 2.

5 G. P. McEntee, *The Social Catholic Movement in Great Britain* (New York: Macmillan, 1927), p. 34.

6 J. H. Whyte, *Church and State in Modern Ireland* 1923–1970 (Dublin: Gill and Macmillan, 1971), pp. 68–71.

7 J. J. Lee, *The Modernisation of Irish Society 1848 – 1921* (Dublin: Gill and Macmillan, 1973), p. 45.

8 T. Garvin, *Preventing the Future: Why Was Ireland so Poor for so Long?* (Dublin: Gill and Macmillan, 2005), p. 30.

9 L. McBride, *The Greening of Dublin Castle: The Transformation of Bureaucratic and Judicial Personnel in Ireland, 1892–1922* (Washington, DC: Catholic University of America Press, 1991).

10 For a full summary of this argument, see F. Campbell, *The Irish Establishment 1879–1914* (Oxford: Oxford University Press, 2009), pp. 297–301.

11 M. Elliott, *When God Took Sides: Religion and Identity in Ireland – Unfinished History* (Oxford: Oxford University Press, 2009), p. 210.

12 D. P. Moran, *The Philosophy of Irish Ireland*, ed. Patrick Maume (Dublin: University College Dublin Press, 2007, [original 1905], p. xxvii.

13 K. Whelan, 'An underground gentry? Catholic middlemen in eighteenth-century Ireland', *Eighteenth-Century Ireland*, 10 (1995), p. 25.

14 S. Pašeta, *Before the Revolution: Nationalism, Social Change and Ireland's Catholic Elite, 1879–1922* (Cork: Cork University Press, 1999).

15 J. Hutchinson, *The Dynamics of Cultural Nationalism: Gaelic Revival and the Creation of the Irish Nation State* (London: Allen and Unwin, 1987); T. Garvin, *Nationalist Revolutionaries in Ireland 1858–1928* (Oxford: Clarendon, 1987).

16 A. O'Day, 'Ireland's Catholics in the British State, 1850–1922', in A. Kappeler, F. Adanir and A. O'Day, *The Formation of National Elites:*

Comparative Studies on Governments and Non-Dominant Ethnic Groups in Europe, 1850–1940 (Dartmouth, NY: New York University Press, 1992), p. 41.

17 J. McConnel, 'John Redmond and Irish Catholic Loyalism', *English Historical Review*, 125(512) (2010), p. 87.

18 The standard reference works are J. Coolahan, *Irish Education: Its History and Structure* (Dublin: Institute of Public Administration, 1987); T. J. McElligott, *Secondary Education in Ireland, 1870–1921* (Dublin: Irish Academic Press, 1981); J. H. Murphy (ed.), *Nos Autem: Castleknock College and Its Contribution* (Dublin: Gill and Macmillan, 1996); P. Birch, *St Kieran's College Kilkenny* (Dublin: M. H. Gill, 1951); P. Costello, *Clongowes Wood: A History of Clongowes Wood College, 1814–1989* (Dublin: Gill and Macmillan, 1989); D. Raftery and S. M. Parkes, *Female Education in Ireland 1700–1900: Minerva or Madonna* (Dublin: Irish Academic Press, 2007).

19 At Downside College, near Bath, the percentage of Irish-born boarders was as high as 36 on average in the 1870s. See Downside Abbey Archives, 'Register of Students at Downside', C/52/H; *List of Boys at St Gregory's* (Downside Abbey, 1972).

20 For more on the Irish educated on the continent, see T. Ó Fiaich, *The Irish Colleges in France* (Dublin: Veritas Publications, 1990); D. Keogh and A. McDonnell (eds), *The Irish College, Rome and Its World* (Dublin: Four Courts Press, 2008); Cathaldus Giblin, 'Irish exiles in Catholic Europe', in P. J. Corish (ed.), *A History of Irish Catholicism* (Dublin: Gill, 1971); T. J. Walsh, *The Irish Continental College Movement* (Dublin: Golden Eagle Books, 1973); E. Larkin, *The Pastoral Role of the Roman Catholic Church in Pre-Famine Ireland 1750–1850* (Dublin: Four Courts Press, 2006), pp. 31–9.

21 Practically no work whatsoever has been done on these continental schools such as the Irish Benedictine Abbey at Ypres (1665–1914), which until its recent closure was housed at Kylemore Abbey, Connemara. An example of a relatively recent schooling in France is preserved for posterity in F. de Burca, *Fionnuala in France: Being the Diary of a Sixteen-year-old Girl in a French Convent School* (Dublin: P. J. Bourke, 1959).

22 Moore himself claimed that his expulsion from the school was due to a sexual indiscretion. See Robert Welch, 'George Augustus Moore (1852–1933)', *Dictionary of Irish Biography* (Cambridge: Cambridge University Press, 2009), vi, pp. 634–9.

23 The fees were sometimes much higher when extras such as music were taken into consideration. The well-known playwright Edward Martyn boarded at Beaumont for a total cost of £175 between September 1873 and August 1874. Archives of the British Province of the Society of Jesus, Beaumont College Archives, 'Beaumont College Accounts 1870–1874', 5/2/9, pp. 251–2.

24 F. Campbell, *Land and Revolution: Nationalist Politics in the West of Ireland 1891–1921* (Oxford: Oxford University Press, 2005), p. 10.

25 Arthur Griffith referred to Meagher's accent as 'one which grated on the ears of his countrymen when he addressed them on the tribune'. A. Griffith (ed.), *Meagher of the Sword: Speeches of T. F. Meagher in Ireland, 1846–1848* (Dublin: M. H. Gill, 1916), p. v.
26 As Lawrence White has noted, Joseph Mary Plunkett was the most moneyed of those executed in 1916, which tallies with his presence at the school L. W. White, 'Joseph Mary Plunkett (1887–1916)', *Dictionary of Irish Biography*, viii, pp. 183–7.
27 Lucien Bonaparte-Wyse to his mother, Ellen Bonaparte-Wyse, 29/05/1881, Bonaparte-Wyse Papers, National Library of Ireland (NLI), MS 41, 615/17.
28 For the 1840s school register, see 'An old census return', *Downside Review*, 10 (1892), pp. 246–64.
29 It is unclear where Beauclerk Upington was born, but his entry in the *Standard Encyclopaedia of South Africa* indicates he arrived there aged 1, returned to the northern hemisphere for his education, and received a qualification from Trinity College, Dublin. He then returned to South Africa to become one of the most famous lawyers of his generation D. J. Potgieter *et al.* (eds), *Standard Encyclopaedia of Southern Africa* (Cape Town: NASOU, 1970), v, p. 99.
30 He continued the family connection to local government, however, serving as chairman of the North Tipperary Co. Council and was even a founding director of the Roscrea Bacon Factory, objected to in parliament in 1906 Hansard, HC Deb. 154, 825–6 (26 Mar. 1906).
31 His youngest son was Frank MacDermot, who attended Downside in the 1890s and was later elected an Independent TD for Roscommon in 1932. Kyran FitzGerald, 'Francis Charles "Frank" MacDermot (1886–1975)', *Dictionary of Irish Biography*, v, pp. 902–3.
32 Unless stated otherwise, figures for landholdings will be taken from both J. Bateman, *The Great Landowners of Great Britain and Ireland* (London: Harrison, 1878) and U. H. H. De Burgh *The Landowners of Ireland* (Dublin: Hodges, Foster and Figgis, 1874).
33 G. P. L. Mansfield had been educated at Oscott, as was his father Alexander, whose school diary of 1801 contains notes on the character of Oliver Cromwell and Walter Raleigh (NLI, Mansfield Papers, MS 38, 399/1–2).
34 W. Sherlock, 'The Lattin and Mansfield Families in the Co. Kildare', *Journal of the Archaeological Society of County Kildare and Surrounding Districts*, 3 (1899–1902), pp. 186–90.
35 NLI, Mansfield Papers, 'Pocket Diary of G. P. L. Mansfield 1837', MS 38, 412/2.
36 C. Costello, *A Class Apart: The Gentry Families of County Kildare* (Dublin: Nonsuch, 2005), pp. 65–6.
37 NLI, Mansfield Papers, MS 38, 427/1.
38 L. Stone and J. C. Fawtier Stone, *An Open Elite? England 1540–1880* (Oxford: Oxford University Press, 1984); D. Cannadine, *Lords and Landlords: The Aristocracy and the Towns* (Leicester: Leicester University

Press, 1980); *The Decline and Fall of the British Aristocracy* (London: Papermac, 1992, pbk, 1996).

39 Advertisements, *The Times*, 29 Nov. 1880.

40 'Dublin merchant makes £100,000 in four years and loses it again', *Freeman's Journal and Daily Commercial Advertiser*, 16 Jan. 1891.

41 Mary Scally married John Robert O'Connell, owner of a magnificent period house in Killiney, Co. Dublin. O'Connell was a member of the Royal Irish Academy, a prominent Dublin barrister and a vice-president of the Incorporated Law Society of Ireland. Mary died in 1925, and her widowed husband became a secular priest. 'John Robert O'Connell', *The Times*, 8 Jan. 1944.

42 N. C. Fleming, 'Review of *The Irish Establishment 1879–1914* by Fergus Campbell', *Twentieth Century British History*, 21(3) (2010), p. 422.

16

The Esmonde family of Co. Wexford and Catholic loyalty

Richard Keogh and James McConnel

In 1942, Lieutenant-Commander Eugene Esmonde (1909–42), who had earlier been decorated for his part in the air-attack on the German battleship *Bismarck*, was posthumously awarded the Victoria Cross for leading the 825 Swordfish Squadron of torpedo bombers in a forlorn attack on two German battle cruisers in the English Channel.[1] At the time, allies and enemies alike expressed their admiration for the squadron's valour in the face of overwhelming odds;[2] but it was its commander's Irishness which later attracted the particular attention of Britain's wartime Prime Minister, Winston Churchill, whose end-of-war radio address in May 1945 singled out Esmonde for having redeemed neutral Ireland's tarnished honour.[3]

But Esmonde's war service cannot simply be fitted into the 'story of the many Irish volunteers who served the Allied cause in the Second World War in the British forces'.[4] After all, he was, as one comrade later recalled, 'a most unusual man – perhaps only his rather rare species – Irish, Catholic *and* "upper class" (for want of a better word) – could have produced him'.[5] This background distinguished Esmonde from the great majority of the 100,000 or so other Irishmen and women from both sides of the border who fought in Britain's armed forces during the Second World War.[6] Because in volunteering to fight against Germany Esmonde drew on a family tradition of martial service to the crown which stretched back centuries. It was a tradition which, by the time George V posthumously awarded Esmonde's VC to his mother Eily at Buckingham Palace in 1942, had already seen the family loyally serve the English crown since the twelfth century, not only as soldiers but also as magistrates, officials and members of parliament.

The Esmondes were not mercenaries. Indeed, this essay examines their family tradition of service in terms of the wider phenomenon of Irish Catholic loyalty. It does so in the knowledge that this is a largely under-researched area of modern Ireland's social and political history,[7] preference having long been given to studying Catholic 'resistance, struggle and confrontation' to the British state.[8] Whereas Irish Protestant loyalty has been the subject of sustained scholarly investigation, Catholic loyalty has either been overlooked or understood in terms of pragmatic self-interest. But while the Esmonde family's history certainly demonstrates that adaptation and evolution to the changing coordinates of Anglo-Irish relations was an essential feature of elite Catholic politics, it also suggests that their loyalty was sustained and by no means insincere. This is not to say that this loyalty was unconditional or reflexive; rather, it was conditioned by family traditions of Catholic lay leadership and a strong commitment to the restoration of Catholic interests, by a sense of status linked to land ownership, by an elite commitment to the profession of arms, by notions of gentlemanliness and by a trenchant support for monarchical government over and above allegiance to a particular dynasty. Combined, these characteristics produced a strong sense of duty, service, and loyalty, which was augmented (and sometimes complicated) by the family's Whiggish patriotism. Even when the 11th baronet seemingly broke with this tradition, other family members continued it for decades afterwards.

I

Loyalty to the crown was deeply ingrained in the Esmonde family's history. After all, the Esmondes claimed descent from Sir Geoffrey Esmonde, who was one of the thirty knights who landed with Robert Fitzstephen in Wexford in 1169. His descendants settled in the southern Barony of Forth, built Johnstown Castle and formed part of the close-knit Old English community which developed in Co. Wexford. Like many Anglo-Norman families, the Esmondes did not convert to Protestantism, though they remained loyal to the crown. Thus William Esmonde died as a Catholic fighting for Queen Elizabeth during the Nine Years War. But it was in the person of his second son, Lawrence Esmonde (d.1645), 'Soldier, Statesman, Patriot, a Terror to Rebels in his Time, [and] a Protector to loyal subjects', that the family became prominent.[9] Unlike his father, Lawrence conformed religiously and prospered thereafter. Following service in the Low Countries and the Nine Years War he was knighted, granted lands for his military services and made a major general. After 1611 he was involved in the plantation of Wexford and eventually received considerable lands, mostly at the expense of the Old English and the native Irish. In 1613 he was elected MP for Co. Wicklow and in 1622 he was made Baron Lymbricke.[10]

Lawrence's only son, Thomas (d.1665), was the result of his marriage to Margaret O'Flaherty, the sister of Morrough, dynast of lar-Chonnact.

Concerns that Thomas might be brought up as a Protestant led his mother to leave Lawrence and raise her son among her own family. As an adult, however, Thomas conformed, and like his father he became a soldier. Service in the king's armies in France in 1626–27 led to a knighthood in 1628 and a baronetcy the following year. In 1629 he fought with an Irish regiment for the king of Sweden during the Thirty Years' War.[11] Ten years later he was elected to represent the borough of Enniscorthy in the house of commons.

Although one authority has claimed that with the outbreak of the 1641 rebellion Baron Esmonde maintained an 'ambivalent neutrality between king and parliament',[12] he told his father-in-law, the earl of Ormonde, that: 'My loyalty rests in my last drop of blood' and sided with the king. It was as the governor of Duncannon Fort that Esmonde was besieged by the Leinster army of the Confederation, to which he capitulated shortly before his death in 1645.[13] In contrast, though Sir Thomas initially wavered, his financial woes and the superiority of the Confederate forces seem to have persuaded him to join the rebels and convert back to Catholicism.[14] In 1646 he attended the Council of Kilkenny at which the papal nuncio, Archbishop Rinuccini, advised that Esmonde should be consulted on all military matters.[15] He reportedly threw himself wholeheartedly into the rebellion,[16] though after 1660 he claimed – in a bid to retrieve his estates – that he had been forced to join the rebels. In fact, as a result of the Confederacy's alliance with King Charles, Esmonde was able to fulfil the family's customary service to the crown. Notwithstanding Cromwell's invitation to join the Parliamentarians, he fought for 'freedom of worship and loyalty to the legitimate sovereign'.[17]

In fighting for the king, Sir Thomas fought alongside his son and heir, Lawrence (d.1688), who 'manifested signal demonstrations of valour ... in some conflicts against the Cromwellians', and thereby demonstrated his 'inviolate innate Loyalty to his King'.[18] As a consequence of this service, Sir Thomas's estates were confiscated and he was transplanted to Connacht as part of the Cromwellian settlement.[19] Following the Restoration, he petitioned the king to restore his family lands,[20] but this was only finally achieved after Sir Thomas's death and following protracted litigation.[21]

According to one recent assessment, after 1688 the Esmonde's were 'strongly Jacobite' and it was only 'sheer luck' that allowed them to survive the Williamite wars relatively unscathed.[22] Although Sir Laurence Esmonde, the second baronet, served as sheriff of Co. Carlow in 1686, he died before the revolution and while an Esmonde fell at the Siege of Derry fighting for James II,[23] the fact that the 3rd baronet was sent to

France for his education between 1689 and 1692 provided something of an alibi against repeated charges that he was a Jacobite and had actually served in the Irish Brigade for two years.[24] That said, while the 3rd baronet (d.1720) took steps to mitigate the effects of the penal laws, his ultimate success in regaining the family estate 'crippled his family for generations' and forced 'the sale of a great part of the estate'.[25]

Notwithstanding his initial success in persuading the crown that he was a 'loyal subject',[26] the 3rd baronet was detained during the invasion scare of 1708 because he was seen as a 'recalcitrant' Jacobite.[27] The 4th baronet, Sir Laurence (d.1739), was more conciliatory and was associated with other leading Catholics in petitioning the lord lieutenant to mitigate the effects of the penal laws.[28] However, these efforts may have been undermined by the service given by successive generations of Esmondes to the armies of France, Spain and Austria during the eighteenth century. Sir John, the 5th baronet (d.1758), served as a captain of dragoons in the Spanish army in the 1730s, while his cousin James, 7th baronet (1701–67), served in the French army.[29] His uncle Patrick, Chevalier d'Esmonde, was in the Austrian service (and spent seven years in a Turkish prison)[30] along with his son Maurice, while as late as the nineteenth century, one of the 9th baronet's brothers, Laurence, Chevalier D'Esmonde (1797–1883), was a colonel in the French army.[31]

From the mid-eighteenth century many 'well-to-do' Catholics sought some form of accommodation with the Hanoverian state.[32] From the 1780s, Sir Thomas Esmonde (the 8th baronet, 1758–1803), took a part in these efforts. Although as a gentleman member of the Catholic Committee he was not particularly prominent,[33] in an effort to rescind the remaining penalties against Catholics he joined other leading members of the Catholic gentry in 1792 in declaring themselves 'his Majesty's most dutiful and loyal subjects ... desirous at all times to declare unequivocally our sentiments of loyalty to our most gracious Sovereign'.[34] During the 1798 rebellion he was a member of the yeomanry and was said to have distinguished himself at the battle of Arklow.[35] Nevertheless, he was arrested afterwards due to the conduct of his brother, John Esmonde (1760–98).

Although John's participation in the 1798 rebellion was later attributed variously to the murder of a priest who was related to the family or because he was 'a sympathetic man assisting his tenants',[36] John Esmonde had long since left the moderate politics of the Catholic Committee behind him, having become a leading member of the Society of United Irishmen during the 1790s. Thus, in 1798 he commanded rebel forces in the barony of Clane and led the attack on Prosperous.[37] Later accounts – particularly that of Musgrave – depicted Esmonde as a traitor who adopted a 'semblance of loyalty' in his capacity as a lieutenant in the yeomanry to betray crown forces.[38] After his arrest Esmonde himself protested that he was a 'loyal subject', but the crown was convinced that he was a leading rebel and following a court martial he was hanged on Carlisle Bridge.[39] John's cousin, Esmonde Kyan, was also a United Irishman who assumed military command during the rebellion in Wexford. Likewise he too was hanged.[40]

II

The children of John Esmonde who came to adulthood in the early decades of the nineteenth century embodied the transitional circumstances of the Irish Catholic aristocracy at that time. Whereas Laurence Esmonde harked backwards to the eighteenth century through his service in the French army, his brothers John and James (1791–1842) served in the Royal Navy, though John only achieved senior rank through his service in the Chilean navy during the war of independence against Spain.[41] Their brother Bartholomew (1789–1862), by contrast, represented a different strand of the family's history, since he joined the Jesuits and was associated with their centre at Stonyhurst, Lancashire, before helping to establish Clongowes Wood College, Co. Kildare.[42] Although the family largely eschewed holy orders thereafter, successive Esmondes were noted as devoted members of their church and the 11th baronet became a papal chamberlain.

John Esmonde's eldest son, Sir Thomas (9th baronet, 1786–1869), remembered the events of 1798 and the death of his father well. Arguably this had a profound impact on his political outlook, and for the rest of his life he was a staunch supporter of the Union and a loyal subject of the crown.[43] Born in 1786, Thomas inherited the baronetcy and family estates from his uncle in 1803. As a young man Esmonde rose to prominence through his association with the campaign for Catholic emancipation, and he frequently chaired the meetings of eminent laymen in support of Catholic relief and petitioning the crown.[44] In anticipation of emancipation, the Catholic Committee dissolved itself with Esmonde in the chair, in an act calculated to 'conciliate the regard of all rational Englishmen'.[45] Thereafter he refused to support any further agitation in the belief that his actions 'might thereby impede' emancipation.[46] In 1829 Esmonde publicly declared his gratitude to both the monarch and the cabinet in reaching a '*satisfactory settlement of the Catholic question*'.[47]

Esmonde remained active in politics after 1829,[48] and regularly attended viceregal levees and other social events at Dublin Castle.[49]

Upon entering parliament in 1841 he was regarded as a 'radical',[50] though this did not prevent him from supporting the Union.[51] Indeed, Esmonde's politics alienated many of his former colleagues, some of whom followed O'Connell into the ranks of the Repeal party. While O'Connell had a 'very great respect' for Esmonde, he did not consider him a suitable representative of the people of Wexford owing to his stance after 1829.[52] Esmonde's loyalty, however, was not unconditional. In 1844, when officers of the crown struck the names of Irish Catholics off a special jury selected to act on state trials, Esmonde joined with a number of laymen in protesting to the crown. On this occasion, he revealed that in 1829 he had hoped that the emancipation campaign would see the end of Catholic agitation, though even then he had accepted that further efforts might be necessary if Catholics were not afforded religious and civil toleration.[53] Still, his faith in the Union remained intact (even during the Famine).[54] Sworn as an Irish privy councillor in 1847, shortly after his death he was described as 'one of the most worthy and respected landowners in the south of Ireland' and a leader of 'that moderate Roman Catholic party ... men who, when O'Connell's magic influence was at its highest, always lent their influence to the side of order and constitutional government'.[55]

Sir Thomas Esmonde's nephew (the 10th baronet) followed the unionist traditions of his uncle. While John Esmonde (1826–76) did not inherit the baronetcy until 1869, he had already achieved political prominence in Ireland as a young man. Educated at Clongowes Wood (which his uncle had helped establish), he proceeded to Trinity College, Dublin, where he graduated with a BA in 1848.[56] Although an Anglican preserve and a staunchly unionist institution throughout the nineteenth century,[57] the Catholic hierarchy tolerated the attendance of men like Esmonde.[58] Thereafter, he followed a typical professional trajectory and was called to the Irish bar in 1850, though rather than pursuing a legal career, he followed his uncle into parliament under 'free trade and liberal colours'.[59]

Entering Westminster in 1852, Esmonde was to remain Co. Waterford's representative until his death in 1876. While his acceptance of the aims of the tenant league and appointment to the committee of the friends of religious equality in 1852 might suggest that his sympathies lay in the direction of the Irish Independent Party, he did not vote as such in the house of commons.[60] Instead, he was a member of the 'Catholic Whigs', who represented a unique mix of 'Unionism, liberalism and Catholicism' in their attempt to preserve Ireland's position within the Union.[61] His wedding party in 1861 was a who's who of Catholic grandees and was also attended by the then lord lieutenant.[62]

Esmonde's voting record in the house of commons between 1852 and 1874 confirmed his status as a Whig, and he was consistent in his support for the Liberal party.[63] For this support he was rewarded with an appointment as high sheriff of Co. Wexford and a short-lived junior lordship of the treasury in 1866.[64] Such support of the Liberals did not preclude his engagement with Irish issues regarding land,[65] national education for Catholics,[66] and the disestablishment of the Church of Ireland.[67] Indeed, Esmonde's attachment to the Catholic Church was such that in 1874 he was one of thirteen Catholic MPs who joined the 'Catholic Union of Ireland', 'a compact body of Catholic members, working together in the interests of religion'.[68]

In Esmonde's case then, enthusiastic Catholicism did not go hand in hand with a strong sense of Irish nationalism. When, for example, the lord lieutenant visited Waterford in 1873 Esmonde was among the 'principal personages' who welcomed him.[69] Nonetheless, he was alive to shifts within Irish Catholic opinion. As a result there was confusion about Esmonde's political loyalties at the general election of 1874. He had declared himself in favour of 'any well defined system which shall (without endangering the integrity of the empire) transfer to Irishmen the management of purely Irish affairs'.[70] The *Freeman's Journal* considered his statements 'supererogatory', and urged his re-election. However, the *Nation* called for his rejection as a 'pure and simple ministerialist'.[71] Esmonde did, in fact, contemplate home rule, and was present at some of the party's early meetings after his election in 1874.[72] However, a closer reading of his loyalties suggests that he was reluctant to support any reconfiguration of the Union. On the eve of his 1874 re-election Esmonde had begged Gladstone for a peerage, pointing to the 'unflinching services of ... [his] family to the Liberal Party ever since Catholic Emancipation', and shortly afterwards he declined to attend a meeting which called together the fifty-nine 'members' of the nascent movement.[73] Such caution reflected Esmonde's reluctance to rely upon the support of an electorate which was becoming increasingly aligned along nationalist political lines. That said, while he was not prepared to vote for the legislative renegotiation of the Union in the house of commons, he was willing to concede to an inquiry into its potential.[74] Esmonde was clearly uneasy about the prospect of a reconfigured Union, and it is in this sense that his lacklustre support for home rule should be viewed.

After his death Esmonde was considered both a 'Home Ruler'[75] and 'one of the Irish Liberals who refused to accept Home Rule'.[76] Such confusion reflected the inchoate nature of the early home rule party, the uncertainty around which enabled Esmonde to maintain his political position until his death, thereby escaping having to choose between a radicalised home rule movement and the political oblivion which the great majority of Catholic Whigs experienced after the 1870s. Esmonde would, arguably, have found the choice a difficult one, since he was fundamentally a loyalist. After all, as the *Irish Times* reported in 1873, following an election contest in Waterford, it was Sir John who 'gave the usual loyal toasts'.[77] Earlier, in 1866, he had been appointed the high-sheriff for Co. Wexford; he was also the deputy lieutenant for Wexford, and a magistrate for Waterford, Wexford and Wicklow.[78]

The loyalties of the last generation of Whig Esmondes were also expressed through the profession of arms. Sir John's father, James Esmonde, had been a commander in the Royal Navy,[79] and his sons maintained this tradition of service to the crown. John held a commission in the Waterford Artillery Militia as a captain, from 1854,[80] while his second son, Laurence Grattan Esmonde (1863–1943), became a professional soldier and attained the rank of lieutenant colonel.[81] While it has been claimed that the Irish militia was more palatable to some Irish Catholics who viewed it as distinct from the British army,[82] the Esmondes' participation should probably not be viewed in this manner. The British army provided a professional outlet for many elite Catholics, their tradition of service confirming and reinforcing their loyalty, while their commissions in the militia permitted them to fulfil their traditional role in Irish county life.[83]

The most prominent member of the family to join the British military in the nineteenth century was Thomas Esmonde (1831–73), Sir John's younger brother. Rather than serving in the militia he entered the regular army, where Catholic officers consistently formed less than 5 per cent of the Anglican-dominated officer class between 1827 and 1865.[84] There were considerable obstacles for Catholics who desired a commission in the British army, which took both a religious and financial form. Prior to 1871, the majority of commissions were purchased, a tradition that reinforced the gentlemanly status of British army officers. Commissions were expensive and beyond the reach of many Catholics. Instead, the army provided a suitable professional outlet for the second and third sons of wealthy Protestant Irishmen, since a place in the officer corps entitled an individual to 'gentleman's company' and offered a vehicle for upward social mobility.[85]

The Esmonde family's relative wealth meant that financial pressures did not concern Thomas, and in 1851 he purchased a commission as an ensign in the 77th Regiment of Foot, before being transferred to the 18th Regiment of Foot (later the Royal Irish Regiment) in the same year.[86] In 1854 he was promoted to the rank of lieutenant without purchase,[87] and to captain the following year.[88] Esmonde's rank of brevet-major, unattached, was converted to substantive rank in 1858,[89] and in 1868 he was promoted to the rank of lieutenant colonel.[90] Esmonde's unusual success can be attributed to his distinguished service during the Crimean war, for which he was awarded the Victoria Cross.[91]

Upon returning to Ireland from the Crimea, Thomas Esmonde was further rewarded for his bravery by his appointment to the office of Assistant Inspector-General in the Irish Constabulary (though some resented this exercise of patronage).[92] Esmonde was promoted to Deputy Inspector-General in 1865.[93] Former army officers were often appointed to senior positions within the constabulary,[94] but the appointment of a Catholic to such a high position was unusual. Indeed, one recent study estimates that Catholics formed just 20 per cent of the senior police officers in Ireland between 1881 and 1911,[95] while Catholics in the highest ranks were even more unusual.[96] Esmonde distinguished himself in 1864 during the Belfast riots of that year and retired in 1867. He died in 1873 after he was involved in a hunting accident.[97]

III

When the 23-year-old Sir Thomas Henry Grattan Esmonde (the 11th baronet, 1862–1935) was selected as the Parnellite candidate for the south Co. Dublin constituency in 1885 it caused quite a stir since it was one of 'the first appearance[s] of a man of the landowning class on the side of the New Nationalist movement'.[98] Although the *Freeman's Journal* pointed out that 'Ireland has found some of her noblest and bravest sons in the ranks of the aristocracy, from Lord Edward Fitzgerald ... down to Parnell',[99] the 'Chief' himself acknowledged that 'it was hard undoubtedly for an Irish landlord to be a good Nationalist in these days'. Several leading home rulers – notably Michael Davitt – went further and expressed their strong opposition towards Esmonde's adoption.[100] The 11th baronet was, after all, not only a landlord, but also a member of the Kildare Street Club and a commissioned officer of the South Irish Division Royal Artillery.[101] Moreover, he rode to hounds (a pastime which had become highly politicised during the recent land war),[102] and his uncle was to be boycotted in King's Co. the following year owing to his involvement in an eviction.[103] That Esmonde prevailed was in no small part due to his unqualified condemnation of landlordism and his invocation of his maternal and paternal great-grandfathers – Henry Grattan, the Irish patriot, and John Esmonde, who 'in the dark days of '98 ... testified with his blood his devotion to his country'.[104]

If nationalists were rather suspicious of Esmonde's espousal of home rule, then Conservatives were left confused and angry by it. After all, as

Vanity Fair claimed, 'all his belongings are Whigs'.[105] Indeed, the *Leeds Mercury* was convinced that Sir Thomas's 'ancestors would be ashamed if they had witnessed the degenerate action of their son'.[106] By this reading, then, Sir Thomas was a 'hereditary rascal' whose political conversion was unprincipled and who dishonoured his family name and the uniform he wore.[107] As a 'Loyal Officer' wrote to *The Times*, 'May I ask if the War Office ... consider his openly joining the party of revolt and sedition ... to be consistent with the loyalty due by an officer ... serving Crown and State?'.[108]

While Esmonde's conversion to Nationalism and his strategic invocation of his great-grandfathers may have been pragmatic at some level, his apparent conversion from his family's Whiggish patriotism was nonetheless thoughtful and considered. To those who regarded him as disloyal he responded, 'Loyalty to whom or to what?'. Denying that the crown entered into the question of Irish self-government, he dismissed as ridiculous and hypocritical Ulster Protestant claims of loyalty given that they had 'kick[ed] the crown of their sovereign into the Boyne'. He strongly denied that he owed any sort of loyalty to Dublin Castle, since loyalty 'is devotion to a righteous cause', and he 'refuse[d] to recognise' that loyalty 'to the class to which I belong' might mean 'such a caste as standing apart from the nation'.[109] Significantly, he drew a sharp distinction between himself and Catholic unionists (whose position he constructed largely in terms of their relationship to Dublin Castle). Thus, he declared that his Conservative opponent was welcome to 'the Catholic JPs of the Masonic and Orange Schools' who supported the Tories. And he added, 'The cause which a traitor to country or to religion espouses must be a bad cause, and the advocacy of renegades of this type is its weakness'.[110] So, while Esmonde rejected accusations of his own disloyalty, he himself levelled equivalent claims against those who he called 'recreant Catholics',[111] thereby further emphasising his alignment of faith with fatherland. That said, his insistence that the gentry should stand with the people was, in a sense, a restatement of the classic Parnellite formulation of a patriotic gentry allied with the Irish people (which was more conciliatory).[112] Indeed, though he played a part in the Plan of Campaign (which in Co. Wexford he linked explicitly to the 1798 rebellion), there was never any real question – contrary to Tim Healy's claim at Esmonde's election in 1885 – of him 'leaving his class'.[113] Esmonde remained a gentlemen: he continued to live in his 'Big House' (Ballynastragh) and was among those invited to hunt with Parnell on his Co. Wicklow estate.[114] And during the 1890s he served as a member of the Commission on Horse Breeding in Ireland and he was one of several 'ardent votaries of the rod' appointed to the Commission on the Inland Fisheries of Ireland in 1899.[115] In 1920 he published a book entitled *Hunting Memories of Many Lands*.[116]

And if Esmonde was not 'loyal' in the sense which his immediate ancestors had been, his nationalism was of a highly individualistic strain which drew much from the Whiggish patriotism of his family. At the Split 'he wavered for a while', before aligning himself with the Healyite wing of the divided Irish Parliamentary Party.[117] Esmonde subsequently worked with both unionists and independent nationalists in his capacity as co-founder and chair of the General Council of Irish County Councils after 1899.[118] While orthodox nationalists feared that he thereby sought to 'create an assembly of notables that could rival the party', some unionists argued that 'Ireland has more to expect from her Plunketts and Esmondes than any number of hysterical firebrands'.[119] And in 1907 he was the most senior member of the IPP to – albeit briefly – defect to the 'monarchist' Sinn Féin party.

After 1907 and his botched defection to Sinn Féin, Esmonde was consigned to the party's backbench. Even so, when John Redmond – another scion of an old Wexford gentry family – developed the 'imperially minded conciliatory nationalism' which historians have termed 'Redmondism',[120] Esmonde proved sympathetic. In 1912, for instance, he told parliament that: 'We Irish people have no rooted antipathy to the empire. The empire is quite as much our empire as yours ... But we must be allowed a proper position in [it]'.[121] Two years later, he agreed to be nominated as the deputy lieutenant for Co. Wexford and, in fact, did not resign until 1920 following the death of Terence MacSwiney.[122] That said, Esmonde did not follow Redmond after August 1914 in embracing a form of neo-Catholic loyalty.[123] Nor did he actively encourage Irishmen to enlist in the British armed forces. Still, during the war itself he called for Irish soldiers to receive proper recognition for their gallantry and lobbied for Ireland to receive more army contracts,[124] while Lady Esmonde helped welcome Belgium refugees to Wexford.[125] As a result it was left to others to uphold the family's martial tradition. Sir Thomas's brother, Laurence (the future 13th baronet) was a veteran of the Boer war and during the Great War he commanded the 4th Battalion of the Tyneside Irish Brigade for a time.[126] Sir Thomas's second son was a midshipman who died at Jutland in 1916 while his cousin, Dr John Esmonde (also a Nationalist MP), became a captain in the Royal Army Medical Corps.[127] In turn, John's eldest son (also an IPP MP) served as a captain in the Royal Dublin Fusiliers during the war, while another son, Lieutenant Geoffrey Esmonde, was killed serving with the 4th Tyneside Irish Battalion. Eugene Esmonde, VC, was John's youngest son by his second marriage and also a product of Clongowes Wood College.

Despite his pre-war associations with Sinn Féin, Sir Thomas Esmonde went 'down with the ship of constitutional nationalism' in 1918. In the years which had followed the 1916 Easter Rising he had became increasingly bitter, telling the British press in 1918 that the 'great majority of Irish Nationalists are friends of your people, and friends of the Empire ... You are now destroying the work of our lives'.[129] And while another son, Osmond Esmonde (the future 12th baronet), served as a 'roving Sinn Féin diplomat' after the Great War,[130] during the War of Independence Sir Thomas was involved in unsuccessful efforts by moderate nationalists and unionists to find a compromise.[131] Eventually reconciled to the new Free State, Esmonde served briefly in the Irish Senate, which in turn led to the burning down of his house by Irregulars in 1923.[132]

IV

In a recent study of the Irish 'establishment', Fergus Campbell has identified the existence of a small group of Catholics who were 'loyal, landed and loaded' and who thereby entered the Irish 'establishment'.[133] For much of the nineteenth century the Esmonde family were also wealthy, landed and loyal. And yet, they were different from the cadre described by Campbell. Indeed, their ancient title, their retention of land and their pursuit of martial distinction insulated them against becoming Catholic clients to Dublin Castle (in the way that so-called 'Castle Catholics' did), while their Whig patriotism prevented them losing touch entirely with changing currents in Irish politics. Perhaps crucially, their leadership role as Catholic laymen did not give way to the corrosive anticlericalism which characterised some Catholic loyalists.

Notwithstanding the presence then of Confederates, Jacobites, Jacobins and republicans among its members, successive generations of the Esmonde family espoused a form of loyalty which was rooted in *ancien régime* Ireland, in the family's land ownership, and prevailing gentlemanly notions of service and duty. Families like the Esmondes were loyal to the house of Stuart and after 1766 they negotiated new loyalties to the house of Hanover and its successors. Even after 1789 and the spread of secular and republican concepts of government, the Esmondes continued to support and identify with the dominant social and political order. This was not only because of the strength of their pan-class identifications but also due to the fact that until the final quarter of the nineteenth century the benefits of loyalty outweighed the costs. By aligning themselves with the crown, successive generations of Esmondes were able to fulfil the military and social imperatives of their caste. Even Sir Thomas Esmonde, who seemingly broke with the family's tradition of loyalty in 1885, was unable or unwilling to subjugate his keen sense of independence or to abjure the leadership role which his family had established over many generations. Indeed, another two generations of Esmondes were to serve the crown in the two world wars after the 11th baronet, while the family's political traditions saw Esmondes serve in the Dáil until as late as 1977.

Notes

1 N. Miller, *War at Sea: A Naval History of World War II* (New York and London: Scribner, 1995), pp. 300–1.
2 R. Doherty and D. Truesdale, *Irish Winners of the Victoria Cross* (Dublin: Four Courts Press, 2000), pp. 163–4.
3 L. Broad, *Winston Churchill, 1874–1951* (London: Hutchinson, 1951), p. 535.
4 R. Doherty, *Irish Men and Women in the Second World War* (Dublin: Four Courts Press, 1999), p. 26.
5 C. Bowyer, *Eugene Esmonde, VC, DSO* (London: William Kimber and Co., 1983), p. 200.
6 *Irish Times*, 13 Jun. 2009, p. 3.
7 The only dedicated study of this phenomenon is J. Biggs-Davison and G. Chowdharay-Best, *The Cross of Saint Patrick: The Catholic Unionist Tradition in Ireland* (Bourne End: Kensal Press, 1984). Also see J. Murphy, *Abject Loyalty, Nationalism and Monarchy in Ireland During the Reign of Queen Victoria* (Cork: Cork University Press, 2001); J. Loughlin, *The British Monarchy and Ireland: 1800 to the Present* (Cambridge: Cambridge University Press, 2007); M. Potter, *William Monsell of Tervoe 1812–1894: Catholic Unionist Anglo Irishman* (Dublin: Irish Academic Press, 2009); F. Campbell, *The Irish Establishment 1879–1914* (Oxford: Oxford University Press, 2009).
8 S. B. Cook, 'The Irish Raj: social origins and careers of Irishmen in the Indian civil service, 1855–1914', *Journal of Social History*, 20 (1987), p. 507.
9 H. F. Hore, 'An account of the Barony of Forth, in the County of Wexford, written at the close of the seventeenth ...', *Journal of the Kilkenny and South-East of Ireland Archaeological Society*, 4 (1862–63), p. 78.
10 J. McHugh, 'The Esmonde family of Lymbrick and Ballytramont: an Old English family', *The Past: The Organ of the Ui Cinsealaigh Historical Society*, 23 (2001), pp. 23–5.
11 A. Norman, *Gentlemen! The Queen!* (Dublin: Levins, 1926), p. 2.
12 J. J. N. McGurk, 'Esmonde, Laurence, Baron Esmonde of Limerick (*c.*1570–1645)', *Oxford Dictionary of National Biography*, Oxford

University Press, Sept. 2004; online edn, Jan 2008: www.oxforddnb.com/view/article/8884, accessed 12 Aug. 2010.

13 McHugh, 'Esmonde Family', p. 25.

14 *Ibid.*, p. 33; Jason McHugh, 'The North Wexford Gentry and the Rebellion of 1641', *The Past: The Organ of the Ui Cinsealaigh Historical Society*, 24 (2003), p. 36.

15 J. D'Alton, *King James's Irish Army List*, 2 vols (London: J. R. Smith, 1861), ii, p. 397.

16 McHugh, 'North Wexford Gentry', 36; D'Alton, *King James's Irish Army List*, p. 680.

17 A. J. Thebaud and J. Habberton, *Ireland Past and Present* (New York: Collier, 1899), p. 267; Norman, *Gentlemen!*, p. 7.

18 J. D'Alton, *The History of the County of Dublin* (Dublin: Hodges and Smith, 1838), p. 559; Hore, 'An Account of the Barony of Forth', p. 79.

19 J. G. Simms, 'Mayo landowners in the seventeenth century', *Journal of the Royal Society of Antiquaries of Ireland*, 95(1/2) (1965), p. 242.

20 McHugh, 'North Wexford Gentry', p. 37.

21 J. G. Simms, *The Williamite Confiscation in Ireland, 1690–1703* (London: Faber and Faber, 1956), p. 9; D'Alton, *King James's Irish Army List*, p. 681; C. C. Trench, *Grace's Card: Irish Catholic Landlords, 1690–1800* (Dublin: Mercier Press, 1997), p. 139.

22 Trench, *Grace's Card*, 39.

23 Norman, *Gentlemen!*, p. 13.

24 E. Bateson, *Calendar of State Papers of the Reign of William III, 1 April 1700–8 March 1702* (London: Eyre & Spottiswoode, 1937), p. 89.

25 Trench, *Grace's Card*, pp. 63, 140.

26 E. Bateson, *Calendar of State Papers of the Reign of William III, 1 January 1699–31 March 1700* (London: Eyre and Spottiswoode, 1937), p. 292.

27 T. Doyle, 'Jacobitism, Catholicism and the Irish Protestant elite, 1700–1710', *Eighteenth-Century Ireland*, 12 (1997), p. 39.

28 S. S. de Val, 'Some Eighteenth-Century Petitions', *The Past: The Organ of the Ui Cinsealaigh Historical Society*, 9 (1972), p. 23.

29 O'Moore Creagh and Edith M. Humphris, *The Autobiography of General Sir O'Moore Creagh, VC*, 3 vols (London: Hutchinson, 1924), i, p. 29.

30 Norman, *Gentlemen!*, p. 35.

31 *Burke's Genealogical and Heraldic History of the Peerage, Baronetage, and Knightage, Privy Council, and Order of Preference* (London: Shaw, 1938), pp. 906ff.

32 T. Bartlett, *The Fall and Rise of the Irish Nation: The Catholic Question, 1690–1830* (Dublin: Gill and Macmillan, 1992), p. 60.

33 L. Chambers, 'John Esmonde', in Seamus Cullen and Hermann Geissel (eds), *Fugitive Warfare: 1798 in North Kildare* (Kilcock: Lord Edward Fitzgerald 1798 Committee in conjunction with CRS Publications 1998), p. 87.

34 *Morning Chronicle*, 6 Jan. 1792, p. 4.

35 *Bell's Weekly Messenger*, 24 Jun. 1798, p. 1.
36 Trench, *Grace's Card*, p. 287; Chambers, 'John Esmonde', p. 89.
37 Chambers, 'John Esmonde', p. 89.
38 R. Musgrave, *Memoirs of the Different Rebellions in Ireland* (2nd edn, Dublin: J. Archer, 1802), pp. 234–5, 239–40.
39 Chambers, 'John Esmonde', p. 90.
40 N. Furlong, 'Kyan, Esmonde (1750–1798)', *Oxford Dictionary of National Biography*, online edn, May 2006 www.oxforddnb.com/view/article/15812 accessed 12 Aug. 2010.
41 *The Times*, 23 Jan. 1822, p. 3.
42 Anon., 'To Palermo and back', *Irish Monthly*, 9(98) (1881), p. 441.
43 *The Times*, 2 Jan. 1869, p. 9.
44 *Morning Post*, 2 Apr. 1814, p. 3; *The Times*, 3 Aug. 1825, p. 3; 4 Aug. 1828, p. 2; 28 Apr. 1825, p. 2.
45 *The Times*, 13 Feb. 1829, p. 3; 16 Feb. 1829, p. 5.
46 *The Times*, 17 Mar. 1829, p. 1.
47 *The Standard*, 27 Sep. 1836, p. 4.
48 *The Times*, 27 Nov. 1834, p. 5; 9 Apr. 1839, p. 6.
49 *Freeman's Journal*, 6 Apr. 1839, p. 2: *The Times*, 25 Jun. 1840, p. 7.
50 *The Times*, 15 Jul. 1841, p. 3.
51 *Freeman's Journal*, 11 Jun. 1841, p. 2.
52 *The Times*, 26 Jul. 1845, p. 6.
53 *The Times*, 15 Jan. 1844, p. 6.
54 A. Breen, 'The history and administration of the Gorey Poor Law Society, 1840–49', *The Past: The Organ of the Ui Cinsealaigh Historical Society*, 28 (2007), p. 64.
55 *The Times*, 2 Jan. 1869, p. 9.
56 *A Catalogue of Graduates who have Proceeded to Degrees at the University of Dublin from the Earliest Recorded Commencements to July 1866, with Supplement to December 16, 1868* (Dublin: Hodges, Figgis and Co., 1869).
57 R. B. McDowell and D. A. Webb, *Trinity College, Dublin, 1592–1952: An Academic History* (Cambridge: Cambridge University Press, 1982), p. xx.
58 S. Pašeta 'Trinity College, Dublin, and the education of Irish Catholics, 1873–1908', *Studia Hibernica*, 30 (1998/99), p. 7.
59 *The Times*, 18 Jun. 1852, p. 8.
60 J. H. Whyte, *The Irish Independent Party, 1850–9* (Oxford: Oxford University Press, 1958), pp. 180–3.
61 Potter, *William Monsell*, p. 2.
62 *Irish Times*, 13 Apr. 1861, p. 3.
63 D. T. Horgan, 'The Irish Catholic Whigs in parliament, 1847–74', Ph.D. thesis, University of Minnesota, 1975, pp. 131–5, 137.
64 *Irish Times*, 27 Dec. 1866, p. 3.
65 *The Times*, 27 Jan. 1859, p. 10; 27 Jan. 1870, p. 3.
66 *The Times*, 10 May 1861, p. 6; 25 Jun. 1869, p. 5.

67 *The Times*, 14 Dec. 1867, p. 8.
68 *Freeman's Journal*, 20 Feb. 1874, p. 5.
69 *The Times*, 16 Aug. 1873, p. 5.
70 D. Thornley, *Isaac Butt and Home Rule* (London: MacGibbon and Kee, 1964), p. 186.
71 *Freeman's Journal*, 6 Sep. 1874, p. 5; *The Nation*, 7 Feb. 1874, cited in Thornley, *Isaac Butt*, p. 186.
72 *Pall Mall Gazette*, 21 Mar. 1874, p. 7.
73 Thornley, *Isaac Butt*, pp. 197, 212.
74 *Ibid.*, p. 284.
75 *Nottinghamshire Guardian*, 15 Dec. 1876, p. 4.
76 *Barrows Worcester Journal*, 16 Dec. 1876, p. 6.
77 *Irish Times*, 4 Jul. 1873, p. 2.
78 *Belfast News-Letter*, 12 Dec. 1876, p. 3.
79 J. Herlihy, *Royal Irish Constabulary Officers, A Biographical Dictionary and Genealogical Guide, 1816–1922* (Dublin: Four Courts Press, 2005), p. 126.
80 Colonel H. G. Hart, *The New Army List and Militia List* (London: John Murray, 1864), p. 434; *Irish Times*, 20 Nov. 1873, p. 2.
81 F. C. Burnard, *The Catholic Who's Who and Year Book, 1908* (London: Burns & Oates, 1908), p. 136.
82 T. Denman, *A Lonely Grave: the Life and Death of William Redmond* (Dublin: Irish Academic Press, 1995), p. 20.
83 *Ibid.*, p. 20.
84 See V. L. J. Fontana, 'Some aspects of Roman Catholic service in the land forces of the British crown', *c.*1750–*c.*1820', Ph.D. thesis, University of Portsmouth, 2002, appendix A, pp. 54–60; data compiled from *Monthly Regimental Returns*, NA WO17/404–784.
85 S. J. Connolly, *Religion, Law and Power: The Making of Protestant Ireland, 1660–1760* (Oxford: Clarendon, 1992), p. 63; A. Jackson, 'Ireland, the Union, and Empire, 1800–1960', in K. Kenny (ed.), *Ireland and the British Empire* (Oxford: Oxford University Press, 2004), p. 140.
86 *Morning Chronicle*, 22 Nov. 1851, p. 2; *Morning Post*, 6 Dec. 1851, p. 3.
87 *Morning Post*, 4 Mar. 1854, p. 6.
88 *The Standard*, 7 Apr. 1855, p. 1.
89 *Glasgow Herald*, 7 Jun. 1858, p. 7.
90 *Morning Post*, 23 Dec. 1868, p. 6.
91 S. L. Gwynn, 'Irish regiments', in Felix Lavery (ed.), *Great Irishmen in War and Politics* (London: Andrew Melrose, 1920), p. 163; *Daily News*, 26 Sep. 1857.
92 Herlihy, *Royal Irish Constabulary Officers*, p. 126; *Irish Times*, 2 Dec. 1859, p. 3.
93 Herlihy, *Royal Irish Constabulary Officers*, p. 126.
94 *The Times*, 28 Nov. 1859, p. 5; *Freeman's Journal*, 28 Nov. 1859, p. 3; *Pall Mall Gazette*, 5 Jun. 1867, p. 8.

95 Campbell, *Irish Establishment*, p. 107.
96 *Ibid.*, pp. 105–6.
97 *Irish Times*, 18 Aug. 1864, p. 3; Herlihy, *Royal Irish Constabulary Officers*, p. 126.
98 *The Times*, 16 Sept. 1935, p. 14.
99 *Freeman's Journal*, 14 Oct. 1885, p. 5.
100 *Ibid.*, pp. 4, 5.
101 *Irish Times*, 20 Sept. 1882, p. 6.
102 *County Gentleman*, 25 Nov. 1882, p. 22; L. P. Curtis, 'Stopping the hunt, 1881–1882: an aspect of the Irish land war', in C. H. E. Philpin (ed.), *Nationalism and Popular Protest in Ireland* (Cambridge: Cambridge University Press, 1987), pp. 349–402.
103 *John Bull*, 5 Jun. 1886, p. 359.
104 *The Times*, 14 Oct. 1885, p. 10.
105 *Western Mail*, 17 Oct. 1885, p. 2.
106 *Leeds Mercury*, 15 Oct. 1885, p. 4.
107 *United Service Magazine*, 165 (1885), p. 468.
108 *The Times*, 16 Oct. 1885, p. 6; also see *Belfast News-Letter*, 24 Oct. 1885, p. 5.
109 *Freeman's Journal*, 9 Nov. 1885, p. 6.
110 *Freeman's Journal*, 26 Nov. 1885, p. 6.
111 *Freeman's Journal*, 28 Nov. 1885, p. 7.
112 T. Claydon, 'The political thought of Charles Stewart Parnell', in D. G. Boyce and A. O'Day (eds), *Parnell in Perspective* (London: Routledge, 1991), p. 163.
113 *The Standard*, 14 Oct. 1885, p. 3.
114 *Birmingham Post*, 17 Dec. 1886, p. 8; *The Times*, 23 Feb. 1887, p. 4.
115 *The Times*, 25 Nov. 1896, p. 5; *Belfast News-Letter*, 14 Aug. 1899, p. 5.
116 Sir Thomas H. G. Esmonde, *Hunting Memories of Many Lands* (Dublin: Simpkin, Marshall, Hamilton, Kent, 1920).
117 *The Times*, 16 Sept. 1935, p. 14.
118 P. Maume, *The Long Gestation: Irish Nationalist Life, 1891–1918* (Dublin: Gill & Macmillan, 1999), pp 30–1.
119 *Ibid.*, p. 31; *Pall Mall* Gazette, quoted in *Freeman's Journal*, 26 Aug. 1899, p. 4.
120 C. Reid, 'Stephen Gwynn and the failure of constitutional nationalism in Ireland, 1919–1921', *Historical Journal*, 53(3) (2010), p. 724.
121 Hansard, HC (series 5), vol. 36, col. 1490, 11 Apr. 1912.
122 *Irish Independent*, 7 Feb. 1914, p. 5.
123 J. McConnel, 'John Redmond and Catholic loyalism', *English Historical Review*, 125(512) (2010), pp. 83–111.
124 *Irish Independent*, 29 Nov. 1915, p. 5; 21 Aug. 1916, p. 2.
125 *Freeman's Journal*, 7 Dec. 1922, p. 4.
126 *The Times*, 2 Feb. 1943, p. 6.
127 *Irish Independent*, 9 Jun. 1916, p. 4; *Waterford News*, 29 Jan. 1915, p. 8.

128 M. Wheatley, *Nationalism and the Irish Party: Provincial Ireland, 1910–1916* (Oxford: Oxford University Press, 2005), p. 136.
129 *Irish Independent*, 25 Jun. 1918, p. 2.
130 M. Kennedy, '"In spite of all impediments": the early years of the Irish diplomatic service', *History Ireland*, 7(1) (1999), p. 18.
131 *Irish Independent*, 27 Aug. 1920, p. 12. On this see Reid, 'Stephen Gwynn', pp. 723–45.
132 *Irish Independent*, 12 Mar. 1923, p. 5.
133 Campbell, *Irish Establishment*, p. 231.

17

Catholic Unionism: a case study: Sir Denis Stanislaus Henry (1864–1925)

Éamon Phoenix

In the quiet Catholic churchyard at Straw, near Draperstown, Co. Derry, a plain rectangular stone marks the grave of the Rt Hon. Sir Denis Henry, Bart., the only Roman Catholic ever to have become an Ulster Unionist MP and the first lord chief justice of Northern Ireland. Denis Stanislaus Henry was born on 7 March 1864, in the townland of Cahore, Draperstown, Co. Derry, the sixth son of James Henry, a wealthy merchant and landowner, and his second wife, Ellen (née Kelly). Of his fifteen siblings (nine brothers and seven sisters) two brothers and two sisters were to enter religious life; one brother was a Marist priest while another, Revd William Henry, SJ became rector of the Jesuit Novitiate at Tullamore in King's Co. (now Co. Offaly). Two other brothers became solicitors.[1]

The Henrys were a well-established, wealthy family in a largely Catholic farming district which had been planted by the Drapers' Company of London during the seventeenth century Plantation. The village in the foothills of the Sperrins had been laid out in 1845 by the Company. The district suffered considerably during the Great Famine but, thanks to the establishment of a railway connection in the 1850s, Draperstown was a flourishing market town by the time of Denis's birth. In 1862 a deputation from the Drapers' Company recorded that the village was 'flourishing'. Henry's father, James is not mentioned by name but he was undoubtedly the unnamed 'owner of the townland of Cahore' who, the report noted, 'had rebuilt … his part of the town … giving it a most respectable appearance'. The Henrys lived in a substantial Georgian villa known as 'The Rath' with a coach house and servants' quarters attached.[2] In a memoir his Jesuit older brother, William recalled that their father was 'a landlord'.[3]

The young Denis Henry received his early education at the local Boys' National School where he was enrolled as a Catholic pupil in a school which had some Protestant boys as well. He proceeded to the Marist College in Dundalk, transferring in 1878, along with his brother, Patrick, to the Jesuit College of Mount St Mary's in Spinkhill, near Chesterfield., Derbyshire. The choice of an English, rather than an Irish Catholic public school was probably due to the fact that Denis's late uncle, Father William Henry, SJ had been a pupil there – further evidence of the family's status. Denis would appear to have been an average student. Interestingly his period at Mount St Mary's overlapped with the teaching career there of the poet, Gerard Manley Hopkins.

Henry proceeded to Queen's College, Belfast, where he read law. This was an unusual choice for an Ulster Catholic in the 1880s when the hierarchy was railing against 'godless colleges'. After an outstanding academic career, in which he achieved the distinction of winning every available law scholarship possible, he was called to the Irish bar in 1885 at the early age of 21.[4]

A keen legal mind – attested to by his contemporaries – together with a 'captivating appearance' and 'a fine musical voice' assisted his rapid progress at the bar. Henry quickly established himself on the north-west circuit – extending from Westmeath to Derry, Tyrone and Donegal – eventually taking silk in 1896 as a youthful 32-year-old. Two years later he was elected a Bencher of King's Inns. He was thereafter much in demand as a prosecutor and in 1898 he appeared for the Crown in three murder cases in Belfast, securing convictions in each case.

It was not until he had already established himself as a successful advocate that Henry began to consider the attractions of a career in politics. However, when he finally entered political life, he aligned himself not with the home rule party – soon to be reunited under John Redmond after the bitterness of the Parnell split – but with the Conservative and Unionist Party. Indeed his family background, though intensely Catholic, was strongly conservative and pro-Union. As his political adversary, T. P. O'Connor, the celebrated home rule MP for Liverpool, later observed:

> He was of a somewhat unique type in Irish life, Catholic by descent and personally .... yet he was entirely at variance with the politics of his co-religionists. His family had always belonged to the prosperous middle classes of Ulster. They shared none of the enthusiasms of his co-religionists and it was in this realistic atmosphere that he was brought up.[5]

The Henry family, as landlords in mid-Ulster, were remembered as opponents of the Land League in the 1880s. Like many middle-class Ulster Catholics and Presbyterians they had been Liberals but, according to Denis Henry in a 1906 speech, had shown 'a reluctance to go with Mr Gladstone when he took up Home Rule'. Thus while the bulk of Catholics in the north of Ireland rallied to the revitalised home rule party under Parnell in the so-called 'invasion of Ulster' of 1885, the Henrys gravitated to liberal unionism, placing themselves in the same camp as the great mass of former Presbyterian Liberals.[6]

As early as the 1895 general election Henry publicly endorsed the unionist nominee in South Derry. In that election the rising advocate spoke on unionist platforms in East Donegal on behalf of the local landed magnate, E. T. Herdman, earning him a scornful rebuke from the nationalist *Derry Journal*. It noted with some disdain how:

> A star of North-West circuit magnitude ... has appeared over the hills of Dark Donegal. Mr Denis S Henry, Barrister, has found time in the midst of his brief ... to rush from the Derry Assizes to East Donegal to save his country.[7]

Speaking to an exclusively Protestant audience, Henry dealt frankly with the issue of his religion:

> While a member of another Church, he was not afraid to stand there and say that he was not ashamed of his religion – (applause) – and that he felt, as an Irishman who had the welfare of his country at heart, he could sink religious differences and support the candidature of Mr Herdman.[8]

Henry's remarks show that at this early stage in his career he subscribed to the broader, more inclusive Irish unionism of Sir Edward Carson rather than the narrower sectarian-based unionism of the north.

Henry attended the inaugural meeting of the Ulster Unionist Council on 3 March 1905 as a unionist delegate – one of the very few Catholics to identify with the Orange-dominated movement. Apart from his family background it would seem that Henry's educational experience had played a role in shaping his political outlook. Unlike most nationalists and the future Ulster Unionist leader, Carson, Henry rejected demands for a Catholic university, declaring: 'Mixing was good for everyone as it broadened their views and let them see that other people held as honest opinions as themselves.'[9]

Henry's first attempt to enter parliament came in the 1906 general election when he was selected as the unionist candidate for the highly marginal seat of North Tyrone. The 1906 contest and the by-election which arose there the following year, provide useful insight not only into Henry's personality and outlook, but also into the manner with which Ulster politics was conducted at a local level.

The Catholic unionist's nomination for North Tyrone was significant. The constituency was one of the most peculiar in Ireland at the time. Despite a slender Catholic majority in population terms, the nationalist strength on the register was several hundred votes below that of the unionists. The fate of the seat turned on the votes of some 200 Presbyterian farmers who adhered to the old liberal faith: they would support a Liberal home ruler but could not be relied upon to vote for a full-blooded Irish nationalist. As a result the nationalists had tended to allow the diminutive Liberal Party a clear run and in 1906 William Dodd, KC, a lawyer and Protestant home ruler was the outgoing member and candidate. Thus Henry, the Catholic unionist lawyer, was pitted against Dodd, the Protestant home ruler. In an exciting contest Dodd managed to hold the seat by the narrow margin of nine votes.

The nationalist press showed little sympathy for the Catholic lawyer. The *Irish News* described Henry as 'one of that weird class of creatures known as an Irish Catholic Unionist' whose stance would be anathema to Catholics and whose religion would arouse the worst sectarian feeling among Protestants. Orangeism remained the bedrock of Ulster unionism and Henry's meetings in Orange halls riled the nationalists while the unionist *Londonderry Sentinel* riposted that Henry's attitude reflected his belief that 'the Orangemen of Ireland are a highly constant factor in defending the Union'.[10] Henry deftly ignored the sectarian issue but reiterated his belief in a pluralist, non-sectarian unionism:

> I am opposed to the establishment of any separate legislature for this country or to any legislature which may in any way tend to weaken the Union between this country and the rest of the United Kingdom. Whether this change is sought to be effected by a Home Rule Bill or under the guise of devolution, it shall have my strongest opposition.[11]

During the 1906 campaign Henry elaborated on his views on the Union. At Strabane he stated that it was the finality of home rule which made the measure particularly dangerous and warned that a Home Rule Act could not be repealed or amended. At Castlederg, Co. Tyrone he declared that Ireland was already free enough, with full religious equality. At Plumbridge he stressed that a Dublin government would have little sympathy for Ulster or its industries. The Dublin-based lawyer added that he could see little in common between the north and the rest of Ireland, saying that the south represented 'quite a different community altogether'. This speech marks a clear hardening of Henry's unionism and an overt partitionism, reflecting the more 'Ulster-centric' outlook of James Craig and the Ulster Unionist Council. In 1895 Henry had addressed Donegal unionists as an 'Irishman', yet now he seemed keen to emphasise 'the distinctiveness of Ulster'.[12]

The election result showed that while Henry attracted few Catholic votes, he enjoyed the overwhelming endorsement of the Conservative leadership, including Joseph Chamberlain and the Irish chief secretary,

Walter Long, as well as local Orangemen. Henry's reliance on the Orange Order aroused a mixture of anger and bewilderment among his co-religionists. One leading nationalist parish priest, Revd Philip O'Doherty, referred to the 'incredible state of affairs' in North Tyrone, commenting that while Judge William Kenny, a former Dublin MP, had merely been a Catholic unionist, Henry had embraced the Orange faction too. In the annals of Irish elections, he added, 'it was a thing unknown to have a Catholic supported by the Orange lodges'. In the *Irish News*, a correspondent poked fun at 'Brother Dinish' in doggerel verse:

A Papist beating the Orange drum!
Surely no slavery could be 'maner'?
To what base uses you have come
In the hope of a North Tyrone retainer![13]

In an election generally devoid of rancour, 5,954 voted out of a total electorate of 6,174, 'a remarkable testament to the organisational flair and perhaps the personating ability of both parties'. When the result was announced, Henry rejected the advice of his agent to demand a recount. He congratulated the victorious home ruler and promised to continue their amicable relationship. The election, he observed, had shown that the north of Ireland was as tolerant as anywhere else in the United Kingdom 'although we are technically beaten for the time being'. Henry again fought for North Tyrone in 1907, when a by-election arose following Dodd's elevation to the bench. Unionist suspicions of the new Liberal government were stoked by the introduction of the (ill-fated) Irish Council Bill which promised a measure of devolution. This time Henry lost to the liberal home ruler, Redmond Barry by a majority of seven votes.

As in the previous year, over 90 per cent of votes were cast as the opposing sides spared no effort to maximise their respective votes. One man died in the arms of friends while being lifted out of bed to attend the voting; a Catholic student for the priesthood made a 400-mile round trip from Maynooth seminary to register his vote against Henry. One voter arrived from Buenos Aires, while brandy was administered to one man who managed to vote for Henry before expiring. The defeated unionist once more suppressed his disappointment, enjoining his supporters to desist from violence: 'if you keep the peace you will please me as much as if you had returned me'. Henry could return to the Four Courts in Dublin secure in the knowledge that his unionist credentials had been firmly established for the future.[14]

The Catholic unionist's political ambitions were destined to remain in abeyance for the next decade as he concentrated on his legal career. He declined a nomination in North Tyrone in the 1910 general elections 'owing to increasing professional duties' and took little public part in the anti-home rule struggle of 1912–14 . His unionism remained solid, however, despite the apparent inevitability of home rule, speaking on anti-home rule platforms – in England and Scotland – 'with great effect' according to the London *Times* – to refute the impression that unionism was a sectarian cause.[15] Henry did not sign the Ulster Covenant which was a self-consciously 'Protestant' protest against the third home rule bill. However, speaking in Dublin in November 1912, he argued that an Irish parliament would do little to protect the rights of minorities and that in the thirty years since he had come to Dublin, no unionist had held public office under the corporation. This was a bad augury for a future home rule parliament. If home rule were passed, he said – displaying his characteristic courtroom wit – the loyal minority would be at the mercy of 'metropolitan misfits and provincial pirates'. In a speech which echoed the Tory rhetoric of the 1880s, Henry expressed the hope that the British public 'would decline to hand them over to a party of disorder and ... disloyalists'.[16]

Henry's legal and establishment connections were strengthened in October 1910 by his marriage to Violet Holmes, the daughter of Hugh Holmes, an Irish lord justice of appeal from Co. Tyrone. Despite the fact that his bride was a member of the Church of Ireland the couple were married quietly according to Catholic rites at St Ethelbert's Catholic church, Leominster. The decision to marry outside Ireland may have been politic at a time when the implications of the *Ne Temere* decree and the acrimonious McCann mixed marriage case was exercising Ulster unionism.[17] The marriage was solemnised by Denis's older brother, Revd William Henry, SJ who was then working among the Dublin poor at the Jesuit mission in Gardiner Street. Denis was now 46, his wife 31. They would have five children – James, born in 1911, Denise, Alice, Denis and Lorna. The children were brought up as Catholics while Violet adhered to her Protestant faith.[18]

Henry was now at the top of his profession with a Georgian townhouse in Dublin's fashionable Fitzwilliam Square. In a will dated November 1910 he was able to bequeath to his wife the substantial sum of £16,000. W. E. Wylie, a later legal adviser to the British government in Ireland, recalled him as 'the quickest thinker and most brilliant advocate' he ever knew, a view was shared by A. M. Sullivan, who defended Roger Casement in 1916. Sullivan believed that Henry was 'the best man the Irish bar produced' in his time.

Henry remained on cordial terms with political opponents such as

Tim Healy, KC, the maverick nationalist MP, and T. P. O'Connor. One nationalist legal colleague recalled the lack of rancour at the pre-partition Irish bar: 'To listen to the circle often formed around Tim Healy or Denis Henry ... was to enjoy a feast of reason ... The [Law] Library was a microcosm of the life of Ireland ... political foes sat cheek by jowl ... good companions all.'[19]

Henry's legal standing was recognised in January 1914 when he was one of two counsel appointed to head an inquiry into the famous Dublin lock-out of 1913 when a clash between police and strikers resulted in two deaths. His final report exonerated the police though some twenty members were found to have committed unjustifiable assaults.

An unexpected opportunity for Henry to redress his earlier political disappointments came in April 1916 when the South Derry seat became vacant. With a wartime political truce in force, Henry's selection and return for his native constituency seemed a foregone conclusion. This was not the case, however. He won the nomination only after a third ballot against Colonel Robert Chichester, the local squire, and D. D. Reid, a fellow barrister, and had to face a contest against a maverick independent candidate from Scotland, Dr Arthur Turnball, a critic of the government's handling of the war. While Henry once more enjoyed the support of the Orange Order, the brief campaign which followed suggested a softening of nationalist asperities towards him. A local Catholic curate, Revd P. McGeown of Kilrea went so far as to welcome Henry's election:

> At present it matters not whether a man is a nationalist, a unionist or a liberal, but to us it does matter very much that he should be a Catholic. And Mr Denis Henry, KC, is a Catholic. We feel that when our interests, or the interests of our religion are at stake we shall a supporter in our future MP.[20]

Interestingly, this was the first by-election in Ireland following the Easter Rising, with the poll coming a mere eleven days after the final executions and in an atmosphere of martial law.[21] Henry's early parliamentary career was low-key though he served on the royal commission into the deaths of three innocent civilians including the pacifist, Francis Sheehy-Skeffington during the Rising. In November 1918 he was appointed solicitor-general for Ireland in the Lloyd George coalition.

In the subsequent general election, which saw Sinn Féin sweep the polls in nationalist Ireland, he successfully defended his South Derry seat against Louis J. Walsh of Sinn Féin (who was, ironically, a distant cousin), and a home rule candidate. Selected in Kilrea Orange Hall, Henry was publicly endorsed by Carson as 'a most loyal and devoted colleague' while the orange grandmaster in the constituency called on every member of the order to support him. Henry warned his supporters that his Sinn Féin opponent represented 'everything that was abominable to their loyalty and allegiance'.[22] With Sinn Féin and the nationalists focusing on the growing threat of partition, Henry showed no enthusiasm for it. He told a meeting in Magherafelt that he felt deeply for his fellow unionists in the south and west and stated that he would prefer to see the present constitutional arrangements unchanged so that unionists and nationalists could 'enjoy the blessings and benefits of ... the Union'. Unionists, he declared, would never submit to a Dublin legislature. A young nationalist who heard Henry speak recalled him as 'an accomplished and convincing orator' who spoke with 'a refined, cultured Dublin accent'.[23] The fatal split in the Catholic vote combined to give Henry a comfortable majority of nearly 5,000 votes over his nearest opponent, the constitutional nationalist, John Conway. Yet the South Derry election of December 1918 represented the last occasion in which a Catholic won a unionist seat in Ulster.

The return of the Tory-dominated Lloyd George coalition in 1919 with its explicit commitment to partition enabled, Craig and the Ulster unionists to accept four junior ministries. These included Henry, now promoted to the post of attorney-general for Ireland, a position he held throughout the violence of the Anglo-Irish War. The first meeting of Dáil Eireann in January 1919 coincided with the opening shots in the independence struggle. Henry, the superb advocate whose mastery of his brief had been his hallmark, now found himself in the invidious position of having to defend the government against a background of mounting insurgency and increasing militarism by the security forces. He served two Irish chief secretaries: Ian Macpherson and, following the latter's resignation in April 1920, Sir Hamar Greenwood. Throughout this tempestuous period, Henry had to respond to persistent allegations of misconduct by crown forces, the revelation of British reprisals, the introduction of coercive legislation and the deployment of the Black and Tans and Auxiliaries. His discomfiture was not eased by Greenwood's frequent absences from the house of commons and the mounting indictment of the government from the British press, the Labour party and the rump of the nationalist party under 'Wee Joe' Devlin.[24]

One of Henry's first major challenges was a hunger-strike by Sinn Féin prisoners in Mountjoy Jail in April 1920. The attorney-general's palpable lack of reliable information on the condition of the hunger-strikers left him struggling at the despatch box. With *The Times* calling for decisive action (the prisoners were eventually released) Henry admitted in cabinet that the whole affair had been 'badly managed'.

In his sensitive position as chief Irish law officer at this critical juncture Henry was closely involved in the formulation of the British government's controversial Irish strategy spanning partition and the ending of the Anglo-Irish war. As the IRA campaign escalated and a system of republican courts displaced the crown courts, he remained unrepentant in his vindication of government policy, telling the house of commons in February 1920 that Ireland was virtually in a state of war: 'It was not an attack on one party, it is not an attack on the Coalition government, it is an attack on your nation. It is an attempt to drive your nation out of Ireland'.

Henry was responsible for introducing the draconian Restoration of Order in Ireland Act (ROIA) which became law in August 1920. The *Irish News* condemned the proposal to establish military courts-martial with the power to impose the death penalty while Joe Devlin's bitter attack on the measure result in his suspension from the house of commons. In a heated exchange with T. P. O'Connor, Denis Henry denied any ill-treatment of prisoners by military authorities. The government, said Henry, had striven 'for a better state of affairs' and the ROIA was a last resort. He regarded those engaged in violence as 'rebels' and 'traitors' and declared that the government was entitled to deal with them on that basis.[25]

Such stridency, however, could not conceal the fact that Henry's parliamentary responses to allegations of atrocities by crown forces were unconvincing and 'perhaps the least satisfying aspect of [his] term of office'.[26] Badly briefed and evasive, he was forced to rely on Royal Irish Constabulary and military reports on incidents involving alleged reprisals and unwarranted shootings by crown forces. As the conflict escalated in the early months of 1921 the political and personal pressures on Henry were intense. When he refused to discuss the alleged murder of men under army escort, his silence provoked vigorous protests by Liberal and nationalist MPs. Henry was also criticised by an official in Dublin Castle, Mark Sturgis, who alleged that he 'sat in London, afraid to set a foot in Ireland' at the height of the IRA campaign.[27] However, Henry's characteristic willingness to stand against the tide of Irish Catholic opinion and his later state-building role in Northern Ireland suggest that he did not lack courage.

With James Craig and his Ulster unionist colleagues Henry pointedly abstained on the second reading of the Government of Ireland Act (1920) which provided for partition and separate home rule parliaments, north and south. In the spring of 1921, as the government and Sinn Féin 'skirmished on the extreme edge of negotiation', he was among those in the cabinet in May 1921 who opposed a truce until the IRA had been defeated militarily. In the event of Sinn Féin refusing to operate the proposed southern Irish parliament he was prepared to contemplate drastic action in the form of crown colony government.[28]

T. P. O'Connor, who knew Henry at Westminster during this period, remembered him as:

> a tall, stout, red-faced man with a mane of hair rising high above his head and, in later years, very white. He had a strong face with a large nose and a very powerful jowl. If you did not know he was a distinguished lawyer you might take him for a squire of County Galway who had stood as a model to [the novelist] Charles Lever. The face indicated the nature, for though he was good-natured, he was also keenly alive to the good things of life, especially high position in his profession. These things he attained, but he had to go almost through blood and tears to reach them for he lived through a very stormy time in the history of his country.[29]

O'Connor added that, although Henry was the subject of invective from nationalist MPs, he and they remained on friendly terms: 'they hated his politics but they did not – nobody could – hate the man.'

Any expectations of a respite from the pressures of public life were dispelled when, in August 1921, Henry was Craig's first choice for the position of lord chief justice of Northern Ireland. He was created a baronet in the same year. Henry's appointment came against the background of the July truce between the IRA and the British government, the Treaty negotiations, and the transfer of law and order to Belfast in November 1921. Northern nationalists continued to hope that the London negotiations would produce a united Irish state and took little interest in the appointment of a Catholic as head of the new judiciary. Dismissing Henry's appointment to 'the absurd northern judiciary' the *Irish News* commented caustically in August 1921: 'Sir James Craig's government cannot undertake any work with the degree of permanency attaching to it because they know that there can be no permanency in this partition.'[30]

To the deepening political uncertainty and politico-sectarian violence was added the urgent task of establishing new legal structures. The gargantuan task of creating the machinery of a new court system fell to Henry, now aged 57. He was active in the recruitment of officials to staff the new northern judiciary, liaising with Dublin Castle and James Craig for whom he had 'a profound admiration' according to Lady Henry. As lord chief justice, Henry was involved in several highly controversial cases which reflected the turbulent birth-pangs of the new state. In July 1922 he ruled against the plaintiff in a landmark case (O'Hanlon v Governor of Belfast Prison) challenging the legality of the unionist government's Special Powers Act. In November 1923 he rejected claims for compensation for the victims arising over a notorious incident in Cushendall, Co. Antrim on 23 June 1922 when three Catholic youths were shot dead by members of the 'A' Special Constabulary within hours of the IRA assassination of Sir Henry Wilson in London. While the police claimed that the men had been engaged in a paramilitary ambush, witnesses alleged they had been innocent while a private investigation by F. T. Barrinton-Ward, the Recorder of Hythe in Kent, rejected the Specials version: 'My conclusion is that no one except the police and military even fired at all ... I am unable to accept the evidence of the Special Constabulary.'[31] In his judgment Henry referred to the 'extraordinary conflict of testimony' between the police and the nationalist witnesses but he rejected the claim for compensation on the grounds that the deaths arose out of an unlawful assembly.[32] Such adjudications reflected Henry's earlier defence of emergency legislation and his instinctive support for the forces of law and order.

The stresses and strains of the Irish revolution years had taken their toll on Henry. He died, following a seizure, on 1 October 1925, at his home, 'Lisvarna', Windsor Avenue, Belfast. He was 61. In his final illness he received the last rites of his church from the local parish priest, and from the Rector of Ardoyne Passionist Monastery in Belfast. Tim Healy claimed that the dying judge 'had a priest after sixty years', suggesting that he had long abandoned his religious practice. After a private Mass in the family home celebrated by his brother, William, Denis Henry was buried in his native place. In a tribute Craig described him as 'one of Ulster's most distinguished sons'. His political opponents paid tribute to his personal qualities, his legal acumen and his compassion as a judge. But, as O'Connor remarked in a obituary, 'there remained some resentment among his co-religionists – and among nationalists generally – that this man of Celtic blood and of the Catholic creed should range himself in the ranks of the Orangemen'.[33]

The career of Sir Denis Henry remains unique in an island where religious and political allegiances are often synonymous. Previous Catholic unionists like William Kenny and Father John Healy of Little Bray had come from the south of Ireland. Northern Catholic unionists were in short supply. Henry's name was largely forgotten until the late 1960s when, in response to civil rights claims of anti-Catholic discrimination, unionist propagandists trumpeted that the first lord chief justice of Northern Ireland had been a Catholic. Yet attempts to broaden unionism beyond its traditional Protestant base had little success in the divided state after his death and it was not until 1998 that another Catholic unionist was elected to the Northern Ireland Assembly.[34]

Notes

1 A. McDonnell, *The Life of Sir Denis Henry, Catholic Unionist* (Belfast, Ulster Historical Foundation, 2000), pp. 1–2; *Belfast Telegraph*, 2 Oct. 1925.

2 *Irish News*, 26 Feb. 2010.

3 McDonnell, *Sir Denis Henry*, pp. 3–4; memo by Revd W. Henry, SJ, Irish Jesuit Archives, Dublin (IJA).

4 *Ibid.*; *Londonderry Sentinel*, 3 Oct. 1925.

5 *Belfast Telegraph*, 2 Oct. 1925.

6 *Londonderry Sentinel*, 6 Jan. 1906.

7 *Derry Journal*, 29 Jul. 1895.

8 *Ibid.*

9 J Biggs-Davison and G Chowdharay-Best, *The Cross of St Patrick: The Catholic Unionist Tradition in Ireland* (Bourne End: Kendal, 1984), p. 290.

10 McDonnell, *Sir Denis Henry*, pp. 11–16.

11 *Londonderry Sentinel*, 2 Jan. 1906.

12 McDonnell, *Sir Denis Henry*, p. 14; Alvin Jackson, 'Irish Unionism', in P. Collins (ed.), *Nationalism and Unionism: Conflict in Ireland 1885–1921* (Belfast Institute of Irish Studies, 1994), pp. 40–1.

13 McDonnell, *Sir Denis Henry*, pp. 15–16; *Irish News*, 2 Jan. 1906.

14 McDonnell, *Sir Denis Henry*, pp. 20–6. In 1944 an Irish Catholic chaplain attached to British forces in Italy ministered to Captain James (later Sir) Henry, a wounded officer in the Royal Navy and the eldest son of Denis Henry. At James Henry's request the priest wrote to the officer's 'black Protestant uncle', E. S. Murphy, a Belfast judge and former Ulster Unionist MP, informing the family that James Henry was wounded but alive. The priest added humorously: 'He was very grateful that I should go so far to see him but I explained that I had once gone much further (from Maynooth as a student) to vote against his father in North Tyrone ... Young Henry ... is such a decent fellow that I was almost sorry I voted against his father.' (Revd W. Devine (Naval Chaplain) to Judge E. S. Murphy, 13 Mar. 1944 (in possession of author) Murphy, a prominent Orangeman, had a sister of Denis Henry's widow and had been a close friend of the Catholic unionist's).

15 *The Times*, 2 Oct. 1925.

16 *Northern Whig*, 20 Dec. 1909; Biggs-Davison and Chowdharay-Best, *The Cross of St Patrick*, p. 292.

17 The *Ne Temere* decree on mixed marriages was promulgated by Pope Pius X in 1908. It required mixed marriages between Catholics and non-Catholics to be solemnised in a Roman Catholic church and a commitment from the Protestant partner that any children of the marriage would be brought up in the Catholic faith. The decree was not applied to Germany but it was applied to Ireland, where it was dramatised by the McCann case in Belfast in 1910 at the beginning of the third home rule crisis. The case involved the break-up of the marriage of Alexander McCann, a Catholic, and Agnes McCann,

a Presbyterian, following the alleged interference of a priest armed with the *Ne Temere* decree. Alexander McCann disappeared with his two young children and was never heard of again. The case provoked an outpouring of religious and political protest in the north of Ireland and Britain. In 2012 the McCanns' great-grandchildren visited Ireland to reveal that McCann had fled to Pittsburgh, and had changed his name.

18 Certificate of Henry's marriage, 1 Oct. 1910 (General Register Office, London); obituary of Revd W. Henry, *Province News* (Irish Jesuits), Jun. 1928, pp. 73–5 (IJA).

19 McDonnell, *Sir Denis Henry*, pp. 30–1; T. J. Campbell, *Fifty Years of Ulster 1890–1940* (Belfast: Irish News, 1941), p. 136.

20 Cited in McDonnell, *Sir Denis Henry*, p. 37.

21 McDonnell, *Sir Denis Henry*, pp. 36–42.

22 *Northern Constitution*, 7 Dec. 1917.

23 McDonnell, *Sir Denis Henry*, pp. 45–50; Eoin Walsh letter to *Irish News*, 13 Jul. 1984.

24 McDonnell, *Sir Denis Henry*, pp. 53–60.

25 Hansard HC Debates 127 (12 Apr. 1920), 1487; (19 Feb. 1920), 1171; (25 Apr. 1920), 2046–7.

26 McDonnell, *Sir Denis Henry*, p. 71; M. Hopkinson (ed.), *The Last Days of Dublin Castle: The Diaries of Mark Sturgis* (Dublin: Irish Academic Press), p. 48.

27 *Diaries of Mark Sturgis*, p. 72;

28 K. Middlemas (ed.) *Thomas Jones, Whitehall Diary*, 3 vols (London: Oxford University Press, 1969–71), *Ireland 1918–1923*, iii, pp. 59, 71; McDonnell, *Sir Denis Henry*, pp 66–7.

29 *Belfast Telegraph*, 2 Oct. 1925.

30 Biggs-Davison and Chowdharay-Best, *Cross of St Patrick*, p. 355; *Irish News*, 6 Aug. 1921.

31 Michael Farrell, *Arming the Protestants: The Formation of the Ulster Special Constabulary and the Royal Ulster Constabulary, 1920–17* (London: Pluto, 1983), pp. 163–5.

32 McDonnell, *Sir Denis Henry*, pp. 107–14.

33 *Belfast Telegraph*, 2 Oct. 1925.

34 Sir John Gorman, a former senior RUC officer was elected in North Down as an Ulster Unionist, supportive of the Good Friday Agreement in 1998.

VII

Contemporary expressions of Catholic and Irish identity

18

Identity and political fragmentation in independent Ireland, 1923–83

Louise Fuller

The centrality of Catholicism to Irish identity in the post-independence era has to be understood against the background of nineteenth and early twentieth century Irish history. The mobilisation of bishops, priests and Catholic laity by Daniel O'Connell from the early nineteenth century led to Catholic emancipation and from that time the Catholic community was increasingly politicised. A chief priority for the bishops throughout the nineteenth century was the securing of education rights for Catholics. To this end they were prepared to support Parnell and the Irish Parliamentary Party to secure home rule and a resolution of the land question. Thus the Catholic faith became inextricably linked to the Irish nationalist cause. This was precisely at the time when the Irish language and Gaelic culture were in decline.

After the Parnell crisis, the subsequent split in the Irish Parliamentary Party and the failure of the second home rule bill a number of groups emerged in the late nineteenth century to fill the vacuum in Irish politics and they were concerned to address this situation. In their various ways they were conscious that the Irish had lost their cultural identity and aimed to revive the Gaelic cultural heritage. These groups became the nursery of the independence movement which led to the 1916 revolution. The Anglo Irish treaty, partition and a bitter Civil War followed. The outcome fell far short of their dreams of national unity and a republic and the country was left politically fragmented. The identification of Irish and Catholic, already well in place by the time of independence, now took on additional significance in the search for national identity and several factors served to reinforce this synthesis post-independence.

Partition left the country polarised along religious lines – southern Ireland was overwhelmingly Catholic in its population. Each census from 1926 to 1961 recorded an increase in the Catholic population. A very close alliance developed between church and state and the essential Catholicity of the state was reinforced in all sorts of ways by successive governments between the 1920s and 1950s. Politicians in the new state were also very concerned to further the aim of restoring the Irish language and culture to its rightful position and they did this chiefly by means of the education system. Church and political interests had the same vision of the purity and distinctiveness of Irish culture and were equally concerned to restore, maintain and protect what was seen as the unique Irish Catholic identity from what were perceived to be alien influences emanating from abroad. Independence made it possible to copper-fasten Catholic identity and politicians across the spectrum legitimated the Catholic ethos by their actions, public appearances, rhetoric and crucially by legislation. An early example was in 1923, when the possibility of making divorce available in the Irish Free State was raised, W. T. Cosgrave sought and complied with the advice of the hierarchy that 'it would be altogether unworthy of an Irish legislative body to sanction concession of such divorce'.[1] The Film Censorship Act of 1923 and the Censorship of Publications Act later in 1929 were designed to protect what was seen as the distinctive Irish Catholic way of life from alien influences.

Two important occasions provided early opportunities to emphasise Catholic identity. The commemoration in 1929 of Catholic emancipation and the triumphant celebrations at the time of the Eucharistic Congress in 1932 publicly underlined Ireland's Catholic identity. In a St Patrick's day broadcast to the United States in 1935, de Valera left no doubt as to the Catholic character of the nation when he declared:

> Since the coming of St Patrick, fifteen hundred years ago, Ireland has been a Christian and a Catholic nation. All the ruthless attempts made through the centuries to force her from this allegiance have not shaken her faith. She remains a Catholic nation.[2]

De Valera's vision of Irish identity was entirely in keeping with the sentiments expressed in Irish bishops' pastoral letters, which in turn were influenced by papal encyclicals and pronouncements since Pope Leo XIII's promulgation of *Rerum Novarum* in 1891. These were concerned with the adverse consequences of the industrial revolution – resulting from industrialisation, urbanisation and mechanisation. Such ideas were distilled by de Valera again in his 1943 St Patrick's day broadcast to the Irish people, where his vision was of 'a people who valued material wealth only as a basis of right living, of a people who were satisfied with frugal comfort and devoted their leisure to things of the spirit'.[3] The 1937 constitution reflected Catholic ideals and recognised in Article 44 the 'special position' of the Catholic Church. For de Valera the logic was simple; in the Dáil he pointed out that 'ninety-three per cent of the people in this part of Ireland and seventy-five per cent of the people of Ireland as a whole … belong to the Catholic Church'.[4] As far as he was concerned, the constitution reflected the political and social landscape that prevailed. At the same time he was also well aware that the 'special position' clause was not by any means the Catholic ideal as regards the relationship between church and state. It was something of a compromise to suit local political and religious circumstances and conferred no legal status on the Catholic Church.

The two main groupings who might have challenged the prevailing synthesis were the minority Protestant tradition, and the Labour movement. Against the background of successive governments' pursuit of a nationalist Catholic agenda, the minority Protestant tradition retreated, and for much of the period after independence there was little overt questioning by Protestants of the prevailing Catholic ethos. The Labour Party's decision not to contest the 1918 or 1921 elections, to allow the electorate to focus attention on the national question, relegated the party to the sidelines of Irish politics. Church warnings about the dangers of communism and socialism further ensured that there was little chance that the Labour Party would make electoral inroads. The French sociologist Jean Blanchard, who conducted research in Ireland in the mid-1950s, wrote of the essential homogeneity of social and political life in Ireland: 'The family life of Irish Catholic workers and employees, with few exceptions, is steeped in Catholicism … The majority of them support the national parties, rather than the Labour Party'.[5] The *Irish Catholic Directory* bore testimony to this, when it recorded the 'huge turn-out of trade union organisations' at the Marian year procession in 1954, which 'passed through O'Connell Street, where all traffic was suspended for more than two hours as crowds twenty-deep packed the processional route.'[6]

Cultural theorists point to the importance of rituals, songs, ceremonies and processions in cultivating an ethos. 'Faith of Our Fathers', sung in conjunction with the national anthem at all-Ireland football finals, reinforced the dual identity of Irish and Catholic. This, and the fact that the archbishop of Cashel, patron of the Gaelic Athletic Association since its foundation in 1884, threw in the ball at the beginning of the match represented a public ceremonial language, which served to define the community and sustain a way of looking at things. On the one hand such rituals took collective sentiments for granted and they also served to affirm them, thus reinforcing the individual's social identity within these parameters. The communications media, radio and press played a key role in legitimating the Catholic ethos. The ringing of the Angelus bell broadcast at six o'clock each evening by Radio Éireann and the extensive coverage given to news of Catholic interest by the

Irish Independent, the newspaper with the largest daily circulation, all signalled the centrality of Catholicism in the Irish way of life.

The first cracks emerged in the church-state consensus during the tenure of office of the first inter-party government 1948–51. The controversy surrounding Noël Browne's, the minister for health, attempts to introduce free medical care for mothers and children up to the age of 16 regardless of means and the hierarchy's objections to the scheme – the so-called 'Mother and Child' controversy – marked a turning point. The proposals were opposed by the medical profession for their own reasons and by the church on the grounds that they were contrary to Catholic social teaching. Browne believing that he had dealt with the objections of the hierarchy, pressed on with the scheme. But the cabinet refused to support him and he resigned in April 1951. There are more ramifications to the episode and the outcome than are possible to outline here, not least among them the opposition of the Irish Medical Association and Browne's poor relations with cabinet colleagues and in particular his own party leader Seán MacBride.[7] So it would be an oversimplification to present the mother and child episode as a straightforward conflict between church and state, but it undoubtedly raised questions about church–state relations in Ireland and the influence of the hierarchy. It was remarkable for the way that the major players were at pains to profess their allegiance to the Catholic Church. Taoiseach John A. Costello asserted in the Dáil: 'I as a Catholic, obey my Church authorities and will continue to do so, in spite of the *Irish Times* or anything else.'[8] In his resignation speech, Browne himself declared 'I as a Catholic accept unequivocally and unreservedly the view of the hierarchy on this matter'.[9] That said he sent to the newspapers on the day of his resignation the text of the correspondence that had passed between himself, the hierarchy and the Taoiseach. This was a revolutionary move, which meant that for the first time in the history of the independent state the role of the church was under public scrutiny. Two pertinent observations capture the mood of the debate which followed. On the day after Noël Browne's resignation, the *Irish Times* leader writer observed: 'the Roman Catholic Church would seem to be the effective government of the country.'[10] And defending the bishops' right to intervene in the matter, Dr Alfred O'Rahilly remarked that 'for a Protestant organ such as the *Irish Times* to launch an attack on this right' was 'plain totalitarianism'.[11] Observations by both Costello and O'Rahilly reflected perceptions of the *Irish Times* as a Protestant organ, and as such not representative, and not entitled to offer an opinion on matters at issue. Later in 1951 in an address to the Catholic Truth Society of Ireland, Archbishop John D'Alton of Armagh expressed his view that 'we have a right to expect that our social legislation will not be in conflict with Catholic principles'.[12] This had been the position since the foundation of the state – but from now on this absolute right of Catholicism to be the informing spirit of Irish culture, and supported by legislation, would increasingly be called into question.

The interpenetration of church and state was nowhere as obvious as in the field of education. The importance of education for the transmission of culture had always been recognised by all churches. Concerns in relation to education had been central to the Catholic bishops' involvement in the political struggles of the nineteenth century, which led directly to their subsequent dominant position in Irish social and political life after independence. Successive governments were happy to leave educational matters to the churches. In so far as successive governments tried to influence policy, their primary interest was the restoration of the Irish language.

Richard Mulcahy put it succinctly in 1956, when he pointed out that teachers, syllabuses and textbooks in every branch of education should be informed by the 'spirit' underlying the Catholic conception of education.[13] The Council of Education reports on primary education in 1954 and on the secondary school curriculum in 1962 reflected this position. The former report pointed out that 'a religious spirit should inform and vivify the whole work of the school'[14] and, in the latter report, the dominant purpose of schooling was seen as the 'inculcation of religious ideals and values' and 'the preservation and transmission' of the cultural heritage.[15]

As regards the Irish language, by the 1960s it was obvious that the aim of restoring Irish as the first language was not viable and the schools-based revival policy was discredited.[16] However there were also more urgent practical educational issues to be faced. In the post-war era Ireland lagged behind Britain, America and mainland Europe in terms of social and economic development. The country had gained independence, but emigration figures, which soared through the nineteen-fifties, made it all too clear that the state had singularly failed to create an economic base that could sustain its own population and education was beginning to be seen as part of the problem. *The Programme for Economic Expansion*, published in 1958[17] signalled a decisive shift in Irish politico-economic thinking which, in a matter of years, was to turn the Irish economy around. It highlighted the importance of education, and in particular vocational education, for economic success. An OECD review of Irish education took place from 1962–65 and the result was a historic groundbreaking report *Investment in Education* published in 1966.[18] Whereas religious imperatives had been central to the Council of

Education's definition of worthwhile curricular knowledge, a key policy which emerged from the 1966 report was the importance of aligning the school curricula to the needs of an industrial economy. This was articulated by politicians and a variety of vested interest groups from the 1960s and from that time governments adopted a more independent line on education policy making. Over time concepts emphasising the importance of fostering an 'enterprise culture' and 'wealth creation' displaced religious ideals. This was reinforced and became part of received wisdom as time went by. It represented a profound change in the ideology underpinning education and was set to have a major impact on the definition of Irish identity from then on.

By the 1960s, many social, economic and political developments would cause cracks to appear in the too cosy coalescence between Irishness and Catholicism. Developments in tourism, opportunities to travel abroad and the radically different approach to the church taken by the new Irish television station from 1962 all led to a more open Irish society. Church figures had always been wary of the communications media. From the early years of the state politicians and Catholic Church leaders had been keen to protect Irish society from what were perceived as alien ideas and influences. In his Lenten pastoral letter after the inauguration of the national television station, Cardinal D'Alton expressed his fears: 'We no longer enjoy our isolation of former days ... In this world, through the medium of the press, the radio, and the T.V., we are subject to the impact of views wholly at variance with Catholic teaching.'[19] Television from the outset questioned the status quo. In a changing socio-cultural climate the rigid censorship policy was no longer sustainable. Between 1964 and 1967 the minister for justice, Brian Lenihan, carried through sweeping changes, all of which led to more questioning of traditional Catholic thinking and concepts of identity.

But the changes were not restricted to the secular or the local sphere. The Second Vatican Council took place between 1962 and 1965 and after centuries of resistance the universal Catholic Church began to embrace the modern. The church engaged in its own programme of '*aggiornamento*' and reinvented itself in terms of its image and fashioned a 'new' theology. Eternal truths, certainties and traditions which had been handed down in a dogmatic fashion were the subject of disagreement during the council and this called the church's absolute authority into question. This had profound implications for those who accepted without question the church's authority, as many did in Ireland. The idea that the church had answers to all the central questions of life was dispelled at the time of the council. It led to a crisis of authority for the Catholic Church. The full extent of this crisis sank home in 1968 when

Pope Paul VI promulgated *Humanae Vitae* reaffirming the church's traditional teaching on birth control. It was known that he was going against the majority opinion of the commission that had been set up to advise the church on the matter. The monolithic confident church was no more – it was fragmented and seen to be so. Another indication of the failure of confidence was the decline in vocations which made itself felt from the late 1960s.[20]

The late 1960s was a time of considerable social and political unrest internationally. The Berkeley and Paris student revolts had their parallel in Ireland. The so-called 'gentle revolution' took place in the spring of 1969, when students in University College Dublin protested against the manner in which the move to the new campus at Belfield was being handled. Such were the profound changes in the air that in the general election campaign held in 1969, a Labour Party slogan could confidently proclaim that 'The Seventies will be Socialist'.[21] Hitherto this would have constituted political suicide in Ireland. The feminist movement emerged in Ireland about that time and before long it confronted confessional positions in particular relating to sexual morality. Taken for granted ideas about national identity were being challenged from another perspective also in the 1960s. A historiographical revolution had been in progress since the 1930s, whereby received versions of Irish history and identity were challenged by historians.[22] Syntheses of Gaelic, nationalist and Catholic were called into question, to be replaced by altogether more complex notions of what formed identity. New paradigms in intellectual and cultural discourse were finding their way into political discourse and by the seventies into the history curriculum of schools.[23] When combined with curricular changes and new teaching methods, which emphasised child-centred learning as opposed to the rote-learning hitherto typical of Irish education, it would lead to a more questioning approach to all authority figures, received values and ideas formerly accepted as immutable and sacrosanct. The 1969 election was not as mould-breaking as had been anticipated, but it did see the arrival on to the political stage of Dr Garret FitzGerald as a Fine Gael TD and Dr Conor Cruise O'Brien as a Labour TD, both of whom were to make their presence felt in the following years, as champions of a more pluralistic society. In an article in *Studies* in 1964[24] FitzGerald signalled his vision of a new Ireland, which would be the product of the combined Christian, liberal and socialist traditions. The new Irish society, he wrote, would glory 'in our mixed inheritance, despising none of it, and elevating no part to a position of pre-eminence over the rest'.[25] Identity issues were to take on added significance sooner than anyone thought.

The eruption of the 'Troubles' in Northern Ireland in 1969 lent a new urgency to the necessity to continue with such questioning. Southerners were forced to confront received assumptions and uncomfortable realities in relation to identity and allegiance. Partition of the island had profound implications for the political cultures that developed on either side of the border. North of the border the consequences were tragic. Traditional versions of the Irish historical narrative, many now felt, had served to entrench sectarian animosities. In the Republic little thought had been given down the years, by either churchmen, or politicians, to the implications of legislative and constitutional provisions which reflected a Catholic ethos, for aspirations towards national unity, or indeed for relations with the Protestant population of Northern Ireland. In the aftermath of the Lemass visit to the north in 1965, an All-Party Committee of the Dáil was set up to review the constitution. It reported in December 1967 and referred to the prohibition of divorce, noting that it took 'no heed of the wishes of a certain minority of the population who would wish to have divorce facilities',[26] and regarding the clauses of Article 44, which recognised the 'special position' of the Catholic Church and certain other religious denominations by name, it pointed out that 'these provisions give offence to non-Catholics and are also a useful weapon in the hands of those who are anxious to emphasise the differences between North and South'.[27] When the possibility of amending article Article 44 was raised, Cardinal William Conway, archbishop of Armagh, reacted by saying that he 'personally would not shed a tear' were the relevant sub-sections to disappear adding that it conferred 'no legal privilege whatever on the Catholic Church'.[28] A short time later after the bishops' autumn meeting, it was stated officially that the matter had been discussed and that the statement made by the cardinal represented the views of the bishops.[29] A referendum proposal to delete the clause relating to the 'special position' of the Catholic Church was put to the electorate on 7 December 1972. The proposal was carried by 88.4 per cent of those who voted and the result was very significant at a symbolic level.

That said, the findings of the first major survey into Catholic practice, attitudes and beliefs a few years later, on the face of it, might have suggested that nothing had changed in Irish Catholic culture. But this was not so – whereas surveys of Irish Catholicism in the 1970s and 1980s indicated a very high level of religious practice relative to other countries, they also recorded a decline in practice among younger people, especially males, and the urbanised. It was also found that when it came to moral teaching which had a bearing on how Catholics lived their lives, such as the prohibition of contraception and divorce significant numbers of Catholics did not fully accept the teaching of the church.[30] The findings confirmed without doubt that the nature of religious identity in Ireland was changing. The term *à la carte* Catholicism was now being employed by some to capture what was a very new phenomenon in Irish Catholic culture. One of the many symptoms of more liberal and independent attitudes was the fact that in spite of a ban on Catholics attending Trinity College many were ignoring it. At the conclusion of their meeting in Maynooth in June 1970, the bishops issued a statement to the effect that they had 'decided to seek approval from the Holy See for the repeal of statute 287 of the Plenary Synod', by which synodal decree 'for over one hundred years the Irish hierarchy has felt obliged to restrict ... the entry of Catholics into Trinity College, Dublin'.[31]

By now Irish society was more ideologically fragmented and following patterns of secularisation long documented in other countries, but Catholic moral precepts were still upheld in legislation. The issue of access to contraception was to dominate the 1970s. In spite of legislation still in place prohibiting the sale of contraceptives, the Irish Family Planning Association was established in 1969. A non-profiting making organisation, it provided contraceptives and gave advice to patients about the planning of families. The law was challenged by a group from the women's movement who went by train to Belfast on 22 May 1971 and flouted the law by bringing contraceptives back through customs in Dublin. Thus the momentum for change built up and in 1972 a government-appointed Commission on the Status of Women asserted that parents had a right to 'regulate the number and spacing of their family' and that the methods that they chose 'must remain a matter for their mutual selection and be influenced by their moral conscience'.[32]

Several attempts were made through the 1970s to change the law relating to contraception, all of which were resisted by the bishops. However they did modify their thinking, maintaining in 1973 that 'there are many things which the Catholic Church holds to be morally wrong and no one has ever suggested, least of all the Church herself that they should be prohibited by the State'.[33] This was a major turning point, but the statement was somewhat disingenuous, as this was precisely what had been expected up to this time. That said, the fact that the Taoiseach Liam Cosgrave and six other Fine Gael TDs voted against their own government's bill in 1974, was a measure of how traditional attitudes held firm. The issue led to a debate on church-state relations, secularisation and the question of Catholic moral precepts being upheld by law. In 1976 Bishop Jeremiah Newman of Limerick stated that his personal position was that 'the Catholic people of our state have a right – a political right – to the provision of the kind of social framework that supports them in the living out of their moral and religious principles'.[34] While the hierarchy as a whole were distancing themselves from this position, it was not too far removed from their position in the past. Garret FitzGerald (now minister for foreign affairs in a Fine Gael–Labour coalition government) and Conor Cruise O'Brien (minister for posts and telegraphs) argued that Newman's position was sectarian. O'Brien defined the secular state as one which takes into account the views of all citizens, whether they adhere to a religion whose members are in a majority, or to religions whose members are in a minority, or those professing no religion.[35] Newman rejected outright such a position, stating that 'we have got to give leadership to the people to stand up against the secular state and those who represent it'.[36] But the authoritarianism of the past was no longer acceptable. Attitudes and values were being formed increasingly by more secular, liberal views of morality and the contraception issue forced the bishops to reassess their role in the new Ireland that was taking shape. The Family Planning Act was passed just two months before the pope's visit in July 1979.[37] It represented the first step in the process of dismantling of legislation and constitutional provisions which had underpinned the Catholic ethos in the Republic. The impressive crowds, who turned out at all the venues that Pope John Paul II visited, might have conveyed the impression that nothing much had changed in Ireland – but much had indeed changed.

Throughout the 1970s the situation in the north of Ireland continued to deteriorate. Hunger strikes in which ten republican prisoners died before they were called off on 3 October 1981 further polarised the unionist and nationalist communities. There was a growing awareness in political quarters that major changes would have to be made to develop a more pluralistic society in the south, if stereotypes of the Republic as a confessional state were to be tackled. In the course of a radio interview in September 1981 Garret FitzGerald, now Taoiseach, announced his intention to pursue a 'crusade' for constitutional reform, pointing out that in the Republic 'our laws and our constitution, our practices, our attitudes reflect those of a majority ethos and are not acceptable to Protestants in Northern Ireland'.[38] The Anglo-Irish summit took place in 1980 and since then there was a recognition that any possibility of peace and stability in the north would require a development of the unique relationship between Britain and Ireland. This led to the establishment of the New Ireland Forum which began on 30 May 1983. The idea of the Forum was to explore the nature of Irish society, with a view to bringing about the kind of social and cultural changes, which would allow all traditions on the island to live in peace and harmony.

However, realising such ideals was not going to be straightforward. The pope's visit in September 1979 provided the catalyst which led to the consolidation of conservative lay Catholic groups who, from that time, increasingly resisted liberalising tendencies. These groups were fiercely opposed to FitzGerald's constitutional 'crusade'. Pope John Paul in all of his speeches was critical of liberal influences, which had come to prevail in Irish society from the late 1960s. At his Mass in Limerick he challenged his audience: 'Irish people have to choose today their way forward' whether that be the path of materialism or of 'the things of the spirit'.[39] His remarks echoed de Valera's 1943 St Patrick's day speech[40] and constituted a direct challenge to the Irish as to how they chose to define themselves. But erstwhile images of Irish identity no longer resonated. In 1973 Ireland had joined the then European Economic Community. Irish society was becoming more secularised like other countries of western Europe, increasingly defined by materialistic values and polarised along rural conservative and urban liberal lines. The extent of the fragmentation became very obvious at the time of the Pro-Life Amendment campaign. In April 1981 an anti-abortion lay pressure group was formed calling itself the Pro-Life Amendment Campaign. Known as PLAC, it campaigned with a number of like-minded groups for an amendment to the constitution which would prevent abortion being introduced. In September 1983, a pro-life amendment to the constitution was carried by a margin of 66.45 per cent in favour to 32.87 per cent against, after a particularly acrimonious and divisive campaign.[41] Seen as a victory in some quarters for the more conservative Catholicism of pre-conciliar times, it also indicated a new and deep urban–rural divide in Irish society. Predominantly rural constituencies voted overwhelmingly yes and urban, largely middle-class areas displayed the strongest resistance to the amendment. In Dublin the margin was very close (51.6 per cent Yes and 48.3 per cent No) and five constituencies opposed the amendment. The seamless Catholic culture of the past was well and truly gone.

To a great extent the pro-life amendment campaign overshadowed the New Ireland Forum taking place in Dublin Castle. The Forum gave the bishops an opportunity publicly to address their position in relation to issues which had become highly contentious. Cahal Daly, bishop of Down and Connor and leader of the bishops' delegation stated categorically that 'we do not seek a Catholic state for a Catholic people'.[42] The Forum Report pointed out that 'public legislation must have regard for the conscientious beliefs of different minority groups', and that this called for a 'deepening and broadening of the sense of Irish identity'.[43] This clearly signalled that erstwhile definitions of Irish identity would have to be re-formulated to take account of 'diversity' and this would involve a radical re-thinking of the relationship between religion, society and the law. The proceedings gave Garret FitzGerald some confidence to press forward with his 'crusade' for constitutional reform. His government's bill to further liberalise the family planning legislation in 1985 passed by a narrow margin in the Dáil. Again it was obvious that there were conservative groups in Irish society, who felt that liberal reforms were threatening their vision of Irish identity. Three Fine Gael deputies and one Labour deputy voted against the bill. The official position of the bishops was to keep to the line they had enunciated in their 1973 statement, but not all bishops were happy to do so. In due course FitzGerald announced his coalition government's intention to hold a referendum to remove the constitutional ban on divorce on 26 June 1986. He presented the proposed change in the context of his 'crusade' for a more pluralist Ireland, which would improve relations with Northern Ireland and also relations between the nationalists and unionists north of the border. Until about a week before the referendum, opinion polls indicated that increasing numbers supported the introduction of divorce. But once again results on the day reflected the resilience of traditional Catholic values – 63 per cent of those who voted rejected the government's proposal.[44] Again, Dublin constituencies voted narrowly in favour of divorce whereas the majority of rural constituencies voted overwhelmingly against the amendment.

Fragmentation along rural conservative–urban liberal lines was set to become an enduring feature of Irish life henceforth, as evidenced in the results of two further referenda on divorce in 1995 and abortion in 2002. By the early 1980s the emphasis was on diversity and the accommodation of different cultural and political traditions. The automatic synthesis of Irish and Catholic was no longer sustainable and would be a thing of the past as the twentieth century came to a close.

Notes

1 R. Fanning, *Independent Ireland* (Dublin: Helicon, 1983), p. 56.
2 *Irish Press*, 18 Mar. 1935.
3 *Irish Press*, 18 Mar. 1943.
4 *Dáil Debates*, 67, col. 1890 (4 Jun. 1937).
5 J. Blanchard, *The Church in Contemporary Ireland* (Dublin: Clonmore and Reynolds, 1963), p. 30.
6 *Irish Catholic Directory* (*ICD*), 1955 (16 May 1954), p. 632.
7 In 1953, James Ryan, Browne's successor in a Fianna Fáil government led by de Valera, dealt with objections and introduced a broadly similar

scheme making health care provision free to 85 per cent of the population, as opposed to the entire population as originally planned.

8 *Dáil Debates*, 125, col. 784 (12 Apr. 1951).
9 *Ibid.*, 125, col. 668 (12 Apr. 1951).
10 *Irish Times*, 12 Apr. 1951.
11 *Standard*, 20 Apr. 1951.
12 *ICD*, 1952 (10 Oct. 1951), p. 709.
13 Cited in J. Mescal, *Religion in the Irish System of Education* (Dublin: Clonmore and Reynolds, 1957), pp. 136–7.
14 *Report of the Council of Education on (1) The Function of the Primary School (2) The Curriculum to Be Pursued in the Primary School* (Dublin: Stationery Office, 1954), para. 132.
15 *Report of the Council of Education on the Curriculum of the Secondary School* (Dublin: Stationery Office, 1962), paras 150, 164, 80, 88.
16 A. Kelly, *Compulsory Irish: Language and Education in Ireland 1870s–1970s* (Dublin: Irish Academic Press, 2002), pp. 132–41.
17 *Programme for Economic Expansion* (Dublin: Stationery Office, 1958), often referred to as the First Programme.
18 *Investment in Education: Report of the Survey Team* (Dublin: Stationery Office, 1966).
19 *Irish Independent*, 5 Mar. 1962.
20 L. Fuller, *Irish Catholicism since 1950: The Undoing of a Culture* (Dublin: Gill and Macmillan, 2002), pp. 167–8.
21 M. Gallagher, *The Irish Labour Party in Transition 1957–82* (Manchester: Manchester University Press, 1982), p. 91.
22 See C. Brady (ed.), *Interpreting Irish History: The Debate on Historical Revisionism* (Dublin: Irish Academic Press, 1994), pp. 3–31.
23 L. Fuller, 'An ideological critique of the Irish post-primary school curriculum: the economic, socio-cultural and political factors influencing its development', M.Ed. thesis, St Patrick's College, Maynooth, 1990, pp. 124–51.
24 G. FitzGerald, 'Towards a national purpose', *Studies: An Irish Quarterly Review*, 53 (winter 1964), pp. 337–51.
25 *Ibid.*, p. 350.
26 *Report of the Committee on the Constitution* (Dublin: Stationery Office, 1967), p. 43, para. 123.
27 *Ibid.*, p. 47, paras 134, 136.
28 *Irish Times*, 23 Sept. 1969.
29 *Irish Times*, 10 Oct. 1969.
30 See *Ten Years of Research and Development 1971–1980* (Maynooth: Council for Research and Development, 1981), p. 51. See also *Religious Beliefs, Practice and Moral Attitudes: A Comparison of Two Irish Surveys, 1974–1984* (Maynooth: Council for Research and Development, 1984), pp. 35, 96–101.
31 For the full background to this decision, see statement by the Irish Episcopal Conference, Maynooth, 25 Jun. 1970, regarding Trinity College,

Furrow, 21(8) (Aug. 1970), pp. 532–3; *Irish Times*, 26 Jun. 1970; 7 Sept. 1970.

32 *Report of the Commission on the Status of Women* (Dublin: Stationery Office, 1972), p. 225, paras 572–3.

33 Statement of the Irish Episcopal Conference, 25 Nov. 1973, in *Irish Times*, 26 Nov. 1973.

34 See *Irish Times*, 1 Jun. 1976.

35 For an insight into this debate and the issues raised, see *Irish Times*, 29 Mar. 1976; 31 Mar. 1976; 1 Apr. 1976; 29 Apr. 1976; 1 Jun. 1976; 2 Jun. 1976. Refer also to radio interview with Olivia O'Leary, RTÉ, 30 May 1976.

36 Radio interview with Kevin O'Kelly, RTÉ, 30 May 1976; see also J. Newman, *The State of Ireland* (Dublin: Four Courts Press, 1977).

37 Health (Family Planning) Act 1979, No. 20 in public statutes of the Oireachtas, 1979.

38 G. FitzGerald, *All in a Life: An Autobiography* (Dublin: Gill and Macmillan, 1992), pp. 377–8.

39 See *The Pope in Ireland: Addresses and Homilies* (Dublin: Veritas, 1979), p. 77.

40 See *Irish Press*, 18 Mar. 1943; n. 3 above.

41 *Irish Times*, 9 Sept. 1983. See also T. Hesketh, *The Second Partitioning of Ireland: The Abortion Referendum of 1983* (Dublin: Brandsma Books, 1990), p. 364.

42 *New Ireland Forum Report, No. 12*, Public Session, Thursday, 9 Feb. 1984, Dublin Castle (Dublin: Stationery Office, 1984), p. 2.

43 *Ibid.*, p. 23, para. 4.13.

44 See *Irish Times*, 28 Jun. 1986.

19

Secular prayers: Catholic imagination, modern Irish writing and the case of John McGahern

Frank Shovlin

> even now I feel the desperate need of prayer
>
> John McGahern, *The Leavetaking*

In 1929 Liam O'Flaherty, the once student-priest, but by then Ireland's most openly anti-clerical writer, published a scathing attack on the Irish Catholic Church in a short, aggressive book titled *A Tourist's Guide to Ireland*. 'This may seem extraordinary', he wrote, 'but it is true that in remote parts of Ireland, usually the parts of interest to tourists, the parish priest has a finger in every pie'. He goes on to provide a withering condemnation of the role played by the priest in Irish life:

> He is the great and only power in the district. Confident in the blind worship of the peasants and the village loafers and the fishermen of the seaside, he forces the wealthier people to obey him in the most minute matters. He is practically master of the body and soul of every individual. When they are born they are brought before him and he baptizes them for a few shillings. When they begin to go to school they come under his supervision. He hires and sacks their teachers at his discretion, very often at his whim. He flogs them if they mitch from school or if they fail to learn their catechism. When they become striplings, he watches them carefully lest they make love clandestinely.

He concludes that for the peasantry, from 'their first yell at birth until the sod falls on them in their grave their actions and thoughts are under his discretion'.[1]

O'Flaherty, though the most hysterical, was far from the first major Irish Catholic writer to denigrate his church. George Moore's *Parnell and his Island* (1887) takes a similar unforgiving approach to the country and its shortcomings, while his novel, *The Lake* (1905), and book of short stories, *The Untilled Field* (1903), are peopled with a range of sometimes cruel, sometimes deranged, sometimes merely hapless priests. Patrick MacGill's *Children of the Dead End* (1914) sees the parish priest of Glenmornan (a town based closely on his native Glenties) hand in glove with the usurious gombeen man. Though today the annual summer school named in MacGill's honour has become a kind of proxy parliament in exile in the hills of Donegal, at the time of writing, his novel's unflattering portrayal of a corrupt church made him an unwelcome visitor back on his home patch: he died an American exile, forgotten and unregarded, in 1963. Even worse opprobrium was heaped on Brinsley MacNamara after the publication in 1918 of his melodramatic novel, *The Valley of the Squinting Windows*, which follows the regression of a young seminarian from devoted mother's boy to lovelorn, fratricidal alcoholic. The book was famously burnt in public by the people of Delvin, Co. Westmeath, the village on which MacNamara had based his dreary Garradrimna. MacNamara's father's school was boycotted by the locals, and the case was taken up by W. B. Yeats, A. E. and others in the first great literary scandal of the Free State.

Today in Ireland, the depiction of a perverse, insane or deviant priest in a work of literature, far from creating outrage, would not raise a murmur. In the wake of a slowly but surely building secularism and the fallout from the spate of sexual scandals of the past twenty years, the Catholic Church could hardly fall much further in popular esteem. Colm Tóibín, one of those contemporary Irish writers to draw on the subject of a sexually abusive church in his short story collection, *Mothers and Sons* (2006), recently described the Catholic Church of his native country thus: 'The Church now has a strange ghostly presence in Irish society. Its hierarchy still meets as though it represents something, including power ... The bishops, priests and nuns are sinking, but have every intention of putting up a struggle before they drown.'[2]

In such an Ireland, the hapless suicide, Fr Walsh, of Martin McDonagh's enormously successful 'Leenane Trilogy' of the late 1990s makes for a nice bit of local colour, and the predatory paedophile, Fr Tiddly, of Patrick McCabe's *The Butcher Boy* (1992) gives us some of the best belly laughs in the book. In these sorts of depictions there is, of course, the danger of falling into what Gus Martin once dubbed 'the clerical cliché', having the priesthood and the broader Catholic Church become as unrealistically monstrous as it once was overly sunny in something like the hugely popular early twentieth-century fiction of Canon Sheehan or the devotional poetry of Katharine Tynan. 'The facile, doctrinaire anti-clericalism which has dominated Irish fiction since George Moore's time', argued Martin in 1965, 'still stands as a mark of our failure'.[3]

On a first, superficial, reading of John McGahern, Ireland's most important fiction writer of the past half century, one might see another contributor to the gallery of malign priests and a gloomy, restrictive

Catholicism. He describes his time in Catholic teacher-training college in stark terms, reminiscent of O'Flaherty:

> Attendance at daily Mass and evening Devotions was compulsory; and, extraordinary in a third-level institution, there wasn't a literary, historical, philosophical or – more surprisingly – even a Gaelic Society: but there were religious societies. We were being groomed as non-commissioned officers to the priests in the running of the different parishes throughout the country, cogs in an organizational wheel, secondary to the priest in all things, including education.[4]

That subordinate role is brought to terrifying life in his short story 'The Recruiting Officer' when the teacher-narrator, a former Christian Brother, witnesses the savage beating of young Walshe by the school manager Canon Reilly with a length of electric cable: 'In a half-circle the beating moves, the boy trying to sink to the floor to escape the whistle and thud of the wire wrapping round his bare legs but held up by the arm, the boy's screaming and the heavy breathing of the priest filling the silence of the faces watching from the long benches in frightened fascination.'[5] McGahern's second novel, *The Dark* (1965), was perhaps the first major work of fiction in Ireland to shine a light on clerical sexual abuse, leading its author to be targeted by then archbishop of Dublin, John Charles McQuaid, and dismissed from his teaching post in a Catholic boys' primary school. Yet despite all of this, to read McGahern as falling into cliché does not do justice to a complex and finely wrought aesthetic sensibility.

Like one of his great literary heroes, James Joyce, McGahern, for the majority of his life, did not believe in God, nor practice the Roman Catholic faith into which he was born. Yet in spite of that, and contra certain influential critical positions, his fiction stands as much the most interesting and lucid engagement with religion generally, and with Catholicism specifically, provided by any Irish writer. Far from having 'no religious feeling', as Seamus Deane writes of McGahern's first four novels, those books, as well as his short stories and later novels, are drenched in religion.[6] Writing to his friend and fellow writer Michael McLaverty in the wake of the banning of *The Dark*, McGahern was pained by the wanton and blinkered misreading that had led to the controversy. 'The Appeal Board have rejected the plea for *The Dark*', he writes. 'I may be asked to leave. I don't see any other alternative than to go to London then. What disturbs me very much is that the book's a religious work if it's anything at all.'[7]

McGahern was similarly insistent on the religious nature of his first published novel *The Barracks* (1963) which features the inner workings of Elizabeth Reegan's mind as she contemplates her coming death from breast cancer. Writing to the trustees of the Macaulay Fellowship while still composing *The Barracks*, he attempts to describe the aims and motivations of the work, 'As it is not a novel, but an attempt to break that form down into a religious poem, I can only hope to indicate some of its tones as it moves to its end. The vision is all that matters in it, and the style, for a banality in it can assume as much importance as the beautiful'.[8] In one of his earliest published interviews McGahern stressed the centrality of religion, describing his work as 'a religious activity which is keeping faith to the sources of one's own being and it is, in the pure sense of the words, a form of praise and of prayer'.[9] Nor does that insistently religious bent of 1960s McGahern dissipate or disappear in the later work. The title of his most celebrated novel, *Amongst Women* (1990), is taken from the 'Hail Mary', that of his final masterpiece, *That They May Face the Rising Sun* (2002), is, in itself, a prayer.

So, why the confusion? How can a writer so drawn to spirituality and religion, so preoccupied with the notion of art as sacred, be still thought of in some quarters as either hostile to, or disinterested in, Catholicism? To answer this question one ought to look first at a book which McGahern frequently cites and which influenced his world-view throughout his writing life: the 1951 study *The Greeks and the Irrational* by E. R. Dodds. Dodds argues for a broadening out of what we understand as 'religion' – if we restrict the meaning of the word, he asks, 'are we not in danger of undervaluing, or even of overlooking altogether, certain types of experience which we no longer interpret in a religious sense, but which may nevertheless in their time have been quite heavily charged with religious significance?'[10] For McGahern, two types of experience in particular – artistic and sexual – take on such religious significance, and a consideration of how these sides of human life impact on his characters makes it easier to see how he might, for instance, insist on *The Dark*'s 'religious' character.

The priestly nature of the writer's art is best exemplified in perhaps the unlikeliest of places, McGahern's experimental 1979 novel *The Pornographer*. Though the unnamed narrator of the book makes ends meet by writing pornographic fiction, his attempts at writing are portrayed in sacramental fashion:

> I washed and changed, combed my hair, and washed my hands again a last time before going over to the typewriter on the marble, and started to leaf through what I had written.
>
> We used to robe in scarlet and white how many years before. Through the small window of the sacristy the sanded footpath lay empty and still between the laurels and back wall of the church ... The wine and water

> and hand linen had been taken out onto the altar. The incessant coughing told the church was full. The robed priest stood still in front of the covered chalice on the table, and we formed into line at the door as the last bell began to ring ... Among what rank weeds are ceremonies remembered, are continued. I read what I had written, to take it up.[11]

The book, owing much to Albert Camus, is a long, existential meditation on the futility of life in the face of inevitable death. And though it is the McGahern novel containing least overt engagement with the church, it retains that insistence which is present throughout his work on the mysterious and magical nature of words placed in the right order, or what we might call literature.

That sense of the transcendental power of good writing is given voice in McGahern's previous novel, *The Leavetaking* (1974), by the character of the narrator's mother, a teacher who is being sounded out by the Mother Superior of her school for a possible life in the church:

> 'Doesn't poetry remain always in some way the unknown, Mother?' she ventured after thought. 'It can be felt, but not known, as we can never know our own life or another's in the great mystery of life itself.'

Such spiritual profundity is beyond the nun's grasp, as it is beyond that of most of her fellow teachers:

> She'd learned too that most teachers read little, had even an instinctive hatred of the essential mystery and magic in all real poetry, reducing it to the factual or sentimental and preferably both, four ducks on a pond and a grassbank beyond.[12]

That the sensitive layperson – sometimes even a non-believing layperson – should be more religious than the man or woman of God is a theme that runs through McGahern and is neatly exemplified in *That They May Face the Rising Sun* when Johnny, home from England for his annual summer visit, remarks unselfconsciously that his sociable parish priest in London 'isn't a bit religious'.[13] Considered closely, the statement seems absurd, yet it goes unnoticed by Ruttledge, the intelligent atheist – just another wise truism of Johnny's.

While poetry or great literature can be seen, then, as one form of religious expression, the other most common forum for such expression lies in the sexual life – and this is where we come back to McGahern's insistence that *The Dark*, with all its explicit and painful exploration of a teenage boy's sexual awakening, ought to be read as a 'religious' novel. Archbishop McQuaid, the book's most powerful censor, would, in McGahern's eyes, have almost certainly fallen into Johnny's category of a cleric who 'isn't a bit religious'. Again, the narrator's mother of

The Leavetaking – very closely modelled on McGahern's own mother – provides a clear example of this merging of the sexual with the religious instinct when she ruminates on her lost virginity the morning after her marriage's consummation:

> 'Has it happened to me?' was all her mind could frame over the tea and toast and brown bread of the North Star Hotel breakfast the next morning, the mind already trying to change the sheets and blood and sexual suck of the night into a sacrificial marble on which a cross stood in the centre of tulips and white candles.[14]

The narrator, while still a young boy, promises his devout mother that he will one day become a priest and say Masses for her. Much of *The Leavetaking* is about how he copes with the guilt of not keeping that promise after his mother's early death. In a key passage he reflects on the choice and on the possibly sacramental nature of sexual instinct:

> The true life was death in life. The sexual life was destruction; the sweet mouth, ruin. In my end was my beginning. One day I would say Mass for her.
>
> Could not the small acts of love performed with care, each normal, mysterious day, be a continual celebration, as much as the surrender of the dream of woman would allow the dubious power of the laying on of anointed hands?[15]

Though framing the statement as a question leaves us in doubt as to the narrator's commitment to the idea, his decision to marry and stay with his lover, an American divorcee, and thus to lose his teaching post is the best example in all of McGahern of the religious, even priestly, nature of sex:

> My love waits for me in a room at Howth. The table will have bread and meat and cheap wine and flowers. Tomorrow we will go on the boat to London. It will be neither a return nor a departure but a continuing. We will be true to another and to our separate selves, and each day we will renew it again. It is the only communion left to us now. Oh soul full of grace, pray for me, now and at the hour, Oh pray for us both; even now I feel the desperate need of prayer.[16]

For McGahern, that stark religious need is sated again and again by the transcendent power of writing.

For the ancient Greeks, argues Dodds, sexual passion could fall into the category of religious experience. For the most dominant theology in the Catholic Church, on the other hand, sex is degraded, shameful and to be avoided except for procreation. This, argues McGahern, is the church's great error, pulling it down into an anti-life whorl. One of the odder but more revealing passages of prose in McGahern's posthumously published essays, *Love of the World* (2009), reflects on this problem:

> We are sexual from the moment we are born, it grows as the body grows and fails with the body until we die: by then it has become part of the mind, the will and the intelligence and heart, which grows in the human act of becoming as the body fails, and suffuses everything we hold precious or dear. The church I was brought up in sought to turn this powerful and abiding instinct into the functional act of procreation, surrounding it with shame and sin, as it directed this human act of becoming modified moment by moment, day by day, year by year.[17]

The piece, which is used, intriguingly, to open the collection, works in the form of a litany, a paragraph worked and reworked five times to produce a slightly different effect on each occasion. But the central message is clear – sexual desire, the sexual self, is at the very heart of what it is to be human; to deny it is fatal. Yet it is also more than that – it is exalted. 'I see sexuality as just part of life', said McGahern in an interview towards the end of his life. 'Either all of life is sacred or none of it is sacred. I'm inclined to think that all of life is sacred and that sexuality is a very important part of that sacredness.'[18]

McGahern, an intensely private man and a writer who believed absolutely in having his fiction reveal its own meaning without prompt or authorial intervention, became more public, more frank as he approached death. The last two books published in his lifetime – *That They May Face the Rising Sun* and *Memoir* (2005) – have an unmistakeably valedictory timbre about them. The same frankness is evident in the greater number of interviews he gave, in the television documentary about his life and work, *A Private World* (2006), and in his essays. One of the last such, 'God and Me', is the single clearest of his pronouncements on Catholicism. Again he remembers the immense power of the church of his youth. 'I grew up in a theocracy in all but name', he writes. 'Churches in my part of Ireland were so crowded that children and old people who were fasting to receive Communion would regularly pass out in the bad air and have to be carried outside. Not to attend Sunday Mass was to court social ostracism, to be seen as mad or consorting with the devil.' In such a world, heaven, hell and purgatory were as real to him as England or America. But this intense, unquestioning belief slipped away from him as an adolescent so that, as he memorably puts it, he awoke one day 'like a character in a Gaelic poem' and realised he was no longer dreaming. 'The way I view that whole world now', he writes, 'is expressed in Freud's essay "The Future of an Illusion"'.[19]

Freud's essay seeks to explain humanity's continuing attachment to religion and to ideas of the divine – a quick examination of it makes for some revealing insights into McGahern's work. Freud argues that the origins of religious belief lie in man's craving for consolation in the face of a hostile, finite world: 'life and the universe must be rid of their terrors'.[20] The invented God's central task is to 'reconcile one to the cruelty of fate, particularly as shown in death'.[21] Practically all of McGahern's fiction is clarified in the light of these insights. Everywhere his characters seek consolation, try to cheat time, escape their inevitable fates. Except very occasionally through sexual love they always fail. And the most common means of failure is a flight to the priesthood. The clearest example of this comes in McGahern's magnificent short story 'The Wine Breath' which follows a day in the life of a country priest who recalls his reasons for entering the church. Though prompted in large part by a sense of love and duty towards his devout mother, he cannot escape the realisation that 'it was out of fear of death he became a priest, which became in time the fear of life'.[22] The story ends with a familiar turn to the sexual, to life:

> Somewhere, outside this room that was an end, he knew that a young man, not unlike he had once been, stood on a granite step and listened to the doorbell ring, smiled as he heard a woman's footsteps come down the hallway, ran his fingers through his hair, and turned the bottle of white wine he held in his hands completely around as he prepared to enter a pleasant and uncomplicated evening, feeling himself immersed in time without end.[23]

But it would be a mistake to read 'The Wine Breath' as an endorsement of the world of sensuous pleasure over that of religious contemplation. McGahern is reluctant to permit simple escape or consolation in the flesh, his fictions peopled by restless, dissatisfied, lonesome lovers. Yes, the priest of this story has made an error, but in a mortal world there may be no way to be right.

Because there can be no final consolation, whether through prayer or art or human solidarity, McGahern never indulges in the knee-jerk hostility to Catholicism so evident in much contemporary thought. There is no sense in which we are invited to despise or dislike the doubting priest of 'The Wine Breath'. He faces the same dilemmas we all face and has gone about attempting a solution in his own ordered way. And while there are several brutish clergyman to be found in McGahern's pages, equally there are hateful laypeople, from the wheedling politician of 'High Ground' to the calculating rapist John Quinn of *That They May Face the Rising Sun*. In fact, for all the power wielded by the clergy of

McGahern's youth, he frequently argues that the ordinary people of the Irish countryside paid them little heed, and 'went about their sensible pagan lives as they had done for centuries'.[24]

Also, and again this is especially true of his later writings, McGahern repeatedly praised aspects of his Catholic upbringing and of the central role the church played in the Ireland of his youth, particularly in education. Though, as we have already seen, his time in St Patrick's training college was more like a prisoner-of-war camp than a third-level institution, he was still able to see some positives and happily accepted an honorary doctorate from the institution in 2003. In his acceptance speech he pointed out an important aspect of church power from his time as a student: 'When so much is being said against the Church, I believe it was the Church that was mainly responsible for the high esteem given to teaching and learning here, an old respect for the schools.'[25] Similarly, he was generous in his praise of the education he had received from the Presentation Brothers of Carrick-on-Shannon in the 1940s and early 1950s: 'The Brothers took me in, set me down and gave me tools. I look back on my time there with nothing but gratitude, as years of luck and privilege, and, above all, of grace, actual grace.'[26]

Such remembrance is a very long way indeed from the more frightening of his fictional accounts of sadism and cruelty in Irish schools such as that previously quoted from 'The Recruiting Officer'; it acts as a useful corrective to increasingly received views of the church's involvement in Irish education. When trying to come to grips with an Ireland that was rushing to secularism a little too quickly for its own good, McGahern feared that the more worthwhile and beautiful aspects of Catholicism would be lost in the race to cosmopolitan modernity. He liked to quote his great literary hero Marcel Proust on this subject. Proust, a hundred years earlier, had witnessed and regretted similar trends towards disregarding the traditions and lifestyles that the French Church had created over centuries, and wrote of his worries in a letter quoted by McGahern:

> I can tell you at Illiers, the small community where two days ago my father presided at the awarding of the school prizes, the *curé* is no longer invited to the distribution of the prizes since the passage of the Ferry laws. The pupils are trained to consider the people who associate with him as socially undesirable ... it doesn't seem to me right that the old *curé* should no longer be invited to the distribution of the prizes, as representative of something in the village more difficult to define than the social function symbolized by the pharmacist, the retired tobacco-inspector, and the optician, but something which is, nevertheless, not unworthy of respect, were it only for the perception of the meaning of the spiritualized beauty of the church spire.[27]

If the church is similarly cast aside in Ireland, what, wonders McGahern, is there to fill the spiritual void? McGahern too, like Proust, though detached from any formal practice, was capable of seeing something worthwhile in the church, something due respect. In that, he has a balance and a nuance absent in many contemporary Irish writers and commentators. 'I never found the church ceremonies tedious', he writes. 'They always gave me pleasure, and I miss them still. The movement of focus from the home and school to the church brought with it a certain lightness, a lifting of oppression, a going outwards, even a joy.'[28]

I would like to conclude with a return to Gus Martin's still relevant 1965 essay 'Inherited Dissent' which chastises Irish writers of the day for failing to escape the influence of the previous generation – the paralysed Ireland of Joyce, the disappointed revolutionaries: Frank O'Connor, Seán O'Faoláin and Liam O'Flaherty. As a result of this tendency, argues Martin, an unrealistically dark and hackneyed picture of Ireland emerges, leading to over easy assumptions about the country in the world beyond. Interestingly, he cites an English Sunday newspaper review of McGahern's first novel *The Barracks* to make his point about the detrimental impact of such cliché:

> In describing the scene around the village church the author mentions an authentic detail – rosary beads twined round the church railings. As every Irishman can tell the beads are lost property which have been picked up off the ground and displayed where their owners may find them. But the reviewer, apparently mistaking the custom for a superstitious rite, wonders sadly what one can do for people who piously twine rosaries round railings. The reader in this case has fallen victim to a *cliché*, because the vision of Ireland which the misreading implies is the result of a powerful and relentless *cliché*. He has seen something in an Irish novel which was not there; he has mistaken John McGahern who was born in 1934 for Frank O'Connor who was born in 1903.[29]

McGahern, Martin could see, even at this very early point in his career, was coming out from under the shadow of Joyce and the paralysed Fr Flynn of *Dubliners* to forge a new and vibrant kind of Irish literature.

That eschewal of didacticism, of ideological certainty, is one of McGahern's great strengths and it is what makes him such a very interesting chronicler and observer of the Catholic Church in Ireland over the past fifty years. His profound love and respect for the written word, both as a writer and as a reader, acted as a form of reverence. Though a non-believer, there are few more religious writers. 'McGahern', writes Declan Kiberd, his one-time student and now one of his most perceptive critics, 'was a slow, ardent reader and his relaxed but vigilant attention was a kind of prayer'.[30]

Notes

1 L. O'Flaherty, *A Tourist's Guide to Ireland* (Dublin: Irish Amer Book, [1929]1998), pp. 19–20.
2 C. Tóibín, 'Among the flutterers', review of A. Quattrocchi, *The Pope Is Not Gay*, *London Review of Books*, 32(16) (19 Aug. 2010), p. 3.
3 A. Martin, 'Inherited Dissent', in A. Roche (ed.), *Bearing Witness: Essays on Anglo-Irish Literature* (Dublin: University College Dublin Press, 1996), p. 94.
4 John McGahern, '*Ní bheidh sibh ar ais*: St Patrick's College Drumcondra', in S. van der Ziel (ed.), introd. Declan Kiberd, *Love of the World: Essays* (London: Faber and Faber, 2009), p. 115.
5 J. McGahern, 'The recruiting officer', in *Creatures of the Earth: New and Selected Stories* (London: Faber and Faber, 2007), p. 72.
6 S. Deane, *A Short History of Irish Literature* (London: HarperCollins, 1986), p. 221. An interesting critical treatment of McGahern's religious sensibility can be found in J. Whyte, *History, Myth, and Ritual in the Fiction of John McGahern: Strategies of Transcendence* (Lewiston: Edwin Mellen Press, 2002), pp. 95–134.
7 *Dear Mr McLaverty: The Literary Correspondence of John McGahern and Michael McLaverty 1959–1980*, ed. J. Killen (Belfast: Linen Hall Library, 2006), p. 42.
8 Quoted in D. Sampson, 'The solitary hero', in John Kenny (ed.), *The John McGahern Yearbook*, 3 (Galway: National University of Ireland, 2010), pp. 75–6.
9 Interview with A. Hamilton (1966), quoted in Whyte, *History, Myth and Ritual*, p. 126.
10 E. R. Dodds, *The Greeks and the Irrational* (Berkeley, CA: University of California Press, 1951), p. 2.
11 J. McGahern, *The Pornographer* (London: Faber and Faber 1979 [pbk, 1990]), pp. 20–1.
12 J. McGahern, *The Leavetaking* (London: Faber and Faber, 1984), p. 38.
13 J. McGahern, *That They May Face the Rising Sun* (London: Faber and Faber, 2002), p. 86.
14 McGahern, *The Leavetaking*, p. 42.
15 *Ibid.*, p. 156.
16 *Ibid.*, *The Leavetaking*, pp. 168–9.
17 McGahern, 'Five Drafts', in *Love of the World*, pp. 3–4.
18 Quoted in E. Maher, 'Religion and art', in J. Kenny (ed.), *The John McGahern Yearbook* (Galway: National University of Ireland: 2008), p. 117.
19 McGahern, 'God and Me', in *Love of the World*, p. 149.
20 S. Freud, *The Future of an Illusion* (London: Hogarth Press, 1928), p. 28.
21 *Ibid.*, p. 30.
22 McGahern, 'The Wine Breath', in *Creatures of the Earth*, p. 116.

23 *Ibid.*, p. 120.
24 McGahern, 'The Solitary Reader', in *Love of the World*, p. 87.
25 McGahern, '*Ní bheidh sibh ar ais*', p. 116.
26 McGahern, 'Schooldays: A Time of Grace', in *Love of the World*, p. 108.
27 McGahern, 'The Church and Its Spire' (*ibid.*, pp. 133–4).
28 *Ibid.*, p. 137.
29 Martin, 'Inherited Dissent', p. 89.
30 Kiberd, 'Introduction', in McGahern, *Love of the World*, p. xxii.

20

Catholic-Christian identity and modern Irish poetry

Bernard O'Donoghue

Modern Irish poetry in English has been dominated by two major figures: both Nobel Prize winners, recognised as the leading practitioners of their time. The first, W. B. Yeats, was a southern Irish Protestant (though for much of his lifetime the northern–southern divide was not such a stark one: he was nearly 60 when the Irish Free State was declared); the second, Seamus Heaney, is a Northern Irish Catholic. So the first notable reflection is that each of them belonged to the ideological (or cultural or religious) minority within their political state. The meaning then of 'Irish identity', or even of the compound 'Catholic-Christian', is far from identical for the two of them. Furthermore, it changes through their lifetimes: Yeats was born in the mid-Victorian period, in 1865. By a neat handing on of the poetic baton, at least in biographical terms, he died in 1939, in January of the year when Heaney was born in April. At the time of writing Heaney is still at the height of his poetic powers, at the age Yeats was in 1937 – then unquestionably still at the height of his, writing his great *Last Poems*.

The differences in identity and culture can quickly be established by quoting a ringing declaration made by Yeats in 1937, two years before his death: 'I could no more have written in Gaelic than can … Indians write in English; Gaelic is my national language, but it is not my mother tongue.'[1] This linguistic difference from Heaney (whose work is very often ghosted by a knowledge of the Irish language) extends into the general cultural area. Yet Heaney too is aware of the distinctions that Yeats is making so trenchantly here, but from the first he is more circumspect about it. Several poems in his great early collection *Wintering Out* display an awareness of such complexity of identity and a sensitivity to it. In 'Traditions' he recalls the confusion of Shakespeare's MacMorris in *Henry V*:

'What ish my nation?'
And sensibly, though so much

later, the wandering Bloom
replied, 'Ireland', said Bloom,
'I was born here. Ireland.'[2]

The Jewish-Irish Leopold Bloom of Joyce's *Ulysses* claims his Irish identity as foundedly as anyone else. Slightly later in *Wintering Out*, Heaney's wonderful poem about religious sensitivities in the north of Ireland, 'The Other Side', portrays a Protestant neighbour tactfully waiting at the corner of the Catholic household until the Rosary was finished. To that Catholic household the Biblical names of their neighbours' observances were equally foreign – 'like loads of hay / too big for our small lanes'.[3]

Twenty years later, rather than the terminology of Christian religion as in these poems, Heaney takes on the internal, spiritual content in religion in his acclaimed volume of poems, *Seeing Things*,[4] playing on the two senses of its title: having visions, or imagining things that are not there. Perhaps surprisingly, the first of these – the transcendent – is the dominant idea in the book, for example in the title-poem which extols the notion of *claritas*: visionary precision. The passage which really establishes the centrality of transcendence in the book comes from the poem 'Fosterling', and it has been much quoted:

Me waiting until I was nearly fifty
To credit marvels. Like the tree-clock of tin cans
The tinkers made. So long for the air to brighten,
Time to be dazzled and the heart to lighten.[5]

The example of a 'marvel' – the tinker's tree-clock which Heaney had already used as the title for a shorter book, *The Tree Clock*,[6] in which 'Fosterling' was the last poem – is not a specifically religious one, but that does not affect the impulse involved. The sense of the 'me' at the start of the quoted passage is 'me of all people': the puzzle is that crediting marvels took so long for the Catholic-Christian Heaney who grew up in the world of marvels and apparitions, a world where the numinous was always immanent, ready to appear.

This spirituality, which is a matter of impulse, rather than being founded on an explicit system of dogma, is of course nothing new in poetry, Irish or otherwise. T. S. Eliot's *Four Quartets*, which are arguably the greatest English religious poems of their century, are concerned with the numinous impulse rather than with an achieved set of beliefs. They end with the great passage drawing on the late medieval mystic Julian of Norwich:

And all shall be well and
All manner of thing shall be well

When the tongues of flame are in-folded
Into the crowned knot of fire
And the fire and the rose are one.[7]

The Dantesque imagery of the last three lines is obviously deeply embedded in the Christian tradition; nevertheless, the meaning of even these lines – and they are the nearest the *Quartets* come to a Christian explicitness – is more a general statement of the spiritual urge towards faith than an exclusive dogmatic pronouncement, whatever the source of its imagery.

This redefinition of the religious, extending its scope beyond the confines of a particular system of belief, had been an important theme in Eliot's thought from the first. What he admired in James Joyce was what Eliot called the 'mythic imagination': the capacity to see the history of thought and literature as a recurrent set of patterns so that, for example, the experience of Leopold Bloom, a twentieth-century Jewish Dubliner, can be seen in the same cultural perspective as Homer's Odysseus in *Ulysses*. One extension of this viewpoint was the way in which Christian models of reality corresponded to contemporary secular–humanist philosophies. Hence we find world-views which combine Marxism with Christianity and the Christian existentialism of Kierkegaard.

This is very different from the reaction to what was seen as the end of the era of faith in the nineteenth century, prompting such poems as Coleridge's 'Dejection Ode', which Matthew Arnold called 'a plangent threnody for a lost wholeness and peace', or Arnold's own 'Dover Beach' with its famous elegiac reflection:

The Sea of Faith
Was once, too, at the full.

In the early part of the twentieth century some Christian thinking evolved in a way that addressed the same problems as the secular philosophies of the earlier century, which had been thought to have superseded Christianity. More significantly, it has become clear that these new post-faith philosophies are addressing the same existential problems as religions address. An obvious case is Heidegger's philosophy of being, which describes humankind's 'thrownness' onto an unsupportive universe in terms similar to those of the Christian Pascal in the eighteenth century: those infinite spaces which terrify us, rather than providing reassurance. Similarly, it has been observed more than once that the 'absent signifier', proposed by the literary philosopher Derrida as an explanation for contingent things which cannot be the explanation of their own being, performs a function strikingly similar to Aquinas's argument for the existence of God based on contingency.

This concern shared among believers and unbelievers is an essential backdrop to the understanding of any serious modern poet. What I am concerned with here is the ways in which this arises as an issue for the Irish poet in particular. Heaney's tree-clock, as a secular response to the religious impulse, is interestingly balanced in this mixed world. There is a further important consideration: given the moral imperative for the responsible Irish writer in the era of the Troubles of the last third of the twentieth century not to align too expressly with either of the two Christian religious traditions which were redefined in combative political terms, it is very useful to have a serious ethical area which does not require an explicit dogmatic alignment. This need is met by the general, rather than the particular, world of the spiritual or numinous.

But the dilemma is that, despite this urge away from particular dogmaticism, the Irish writer, in representing a culture in which the religious has been so pervasive, can hardly be expected to avoid the terminology of the religious. This problem was addressed interestingly, if not entirely satisfactorily, by John F. Deane in the introduction to his valuable anthology *Irish Poetry of Faith and Doubt: The Cold Heaven*.[8] Deane says that his material is:

> poetry that has sprung from a reaction to religious beliefs, that is reaction in terms of acceptance, rejection or suspicion of the existence of a higher, unseen controlling power known as 'God'. I have excluded poetry that is merely devotional, that is a response in terms of service or homage to an already accepted God … Included is poetry that rejects the existence of God, as this, too, is a reaction. But most important … are the poems that spring from hesitation, doubt and 'vacillation', as these appear to be the most common themes over the last hundred years.

I have quoted this definitive passage at some length because I think it sorts out the issues to some extent. When I said that Deane does not solve the anthology's problems entirely satisfactorily (and that, of course, would be a lot to ask), my reservation is that I think this passage, and the anthology as a whole, again slants the discussion too much towards the *terminology* of religion (reactions to the word 'God') rather than its *spirit*. Of course the terminology is important too; but it is striking that Deane uses the term 'reaction' three times (and the synonym 'response' once) in this passage. He confines discussion to the terminology of the religious and reactions to it rather than to the feeling of the religious itself.

This distinction can be clarified by reference to a gifted Northern Irish poet not included by Deane, Tom Paulin, who often draws on the terminology of religion despite being a socialist humanist with a marked political model of the world and no active Christian affiliation:

> O Absalom, Absalom, my son,
> an hour is too long, there are too many people.
>
> ('Inishkeel Parish Church')[9]

This poem, from Paulin's celebrated first collection, *A State of Justice*, ends with a beautiful use of the traditional image of transcendence, the sea:

> There was an enormous sight of the sea,
> A silent water beyond society.

Paulin's work is emphatically political, but the language of his poetry has continued to draw on religious resources. His collection *Walking a Line* has a poem called 'Matins' with a church bell ringing through it, and a 'A Belfast *Bildungsroman*' with the Pentecostal epigraph: 'And suddenly there came a sound from heaven as of a rushing mighty wind and it filled all the house where they were sitting.'[10] In a different spirit, the occasional anti-Christian sardonicism of another compassionate humanist poet, Paul Durcan, falls back on the terminology of religion in poems such as 'The seminary' and squibs such as 'Irish hierarchy bans colour photography'. And Durcan's apparent iconoclasm can be subtle too, as in the wonderful poem on the death of the Punk singer Sid Vicious which suddenly ends in a prayer: 'Jesus, break his fall!'[11] Like many other twentieth-century Irish poets, the language of religion is Durcan's stock in trade, whatever purpose he is putting it to.

Deane's title, however, is very well chosen: faith and doubt are complementary and vacillation is at the centre of the issue. Here, as pretty well everywhere in twentieth-century Irish poetry, the dominant influence is Yeats, and his pronouncements clarify the matter more than anyone else's. He insists on the centrality of the religious impulse, describing himself as someone of spiritual inclination who has been robbed of his Christian inheritance by the rationalism of Tyndale and Huxley. Throughout his life Yeats, in common with many of his contemporaries, attempted to supply this privation by adapting and mixing various creeds, describing the occult as one of the two great passions of his life. From his concerns with the theosophy of Madame Blavatsky in the 1890s, to Irish fairy lore in the Sligo which he always felt was his real home, to the spiritualist revelations of his wife's automatic writing, Yeats was obsessed by matters of belief. Out of this complex and in reaction to the same sense as Eliot's 'mythic imagination', he wrote his strange, eclectic book, *A Vision*, which attempted to pull all the elements together into a single, privately constructed philosophy. At the end of his life, he summarised the impulse in one of his greatest synoptic statements. When asked whether he really *believed* the tenets of this philosophy, he replied: 'Man can embody truth but he cannot know it.'[12]

It is probably not putting it too strongly to say that this statement is the context in which all non-dogmatic discussion of religious issues by Irish poets is to be seen. Deane recognises this in two ways: first, his subtitle is the title of one of Yeats's great poems, 'The Cold Heaven'.[13] (Deane rightly includes it in the anthology though its explicit religious application is not that obvious.) Second, the prominence he gives to the idea of 'vacillation' in the passage quoted above is surely owed to Yeats's mystical poem of that same name, which Deane includes in the anthology. It includes a marvellous passage of secular mysticism:

> My fiftieth year had come and gone,
> I sat, a solitary man,
> In a crowded London shop,
> An open book and an empty cup
> On the marble table-top.
>
> While on the shop and street I gazed
> My body of a sudden blazed;
> And twenty minutes more or less
> It seemed, so great my happiness,
> That I was blessèd and could bless.[14]

It would be hard to imagine a more exact poetic expression of the collaboration of the secular (the shop and the street) with the spiritual impulse (blessing, and the Dantesque image of blazing again).

The passage is also immensely influential; most obviously we recall that Heaney was 'nearly fifty' when he began 'to credit marvels': a reference, no doubt, to the first line here. Heaney, like Yeats, has always considered himself to be by nature of a spiritual disposition (though by no means 'pope-holy', to use a medieval term). The poem which most extensively represents the religious in him is the long sequence 'Station Island' in the collection of that name.[15] This sequence of twelve longish poems describes a fictional journey by the poet through the purgatory of Irish tradition, 'St Patrick's Purgatory' on Lough Derg in Co. Donegal. From the 'hurry of bell-notes' with which the first poem opens to the conclusion in which the shade of James Joyce urges Heaney to strike out for artistic freedom rather than reverting to his 'peasant pilgrimage', the poem is urgently concerned with duty and repentance. The terms in which Joyce's advice is given (more accurately, of course, invented by Heaney for Joyce) are well known:

You lose more of yourself that you do redeem
doing the decent thing. Keep at a tangent.[16]

The language of this does not need labouring in the context of this chapter: the Christian verb 'redeem', or the ethical word 'decent' derived from the dutiful Latin impersonal verb *decet*. And Heaney in his later writings is at least vacillating in the face of Joyce's advice. By the time of *Seeing Things*, as we have seen, he is ready to celebrate the spiritual again, in the seeing of marvels.

Heaney's later poetry (*Seeing Things* in 1991, after all, is mid-career in a poet whose celebrity has been reinforced still further with the Nobel Prize and all the recognitions that the literary world can offer) is shot through with religious reference and reflections of the numinous in the same way. A glance down the contents list of Heaney's titles makes this immediately evident: 'A Transgression', 'St Kevin and the Blackbird', and so on. From his most recent book *Human Chain* (2010), 'Colum Cille Cecinit' translated its twelfth-century source 'Crowds of white angels on their rounds / At every corner', and the wonderful secular–spiritual poem 'Miracle' begins

Not the one who takes up his bed and walks
But the ones who have known him all along
And carry him in ...

The poem ends with the bier-carriers waiting for

Their slight lightheadedness and incredulity
To pass, those ones who had known him all along.[17]

Heaney's nature as a poet of duty and inwardness is not in question. Despite the pull of the public world for a Northern Irish poet of his era, he tells us himself in a television interview with Melvyn Bragg that his 'temperament is not Brechtian'. He is more inclined to the artistic–spiritual than to the political, even if he is not afraid to address that too when the occasion demands. What is less generally recognised, I think, is how steeped in the language of the Christian spiritual tradition is the poetry of the most prominent Northern Irish poet of the semi-generation immediately following Heaney's, Paul Muldoon. Muldoon is a cryptic, elusive, witty writer who has occasionally been accused of ducking major issues by retreating into an elusive world of metaphors and poetic analogies. He expresses the charge against himself in 'Lunch with Pancho Villa', the first poem in his book *Mules*:

'Look, son. Just look around you.
People are getting themselves killed

Left, right and centre
While you do what? Write rondeaux? . . .
You want to get down to something true . . .

"When are you going to tell the truth?"
For there's no such book, so far as I know,
As How it Happened Here,
Though there may be. There may.'[18]

Although the argument here is about whether or not political involvement is a moral obligation, it is couched in decidedly moral terms: 'truth', and the transcendental question of whether such books as *How it Happened Here* exist or not, a question which becomes philosophical by being left open. This discussion, for all its lightness, fits into the existentialist world of uncertainty.

Later major poems by Muldoon draw on Christian-spiritual structures in a much more overt way. This is especially the case in the two long poems with which the next two volumes of Muldoon end, 'Immram', from *Why Brownlee Left* (1980), and 'The more a man has the more a man wants', from *Quoof* (1983). The first of these uses the medieval Irish *immram* form, the saint's *navigatio*, appropriate for Muldoon because one of the Irish medieval prototypes was the *Immram Maelduin* which might be translated as 'Muldoon's pilgrimage'. This modern version of the pilgrimage is decidedly secularised, consisting of a zany, drug-clouded 300-line mini-epic in the style of Raymond Chandler, involving the protagonist's search for an Irish-American father. (It has often been noted – by the critic Edna Longley, for example – that twentieth-century male Irish poets are much preoccupied with fathers: a preoccupation that might easily be translated into a sense of alienation from a traditionally paternalistic God. But that is too far from the subject here.) Again, Muldoon, like Paulin, draws on religious terminology for his titles, if decreasingly so through his career: 'Vespers', 'Good Friday, 1971. Driving westward' (alluding to John Donne), 'Behold the Lamb', 'Lives of the Saints', 'Our Lady of Ardboe', 'Armageddon, Armageddon', 'The Bishop', 'Palm Sunday', 'Holy Thursday'.

The second of the long Muldoon poems I mentioned, 'The More a Man Has the More a Man Wants', is another loose, extensive narrative, but this time with a much more overt and grimmer bearing on Northern Irish politics. This poem contains some slight Catholic references, predictable in its context (the 'Child of Prague', 'Beatrice', 'Someone on their way to early Mass'); but much more significant in this volume, *Quoof*, of which this discovery poem is the climax, is the eclectic, Yeatsian religious impulse, drawing mostly on Native American shamanist myths, one of which provides the volume's epigraph. Muldoon's work, whose stark and disturbing wit has left to its being called 'post-modernist', has a strangely ethical basis. Often this occurs in a perverse form; as in his poem 'Trance', the pseudo-spiritual references in his poetry are often ostensibly accounted for by drugs. *Quoof* begins with 'Gathering Mushrooms', a poem which balances the biographical fact that Muldoon's father *was* a mushroom farmer with the book's interest in conditions of trance induced by starvation (as in the IRA hunger-strikers) or by ingesting hallucinogenic mushrooms. No less than Yeats, Muldoon wants to invoke states of mind beyond the quotidian. Yeats's route to those higher psycho-spiritual realms was the occult: theosophy or séances; Muldoon's is ostensibly through drug-induced trance. But the spiritual objective in both cases is the same: the truth that, to use Yeats's terms again, man can embody but cannot know. I would suggest that this, rather than political evasion, is the ultimate rationale for what has been seen as Muldoon's obscurity, as it was for Yeats's.

The point I am making with Muldoon is that for any Irish poet, however allusive or whimsical, to be taken seriously, he or she must draw on the religious wells of the language and culture. Mention might have been made of a non-central but respected tradition in Irish poetry which has links with existentialism and European modernism, but which uses the language of Catholic Christianity much more overtly. The principal figures in this tradition are Denis Devlin, Brian Coffey and Thomas McGreevy (who was a close friend of Samuel Beckett). But I want to consider finally two poets in the forefront of contemporary Irish poetry, Michael Longley and Medbh McGuckian. Longley is one of the Northern Irish poets who has most stressed the dilemma of the writer in the Troubles: discuss them in poetry and you are accused of exploitation of suffering for the poet's own ends; ignore them and you are accused of heartless, ivory-tower indifference. Longley's solution has often been to give evidence of the gravity and caution with which political suffering must be taken by using hieratic language. In one of his finest poems, 'The Linen Workers', which is a lament for ten linen workers massacred as they drove home from work, Longley strangely begins:

> Christ's teeth ascended with him into heaven.[19]

Another poem in the same series, 'Wreaths', is an elegy for a greengrocer shot in his shop. It ends:

> Astrologers or three wise men
> Who may shortly be setting out
> For a small house up the Shankhill

Or the Falls, should pause on their way
To buy gifts at Jim Gibson's shop,
Dates and chestnuts and tangerines.[20]

We might note in this small masterpiece how religion, like poetry, can work to heal sectarian division (the Protestant Shankhill and the Catholic Falls Road together), despite its co-option into the service of sectarianism. But more particularly here Longley illustrates how spiritual reference is used as a tender of seriousness and sensitivity.

The last – and most cryptic – poet I want to discuss briefly is Medbh McGuckian, to consider whether her obscurity can, like Muldoon's be explained in the context of developments in twentieth-century spiritual thought. Her language has usually been explored, often enlighteningly, in feminist terms (and, in a brilliant study by Clair Wills, in political terms);[21] but there is much to be learned by looking at her poems in the light of traditional religious language, especially given the inclination since Yeats to extend the range of belief into areas beyond what is statable in dogmatic terms. I am selecting a few poems from McGuckians's early book *Venus and the Rain*[22] almost at random. A poem called 'Underground' begins with lines which I find hauntingly evocative in eschatological terms:

The death-linen was a present from my mother-in-law.
I have packed it in a truck which is already too full.

The last poem in the book 'Sabbath Park', begins with the lines reminiscent of the mystical passages from the great fourteenth-century visionary poem *Piers Plowman*:

My absolute address is Sabbath Park,
And the traditional light blue of its
Paradise Lost room, which I took to be
My mother. Sometimes in the evenings
I would ask, a step not easily taken,
Whether the bird learns to build its nest
Like that – a perfect nest from such
Arthritic wood.[23]

Well before its conclusion –

The sewn
Lilies near the ground growing downward

– McGuckian's poem has established its transcendent concerns. Death-linen, light blue and lilies all link inseparably with the Christian iconographic tradition. This is not to say that McGuckian's poetry is not to be read also in personal terms: perhaps more naturally so. The point I want to make, as with Muldoon and Longley, is that this writing achieves its *gravitas* by locating itself within the traditions of religious language and themes.

To end with these poets is more or less random. There are many contemporary Irish poets in whom the terminology and/or spirit of the Catholic/Christian is central, in both the Irish and English languages. Writers in Irish in whom it is particularly embedded are Máire Mhac an tSaoi, Liam Ó Muirthile and Nuala Ní Dhomhnaill: all writers in whom the socially rooted and the mythological are profoundly linked. In English some inescapable figures are Eiléan Ní Chuilleanáin, Ciarán Carson, Martina Evans, Sinéad Morrissey and Leontia Flynn (the predominance of women in the lists in both languages is striking). But no Irish writer in the modern era and idiom is unaffected by it. And of course it is not confined to Ireland: a celebrated early twenty-first century instance is the acclaimed Scottish poet-novelist John Burnside.

In the end, the distinction I made at the outset here between the terminology and the spirit of the spiritual is not sustainable. Language is never value free; it brings with it traces of the tradition to which it belongs. This recalls distantly the old scholastic argument about whether the use of the term 'God' must presuppose God's existence. The greatest existentialist Irish writer, Samuel Beckett, alludes to this when one of the characters in his highly philosophical absurdist play, *Endgame*, observes of God with bitter disappointment: 'the bastard! He doesn't exist!' Irish poets throughout this century have not only gratefully drawn on the traditional language of religious discussion; they have relied on it to express a general sense of the numinous which the post-Enlightenment nineteenth-century poets had despaired of feeling again. It is a fact which has been surprisingly little stressed that the three great poetic influences from the early modernist period in English – Hopkins, Yeats and Eliot – were all of a strongly spiritual disposition. Hopkins' 'The world is charged with the grandeur of God'[24] has remained as true of poetic language as it is of the world. The tinkers' tree-clock of Heaney's poem is only marvellous because it is perceived as such; and the language of Irish poetry since Yeats is always predisposed to meet the transcendent half-way.

Notes

1 W. B. Yeats, 'A general introduction for my work', in *Essays and Introductions* (London: Macmillan, 1961), p. 520.

2 S. Heaney, *Wintering Out* (London: Faber and Faber, 1972), p. 32.

3 *Ibid.*, p. 35
4 S. Heaney, *Seeing Things* (London: Faber and Faber, 1991).
5 *Ibid.*, p. 50.
6 S. Heaney, *The Tree Clock* (Belfast: Linen Hall Library, 1990).
7 T. S. Eliot, *Little Gidding*, closing lines, in *Collected Poems 1909–1962* (London: Faber and Faber, 1963), p. 223.
8 J. F. Deane (ed.), *Irish Poetry of Faith and Doubt: The Cold Heaven* (Dublin: Wolfhound Press, 1990), p. 11.
9 T. Paulin, *A State of Justice* (London: Faber and Faber, 1977), p. 15.
10 T. Paulin, *Walking a Line* (London: Faber and Faber, 1994), p. 80. Quotation from Acts 2:2.
11 P. Durcan, *Daddy, Daddy* (Belfast: Blackstaff Press, 1990). A volume of Durcan's which draws on some earlier pieces is brilliantly called *Jesus and Angela* (Belfast: Blackstaff, 1988), combining the Sid Vicious line with the title of an earlier volume *Jumping the Train-tracks with Angela* (Dublin: Raven Arts, 1983).
12 Letter to Lady Elizabeth Pelham, Jan. 1939. See *The Letters of W. B. Yeats*, ed. A. Wade (London: Rupert Hart-Davis, 1954), p. 918.
13 *Yeats's Poems*, ed. A. Norman Jeffares (London: Macmillan, 1989), p. 227.
14 *Ibid.*, p. 366.
15 S. Heaney, *Station Island* (London: Faber and Faber, 1984).
16 *Ibid.*, p. 93.
17 Seamus Heaney, *Human Chain* (London: Faber and Faber, 2010), pp. 72, 17.
18 P. Muldoon, *Mules* (London: Faber and Faber, 1977), pp. 11–13.
19 M. Longley, *Poems 1963–1983* (Edinburgh: Salamander Press; Dublin: Gallery Press, 1985), p. 149.
20 *Ibid.*, p. 148.
21 C. Wills, *Improprieties: Politics and Sexuality in Northern Irish Poetry* (Oxford: Oxford University Press, 1993).
22 M. McGuckian, *Venus and the Rain* (Oxford: Oxford University Press, 1984).
23 *Ibid.*, p. 54. The great passage from *Piers Plowman* this draws on is in B-text *Passus*, xi, lines 346–9.
24 N. H. Mackenzie (ed.), *The Poetical Works of Gerard Manley Hopkins* (Oxford: Oxford University Press, 1990), 'God's Grandeur', p. 139.

21

Northern Catholics and the early years of the Troubles

Oliver P. Rafferty

One of the most iconic images to emerge from the thirty-year history of the recent Northern Ireland Troubles is that of then Fr Edward Daly leading a group of people carrying the mortally wounded body of Jackie Duddy in Derry on Bloody Sunday, 31 January 1972. Daly waves a bloodied white handkerchief as a token of peace and as a plea for safety so that the dying Duddy might be given some comfort in the last minutes of his life. Here in brief is a summary of the Catholic Church's relationship with its own community in the context of the wider Troubles between 1969 and 1994.

The church struggled to confront the perceived injustices of Northern Ireland as these were experienced by its members, but also to mediate between Catholics and the forces of violence coming either from the republican or loyalist factions, or from the state itself, in the shape of internment without trial or, at times, repression at the hands of the security forces. It sought to maintain its position as the central element in the life of the Catholic–nationalist community at a stage when indifference and secularisation, which had reduced the church's influence in other parts of Europe and North America, were just beginning to make themselves felt on the Irish scene. But perhaps one of the greatest difficulties the church faced in the early Troubles was its lack of direct political influence over government policy. Its failures to convince successive administrations of the roots of Catholic alienation, and the steps needed to remedy these, meant that its moderating voice in the Catholic community could easily be dismissed by those who thought that violence was the only solution to the community's difficulties. The failures of government to uphold the credibility of institutional Catholicism in the eyes of the Catholic community led to fragmentation in Catholic identity and enabled the 'men of violence' to take the lead in determining Catholicism's relationship with the state authorities in Britain and Northern Ireland.

Despite the church's decline since the peace process as a major force in Irish society, some recent academic analysis would have it that the church still remains the touchstone for how Catholics in Northern Ireland see themselves.[1] Others have argued that the church's historic role had been to preserve a sense of Irish values as the one institution not subjugated by the 'British presence'.[2] By contrast Marianne Elliot has argued that what is central to Catholic identity is not Catholicism per se but rather the history, language and culture of Ireland's past which gave coherence to the Catholic community.[3] Of course a question immediately arises of the historical weight of those factors if one tried to filter out the Catholic dimension: a question that never seems to occur to Elliot.

These issues of the interrelatedness of cultural identity and Catholicism were nowhere more acute in modern Irish history than in the recent Troubles. There is a sense in which for the Northern Ireland Catholic community, prior to the outbreak of the Troubles in 1969, religion was its political identity. And yet owing to internal developments within Catholicism, following Vatican II, where the role of the laity in the church was stressed, and the emergence in the late 1960s of a new and highly articulate political leadership in Northern Catholicism, the scene was set for the potential fragmentation of northern Catholic identity, where the position and role of bishops and priests did not command immediate deference. In such circumstances ecclesiastical leaders struggled to impose their views of what constituted Northern Irish Catholic identity.

Large sections of the Catholic population were at loggerheads with the hierarchy over the analysis of the extent and causes of the problems facing the Catholic community in the early stages of the Troubles. In particular as the purely defensive arrangements as represented by the 'Defence Committees' in Belfast following August 1969 gave way to the murderous activity of the Irish Republican Army (IRA), the hierarchical church distanced itself from the campaign of violence and as a consequence alienated certain elements of the Catholic population from the church and its clergy. The rhetoric in justification of violence was one of defence of the community against the state, aggressive and violent Protestants, and, from 1970, the British army. There is a certain sense in which institutional Catholicism also went along with that rhetoric at least until the emergence of violent republicanism. It is instructive, however, to read that as late as 1987 Fr Denis Faul, no friend of the Provisional IRA (PIRA), could remark that for many in the Catholic community the 'Provos' were 'the last insurance card against the madmen of extreme Protestantism'.[4]

At an earlier stage Bishop William Philbin of Down and Connor, a diocese centred on Belfast could, at times, display a breathtaking naivety in his estimation of the vigilante groups that grew up to protect Catholic areas in Belfast. He would thus assure his opposite number in Dublin, Archbishop John Charles McQuaid, that:

> [O]ur young people, have become mature and responsible citizens overnight, taking over maintenance of law & order & eliminating petty crime as well as picketing and manning barricades, no police being around even yet.[5]

Furthermore Philbin wanted such vigilante groups to exist in every parish supervised by a committee and insisted that they should be affiliated to the executive of the Central Citizens' Defence Committee.[6] It was from these same defence committees that individuals would emerge within months to swell the ranks of the nascent PIRA.

The church's ability to control what was and what was not acceptable behaviour in response to sectarian and state oppression was wrong footed by the conviction of the PIRA that its strategy and outlook were based on Catholic principles.[7] This immediately caused problems for the church which sought to distance itself from such views and which also struggled to demonstrate that the Catholic clergy as a whole were not supporters of the IRA. On the one hand the church was gratified that the new defenders of the Catholic community were not tainted with the aura of communism,[8] on the other it is a complete distortion of the reality of the early Troubles to think that the clergy encouraged in any way 'the emerging Provisionals to break the influence of the Marxists' of the Official IRA.[9] The initial ambiguity of the church's response to the violence in Derry and Belfast in 1969 gave rise to what Mairead Corrigan has described as a 'great ambivalence from all church quarters, there was no strong non-violent message coming from the pulpits'.[10] This was part of a general perception that the Catholic Church did not speak with a loud and univocal voice in the condemnation of violence emanating from the Catholic community.[11] It prompted the archbishop of Westminster, Cardinal John C. Heenan, to urge the archbishop of Armagh, Cardinal William Conway, to draw up and circulate to influential public representatives a privately printed book giving all his and the northern bishops' statements condemning violence in all its forms from 1969 onwards.[12]

The church's ability to set the agenda even to some extent for the IRA at the early stages of the Troubles, was of course predicated on its prestige generally in Irish society and on the fact that, in contrast to the later stages of the conflict, many of those engaged in violence were not only practising Catholics but individuals who looked to institutional

Catholicism for guidance for the problems they confronted. Bishop Philbin could, for example, boast that over 90 per cent of those interned in Long Kesh not only went to Mass but also gathered in the evenings for the communal recitation of the rosary.[13] The church's desire to control the violent and revolutionary propensities of its flock was also seen in the role played by Archbishop McQuaid in brokering the short-lived IRA ceasefire at Christmas 1971. McQuaid described, for the benefit of the papal nuncio to Ireland, Archbishop Gaetano Alibrandi,[14] how he had summoned the various leaders of the PIRA and the Official IRA and asked for a truce which obtained for two days. So far as the PIRA was concerned the leaders spoke to McQuaid 'at length about very secret aspects of their movement. It would be difficult to conceive a more cordial and friendly meeting'.[15] McQuaid also cautioned against seeing the Officials as Marxist since in his opinion they confused social justice issues with Marxist aims and because more especially the 'most formidable man of this group kissed my ring and genuflected with quite spontaneous Faith'.[16] Furthermore when the ceasefire broke down one PIRA operative wrote to McQuaid blaming the British army and pleaded with the archbishop, 'Pray for us as we are suffering to free our land from the English. Please pray for us.'[17] Even British government officials could be caught up in conspiracy theories about the extent of the church's involvement with terrorist organisations. One civil service memo from late 1971 recorded that the government accepted that 'the Vatican has officially severed its connection with the IRA, we do not precisely know in what terms, when and by whom this was done'. The same paper sought to draw parallels with the situation in Cyprus with Archbishop Makarios and the Cypriot terrorist organisation EOKA.[18] Whatever the situation in Cyprus, the analysis about Northern Ireland was purely fanciful. But it is a measure of the unreality of government analysis about the role of the Catholic Church in Northern Ireland at that stage of the Troubles. Years later civil servants could still write that in the earlier years of the Troubles the position of the church on IRA violence was 'equivocal' in the eyes of the government and of Protestant church leaders.[19]

It would be difficult to exaggerate the extent of the problems facing the Catholic community from the summer of 1969 on, when it must have seemed to some that the whole apparatus of the state was bent on facilitating large-scale destruction of Catholic life and property and the repression of the Catholic community. This scenario was intensified by a sense of alienation at the high points of the Troubles on such occasions as the Lower Falls curfew of June 1970, the introduction of internment without trial in August 1971, Bloody Sunday in 1972 and later by the circumstances of political intransigence on all sides surrounding the hunger strikes of 1981.

One of the theoretical issues that institutional Catholicism has been reluctant to face is to what extent the church itself facilitated a situation that enabled IRA activity to emanate from the ranks of the Catholic community. What instruments did the church employ in its attempt to control the narrative of communal identity? It was after all that narrative which not only initially assisted the Catholic community's resistance to state oppression and the violence originating in the Protestant–Unionist community, but which enabled the IRA to exist and thrive among Catholics despite increasingly shrill denunciations of its activities by a combination of the hierarchical church, Catholic constitutionalists, and the British and Irish governments. So far as some British ministerial advisers were concerned, by late summer of 1977, the Catholic clergy were firm supporters of a United Ireland. Furthermore 'at best the majority [of priests] are moderate Republicans; at worst they are {active supporters} sympathetic to the aims of the Provisional Sinn Fein'.[20]

The Catholic community's sense of itself in Northern Ireland was forged most powerfully within the context of the Catholic school system.[21] Even the government recognised that the church's control of education was 'fundamentally a matter of self-interest'.[22] The schools were not only the focus of education, but also the location for the socialisation of Catholics into Catholic practice. It was in school that children were prepared for the sacraments of confession, communion and confirmation. The schools were imbued with religious practice and symbolism but they were also the instruments whereby a sense of Irishness was grounded and manifest in the learning of the Irish language and the inculcation of Gaelic games. Historically, education was the chief area whereby Catholic churchmen were brought into contact with the apparatus of the northern state, a state which many Catholics regarded as inimical to the very existence of Catholicism. Bishops and priests protected the schools and expended a great deal of the community's time and resources on preserving them. Within the schools there was much insistence that a 'Catholic ethos' had at all costs to be maintained. All this seemed self-evident to the Catholic community of the time. The small numbers of parents who refused to send their children to Catholic schools soon felt the sharp end of episcopal displeasure by the refusal, at least in Down and Connor, of the sacraments to their children.[23]

More recently Bishop Edward Daly, although a firm supporter of Catholic schools, has written of his concern that the ethos communicated in such institutions did not prevent many of their alumni from joining the ranks of the PIRA.[24] It is, however, significant in this regard that from the time of direct rule the British government favoured and relentlessly pursued a policy of integrated education in Northern Ireland. Thus, for example, civil servants would, in departmental memos, express appreciation of the activity of Bishop Edward Daly and Bishop William Philbin in denouncing the IRA but would criticise them for the fact that they were not 'on board' so far as integrated education was concerned.[25] Further the government was determined that its work for integrated education would be 'undeterred by any attempt of the church to veto this. We will here be appealing directly to the people ... There may be scope here for using the Peace People.'[26]

This was part of a bigger and grander strategy of the government in relation to the church and the Catholic community. Not only did the government decide it needed to enlist the hierarchy's good offices in its propaganda war against the IRA, but it also saw the need to reduce the institutional church's hold over the Catholic community for altogether other reasons. As one Northern Ireland Office official put it:

> The realisation of our political objectives would result in a pluralistic state in which the Catholic Church's influence would have to compete with other denominational or plainly philistine trends; this would pose a threat to its control over its flock which it jealously guards.[27]

Such thinking would in time fit in with Garrett FitzGerald's ideas of a constitutional crusade in the Republic, whereby the net result would be to reduce the power of institutional Catholicism and achieve a more 'pluralist' society.[28] But it is also clear at least in the Northern Ireland context that Catholic prelates realised they would have to play quite a sophisticated political game to maintain their position vis-à-vis the Catholic community in the very different circumstances north and south of the Irish border.

Cardinal Conway informed Bishop Philbin that any response of the northern bishops to the proposals of the secretary of state, Merlyn Rees, to reform the law in the north on divorce and homosexuality in a more liberal direction, and thus bring it into line with prevailing legislation in the rest of the United Kingdom, would have to be delicately handled so that the bishops' position 'could not be distorted in a debate in the Republic'.[29] Above all, the Catholic ethos of the Republic, over which the bishops had more control, had to be maintained whatever developments might come in Northern Ireland where the bishops had less control but where still, in some respects, they had considerable influence. In a certain sense churchmen were much more skilled and sophisticated in their abilities to handle the different political realities under which they lived than politicians in Britain or on either side of the Irish border. Indeed the bishops were not slow to criticise among themselves what they took to be the evident failures of their political masters. Both Edward Daly[30] and Conway[31] made much of the fact that Rees was no match for his Conservative predecessors William Whitelaw and Francis Pym, owing to his lack of ability to come to terms with the complexities of Northern Ireland life. Subsequently, however, Daly would praise Rees for his political courage in phasing out internment without trial.[32] In general, Catholic prelates, at least until the hunger-strike era, thought the Conservatives made a better job of governing Northern Ireland than did the British Labour party.[33] Even politicians in the Republic could incur espicopal displeasure over northern affairs with Bishop Cahal Daly complaining that the comments of Garret FitzGerald and Conor Cruise O'Brien actually made matters worse in Northern Ireland,[34] and he regarded the record of the Fine Gael–Labour coalition government of 1973–77 on Northern Ireland as 'dismal'.[35]

At the same time politicians and civil servants were not slow to castigate what they took to be the shortcomings of Catholic bishops and priests. Cardinal Conway, as the titular leader of Catholicism on both sides of the border, was often a subject of civil servants' vituperation. At some personal cost so far as his reputation in the nationalist community was concerned, he gave a clear lead by consistently repudiating violence for political ends, but government officials still maintained that given his background as a west Belfast Catholic he was 'blinkered' on issues of Irish politics and had been 'slow to condemn the IRA'.[36]

One of the factors in the animus against Conway on the part of officialdom was that, at least in private, he could be deeply critical of government security and political policy. Along with other Catholic churchmen, in contrast to their Protestant colleagues,[37] he denounced internment, especially its clearly one-sided application. He also felt a deep sense of personal betrayal concerning the government's climbdown in the face of the Ulster Workers' Strike in May 1974, which brought down the power-sharing executive. He was also not slow in pointing out what he took to be human rights abuses on the part of members of the security forces, which he insisted had a deplorable effect on Catholic public opinion. Nor could he understand that while the IRA was rightly an illegal organisation the government seemed unwilling to proscribe Protestant paramilitary groups.

This last touched on one of Conway's deepest concerns. From 1970 until his death in 1977 he maintained that there were two campaigns of violence in Northern Ireland, one carried on by the PIRA and the second a campaign of sectarian assassination mounted by Protestant paramilitaries against innocent Catholics.[38] In this, Conway had the support of the highest level of authority in the Roman Catholic Church. He frequently complained to the Holy See about the assassination of Catholics in Northern Ireland. On at least one occasion Pope Paul VI, as a direct result of Conway's representations, caused the Vatican secretary of state, Cardinal Jean-Marie Villot, to write to the then British prime minister, Harold Wilson, expressing the pope's concern in the matter. Such was the diplomatic finesse in that letter that the foreign office had to explain to Downing Street that when Villot said that the Vatican was confident that serious measures were being taken to combat the campaign of violence against Catholics, 'it means in effect that the Holy See are <u>not</u> confident' that such measures were being taken'.[39] In his reply to Villot, Wilson stressed that both Loyalist and Republican terrorists had been involved in sectarian assassinations.[40]

Vatican officials made a number of representations to the British minister to the Holy See concerning both Catholic sectarian murders and the treatment of Catholics at the hands of the British army. The minister, D. J. C. Crawley, explained that:

> The Vatican was being accused by its own Catholics of partiality in issuing statements condemning the IRA at our request, but of refusing to issue similar statements when Catholics were murdered ... Benelli perhaps has a point here.[41]

The real difficulty in all this was that the church's complaints about the state's relationship with the Catholic minority seemed to exactly mirror the complaints of the PIRA with relation to human right abuses of internees, harassment of the Catholic community and the events of Bloody Sunday. Equally, so far as the state was concerned, the church was a valuable instrument of control over the Catholic population and despite some perception that the hierarchy could not always restrain the more wayward tendencies within the Catholic community, government officials could quite happily talk about the ability of the hierarchy 'to deliver' in the interests of government policy as least so far as the security situation was concerned.[42]

If the Catholic hierarchy could enlist the Vatican to bring pressure to bear on the government to underline its views, the government could equally motivate influential British Catholic opinion to support it in the propaganda war of the 1970s. Basil Hume, soon after his appointment as archbishop of Westminster and cardinal in 1976, could appeal to the home office to brief him about the affairs of Northern Ireland.[43] Groups of British Catholic MPs would routinely come to the government's assistance in denouncing the perceived lack of overt condemnation of

IRA activity by northern bishops.[44] Influential English Catholics would also, at times, pressurise the English hierarchy to plead with their Irish counterparts for a more strident line in dealing with the IRA.[45] This led on at least one occasion to a meeting between representatives of the hierarchies of England and Wales, Scotland and Ireland in an effort to come to some understanding of how the Catholic church in these islands could best deal with the terrorism in its midst.[46]

There were also tensions at a diplomatic level between the papal nuncio in Dublin and his opposite number in London, the apostolic delegate, Mgr Bruno Heim.[47] Heim made no bones about the fact that he distrusted Alibrandi's judgement and that he wanted to feed to the Vatican the British government's view of what was happening in Northern Ireland. In April 1978 Heim assured Roy Mason, the Northern Ireland secretary, that he had jeopardised his own position with the Holy See in order to contradict Alibrandi's views.[48] As a result there was some speculation in the foreign office about upgrading Heim's status to that of a pro-nuncio since:

> Recent contacts have shown that [Heim] could be of value in balancing the influence and attitudes fed to the Vatican by Mgr Alibrandi in Dublin. Diplomatic status could only increase this value to us.[49]

Although the British government was delighted at Heim's willingness to view Northern Ireland from its perspective, namely that the prisoners in Long Kesh were simply 'criminals',[50] officials made clear that they thought Heim as 'more devious than he seems' and that he was 'prone to take himself seriously'.[51] More realistically some officials recognised that although it would be good to have Britain and the Vatican singing from the same hymn sheet nevertheless:

> Positive Vatican statements helpful to us will not have much effect on the laity, at least not in positive terms, whilst the PIRA can instil more immediate fear than can His Holiness.[52]

From that perspective it was more important that the bishops in Northern Ireland would be more vehement in their attempts to wean the Catholic community away from its apparent support for the PIRA.

Government tried to facilitate this by helping the church with social programmes aimed at assisting the unemployed but it was also anxious that the right type of leadership might emerge in the hierarchy that would move the community in the direction in which the government thought it should go. From the government's viewpoint the most important ally in the first ten years of the Troubles was William Philbin of Down and Connor, who consistently analysed the Northern Ireland situation from the government's view point. On one occasion declining an invitation to a memorial service at army headquarters, Lisburn, for soldiers killed in Northern Ireland since 1970, owing to a prior engagement, he remarked to General Sir Frank King that he greatly regretted his absence from the service because he had 'great sympathy for the many young men who have been so ruthlessly killed here in recent years'.[53] On a previous occasion he had told another army commander 'I feel that our relationship generally has been one of mutual understanding'.[54] At the same time the Northern Ireland office recognised that Philbin's position carried little weight with his flock. By contrast they saw that Edward Daly of Derry was more influential in his diocese with regard to the condemnation of IRA violence but that he 'has also had some harsh words for us about the police and the army'.[55]

With the death of Conway in 1977 an opportunity presented itself for the government to attempt to influence the leadership direction of northern Catholicism. Oddly, however, the initiative for this came initially from Garrett FitzGerald, the then foreign minister in the Republic, who wondered aloud to the British ambassador in Dublin if there had ever been an occasion when the British and Irish governments jointly had made representations on who should be the archbishop of Armagh.[56] The Dublin government made clear it own preference for Bishop Cahal Daly of Ardagh and Clonmacnoise. The British government decided initially merely to give to the Vatican a list of the qualities that the new archbishop should have. At a crucial meeting with Archbishop Heim and Cardinal Basil Hume[57] to put its views, Roy Mason departed from his brief to discuss Daly's name, with Hume remarking that he was the outstanding candidate although he maintained that Daly lacked 'charisma'.[58]

The appointment of a man filled with charisma, Tomás Ó Fiaich, was facilitated by the collapse of the coalition government in Dublin and the return to power of Fianna Fáil following the elections on 16 June 1977. Ó Fiaich was clearly a more avowed nationalist than his other episcopal colleagues. His forthright interview with the *Irish Press* the following January in which he said that Britain should make a declaration of its intention to withdraw from Northern Ireland drew rounded criticism from many sides of the Northern Ireland divide. Intriguingly, however, an official of the British embassy in Dublin thought that apart from the remark about the declaration of intent Ó Fiaich 'seems to have dealt effectively and moderately with provocative questions by [the newspaper's editor Tim Pat] Coogan'.[59]

Nevertheless Ó Fiaich's advent onto the national and international scene did serve to underline tensions within the hierarchy over Northern

Ireland affairs and the church response to continuing violence. Such tensions had been in place even in Conway's time over the question of internment. Philbin clashed with Conway over the latter's desire to visit Catholic areas of Belfast that had seen so much violence and disturbance. Philbin said that any such visit would feed into criticism of Philbin's own conduct of affairs and that:

> You will be aware that there were comments on your pastoral visit to Long Kesh which I was known to have refused to make ... Just now in addition, there might be some who would connect a visit with the feature in the *Sunday Press* alleging the failure of 'the three other Northern Bishops ... to make much impact on events since 1969' and supporting your making moves 'to carry out important reorganizations' etc.[60]

More surprisingly, Philbin was to remonstrate with Cahal Daly over the latter's desire to visit internees in Long Kesh. He accused the Co. Antrim born Daly of being an 'outsider' and further:

> I find in much of what you say assertions that blur or are at variance with moral principle, that offer unwise advice to priests and people in my jurisdiction and that are based on conceptions of Irish History that produce uncritically the kind of romanticised glorifying of very questionable aspects of our past – one of the very chief sources of present wrong-headedness on the part of people of which the prisoners in Long Kesh are typical, generally speaking.[61]

As the Troubles progressed Cahal Daly became at a rhetorical level more hard-line in his views on contemporary Irish nationalism, and these views seemed to put him at variance with Ó Fiaich. What is significant is that in the struggle between the church and republicanism for the loyalty and affection of the Catholic community, the church, unlike the republicans, could not always offer a united and coherent front.

The church's opposition to the PIRA was predicated on the fact that violence for political objectives was immoral, that the PIRA had no mandate for its murderous campaign[62] and that it was madness to think that northern Protestants could be forced into a united Ireland against their will.[63] The church was also concerned that the activity of the PIRA if directed against the government south of the border would bring about great instability, possibly even collapse of political structures in the Republic.[64] This led some Catholic bishops to take enormous risks in the early years of the Troubles in seeking out the PIRA in an effort to bring about peace. Both Edward Daly[65] and Cahal Daly[66] met with them in 1975 in rather fruitless discussions which caused Cahal Daly to decide that they were simply evil men, and for the rest of the Troubles he refused ever to meet with them or their political representatives, Sinn Féin, so long as they continued to support the 'armed struggle'.[67] It is also clear that the church considered various stratagems for dealing with violent republicanism even reviewing, as is evident from Conway's papers, the possibility of excommunication for membership of terrorist organisations. The closest the hierarchy came to such decisive action was a proposal to make murder 'a reserved sin',[68] but decided that this would be merely a symbolic gesture and furthermore that 'priests would find it difficult to explain it' to their people.[69] Such was the enormity of the problem facing the church that Cahal Daly at one point concluded that the bishops were 'becoming less rather than more episcopally geared to meet the dangers ensuing for the Church'.[70]

For its part the PIRA accused the church of colluding with 'the continued injustice of the British presence in Ireland'.[71] Sinn Féin/IRA could argue this because the church was anxious to uphold the authority of the state. At the same time the church did share with the republicans a measure of reserve about some of the operations of the state as these appeared to be aimed against the Catholic community. The church was also determined to appeal to a set of transcendental ethical norms which it believed must ultimately condition all social and political life within Northern Ireland and which even governments must obey. William Leonard has persuasively argued that the church's view of what was happening in Northern Ireland at the early stages of the Troubles was determined by its conviction that even the state is subject to the natural law, and in some instances, at least, the Northern Ireland state as a corporate body seemed to violate that law.[72]

What was really at issue was the question of who was best equipped to speak for and articulate the needs, identity and aspirations of Catholics within Northern Ireland. Although the church favoured the constitutional nationalists as its collaborators in this task, too often IRA violence seemed to marginalise moderate voices within the Catholic–nationalist community. From the outbreak of the Troubles, the Catholic Church and the Republican movement were locked in a herculean struggle over the symbols and identity of northern Catholic life. For much of the early years of the Troubles the church sought to prevent the direction and destiny of the community from falling into Republican hands. Its actions and *raison d'être* were often misunderstood and distrusted by government. The state's relative hostility to the church and churchmen, and its lack of response to the church's often penetrating analysis, ultimately contributed to the institutional church's relative impotence in the face of urban guerrilla warfare and meant that the struggle endured much longer than otherwise might have been the case. Because of government mishandling the way was left open for the PIRA rather than church authorities to set the agenda for much of Catholic and nationalist life in Northern Ireland.

Notes

1 C. Mitchell, Religion, *Identity and Politics in Northern Ireland: Boundaries of Belonging and Belief* (Aldershot: Ashgate, 2006), p. 142.

2 W. Crotty, 'The Catholic Church in Ireland and Northern Ireland: nationalism, identity and opposition', in P. C. Manuel *et al.* (eds), *The Catholic Church and the Nation-State* (Washington, DC: Georgetown University Press, 2006), pp. 117–30, 118.

3 M. Elliott, 'Religion and identity in Northern Ireland', in W. A. Van Horne, *Global Convulsions: Race, Ethnicity, and Nationalism at the End of the Twentieth Century* (Albany, NY: State University of New York, 1997), pp. 149–67, 150.

4 Quoted in M. L. R. Smith, *Fighting for Ireland?: The Military Strategy of the Irish Republican Movement* (London and New York: Routledge, 1995), p. 125.

5 Archives of the Archdiocese of Dublin (AAD) McQuaid Papers XV/C/415 Philbin – McQuaid 25 Aug. 1969.

6 Archives of the Diocese of Down and Connor (ADDC) Philbin Papers, EP6/2/71, Philbin to Belfast priests, 22 May 1970.

7 Smith, *Fighting for Ireland*, p. 86.

8 Even Bernadette Devlin was denounced by the cardinal archbishop of Los Angeles for associating with groups of a 'socialist character' during a speaking tour of the United States. ADDC Philbin Papers EP/6/2 J. Francis McIntyre – Philbin 10 Sept. 1969.

9 P. Devlin, *Straight Left: An Autobiography* (Belfast: Blackstaff Press, 1993), p. 111.

10 D. Sharroch and M. Devenport, *Man of War, Man of Peace: The Unauthorised Biography of Gerry Adams* (London: Macmillan, 1997), p. 139.

11 This was the view of some officials in the Northern Ireland Office as late as 1977. See the National Archives (London) (TNA) CJ4/1546 (98) 22 Aug. 1977.

12 Archives of the Archdiocese of Armagh (AAA) Conway Papers 24/2, Conway to Secretary of State William Whitelaw 17 Oct. 1972 enclosing a copy of the booklet 'in order to refute the canard that the Catholic bishops have largely kept silent during this terrible time. I hope at least it will demonstrate that we have ceaselessly condemned the IRA campaign ... in the strongest and most unqualified language'.

13 ADDC Philbin Papers, EP6/2/71 Philbin – Archbishop George Patrick Dwyer (of Birmingham) 2 Dec. 1971.

14 According to IRA sources Alibrandi was the only bishop in Ireland who

understood them. See E. Daly, *A Troubled See: Memoirs of a Derry Bishop* (Dublin: Four Courts, 2011), p. 49.

15 AAD McQuaid Papers, McQuaid – Alibrandi 23 Dec. 1971

16 *Ibid.*

17 Quoted in J. Conney, *John Charles McQuaid: Ruler of Catholic Ireland* (Dublin: O'Brien Press, 1999), p. 426. I was unable to discover the original letter in the AAD.

18 TNA, CJ4/1107 (35) 19 Nov. 1971.

19 TNA CJ4/1556 (98) 22 Aug. 1977.

20 TNA CJ4/1546 (118) 31 Aug. 1977. The words in brackets { } have been pencilled out in the original draft of this memo.

21 Although now slightly dated, one of the best treatments of Catholic education in Northern Ireland remains M. McGrath, *The Catholic Church and Catholic Schools in Northern Ireland* (Dublin: Irish Academic Press, 2000).

22 TNA CJ4/1546 (98) 'Memo on HMG and RCC in NI', 22 Aug. 1977.

23 C. de Baroid, *Ballymurphy and the Irish War* (London: Pluto, 1990), pp. 141ff. See also his *Down North: Reflections of Ballymurphy and the Early Troubles* (Belfast: Ogham Press, 2010), pp. 49–50; Daly, *A Troubled See*, p. 36. Daly administered confirmation to some children in these circumstances, much to the chagrin of Philbin.

24 Daly, *A Troubled See*, p. 214.

25 CJ/1546 (89) 21 Jul. 1977.

26 TNA CJ4/ 1546 (118) 31 Aug. 1977.

27 TNACJ/1546 (90) 2 Aug. 1977.

28 G. FitzGerald, *All in a Life: An Autobiography* (Dublin: Gill and Macmillan, 1991), pp. 336–7.

29 ADDC Philbin Papers, EP6/5 Conway – Philbin 23 Feb. 1977. Conway was grateful for a long letter published in the newspapers by Lord MacDermott, the former lord chief justice of Northern Ireland on 21 Feb. 1977, opposing the reforms to divorce law.

30 Archives of the Diocese of Derry (ADD) Daly papers 3/1 Daly – Conway 30 Jul. 1974.

31 AAA Conway Papers 24/2; memo Conway prepared 23 Dec. 1974 in which he expresses this view. He also wrote that Edward Heath, the former prime minster, was of the same opinion. Conway fed this view to the Vatican which in turn became the position of the Holy See. See TNA CJ4/1108 D. J. C. Crawley, British legation to Holy See – Foreign office, 25 Oct. 1974. To be fair to Daly and Conway, both praised James Callaghan's handling of the situation when he was home secretary (1969–70).

32 ADD Daly Papers 11/1 Daly – Rees 6 Dec. 1975.

33 See AAA Conway Papers 14/1 Conway – Heenan 27 Nov. 1973, and DDA. This also represented Vatican thinking on the matter. TNACJ4/1108 R. M. Purcell – Foreign office, 16 Oct. 1974. Purcell was a member of the British legation at the Holy See. Of course this was simply a reflection of Conway's views. He was, understandably, the source the Vatican most trusted on

Northern Irish affairs. See D. J. C. Crawley – Foreign office, 25 Oct. 1974.

34 AAA Conway Papers 16/3–2 Daly – Conway 31 Jun. 1975.

35 *Ibid.* Daly – Conway 31 Jan. 1975.

36 TNA CJ4/1108 2 Jul. 1976.

37 The leaders of the three main Protestant Churches accepted 'with regret' the need for internment (*Irish News*, 10 Aug. 1971).

38 Conway expressed this constantly to British ministers and officials and also to Pope Paul VI. AAA Conway Papers 11/2 – 1/6 Memo presented to the pope 24 Oct. 1974.

39 TNA CJ4/1108 Foreign office to Lord Bridges 28 Nov. 1974, emphasis in original. Bridges was an adviser to Number 10 Downing Street and subsequently British ambassador to Italy. The secretary of state is in effect the Holy See's prime minister. This fact had to be explained by the foreign office to Harold Wilson's advisers.

40 A copy of this letter is in AAA Conway Papers 11/2–1, dated 23 Dec. 1974.

41 TNA CJ4/1108 Crawley – Foreign office, 29 Nov. 1974. Archbishop Giovanni Benelli, sometimes called the 'Vatican's Kissinger', was the substitute or deputy secretary of state of the Holy See.

42 TNA CJ/1546 (89).

43 TNA CJ4/1107 (14). Hume to the home office, 9 Jun. 1976.

44 Thus for example Bob Mellish, the government chief whip, Shirley Williams, a cabinet minister and James Dunn a junior whip, meet the English and Welsh hierarchy in November 1974 to ask that a tougher line be taken by bishops in denouncing IRA atrocities. TNA CJ4/1108 Mellish to Merlyn Rees 27 Nov. 1974. See also Mellish to Harold Wilson TNA PREM 16/451 27 Nov. 1974.

45 See for example the letters of the well-known economist Barbara Ward (from 1976 Baroness Jackson), to Heenan who in turn passed them on to Conway. AAA Conway Papers 14/1 Heenan – Conway 6 Sept. 1974.

46 A copy of the minutes of this meeting of 9 Jan. 1975 is preserved in the Daly Papers in ADD.

47 TNA CJ/1546 (76) report from N. C. Abbott to secretary of state for Northern Ireland 7 Jul. 1977.

48 TNA CJ4/2036/1 (51) memo 'Lunch with the Apostolic delegate and the SSNI', 27 Apr. 1978.

49 *Ibid.* (35) 10 Mar. 1978.

50 TNA CJ4/2036/1 (17).

51 TNA CJ4/2036/1 (15a). Briefing paper for interview between Heim and Mason on 15 Feb. 1978.

52 TNA CJ4/2036/1 (23a) Feb. 1978.

53 ADDC Philbin Papers, EP6/2/73 Philbin – King 29 Nov. 1973

54 *Ibid.*, Philbin to Sir Harry Tuzo 31 Jan. 1973.

55 TNA CJ/1546 (89) memo dated 21 Jul. 1977.

56 *Ibid.* (38) Ambassador W. R. Hayden – Foreign office, 11 May 1977.

57 The meeting was in itself a lapse of protocol. All Catholic ecclesiastical matters from the church's viewpoint are dealt with on an all-Ireland basis, and so Mason ought to have made his representations to the papal nuncio in Dublin.

58 *Ibid.* (75) see also memos (43) and (81).

59 TNA CJ4/2036/1 (7) R. M. Harris – Foreign office, 26 Jan. 1978.

60 ADDC Philbin Papers, EP/2/1972 Philbin – Conway 7 Dec. 1972.

61 Daly sent a copy of this letter to Conway. See AAA Conway papers 16/3–2 Philbin – Daly 30 Aug. 1974. Philbin had perhaps a point. Daly could write of the War of Independence that he was 'personally convinced that our fight for national freedom was just and necessary'. Ideas to which the contemporary PIRA would also subscribe. See Daly, *Violence in Ireland and Christian Conscience* (Dublin: Veritas, 1973), p. 31.

62 *Ibid.*, p. 67. When Sinn Féin began to field candidates in elections in the north bishops not only argued that voting for them was a 'serious sin' but they also changed tack. Daly declared that: 'It is rankly dishonest to appeal for votes in support of political and social aims and then declare that those votes are votes for violence' (Daly, *War: The Morality, the Reality, the Myth* (Belfast: Queen's University, 1984), p. 25).

63 Joint Statement of the Ulster Bishops 12 Sept. 1971. See statements by Cardinal Conway and Joint Statements on the Northern Ireland Situation 1968–72, p. 26.

64 AAA Conway Papers 16/3–2 Daly – Conway 31 Jan. 1975.

65 Daly, *A Troubled See*, pp. 47–8, who gives a more positive estimation of the meeting. Bishop Patrick Lennon of Kildare and Leighin was also present.

66 When the Irish police called on Daly at his home in Longford to ask about the meeting Daly had 'no compunction whatever in denying' that he had been approached by the PIRA. He also thought the Irish government had 'a cheek' in making such enquiries through the police. AAA Conway Papers 16/ 3–2 Daly – Conway 31 Jan. 1975. See also ADD Daly – Daly 31 Jan. 1975. One curiosity is that Cahal Daly says that the meeting took place around 7 Jan. 1975. Daly, *A Troubled See*, p. 47, says it took place in April. It could be that the bishops met the PIRA twice that year or that Edward Daly has simply misremembered. In an email exchange Daly has confirmed that Cahal Daly's dating is more likely to be correct.

67 B. Fitzgerald, *Primate: A Portrait of Cardinal Cahal B. Daly* (London: Fount, 1992), p. 116.

68 This is a provision in Catholic canon law whereby confession of certain sins can be made only to a bishop or to a priest especially nominated by him for that purpose. It is thought that such a procedure operates as a disincentive to commit the specified sin.

69 AAA Conway Papers16/1 'Summary of a meeting of N. bishops at *Ara Coeli* [the cardinal's house in Armagh]', 23 Jan. 1974.

70 ADD Daly Papers, Daly – Daly 15 May 1978.

71 This from Martin McGuiness. See A. Y. Devine, 'A study of the relationship

between the Catholic Church, nationalism and republicanism with particular reference to the Northern Ireland conflict since 1968', Ph.D., University of Ulster, 1997, p. 277.

72 W. A. Leonard, 'Churches, states and violences: how the Roman Catholic and Presbyterian Churches addressed the violence of the Northern Ireland Troubles, 1968–1994', Ph.D., University of Ulster 1997, p. 252.

22

Irish identity and the future of Catholicism

Niall Coll

It is a truism to say that the Catholic Church came to dominate both the public identity and the personal values of the great majority of the Irish people from the middle of the nineteenth century until recent times. Now, in the wake of the gradual rise of urban, secular Anglo-American cultural norms on the one hand and the clerical abuse crisis on the other, that dominance has been shattered.[1] Dermot Keogh has written that the Catholic Church in Ireland now faces its 'greatest crisis of credibility' in the last three centuries.[2] Roy Foster has asserted that 'by the turn of the twenty-first century the authority of the Catholic Church in Irish civil society has been comprehensively destroyed'.[3] Fintan O'Toole is of the settled judgement that 'the church has ceased to be *us* and become them' and that there is no going back. The church, he concedes, may still have its adherents 'but it will never, ever be woven back into the fabric of what it means to be Irish'.[4] Beneath these visible and measurable social changes, reflected in falling levels of Mass attendance and attitudes to church teaching, there has been a deep process of secularisation.[5] The Nobel Prize-winning poet, Seamus Heaney, has spoken of his personal loss of faith, of belief in God and the afterlife, and seems to assume that his experience is the norm,[6] a sentiment encapsulated in one of his poems, 'Out of This World',[7] when he noted that 'The loss occurred off-stage', and, one might add, in his case, quietly, profoundly.[8]

So, is that it: will the Irish Catholic Church succumb in the face of modernity's challenges, the abuse crisis and the ways in which it has been mishandled by church authorities? Or will the church, and not just in Ireland, come in time to recognise these revelations as a moment of catharsis, 'an act of providence' which in the words of Benedict XVI, 'humbles us and forces us to begin all over again'.[9] Will the church find a path of reform and renewal that will allow it to emerge again onto the Irish public square humbler and more credible in its witness to and teaching of the gospel? To answer these questions it will be necessary in this article to explore why the Catholic Church has been so important to Irish identity, to offer some explanation for the ending of this close embrace, and to make some suggestions as to what the church's priorities ought to be now and in the years ahead.

I

The long nineteenth century of the Catholic Church in Ireland can be said to have stretched from the relaxations of the anti-Catholic penal laws in the final decades of the eighteenth century until the beginnings of the 1960s and the changes to church and society ushered in respectively by the Second Vatican Council and the wider cultural and social revolution in the west associated with 'the 1960s'. But the Catholic Church would involve itself in matters which stretched beyond the purely spiritual and pastoral. For one thing, Thomas Bartlett has noted that the failure to grant Catholic emancipation at the time of the Union in 1801 meant that the struggle for political rights became a national struggle with religion at its very heart: 'the Nation of the Irish' pitted against the English parliament and Dublin. Bartlett goes on to assert that this contest would prove to be the crucible in which the Irish Catholic nation was forged.[10] The campaign for Catholic emancipation, which the British government finally conceded in 1829, saw Daniel O'Connell succeed in mobilising the Catholic faithful and politicising the clergy, helping to give the latter an insight into its potential influence in public affairs.[11]

In one way or another, as the nineteenth century progressed, there was a strengthening clerical presence in Irish society and politics, the most outstanding example of which was the increasingly important place occupied by Cardinal Paul Cullen in Irish ecclesiastical and religious life.[12] Brian Fallon has argued that the key to the hold that the church came to exercise over most Irish people until quite recently was that: 'It gave them the only morality they knew, it enriched their often hard, underprivileged lives with its rituals and sacraments, baptised their children, married their young people and buried their dead.' In these and so many other ways it was woven into the texture of daily life, and while it may have terrified people intermittently with the prospect of God's judgement, 'it promised redemption for the sinner and eternal life for all'.[13]

Following the 1916 Easter Rising and the subsequent war of independence a free republic was not achieved. Partitioned dominion and Civil War meant that the new southern state began at low ebb. In this context the Anglo-Irish poet W. B. Yeats acknowledged that in the wake of Civil War violence the Catholic Church was badly needed to restore order and values among young people.[14] The question of identity took on even greater importance. Patrick Corish has commented that at this time 'Nationalist Ireland was never in greater need of identity; it had to be either the Irish language or the Catholic Church, and for most people it was in fact the church'.[15] Meanwhile in the new northern state, the Catholic minority community frequently organised its life in parallel to the society around it, thus giving the impression of being 'a state within a state'.[16] Religious and political identity were arguably even more intimately linked than in the south, and the bishops were conscious of the need to secure and defend Catholic interests, especially in relation to the church's role in education.[17]

The fledgling Free State took on a certain conservative Catholic ethos, made all the easier by the erection of a separate and overtly unionist and Protestant jurisdiction for Northern Ireland. The southern government was as determined as the clergy to preserve what was regarded as traditional values.[18] But things would change: slowly Ireland would become part of what Charles Taylor termed a wider 'large-scale shift in the general understanding of the good' which would become so manifest throughout the west in the 1960s.[19] However, the bishops were clearly not alive to the potency of the new intellectual currents which would soon flood Irish society. This has led Dermot Keogh to judge that 'the leadership of the church in the 1950s notwithstanding John Charles McQuaid, was vey weak. A number of its leaders had excellent negative minds.'[20]

By 1959, however, there came the news that Pope John XXIII was summoning the Second Vatican Council. Its proceedings lasted for four years (1962–65). The Irish bishops were totally unprepared for it, and for the whirlwind of change which would strike the Irish Catholic Church. Louise Fuller noted that for most Irish Catholics, the most visible and dramatic signs of change in Catholic culture were those that related to the liturgy, and that: 'There was a sense in which the bishops feared that Irish Catholics might be disturbed by the changes, and their traditional faith threatened.'[21] The winds of change brought by the council would indeed blow the Irish church off its traditional Counter-Reformation course. Bartlett has asserted that the council's reforms of church teaching especially that on the importance of the laity 'proved painful for those Irish prelates accustomed to fulsome deference, abject obedience and unquestioned authority'.[22] But Ireland was changing in response to other stimuli too, caught up in the cultural revolution of the 1960s with its new approaches to sexual mores and questioning of traditional gender roles.[23]

As the reforms of the Second Vatican Council and the social revolution were breaking on church and society in the west Vincent Twomey arrived at Maynooth College as a student for the priesthood (he was subsequently ordained in 1970). On reflection he has judged that this national seminary, where most of Ireland's future clergy were being trained and formed, was a place where few professors or fellow students 'seemed to be even remotely aware of the void opening up behind the Catholic mask of Irish society or aware of developments in society that would in time led to an impasse'.[24]

Roy Foster seems to be of the view that it was the emerging women's movement in Ireland which finally brought this void into full view. He has written that 'the 1970s feminist saw the social values of Catholicism as a major obstacle inhibiting equal opportunities for women in Ireland, however personally devout they might be'. Catholic opposition to artificial birth control, divorce and abortion – what Foster terms 'pro-creation politics' – would provide the point of departure for tackling Catholic social power head-on.[25] Following the visit of Pope John Paul II to Ireland in 1979 Bartlett has argued that there was a resurgence of traditional Catholic objections to the social progress favoured by liberal Ireland reflected in the acceptance of the 1983 Pro-Life Amendment to the Irish constitution and the defeat of the campaign to legalise divorce in the 1986 referendum.[26] Progressive opinion was outraged and there was intense criticism of the church, especially in the media. The bishops seemed at sea in this new climate, and Keogh has written that 'By the end of the 1980s, the Irish bench of bishops was particularly weak'.[27]

But then the ground shifted with the beginnings of the avalanche of disclosures of cases against priests of sexual abuse, and subsequent mis-handling of allegations by church authorities. These have shattered the church's credibility, held it up to ridicule and served to silence its voice in the public square. A second divorce referendum in 1995 legalised divorce, even if it was passed by the slimmest margin. Constant media scrutiny and exposure of child abuse by clergy and government inquiries Ferns (2005), Ryan (2009), Murphy (2010) and Cloyne (2011) mean that the past two decades 'have been momentous in terms of the diminished standing of the Catholic Church in Ireland'.[28]A highly secularised society has emerged, and the archbishop of Dublin, Diarmuid Martin has conceded that '[t]he Catholic Church in Ireland will inevitably become a minority culture'.[29]

The current Taoiseach Enda Kenny underlined this new reality in his widely reported, emotive and highly undiplomatic Dáil speech, 'more scattergun than sure shot',[30] following the publication of the Cloyne Report when he excoriated 'crozier power' and attacked the Vatican's role in handling clerical sexual abuse allegations. And this in a society already hugely traumatised since 2007 in the face of the worst economic downturn since the Great Famine. Politicians, bankers, developers and financiers are under fire. In what way then is it credible to speak about Irish Catholic identity today? A sharp and amusing perspective on the current confusions and challenges that Irish Catholics and indeed all Irish people face in trying to locate a distinct identity is summed up in Tom Bartlett's observation that:

> By 2010 Irish distinctiveness had apparently vanished, and so too had Irish exceptionalism. Where once just about everything on this island was unfathomable, mysterious or exotic to the outsider, by 2010 all that remained to puzzle the traveller was the undimmed urge of the Irish to attend the funerals of distant acquaintances, the undiminished support for the field sports organised by the GAA, the unquenchable determination to drink to excess, and the near total refusal to speak Irish in everyday conversation. To these we might add, perhaps that the Irish still retained a way with words and music and dance. Were these enough for a distinctive identity?[31]

II

This chapter began with withering judgements on the Catholic Church in Ireland by two of the country's most important public intellectuals, Fintan O'Toole (a former assistant editor of the *Irish Times*) and Roy Foster (the Oxford-based historian). As far as both of them are concerned the Irish Catholic Church is at death's door and will soon cease to have any meaningful role in Irish life. O'Toole in his weekly columns campaigns for a liberal secularity, while Foster has provocatively suggested that such has been their demonstration of individual conscience and judgement that Irish Catholics have effectively become Protestants.[32] It seems fair to say that most media comment shares their determination to write Catholicism out of the picture. So pervasive is this theme in Irish society that, following the publication of the Murphy Report and the pope's letter to the Irish Church in 2010, one of the very few Irish journalists who wrestles sympathetically with faith issues, John Waters, wrote about 'the hostility of the broader culture to the very existence of Catholicism, if not indeed the very existence of Christianity, in this society'.[33]

A discussion of the decline of Irish Catholicism purely in terms of the sexual abuse crisis would be, of course, to overlook the broader secularising societal changes in the west, affecting both Catholics and Protestants. The influential Canadian philosopher Charles Taylor, thinking from the perspective of what he calls north Atlantic civilisation, has provocatively asked, 'Why was it virtually impossible not to believe in God in, say, 1500 in our Western society, while in 2000 many of us find this not only easy, but even inescapable?'[34] Taylor believes that since the 1960s the north Atlantic countries have been living through what he terms the 'age of authenticity' where faith has lost much of its significance for social order and become a matter of personal choice and individual identity.

But in spite of these difficulties, the life of the Catholic Church in Ireland goes on in hundreds of parish communities throughout the country. Two recent surveys, first, the European Social Survey 4th wave (2008–09) puts weekly Mass attendance at 45.2 per cent for the Republic of Ireland, and 59 per cent for the north,[35] and, second, the RedC opinion poll on behalf of the Iona Institute in 2009 found that 65 per cent of people in the south go to Mass at least once a month. Interestingly, David Quinn has commented that this latter poll suggests that church attendance has actually increased since the recession began.[36]

It is no exaggeration to say that Irish Catholicism exists in a state of siege, and that the immediate trigger for the crisis has been the clerical abuse crisis. It also seems clear that the underlying tensions were already apparent in the anger that has built up in liberal Ireland over the last few decades concerning the church's perceived role in delaying reforms in personal and family morality. One might also add that the thirty years of sectarian violence during the Troubles in the north also led some Irish people to regard religion as essentially divisive, and to welcome what they interpret as a more peaceful secularisation. All of this was made possible by the underlying processes of secularisation, globalisation and the communications revolution which have caused a tectonic shift in how the Irish understand themselves. The earlier benign consensus between church, state and broader society about what it meant to be both Irish and Catholic has evaporated. It is not yet clear what has replaced it. Desmond Fennell, representing a strand of opinion not often heard in the public forum, has provocatively commented that from the early 1960s the Irish media in particular agitated successfully 'to cancel piecemeal the established Irish identity, while replacing it with nothing'.[37] Tom Inglis was surely correct in saying that '[i]t is now the media more than the Church that form and inform the consciences and expand the limits of how people perceive the world'.[38] Thus in one way or another, as one looks to the future, there would indeed seem to be firm grounds to support the view that Irish Catholic identity, as opposed to a vague cultural Catholicism, is in jeopardy.

The move to a more individualistic morality was evident in the Celtic Tiger era neo-liberal economic policies of successive Fianna Fáil led (but

Progressive Democrat driven) governments, leaving us with the wrecked Irish banks which had embraced wholeheartedly the unsupervised global markets to finance a housing bubble.[39] It is also reflected in the glaring social inequality in terms of personal taxation, education, health and social services leading Garret FitzGerald to comment that '[t]he harsh truth is that we have allowed far too much of our new wealth to be creamed off by a few influential people, at the expense of the public services our people are entitled to'.[40] As the economic crisis deepened, an editorial in the *Irish Times* opined that things are so bad that 'we have no choice but to begin a profound process of national renewal' as it acknowledged 'the absence of anything resembling authority, competence or courage coming from the institutions of the State, government or the church'.[41]

III

Constantinian Christianity has run its course, Christendom is dead; the church is no longer unassailably part of the power structures in the west. Further, in one way or another fewer people in the west, admittedly more so in Europe than the United States, from the mainline Christian traditions, are attending their respective churches. Sociologists such as Grace Davie, however, are keen to remind people of faith, and that all is not lost. Instead, she points to the importance of what she terms 'vicarious religion' and to the notion of faith lived and celebrated by an *active* minority on behalf of a much larger number, who, implicitly at least, not only understand, but, quite clearly, approve of what the minority is doing.[42] Hence the widespread popularity of faith-based education in Britain and North America. Davie's perspective is reminiscent of Joseph Ratzinger's conviction that a 'soulless, jaded Europe' that lacks 'an orientation to life and to the future' needs what he terms 'creative minorities', believing and active Christians who can demonstrate the attractiveness and goodness of the Christian model of life'.[43] This might mean in Ireland that, even if they are fewer in number than hitherto, committed Catholics have much to offer wider Irish society, not least in terms of an internationally recognised and respected tradition of Catholic education that parents may chose for their children,[44] and an ongoing outreach to the poor and marginalised in Irish society through its various social justice initiatives.[45]

As is well known, the Irish Catholic Church, as it emerged from penal persecution, found itself by the nineteenth century very much at the centre of the nation-building process, and this role was intensified in the wake of independence and partition, in different ways, in both parts of

Ireland. Catholicism as a badge of identity had huge social and political uses. These have turned to dust; confessional allegiance, especially in the south, is now a very personal matter and it is hard to conceive of it being of any advantage socially or politically. In these circumstances there can be no question of a return to business as usual. The Irish Church must take stock and seek to reclaim a deeper awareness of its true identity and mission. It is singularly striking that so many Irish Catholics have experienced their church leadership as being high-handed and patronising, more interested in control than in helping them encounter God in Christ, mediated by word, sacrament and the community of the church. Breda O'Brien has commented that for those Catholics not directly affected by the abuse crisis, 'the greatest failure of the Catholic Church in Ireland may be its failure to respond to the need in human beings for a practical, lived spirituality that encourages service and gives profound meaning to the most mundane of acts'.[46] The church has to find new ways to unlock the many spiritual treasures in its rich and diverse heritage.[47] John Waters, writing in the charged atmosphere following the publication of the Pope Benedict's pastoral letter to the Catholics of Ireland, went as far as to assert that the abuse crisis relates fundamentally 'to the removal, a long time ago, of any sense of Christ from Irish Catholicism'.[48] Whatever the truth of this devastating assessment, Donal Murray was surely correct when he said: 'The antidote to secularism will not be found in condemnation or coercion. It will be found in allowing people to see a Truth which is richer, more satisfying, more liberating, more human, more worthy of wholehearted commitment and effort than anything else.'[49]

The Second Vatican Council is regarded by many as the most important religious event of the twentieth century. Though it ended almost a half-century ago, there is still much dispute as to its meaning. Arguably, the central document of the council was the Decree on the Church, *Lumen Gentium*. In the words of Eamon Duffy it abandoned the defensive, juridical understanding of the church which had dominated Catholic thought for centuries and placed at the centre of its teaching the notion of the people of God, embracing both clergy and laity. This concept moved understanding of the nature of the church out of rigidly hierarchic categories, and enabled a radical and far more positive understanding of the role of lay people in the life of the church.[50]

The Irish theologian Gerry O'Hanlon has argued that the teaching of this council is 'the most authoritative, most modern faith and gospel-based vision of the church that we have at our disposal' and that in the face of the current crisis in Irish Catholicism it is 'our best resource for the kind of renewal that we require'.[51] But he goes on to caution that while the teaching constituted 'a huge shift from the dominant hierarchical and overly juridical vision that was dominant before the council' it remains in large parts 'a shift that has yet to be effected'. Nonetheless, he is clear that the Second Vatican Council's teaching invites us 'to a new way of imagining and being church' and that the current crisis calls us 'to reconsider this vision, to clarify it and to seek for appropriate instruments of implementation'. O'Hanlon prioritises the importance of truly receiving the council's teaching on the centrality of baptism in the Christian life and on the universal call to holiness. A model of church overly focused on the clergy is to be consigned to the past and there needs to be real collegiality and co-responsibility and sharing in governance extending to all the faithful, including a strong voice for women.[52]

IV

It is abundantly clear that the Irish Catholic Church urgently needs a forum where representatives of the Catholic faithful, lay and ordained, can debate, pray, discern and plan for the future together. Noel Coghlan, writing from a Church of Ireland perspective with its experience of annual diocesan and national synods, has counselled wisely when he wrote that active discipleship flourishes best in a consensual community, one that is open to change and which comes with transparency in decision making, 'a community in which different voices can be heard, a community of love rather than of laws'.[53] Whether or not, as some theologians have argued, a national assembly is a viable option for the Irish Catholic Church in the short to medium term,[54] Eugene Duffy has noted that many Irish dioceses have been thinking about how best to plan and manage pastoral activities in a church where there will be fewer clergy and a much greater appreciation and reliance on lay ministry.[55] This will become a much more pressing issue in the years ahead.

While accepting that the long-surviving Catholic Church is often said to think in centuries rather than days, and asserting that the all-encompassing nature of Catholicism is 'like a mother's love for her child', Patricia Casey has noted that the Irish Catholic Church is 'poor at communicating and even poorer at rectifying errors it has made in the past'.[56] The serious failures made in the past to confront properly the abuse that is so painfully documented in the Ferns, Murphy, Ryan and Cloyne reports are an open wound. Fergus O'Donoghue, in commenting on Benedict XVI's hope for a revival of the Irish Church,[57] noted that 'healing will not happen if the solutions are too clerical in outlook and Roman rather than local in spirit'. He went on to say that the great spiritual energy in the laity needs to be rediscovered and encouraged.[58]

It would be foolish indeed to think that any real renewal can take place behind clerical closed doors, or be imposed from above. Thankfully, Archbishop Diarmuid Martin realises this and he has said that 'more participation of laymen and laywomen is needed to avoid a false culture of clericalism'.[59]

Nuala O'Loan, the former Northern Ireland Police Ombudsman, is one of Ireland's few public Catholic intellectuals today and she has repeatedly called for serious reflection on how the church is governed, on the importance of transparency and accountability for the way in which power is exercised in the church in terms of processes, decisions and probity.[60] She observed a good start being made in the new structures for handling allegations of child abuse, if properly implemented and monitored and acknowledged that '[t]hey have involved a transfer of power from bishops to people. They are a model for accountability, and the principles which underpin them are transferable to other areas of church life.'[61] Effective governance procedures would mean some mechanisms for discussion and consultation at parish, diocesan and national levels. Parish pastoral councils and diocesan pastoral councils where they exist are a good start. There ought to be systematic accountability, including annual reporting at diocesan and parish levels and properly constituted complaints procedures.[62] One might add that such steps forward in developing new and better approaches to church governance in Ireland may in time be seen as models which will be valued and emulated throughout the Catholic world.

Timothy Radcliffe has written that '[t]he point of Christianity is to point to God as the meaning of our lives'.[63] The academic discipline which seeks to explore our experience of God is theology; it is, in the time-honoured words of St Anslem, 'faith seeking understanding'. One of the key weaknesses of Irish Catholicism that lies so exposed today is its impoverished theological culture. Fr Bruce Francis Biever, a US sociologist, writing in the early 1960s on Irish Catholicism, identified an endemic authoritarianism which emphasised legalism at the expense of a reasoned conviction as the basis of faith.[64] Fr John C. Kelly, writing in 1959, worried that too many people in Ireland at that time were 'trying to make do with a peasant religion' when they were no longer peasants. He went on: 'We are growing and developing a middle-class nation, acquiring a middle-class culture, and we must have a religion to fit our needs.'[65]

Vincent Twomey has wondered if the almost totally dismissive and rancorous attitude to the church and it spokespeople in the Irish media is partly explained by the church's 'failure to produce a theologically literate laity'.[66] It is deeply ironic that a church that was so overwhelmingly involved in school provision and management over a few generations presided over a system (in the Republic) where religious education was not examined at secondary level until very recently,[67] thus ensuring that in too many Catholic schools it lacked depth and academic respectability.[68] The faith, then, was not really explained or taught, it was said to be 'caught'. The unspoken assumption seems to have been that the faith could be taken for granted and that schools were to prepare students to go to university and get jobs, helping them pursue those great goals of nineteenth-century Irish Catholics, social advancement and respectability.

It should be abundantly clear, then, that one of the most pressing needs today is to develop a genuinely vibrant theological culture in Ireland. The whole people of God, lay faithful, religious and clergy, urgently require a more profound intellectual grounding in what precisely constitutes the nature and mission of the church and a deeper personal experience of the transcendental dimension of life. In our well-educated, well-travelled – and in spite of the current economic crisis – relatively affluent society, the Irish Catholic Church, long overinvested in the task of nation building, must rediscover its core identity and mission. Whereas in the past the clergy wanted the people to believe, to 'keep the faith' first and last, and, in contrast, the liberal intellectuals wanted them to think and to question,[69] now the church urgently wants the people to explore and think beyond the constraining framework of the dominant secular, individualistic culture. The church will need to put much energy and resources in the future into its teaching and evangelising ministries. Theological and broader spiritual and pastoral formation courses at parish and diocesan levels will be critically important.

The excesses of the Celtic Tiger years and the shameful unfairness in Irish society in terms of two-tier education and health-care systems point to the pressing need for such critical voices in Irish society. Meanwhile the church's continuing work, so often hidden from public view, among the poor and socially deprived, through agencies like the Society of St Vincent de Paul and the Dublin Diocese's Crosscare, play a vital role in Irish life today.

It is most unlikely that Catholicism will ever again be woven into the fabric of what it means to be Irish. Some of the main reasons, social, political and religious, for such a close identification in the past and the causes of its unravelling have been surveyed here. Now in the face of the emergence of a more heterogeneous, secular and ethnically and religious diverse society, the Irish Catholic Church must adapt to its new environment. It will need space and time to adjust to these new realities, and, moreover, to respond credibly and effectively to the abuse crisis and wider secular critique. But respond it must. A renewed church which is both humble and truly evangelical would have much to contribute as it seeks again to harness the Christian impulse which has been such an enduring feature of Irish life for more than fifty generations.

Notes

1 F. O'Toole, *Ship of Fools: How Stupidity and Corruption Sank the Celtic Tiger* (pbk edn, London: Faber and Faber, 2010), p. 182.
2 D. Keogh, 'The Catholic Church in Ireland since the 1950s', in Leslie Woodcock Tentler (ed.), *The Church Confronts Modernity: Catholicism since 1950 in the United States, Ireland, and Quebec* (Washington, DC: Catholic University of America Press, 2007), pp. 93–149, at p. 94.
3 R. F. Foster, *Luck and the Irish: A Brief History of Change c.1970–2000* (London: Allen Lane, 2007), p. 66.
4 F. O'Toole, 'Everything and nothing has changed', *Irish Times*, 12 Mar. 2011.
5 See T. Inglis, 'Catholic Identity in Contemporary Ireland', *Journal of Contemporary Religion*, 22(2) (2007), pp. 205–20.
6 See J. Water's searching criticism of Heaney's position, what the former terms 'The Poetics of Nothing', in *Beyond Consolation* (London: Continuum, 2010), pp. 115–36.
7 S. Heaney, *District and Circle* (London: Faber and Faber, 2006), p. 47.
8 Michael Paul Gallagher reflects interestingly on Heaney's 'eclipse of faith' as an example of that process of secularisation discussed by Charles Taylor. See M. P. Gallagher, 'Translating Taylor: Pastoral and Theological Horizons', in I. Leask *et al.* (eds), *The Taylor Effect: Responding to a Secular Age* (Newcastle upon Tyne: Cambridge Scholars, 2010), pp. 113–23, at p. 116.
9 Pope Benedict XVI, *Light of the World: The Pope, the Church, and the Signs of the Time. A Conversation with Peter Seewald* (San Francisco, CA: Ignatius Press, 2010), p. 35.
10 T. Bartlett, *Ireland: A History* (Cambridge: Cambridge University Press, 2010), p. 242.
11 D. A. Kerr, *Peel, Priests and Politics* (Oxford: Oxford University Press, 1982), p. 6.
12 C. O'Carroll, *Paul Cardinal Cullen: Portrait of a Practical Nationalist* (Dublin: Veritas, 2008), p. 17.
13 See B. Fallon, *An Age of Innocence: Irish Culture 1930–1960* (Dublin: Gill and Macmillan, 1998), p. 189.
14 *Ibid.*, pp. 188 and 280, n. 7.
15 P. J. Corish, *The Irish Catholic Experience: A Historical Survey* (Dublin: Gill and Macmillan, 1985), p. 244.
16 O. P. Rafferty, *Catholicism in Ulster: An Interpretative History* (Dublin: Gill and Macmillan, 1994), p. 221.

17 See M. McGrath, *The Catholic Church and Catholic Schools in Northern Ireland: The Price of Faith* (Dublin: Irish Academic Press, 2000), p. 2.
18 Corish, The Irish Catholic Experience p. 244.
19 Taylor, *A Secular Age*, p. 474.
20 *Ibid.*, p. 105.
21 L. Fuller, *Irish Catholicism since 1950: The Undoing of a Culture* (Dublin: Gill and Macmillan, 2002), pp. 109–10.
22 Bartlett, *Ireland*, p. 494.
23 D. McCulloch, *A History of Christianity: The First Three Thousand Years* (London: Allen Lane, 2009), p. 998.
24 D. V. Twomey, *The End of Irish Catholicism?* (Dublin: Veritas, 2003), p. 48.
25 Foster, *Luck and the Irish*, pp. 47–8.
26 Bartlett, *Ireland*, pp. 530–1.
27 Keogh, 'The Catholic Church in Ireland', p. 120.
28 J. Littleton and E. Maher. 'Introduction', in J. Littleton and E. Maher (eds), *The Dublin/Murphy Report: A Watershed for Irish Catholicism* (Blackrock: Columba Press, 2010), pp. 7–16, at p. 7.
29 D. Martin, 'Keeping the show on the road: is this the future of the Irish Catholic Church?', speaking notes to the Cambridge Group for Irish Studies, Magdalene College, Cambridge, 22 Feb. 2011; www.dublindiocese.ie/index.php?option=com_content&task=view&id=2293&Itemid=372; accessed 29 Aug. 2011.
30 D. Keogh, 'Nuncio's recall is serious for church–state ties', *Irish Times*, 29 Aug. 2011. See also the Vatican's 'Response to Mr Eamon Gilmore, *Tánaiste* and Minister for Foreign Affairs and Trade of Ireland, concerning the Cloyne Report', www.vatican.va/resources/resources_risposta-gilmore_20110903_en.html; accessed 10 Sept. 2011.
31 Bartlett, *Ireland*, pp. 473–4.
32 Foster, *Luck and the Irish*, p. 66. Foster, in his wider discussion here, demonstrates a rather reductionist view of what constitutes Protestantism, seeming to equate it with only its liberal, post-Enlightenment expression.
33 J. Waters, 'Can Christianity survive in our society?', *Irish Catholic*, 25 Mar. 2010.
34 Taylor, *A Secular Age*, p. 25.
35 E. O'Mahony, 'Religious practice and values in Ireland: a summary of the European Values Study 4th wave data', Sept. 2010, www.catholicbishops.ie/wp-content/uploads/images/stories/cco_publications/researchanddevelopment/evs_4th_wave_report.pdf; accessed 29 Aug. 2011.
36 Press release by Iona Institute, 'New poll shows big rise in church attendance', www.ionainstitute.ie/pdfs/Press_Release_by_The_Iona_Institute_2Nov2009.pdf ; accessed 29 Aug. 2011.
37 D. Fennell, 'Making Ireland unlovable; a call to Irish historians', Apr. 2010, www.desmondfennell.com/essay2.htm; accessed 29 Aug. 2011.

38 T. Inglis, *Moral Monopoly: The Rise and the Fall* (Dublin: University College Dublin Press, 1998), p. 246.
39 P. Kirby, *Celtic Tiger in Collapse: Explaining the Weaknesses of the Irish Model* (2nd edn, Basingstoke and New York: Palgrave Macmillan, 2010), pp. 6–7.
40 G. Fitzgerald, 'Short term pain should not blind us to bright future, *Irish Times*, 17 May 2008.
41 Editorial, 'Renewing the Republic', *Irish Times*, 3 Apr. 2010.
42 G. Davie, 'Is Europe the exceptional case', *Hedgehog Review* (2000), pp. 23–32, at p. 24. See also her *Religion in Modern Europe: A Memory Mutates* (Oxford: Oxford University Press, 2000), pp. 69, 80–1, 177–80.
43 See J. Corkery's outline and critique of Ratzinger's position in his, *Joseph Ratzinger's Theological Ideas: Wise Cautions and Legitimate Hopes* (Dublin: Dominican Publications and Paulist Press, 2009), pp. 109–24, esp. pp. 117–19.
44 Catholic Schools Partnership, 'Catholic schools in the Republic of Ireland: a position paper', Maynooth, 2011, www.catholicbishops.ie/2011/04/13/catholic-schools-partnership-position-paper-2011/; accessed 1 Sept. 2011.
45 Further information on these programmes can be accessed at www.catholicireland.net/church-in-ireland/church-organisations#justice.
46 B. O'Brien, 'Catholic Church failing to meet the need for practical spirituality', *Irish Times*, 3 Oct. 2009.
47 T. Rausch, *Educating for Faith and Justice: Catholic Higher Education Today* (Collegeville: Liturgical Press, 2010), p. 155.
48 Waters, 'Can Christianity survive in our society?'.
49 D. Murray, *Let Love Speak: Reflections on Renewal in the Irish Church* (Dublin, Veritas, 2011), p. 168.
50 E. Duffy, *Saints and Sinners: A History of the Popes* (pbk, New Haven, CT and London: Yale University Press, 2006), p. 376.
51 G. O'Hanlon, *A New Vision for the Catholic Church: A View from Ireland* (Blackrock: Columba Press: 2011), p. 12.
52 *Ibid.*, pp. 56–8.
53 N. Coghlan, 'So does religion have a future?', *Studies: An Irish Quarterly Review*, 99:396 (2010), pp. 395–404, at p. 404.
54 Paschal Scallon, eager to tap into an emerging leadership among the laity, has already offered a vision of what such a national assembly might look like and what it might do in assisting all members of the church to assume greater responsibility in its life. P. Scallon, 'Modelling a national assembly of the Catholic Church in Ireland', in N. Coll and P. Scallon (eds), *A Church with a Future* (Blackrock: Columba Press, 2005), pp. 208–19.
55 E. Duffy, 'Clustering parishes: reflections on the practice and theology', E. Duffy (ed.), *Parishes in Transition* (Blackrock: Columba Press, 2010), pp. 92–115, at p. 92.
56 P. Casey, 'Catholicism: finding personal meaning', in J. Littleton and

E. Maher (eds), *What Being Catholic Means to Me* (Blackrock: Columba Press, 2009), pp. 133–40, at pp. 139–40.

57 Pope Benedict XVI, 'Letter to the Catholics of Ireland', 19 Mar. 2010, www.vatican.va/holy_father/benedict_xvi/letters/2010/documents/hf_ben-xvi_let_20100319_church-ireland_en.html.

58 F. O'Donoghue, 'Editorial', *Studies: An Irish Quarterly Review* 99(395) (2010), pp. 265–6, at p. 265.

59 Archbishop Diarmuid Martin, 'Homily for the fifth Sunday of Lent', 1 Apr. 2010; www.dublindiocese.ie/index.php?option=com_content&task=view&id=1838&Itemid=372; accessed 29 Aug. 2011.

60 N. O'Loan, 'Transparency, accountability and the exercise of power in the church of the future', *Studies: An Irish Quarterly Review*, 99(395) (2010), 267–75, at pp. 267–9. Séamus Murphy has drawn attention to the failure of the Irish bishops in governance not only in relation to civil, but also canon law: 'they generally failed to apply to those abusers the very law that they were themselves responsible for enforcing. This was a very serious failure in governance' ('No cheap grace: reforming the Irish Church', *Studies* 99(395) (2010), pp. 303–16, at p. 307).

61 O'Loan, 'Transparency, accountability', pp. 269–70.

62 N. O'Loan, 'Governance: the challenge for church and state', unpublished Annual *Le Chéile*-Together Lecture, St Mary's University College, Belfast, 3 May 2011.

63 T. Radcliffe, *What Is the Point of Being a Christian?* (London: Continuum/Burns and Oates 2005), p. 3.

64 B. F. Biever quoted in Keogh, 'Catholic Church in Ireland', p. 108.

65 J. C. Kelly, SJ, quoted in Fuller, *Irish Catholicism*, p. 61.

66 Twomey, 'End of Irish Catholicism?', p. 69.

67 Since 2003 religious education has been introduced as a subject in the Republic's leaving certificate syllabus.

68 This point is discussed at greater length in N. Coll, 'After the wake: an alternative to Cullen's church', *The Furrow* (1999), pp. 98–106, at pp. 104–5.

69 Fallon, *An Age of Innocence*, pp. 190–1.

Index

CPSIA information can be obtained at www.ICGtesting.com
Printed in the USA
BVOW11s0503190515

400333BV00003B/8/P

9 780719 097317